DR. TOM DOOLEY'S THREE GREAT BOOKS

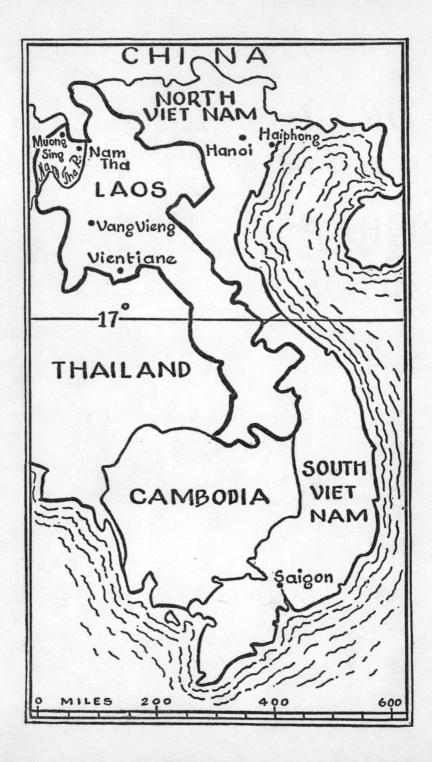

DR. TOM DOOLEY'S THREE GREAT BOOKS

Deliver Us from Evil

The Edge of Tomorrow

The Night They Burned the Mountain

New York
FARRAR, STRAUS & CUDAHY

DELIVER US FROM EVIL

TO THE MEN OF THE U. S. NAVY AND TO THE COURAGEOUS ESCAPEES OF NORTH VIET NAM WHO, TOGETHER, HAVE SHOWN ME THE TRUE NOBILITY OF LIFE.

FOREWORD

by ADMIRAL ARLEIGH BURKE,

U. S. Navy, Chief of Naval Operations

The United States Navy has always been proud of its men, proud of their character, of their American ideals and convictions.

The heart of the Navy is found in its men—skilled, imaginative, courageous, alert, enthusiastic and kindly men. No organization in the world depends so much upon the individual initiative of its men as do we in the Navy.

The Navy is essentially a combat organization but one whose primary purpose is to support our government to the utmost both in peace and war. As a result, Navy men must continuously train thousands of other men to accomplish skillfully a myriad of undertakings. The Navy's training program is a never-ending chain. It teaches the real meaning of service to one's fellow men. It also teaches men to become technically proficient and to utilize the most modern tools in existence.

Today's naval traditions have been built by generations of men like young Doctor Dooley who have served their country well under arduous and challenging circumstances. The American sailor is ofttimes (as was Doctor Dooley) confronted with situations in which proper courses of action could not have been pre-planned or pre-determined.

Therefore in his training, whether as line officer, doctor or boatswain's mate, each individual must have prepared himself to assume responsibility and to act in accordance with his best judgment. Every Navy man must know that the life of his ship, and the success of his country, may sometimes depend upon his willingness and his ability to act boldly and independently for the common good.

Hence sailors will read with pride, as will all Americans, the courageous exploits of the young lieutenant, Doctor Dooley. His humanitarian actions are the kind of good deeds that will remain indelibly impressed in people's hearts—good deeds that neither propaganda nor brainwashing will ever stain.

Through the tireless work of his small naval unit in the huge refugee camps of the hostile and turbulent North Viet Nam country, he has won for America the love and admiration of thousands and thousands of refugees who passed through these camps on their historic march to freedom.

Lieutenant Dooley, a naval medical officer on independent duty, contributed greatly to the welfare of mankind and to an understanding of the fundamental principles of the United States, as he participated in this epoch-making period of world history. In DELIVER US FROM EVIL he has written that story with freshness, clarity and force. It is a story that will be told and re-told.

It is a story of which the United States Navy is proud.

CONTENTS

DELIVER US FROM EVIL

ONE ·
ENSIGN POTTS CHANGES HIS MIND

The Hickham Field airport terminal was jammed with military personnel and their dependents. November in Hawaii is lovely; when a light misty rain is falling, the Islands are enchanting. And I was going home. I was going *home*. Two weeks in Hawaii, winding up my two-year overseas stint, went fast and gave me two great moments. The second moment occurred right at Hickham Field.

The scene of my first was a U. S. Navy holy-of-holies—the Command Conference Room for Pacific Fleet Headquarters at Pearl Harbor. There I was to brief Admiral Felix B. Stump's staff on my recent experiences in Southeast Asia. Admiral Stump was the Commander-in-Chief of the Military Forces of the Pacific. I was just a twenty-eight-year old Lieutenant (recently junior grade) in the Navy Medical Corps, in command of nothing whatsoever.

But I had had rich duty in the Orient. I had been stationed in the city of Haiphong, in North Viet Nam, Indo-China, and assisted in the epic "Passage to Freedom" that moved some 600,000 Vietnamese from the Communist North to the non-Communist South.

Indo-China had been a French colony. But on May 7, 1954, after eight years of bloody colonial and civil war, the key fortress of Dien Bien Phu had fallen to the Communists, and soon thereafter, at Geneva, the Red victory was nailed down in a peace treaty that arbitrarily split an ancient country in half. One of the treaty's terms said that, if they wished, non-Communists in the north would be allowed to migrate to the south. Hundreds of thousands desperately wished to do so and most of those who made the trip traveled through Haiphong. And that was where I came in.

Needless to say, Admiral Stump's staff had received regular reports on the operations at Haiphong, probably with frequent enough mentions of a young Irish-American doctor named Dooley. But evidently they wanted more, or at any rate Admiral Stump thought they did. So I was ordered to stop over on the way home to deliver a briefing, which is a lecture in uniform.

It was delivered in a room that collects stars. On this day, when I addressed some eighty officers for one packed hour, I counted sixteen of those stars on the collars in the front row. Captains filled the next few rows. Commanders brought up the rear.

Rank doesn't scare me too much, but when it gangs up on a man in this wholesale fashion it does shake him a little. But I told these men about the hordes of refugees from terror-ridden North Viet Nam and how we "processed" them for evacuation. I told them how these pathetic crowds of men, women and children escaped from behind the Bamboo Curtain, which was just on the other side of Haiphong, and of those who tried to escape and failed. I told of the medical aid given them in great camps at Haiphong and of how, in due course, they were packed into small craft for a four-hour trip down the Red River, to be reloaded onto American ships for a journey of two days and three nights 1,000 miles down the coast to the city of Saigon, in South Viet Nam.

I told them individual tales of horror that I had heard so many nights in candlelit tents, in the monsoon rains of that South China Sea area. I even got in some complaints. Why hadn't certain missions been carried out more effectively? Why had American naval policy dictated such and such a course? So for one hour I talked. They all listened intently.

I suppose one measure of a lecturer's hold on his audience is the length of time it takes for the questions that follow his speech. I must have had a pretty good hold because the questioning lasted more than seventy minutes. Finally three stars in the front row spoke up. "All right, Dr. Dooley," he said. "You have given us a vivid picture and told us moving stories of courage and nobility. You have also raised a lot of objections. But you have not offered one solution or one suggestion on what we can or should do in the still-free parts of Southeast Asia."

I responded, perhaps a bit unfairly, that two small stripes could hardly presume to offer solutions, if indeed there are any, to three big stars. My job was to take care of backaches and boils.

Then came my first big moment in Hawaii—the Walter Mitty dream moment that every junior officer has dreamed of since the Navy began. How often I had sat at table in the ship's wardroom saying, "Well, if I were running this outfit. . . ." Or "Why the devil didn't the Admiral do it this way?"

And now the Admiral was saying, "Well, Dooley, what would *you* do if *you* were wearing the stars?"

I took the plunge with a few suggestions, low level and not necessarily new.

"Sir," I said, "I think that American officers ashore in Asia should always wear their uniforms. I think that American Aid goods should always be clearly marked. I think we should define democracy in Asia so that it will be clearer and more attractive than the definitions Asians get from the Communists."

I said a lot more which, to be perfectly truthful, I can no longer remember, and even as I held forth I was worried about my cockiness. You get neither applause nor boos from such an audience, merely a curt "Thank you, Doctor." The only punishment meted out to me when the show was over was a request to repeat the briefing to a lot of other audiences in Hawaii, military and civilian.

Only one man besides myself attended all my briefings. He was the hapless Ensign Potts, a spit-and-polish young officer five months out of Annapolis. He had been assigned to help me with the myriad little things I had to do on my lecture tour of Hawaii.

Ensign Potts baffled me. He saluted me every time I turned around. Riding in a Navy car with me he would invariably sit in the front seat with the driver. When I would ask him to sit in the back with me his response would be: "No thank you, sir, I think it will be better if I sit up front." Sometimes, after I had delivered a lecture in the evening, I would ask Potts to come to the beach with me for a swim. "No, sir, thank you," he would say. "I had better go back to Officers' Quarters."

As we drove to Hickham Air Force base for my flight home, I again asked Potts to sit in the rear seat with me. "No thank you, sir," he started to say, but by this time Ensign Potts was getting on my nerves.

"Mr. Potts," I said, "get in this back seat. I want to talk to you. That is an order."

Stiffly and reluctantly, he obeyed.

"Potts," I said, "what the hell's wrong with you—or with me? I think I get along with most people fairly well, but obviously you don't like me. What's up?"

"May I speak frankly, sir?" he asked.

"Hell yes," I said.

"Then, sir," he said, "allow me to say that I am fed up with you. I am fed up with your spouting off about a milling mass of humanity, about the orphans of a nation, a great sea of souls and all the rest of that junk. And what I am most fed up with, and damn mad about, is that most of the people you spout at seem to believe you."

Ensign Potts stopped a moment to observe my reaction. When he saw I was listening, he continued:

"You talk of love, about how we must not fight Communist lust with hate, must not oppose tyrannical violence with more violence, nor Communist destruction with atomic war. You preach of love, understanding and helpfulness.

"That's not the Navy's job. We've got military responsibilities in this cockeyed world. We've got to perform our duties sternly and without sentiment. That's what we've been trained for.

"I don't believe your prescription will work. I believe that the only answer is preventive war."

Evidently he had thought a lot about it. He explained that some 200 targets in Red Russia, Red China and the satellite nations could be bombed simultaneously and that this would destroy the potential of Communism's production for war. Then a few more weeks of all-out war would destroy Communist forces already in existence.

Sure, the toll of American lives would be heavy, but the sacrifice would be justified to rid mankind of the Communist peril before it grew strong enough to lick us. For that matter, maybe it was too late already.

Slowly Dooley was beginning to understand Potts. The Ensign had nothing against me personally; he just didn't like what I was preaching. He himself had a radically different set of ideas, and many Americans, I suppose, share his views. I do not.

The Ensign had not yet said his full say. "Dr. Dooley," he concluded, "the oldest picture known to modern man, one of the oldest pieces of art in the world, is on the walls of a cave in France. It shows men with bows and arrows engaged in man's customary pastime of killing his fellow man. And this will go on forever. Prayers are for old women. They have no power."

With this he fell silent, sucked in a deep breath and slumped in his seat. He had vented his hostility and was appeased.

Just then I noticed that our car was not moving. We had arrived at the terminal, but the sailor chauffering the car was too engrossed in our conversation to interrupt. Potts and I stepped out, disagreeing but friends at last.

And that brings me to the second of my two big moments in Hawaii.

I stood in the misty perfumed rain at the terminal. I was heading home. Things would be quiet now. They would be pleasant and uneventful. I was going to sleep, eat, and then eat and sleep again. There would be no turmoil. No hatred. No sorrow. No atrocities. No straining with foreign languages (I can speak Vietnamese and French, but they take a toll on the nervous system).

The terminal building at Hickham is immense. Preoccupied with thoughts of going home, I did not hear the first shout, but the second one came through loud and clearly. From the other end of the waiting-room someone was yelling: *"Chao Ong Bac Sy My,"* which in Vietnamese means, "Hi, American doctor."

I turned around and was enmeshed in a pair of strong young arms that pinioned my own arms to my side. A Vietnamese Air Force cadet was hugging me tight and blubbering all over my coat. He was a short, handsome lad of perhaps sixteen. Squeezing the breath out of my chest, he was talking so fast that it was difficult to understand what he said. Suddenly there were about two dozen other olive-skinned youngsters in cadet uniforms swarming around me, shaking my hands and pounding me on the back as an air-hammer pounds a pavement. They were all wearing the uniform of the Vietnamese Air Force. And everyone concerned was bawling all over the place.

"Don't you remember me, American Doctor? Don't you remember?" asked the boy who still had me pinioned in his bear-hug.

"Of course I do," I lied—who could remember one face among those hundreds of thousands?—but behold! the lie turned into truth and the old familiar gloom came over me. The boy had no left ear. Where it should have been, there was only an ugly scar. I had made that scar. I had amputated that ear. I might not remember this particular boy, but I would never forget the many boys and girls of whom he had been one. The ear amputation was their hideous trademark.

"You're from Bao Lac," I said, disentangling myself from his embrace. Pointing to others in the group, I added, "And so are you, and you and you."

Each of them also had a big scar where an ear should have been. I remembered that in the Roman Catholic province of Bao Lac, near the frontier of China, the Communist Viet Minh often would tear an ear partially off with a pincer like a pair of pliers and leave the ear dangling. That was one penalty for the crime of listening to evil words. The evil words were the words of the Lord's Prayer: "Our Father, Who art in Heaven, hallowed be Thy name. . . . Give us this day our daily bread. . . . and deliver us from evil. . . ." How downright treasonable, to ask God for bread instead of applying to the proper Communist authorities! How criminal to imply that the new People's Republic was an evil from which one needed deliverance! A mutilated ear would remind such scoundrels of the necessity for re-education.

The boy spoke of his escape from North Viet Nam in November of 1954, when he had come to my camp. There I had amputated the stump of his ear, dissected the skin surfaces of the external canal, then pulled the skin of the scalp and that of the face together and sutured them. The tension was great on the suture line, and I knew the scar would be wide and ugly. But, with the limited time and equipment available, I had no alternative. Would he hear again from that ear? Never. Only from the other ear would he ever hear words, evil or holy.

All of the Vietnamese youngsters now in the Hawaiian terminal had passed through our camps at Haiphong, and many of them bore this trademark. I had put them on small French craft or on sampans which carried them to American ships to be taken to Saigon. There those who had reached the age of sixteen were old enough to join the newly created Air Force of Viet Nam. At sixteen they were men, preparing to regain the north half of their country from the Communists.

Under an American Military Aid Program, this contingent was going to Texas to be trained as mechanics. At the airport in Hawaii they had spotted the American doctor who had helped them a year earlier. They remembered him. I remembered only the scars.

A fairly large crowd, mostly Americans, had been attracted by our noisy and tearful reunion. Some people wanted to know what it was all about. This seemed as good a time as any to begin "briefing" my fellow-citizens, and I made a speech. I told them about these youngsters and their valor; I told them where I had come from and what I had seen, and then I satisfied their curiosity as to why most of these air cadets had only one ear apiece. I suspect I did not succeed in keeping the tears out of my voice. Soon many of those who had been staring at us and who now understood began to find their vision clouding up, just as mine was clouded. Not in many a year had that number of tears hit the deck at Hickham.

And among those who wept and did not bother to hide it was Ensign Potts. The same young officer who half an hour before had scoffed at my softness.

"Mr. Potts!" I commanded. "Pull yourself together, sir."

He came over, grinning through the tears, and shook my hand.

"Mr. Potts," I said, "don't you think these kids would do anything, even at the risk of their lives, because of the way they feel about one American?"

In all the honesty of his enthusiastic heart, Ensign Potts replied: "Yes, Doctor, I think they would. Perhaps you are right. Perhaps there *is* a special power in love."

TWO ·

THIRTY-SIX BRANDS OF SOAP

The Vietnamese cadets had been caught in the inevitable foul-up. They had been at Hickham for days with no one to look after them. Since they knew no English, they had just been wandering around the terminal to kill time. I tracked down the Air Force officer in charge; he told me the kids were due to leave on a flight that night. I asked if I could be put aboard the same plane. That, it seemed, was impossible. Suddenly my new friend, Ensign Potts, moved into line with all guns blazing.

"Sir," he roared, inaccurately, "Doctor Dooley is Admiral Stump's guest, and I have authority to speak for the Admiral. The doctor can have the Admiral's own plane if he wants it. It seems to me the least the Air Force can do is to put him on that lousy flight."

So the Air Force put me on the flight, which wasn't so lousy at that.

The big Constellation was filled with soldiers, sailors and marines. When we were airborne I told them a little about their fellow passengers, the twenty-six olive-garbed Vietnamese. I called up my cadets one by one and asked each to tell his story while I translated. My captive audience, at first indifferent, was soon entranced.

Then I asked the Vietnamese to sing some of their mountain songs. The Tonkin mountain music is melodious, almost eerie, something like the ancient Hebrew liturgical chants. The cadets sang and the Americans on the plane listened with attention.

Next I asked the U.S. servicemen to sing some American songs. "OK, Doc," a sailor said, "how about *Shake, Rattle and Roll?*" The title was tough to translate into Vietnamese, but the singing was great. And so was the singing of *Home on the Range, There's Nothing Like a Dame* and *Deep in the Heart of Texas.*

Thus passed the flight, with a great good deal of singing and laughter.

When we finally came in over the Golden Gate, the Americans shifted seats to let the "foreigners" sit by the windows and excitedly tried to explain the sights below by gestures and sign language. I felt good inside.

We landed at Travis Air Force Base near San Francisco. There I watched my fellow passengers file off the plane, each soldier, sailor and marine with a cadet in tow. After we were processed, the Vietnamese had ten hours to kill before taking off for Texas. The Air Force provided a bus and some of the U.S. servicemen volunteered to come along while I took the kids sightseeing.

When I returned to San Francisco it was as though I had been away for ages. We take too many things for granted in our American way of life; when we are absent from them for a year or two, they become engrossing, wonderful, slightly incredible. Why, hey, say! I learned that American ingenuity had developed an automobile with gears that can be shifted by pushing a button, and a television set on which programs can be turned off and on by sighting it with a Buck Rogers type of ray gun. Such wonders almost floored me because now I saw them through the eyes of the kids.

Downtown San Francisco made them bug-eyed with wonder. When we went into an all-night drugstore for milk-shakes, the Vietnamese wandered around as if in fairyland. Under the glaring lights, at their insistence, I described the contents of some of those colorful packages which were stacked on the shelves. One section was devoted to soaps; a cadet counted thirty-six different brands. "Please explain the differences between them," he said to me, and that one had me stumped. The first bar of soap he had ever seen was one I had given him in Haiphong—and I had only one kind. All his life, until then, he had used a fat preparation. To him, that was soap. An American sailor came to my rescue. "Tell him they have thirty-six different smells," he said, and I translated to the cadet's satisfaction.

We finally returned to Travis Airport where I loaded my charges on a plane bound for the deep heart of Texas. We said "So long" and they thanked me again, individually and collectively. But I think I owed them some thanks too. For one thing, they had taught me to appreciate afresh some of the assets of my country. And not just the material assets either.

At Haiphong, to get supplies for the miserable refugees, I had done some shameless begging, seeking this, that or the other thing from American groups, business concerns and individuals. Now I wanted to spend part of my leave in thanking the people who had responded to this Operation Hat-in-Hand—the pharmaceutical companies, surgical supply houses and such outfits as the International Rescue Committee and the Youth of All Nations.

While I was on the West Coast, I decided to visit the San Diego high school whose senior class had sent my refugees bundles of clothes and other necessities. The principal and teachers arranged it so that I addressed the assembled classes of several San Diego schools.

I looked out over that sea of fresh young faces and felt older than Father Abraham. They were noisy kids, some of them dressed in faded blue jeans and leather jackets, some of the girls wearing full-blown sweaters, and many of the boys with those long duck-butt haircuts. When I stepped out on the platform, wearing my uniform and ribbons, there was a bedlam of wolf-calls and whistles and stomping feet.

They were tough, so I decided to shoot the works. I gave them the whole sordid story of the refugee camps, the Communist atrocities, the "Passage to Freedom," and the perilous future of southern Viet Nam. I talked for an hour—you can see I was getting to be quite a windbag—and you could have heard a pin drop.

When I was through, they asked questions for another hour—earnest, intelligent questions that kept me on my toes. Toward the close, there was one little girl in the rear who had to come down front in order to be heard. She couldn't have been more than thirteen and she took a wad of gum from her mouth before asking her question with intense seriousness.

"Doctor Dooley, what can we boys and girls of the Lincoln Memorial High School *really do* to help improve the social, economic and political situation in Southeast Asia?"

Now that *is* a stopper! But dear little girl, put back your gum and don't be ashamed. I haven't met a single American who hasn't asked something like that once he has heard the facts.

I have no magic formula to offer. What do *I* know about foreign aid in billion-dollar packages? But I do know that American aid, used wisely and generously by individuals, on a people-to-people basis, can create bonds of friendship that will be hard to sever. And we have several million willing American hands around the world, if we want to use them—not in the Navy alone, but in all the services overseas. We can still serve the folks back home—if they want us to—as instruments of the sympathy, generosity and understanding that are hallmarks of the American character.

Unless these intangibles are conveyed to Asian people plainly, I'm afraid the costly programs of material aid are often wasted. And they needn't be. My meager resources and lame efforts in Indo-China did not win the people's hearts, although I know they helped. What turned the trick, when the trick was turned, were those words: *"Day La Vien Tro My"* ("This is American Aid")—and all that those words conveyed. Let us stop being afraid to speak of compassion, and generosity. Christ said it all in the three words of His great commandment: "Love one another."

I then took a train to St. Louis, my home town, because I wanted to see America's fields and mountains, her canyons and plains. I even sat up most of the night looking out the window. I was home. I was back in America— though truly I had never left her at all. She was in my heart. I wore her insignia on my hat, her bold eagle and shield over her Navy's anchors.

At home in St. Louis I answered a thousand questions. How did that evacuation of the north get started? What are these people really like? How the hell did a young man like *you* get into it? What did the President of Viet Nam mean when he said, "Doctor Dooley, you are the only American I have ever met who could speak my language. . . . You are beloved by my people. You were the first American most of them ever saw and by knowing and loving you they grew to understand the American people." If as he said they loved you so damned much, why did they beat you up?

The answers are long and involved. They can only be found by reviewing the whole story of the evacuation, from day one to the end of the eleventh month.

THREE ·

NEW CARGO FOR THE
U.S.S. MONTAGUE

One night, in the spring of 1955, I lay sleepless and sweltering in the dying city of Haiphong, North Viet Nam, asking myself the question that has taunted so many young Americans caught in far-away places, "Whatinhell am I doing here?"

None of the answers that came to mind seemed wholly satisfying. I was on this weird mission under the Bamboo Curtain because—in a way—I had asked for it. Each month the Navy offered me the chance to quit and go back aboard a nice clean ship and perhaps go home. Yet each month I volunteered to stay on in this nightmare for still another thirty days. Why? In my depressed mood I cursed myself for a damned fool.

For as long as I could remember, I had wanted to be a doctor. Now, at twenty-eight, I was an M.D., although a very green one. Moreover, I was a Navy doctor, an added distinction I had coveted since I served as a hospital corpsman in the United States Navy in 1944–46. Finally, I was one young doctor who did *not* lack patients. God knows, I had more cases on my unskilled hands at the moment than the most seasoned doctor has any right to handle.

Out there, in the 140-odd tents of the quagmire I called Camp de la Pagode (there wasn't a pagoda within miles) were more than 12,000 wretched, sick and often horribly maimed Vietnamese, most of them either very young or very old, who were fleeing from the Communists of northern Viet Nam, hoping to reach the doubtful security of Saigon. Many thousands had previously passed through my camps and the number would run into the hundreds of thousands before the tragedy ended.

Sure, I had long known about the fall of Dien Bien Phu, in which world Communism had scored another resounding triumph. At the Yokosuka Naval Hospital in Japan, where I had been stationed only a couple of months, I had followed this news in a casual, impersonal way, like everyone else. If I was a little more interested than most were, it was only because Indo-China was a French colony; I had studied in Paris at the Sorbonne and had an interest in everything French.

Yet, because of Dien Bien Phu, here I was, more by accident than by merit, in practical command of the medical aspects of the gigantic job of evacuation at Haiphong, and its periphery in the Tonkin Delta.

For me, tropical medicine had been a drowsy course at St. Louis University Medical School. Yet now I was crowding more practice in malaria, yaws, beri-beri, smallpox, leprosy and cholera into a month than most doctors see in a long lifetime.

I was only a fledgling surgeon, but already I had performed operations which the textbooks never mention. What do you do for children who have had chopsticks driven into their inner ears? Or for old women whose brittle collar-bones have been shattered by rifle butts? How do you treat an old priest who has had nails driven into his skull to make a travesty of the Crown of Thorns?

I had never before borne real responsibility or authority. But now I had to provide shelter and food, sanitation and some human solace to a flood of humanity, undernourished, exhausted, bewildered and pitifully frightened. My primary task was medical—to stamp out contagious diseases before these hordes boarded our transport vessels, and so to protect our crews against epidemics. But there was no ducking the huge problems of housekeeping and administration for the shifting camp population, normally between 10,000 and 15,000 persons.

And, maybe because I am a glutton for punishment, I chose not to duck larger tasks not set down in my instructions. One was to help refugees to reach our evacuation zone. They had been told, formally, in the Geneva compact, that they could be evacuated when, as and if they wished. But it turned out that they had been told a lie. Another of my tasks was to teach at least some of the refugees, in the brief time they were in my charge, to understand and trust Americans.

I had to do these things, moreover, across barriers of suspicion, fear and often hatred of Americans cunningly instilled by Communist propaganda. My assignment brought me face to face with misery on a horrifying scale, with hideous atrocities—but also with quiet courage, simple nobility and, above all, the miracle of a faith in God that takes the risks of torture and death in its stride.

Yes, cocky young Dooley, whom the profs at medical school had ticketed as a future "society doctor," was learning things the hard way, but he was learning at last. At Notre Dame they had tried hard to teach me philosophy. Now out here in this hell-hole I had learned many profound and practical facts about the true nature of man. I understood the inherent quality that enables tough, loudmouthed sailors to become tender nurses for sick babies and dying old men. I had seen inhuman torture and suffering elevate weak men to great heights of spiritual nobility. I know now why organized god-lessness never can kill the divine spark which burns within even the humblest human.

That night, in my tent at Haiphong, I tossed fitfully on a sweaty cot until, just before dawn, I heard Boatswain's Mate Norman Baker—"lately from New Hampshire, sir, and proud of it"—stumble into my tent.

"Better get moving, Doc," he said. "We've got another batch—800 or maybe a thousand more."

From Baker's tone, I could tell that the newcomers would be like all the rest—filthy, starving, diseased, and maimed in God knows what manner.

Groping for a flashlight and pushing my swollen feet into a pair of muddy boondockers, I instinctively began murmuring the *Our Father*, as I had every day since childhood: "And deliver us from evil." I had to pause in the darkness. Yes, O God, that is the people's prayer—to be delivered from evil. At that moment I think I sensed, however dimly, the purpose behind my being in Indo-China.

The evacuation of North Viet Nam really began, at least for me, in the Philippines.

In the first week of August, 1954, with the one-and-a-half stripes of a Lieutenant (j.g.) on my sleeve, I was assigned to the U.S.S. *Montague*, AKA (Auxiliary Cargo Attack) 98, for thirty days of what the Navy calls TAD. Those letters mean Temporary Additional Duty, and they also happen to be the initials of my name: Thomas A. Dooley. We were to take part in amphibious exercises, and practice landings on the Philippine beaches. Soon we had conquered all the undefended beaches in the area.

(The duty seemed so temporary that I allowed a Navy nurse in Yoko-suka, Japan, my last station, to drive my new convertible while I was gone and I told my roommate that he could wear my brand-new civilian suit. When I got back to Japan, eleven months later, there were 20,000 additional miles on the speedometer and as for the new suit—well, I couldn't have worn it anyway. I had lost sixty of my 180 pounds.)

For a Navy doctor, the maneuvers were not too strenuous and there was amusement on shore. I planned to devote my life to the U. S. Navy and this was my first big chance to get better acquainted with ships and sailors and the sea that is their stern mistress. I had seen plenty of ships before—the *Queen Elizabeth*, the *Queen Mary*, the *Independence*. But in my mind they couldn't compare with an AKA. I admit the *Montague* was not as luxurious as the *Queen Elizabeth* and certainly it did not have the cocktail space of the *Independence*. But to me it was important—important because it was my first ship and important because of the friendships I made. In the Navy friendships are easily made—and difficult to forget.

After we had scrambled down landing nets and stormed ashore repeatedly for a couple of weeks, we reloaded equipment and put in at the big naval base on Subic Bay, across the island from Manila. There most of us were doing "club time" exercises—swimming, sunning, sleeping, or drinking gin and tonic—when our breathing spell in the breathless Philippine summer heat was cut short, very short.

Task Force 90 was ordered to "proceed on 12 August 1954 to Haiphong, Viet Nam, Indo-China, anchor in stream and await instructions." Operation "Passage to Freedom" was getting under steam, we were part of it, and we were not to discuss it with anyone. That last command was easy to obey. Few of us knew anything about Indo-China other than the fact that it was south of China and east of India. And we knew even less of this "Passage to Freedom." Who or what was passing to freedom, and where, and why?

Our "Op Order," the Operation Order detailing a mission, was not to reach us until the day we dropped anchor off Haiphong. The Admiral in charge of the Task Force that included the *Montague* knew the answers, but he did not know them soon enough to draft the order before we left the Philippines.

What we did know, however, was that we were to prepare our ship to transport 2,000 people. We were ordered to prepare for this new type of cargo in two days, then sail. The trip would take another two days. Total, four days. Four days in which to transform the *Montague*, a cargo ship built to transport tanks and trucks, into a ship to carry a cargo of humans, 2,000 at a time.

As the ship's medical officer, I should have sensed the significance of the worried look on Captain William Cox's face; but I was a neophyte, full of animal spirits, and this grueling, around-the-clock chore sounded like a lark.

What we did during the two days at Subic Bay and the two days under sail was unbelievable. We converted this ship into a passenger liner, though without many of the ocean-going luxury items, to be sure.

An AKA is about 460 feet long and has five large holds, with three levels to each hold. These are used to store the trucks, tanks and other vehicles for amphibious landings. There is no ventilation in the holds and the only openings are the hatches or covers which must be replaced after the cargo is loaded. On the tops of the hatches the ship carries landing craft.

Normally, after the lowest level of each hold is loaded, its hatch is closed and the level above gets its cargo. For the Passage to Freedom these holds had to be converted to accommodate men, women and children—something the designers had never anticipated. It was hardly an ideal arrangement.

The first thing we did was to remove the ladders from deck levels and place them between the levels of the holds to provide entry into and egress from their deep recesses. Wooden staircases were constructed for the holds when all the metal ones were used up. Water hoses were rigged into all the holds, along with fans and such other accessories as we could muster. The hatches, of course, could not be left open, for fear that people would plunge down three levels; but every other hatch board was removed to allow air to filter down.

Each division officer tried to imagine what he would need in the way of supplies, and then we headed for the supply depot at Subic Bay. Whatever we thought we needed we piled aboard, overlooking formalities and showing a fine disregard for Supply Corps rules and regulations. Aboard went tons of rice, hundreds of crates of sardines, thousands of drinking cups, 60-gallon drums, empty paint cans to serve as portable toilets, tons of sawdust to be strategically deployed in boxes for the seasick.

We sailed out of Subic Bay on the designated date, full of rice and mystery and scuttlebutt. Every sailor and every officer had the inside dope and was willing to share it with someone else in return for a pledge of secrecy.

Officers held roundtable discussions in the wardroom. Enlisted men held discussions around a stanchion on the fantail. Then we had combined conferences in which each contributed his piddling bit of information. If all this jawing did nothing else, it at least brought one thing to light quite vividly—how little most of us knew about Southeast Asia.

We scoured all the reference books we could find aboard the ship. We dug through old magazines. We looked everywhere for information on Indo-China. We found pitifully little.

Meanwhile, at sea, the ship resounded with hammering and sawing and the shouting of orders. All the facilities ingenuity could contrive were provided for our prospective guests. Sixty-gallon canvas "Lister" bags for drinking water were hung in the holds. Oil drums were scoured and filled with water for washing.

But Captain Cox's masterpiece was the latrine system. Oil drums were split lengthwise, welded end to end, and topped by wooden seats in which the carpenters cut holes of various sizes. When the job was finished, the skipper made an inspection.

I'll never know whether his primary concern was for Vietnamese buttocks, or the tremendous job of splinter-picking that seemed about to devolve on the ship's doctor. But he ordered blocks of sandpaper and stood by until the men had rubbed those latrine seats satin smooth. As things turned out, however, he might have spared the sailors their trouble. Asian toilet habits are decidedly different, as we were to learn.

Now our reconversion was complete. Now we were ready. But for what?

Not until much later did we realize that we were the advance guard in the largest evacuation ever undertaken by the U. S. Navy.

FOUR ·

THE REFUGEES COME ABOARD

The *Montague* glided into the surrealist beauty of the Baie d'Along on August 14, 1954. On the same day several other ships anchored in the stream. By August 15th there were five ships lined up in this slit among the bay's crags and rocks. We were at Position 1; the *Menard*, another cargo ship, was at Position 5.

Anxiously we waited for our first view of the refugees. What would they be like? How many of them would there be? What kind of diseases would they bring with them? We soon found out.

I tried to imagine what conditions must be with hordes of people pouring into the city of Haiphong, beyond the bay four hours upriver, waiting to be carried out to these strange ships standing offshore. Little did I realize that, just beyond that shoreline, lay an ordeal which would scar my memory for a lifetime.

Then I heard a shout and saw the men pointing to a small LCT slowly ploughing along in the angry swells. Such small craft are built to transport four or five tanks and a few dozen men. Their overall length is less than 150 feet. As this one pulled alongside, I looked down into the open deck with horror. I know horror is a strong word, but there were more than a thousand people huddled on the deck, close-packed like fowl in a crate, wet, seasick and exposed to a brutal sun. They were numb with fright. Among them were a multitude of babies.

When the LCT arrived at the side of our ship, huge by comparison, an open gangway was lowered to its deck. This was secured as firmly as possible, fighting the swells and sickening rolls of the bay. The refugees were told to come up. I could see them hesitate, in fear. I supposed that it was merely dread of the unknown. Later I learned that the trouble was more specific—they were in mortal fear of the savage, inhuman Americans against whom they had been very often and very effectively warned.

One old man, probably one of their esteemed elders, took the lead. He started painfully up. He wore a conical straw hat and in one hand clutched a slender brown-crusted bamboo pipe. In the other hand, even more tightly, he held a chipped frame—a picture of the Blessed Virgin. It was clear that these were his most prized possessions. In fact, they were nearly all the possessions he had.

For a few steps he came on bravely, then looked down at the swells smashing inches below the steps. One look was enough. He froze where he stood. When he looked up, many things showed in his wizened face. There was starvation, all too obvious; there was fright at the booming sea; there was sheer terror of what lay ahead.

He was hunched over as if heavily burdened. When, nervously, he removed his hat, his scalp showed patches of scaling fungus. His ribs stood out sharply, stretching the skin of his chest to shiny tautness. I had never before seen such utter dejection. Could this be Viet Nam?

A white-capped sailor went down the steps; he wanted to help, repugnant as the thought of touching that old fellow must have been. But when he did touch the man, it was as if the grandfather had felt the hand of an executioner. Only the press of the people behind finally forced him to mount the rest of the steps to our deck. His trembling fingers were barely able to hold a numbered card another sailor handed him before he was urged, gently, away from the ship's rail.

We stopped the line after a few refugees had come aboard and put a canvas cover over and under the accommodation ladder so that they would not see the ocean breaking beneath the open steps. This, we hoped, would lessen their terror. Nevertheless the others, equally miserable, entered the ladder-tunnel with apprehension.

Many of them carried long balanced poles with large shallow baskets at each end. In these they carried everything they owned. Usually they had some clothes, always a rice bowl and chopsticks, invariably a religious object —a crucifix, statue or sacred picture.

On and on they came through that cavernous tunnel, some of them with eyes lowered, as if not daring to look at us. They had children on their backs and in their arms; even the older kids toted babies. The children were given a tag which, when presented later, entitled them to milk, a nearly unheard-of luxury. The little ones were sweet, and wide-eyed and grave. And very frightened. I saw a sailor, to lighten a mother's load, pick up a brown little bundle of baby and mutter, "God, this kid smells awful."

Then the last of this group of refugees was aboard and the French LCT pulled away with an obvious air of relief. A second French craft pulled alongside and the dismal exchange was repeated.

Somehow, in the confusion, our guests managed to haul aboard a huge barrel of stinking oil. I took one whiff and ordered it tossed overboard. Too late, I learned that the rancid oil was considered a delicacy, indispensable to Tonkinese cookery.

Now more than 2,000 Tonkinese were started on their passage to freedom, the first of the hundreds of thousands who would depart from this harbor before the Bamboo Curtain finally fell. They had made a wholly free choice in tearing up century-old roots and abandoning revered ancestral graves. For the right to continue to worship their God—the decisive motive in nine cases out of ten—they had given up their rice paddies, their homes, their beloved native villages. What lay ahead of them in the south, which would be almost a foreign land to Tonkin Delta folk? Indeed, would these big-nosed and strangely dressed white men ever deliver them to the south at all?

They had been told in great detail by followers of Ho Chi Minh—the fabled Ho Chi Minh who was playing ball with Moscow but whom many of them still regarded as a patriotic nationalist—that Americans were scarcely human. The whole evacuation, they were told, was a trap. American sailors would throw the old people overboard, cut off the right hands of the new-born, and sell the comely girls as concubines to capitalists. They had seen "pictures"—crude but vivid drawings on propaganda leaflets—of just such white-capped sailors as those on this big ship roasting a child alive, pre-sumably for breakfast.

Small wonder that there was not a smiling face, young or old, among these thousands as they clambered awkwardly into the ship's cavernous belly with their sorry belongings. So it seemed a heart-warming miracle, hours later, to notice the blossoming of shy smiles here and there, first among the children, and then among their elders too. The mood of our guests was becoming more tranquil.

We now notified the galley that they would have the mammoth task of feeding these thousands. A number of comparatively clean and healthy-look-ing Vietnamese—and they were not easy to find—were selected to help serve the food. We planned to serve only twice a day, but since the second meal ran into the first, the lines were continuous. Vitamin deficiences were gen-eral, and this was a chance for the Vietnamese to eat their fill, perhaps the first in months.

We cooked the rice in our own fashion, nice and fluffy. Embarrassingly, we discovered that the refugees did not like rice cooked our way. They preferred it when it looked like an inedible ball of congealed mash. When they finally got it that way, they would take extra helpings and press it into sticky chunks to be tucked into their bundles.

Finally the last refugee was aboard and the accommodation ladder hoisted. The "Ready to get underway" reports were submitted to the Skipper, the screws churned the blue-green water and the *Montague,* with its strange cargo, embarked for the south.

Soon the heat became intense and the stench almost overpowering. There was sickness throughout the ship. There were "honey buckets" for toilets in every hold, as well as large latrine troughs on the decks, but at first the refugees did not understand how to use them properly and they just didn't. It wasn't long before Captain Cox called me to his bridge and said, mournfully, "Dooley, look at my latrines!" I looked and howled with insubordinate laughter. There, answering nature's call, were eight or ten refugees, perching on the seats with their feet rather than with the usual portion of their anatomy. That was their way, and there was nothing we could do about it.

With the help of a French-speaking priest and several elders (called mandarins), we tried to make the ship's rules known. This water was for drinking, that water for washing, and so on. As we lectured them I had to struggle to control my nausea. These people were filthy, scabrous, often covered with open sores. They bore scars and disfigurements of mistreatment. From that dimly remembered course in tropical medicine at St. Louis, I was able to recognize symptoms that said I had lots of work cut out for me.

The sailors had been told not to have too much contact with the refugees because of the contagiousness of their multiple diseases. But, when dealing with bluejackets, you are dealing not with creatures of cold logic but with boys of emotion and charity. Many of them spent hours in the nauseous holds trying to ease the anxieties of Vietnamese minds and the ache of Vietnamese bodies.

I held almost continuous sick-call, aided by my few medical corpsmen and by a rough-handed contingent of pipefitters, boiler tenders and machinist mates "sworn in" for the occasion. Most of those boys knew the sick bay only as a place where a skillfully feigned bellyache might get a man excused from duty. Yet, with a minimum of instruction, they were soon performing like veterans, passing out pills, cleaning the repulsive ulcers of yaws and slapping on ointments—sometimes the right ones. And never once upchucking or showing any emotion less fitting than heartfelt sympathy.

For the children, milk was distributed by some of the biggest and toughest sailors aboard. These "Milk Maidens," as we called them, had to be big and tough because when they walked into the holds with huge kettles of milk they would be almost stampeded by clamoring masses of child refugees.

For the newborn babies, bottles were needed. From strange, well-hidden places beer bottles appeared with rubber nipples attached. The nipples came from air hoses in the engineroom. They took care of the kids who couldn't guzzle from paper cups.

One of my corpsmen told me about a child in No. 5 hold who seemed to be dying of fulminating diarrhea. The kid was dead before I could confirm my suspicion that he had the disease we still mention only in a whisper —cholera.

To play safe, we insisted upon immediate burial at sea, and that precipitated a near-riot. The boy's relatives all tried to jump overboard after the body. It took several strong-armed sailors to restrain them. We at last were able to coax them to drink some tea, and soon they were slumbering peacefully on the deck. I had dosed that tea with chloral hydrate.

One group of sailors had the unpleasant detail of trying to urge refugees to carry overflowing honey buckets topside and dump them overboard—on the leeward side, of course. These boys also had an unofficial title, but it would never pass the censor.

Now I was seeing for the first time diseases that had been mere names to me. On the first day I isolated ten cases of smallpox. I saw yaws, leprosy, elephantiasis, skin syphilis and, of course, plenty of malaria.

The right to complain is a firmly established and staunchly defended tradition in the United States Navy. But on the *Montague* there were very few complaints from the crew, who had to endure the stench, the shortage of drinking water, the obstacle course on the decks, the extra watches and lookouts and details.

During the night, in order to persuade the children to come topside to the latrines instead of using the decks of the holds, the men on watch would let them carry flashlights. This thrilled the kids and I am sure that many a boy and girl made night visits far beyond the true call of nature.

On some of the lower-deck levels there were areas used as sleeping quarters by the crew. The refugees were supposed to be kept out of these areas but one compartment in particular fascinated the Vietnamese and they could not stay away from it. It was that funny room, with all the shining porcelain bowls in little booths and the higher basins and the long clean white troughs with water running in them all the time. (Of course, occasionally a sailor could be seen relieving himself there, which the refugees were sure that he shouldn't be doing.) Nevertheless, undaunted mothers would sneak into this white room from time to time to wash their babies in the troughs, so handy, so neat. Perhaps a letter of appreciation should be written thanking the Chinal Urinal Company for the excellent baby bathtubs installed on Navy ships.

We not only introduced the Vietnamese to our porcelain facilities; we introduced them to another American institution as well—the beauty contest. On the evening of the second day a contest was held and a refugee girl chosen as best-looking of the lot was crowned Miss Passage to Freedom. She was selected by the Captain, dressed in a surgical robe from sick bay, and given a crown fashioned by the boys in the radio shack. She sat on a throne built in the carpenter shop and was awarded an extra ration of fruit by the cooks. All this delighted her and she rewarded us with black-toothed, betel-stained smiles.

There was a French liaison officer on each ship and a control team who translated from Vietnamese into French and sometimes into English. They traveled back and forth and were considered part of the crew. Over loud speakers, they explained the strange American habits to the refugees: "Urinals are for urinating, latrines are for latrining and, fear not, the babies will not be eaten alive by the sailors."

The refugees had seen a Communist pamphlet with a picture of a Navy doctor, not unlike Dooley, vaccinating people with deadly germs. But the prize, I think, was a drawing of an LCT (amphibious landing craft) that carried its passengers far out to sea, then opened its giant maw and spewed them overboard.

Now the mandarins shook their heads solemnly over the enormity of such lies and apologized for the people's having believed them. They promised to work diligently to dispel groundless fears. But already a more powerful corrective was working on the people's hearts and minds.

By this time many of the refugees were watching our sailors with bug-eyed wonder. On the faces of the children there was a certain softening that might even be laughter. And why not? I have never seen anything funnier—or more inspiring—than red-necked American sailors seriously performing the duties of baby-sitters and maids-of-all-work.

Other strange things began to happen on the *Montague*. Loaves of bread, enormous quantities of candy, cigarettes, soft drinks and other articles were appearing in the hands of the old and the young. It was not theft—unless a sailor purloining something to slip to his new Tonkinese friends be stealing. I saw one notoriously loud, cursing boatswain's mate on the forecastle, bouncing a brown bare-bottom baby on his knee while stuffing a Baby Ruth into its toothless mouth. It would have pleased their mothers, as it pleased me, to see their sailor sons caring for this shipload.

Throughout the ship, these little acts of spontaneous kindness were happening by the hundreds, and none of them was lost on our fearful and suspicious refugees. This was the force, heartfelt and uncontrived, that finally washed away the poisons of Communist hatred.

On each of the three mornings we were enroute, a priest offered Mass in the various holds. It was poignant to hear these weary, bedraggled exiles, singing softly their thanks to God, who seemed temporarily to be looking away from them. Yet their faith was strong and comforting and made us humble in their presence. I noticed that the sailors, working on deck with unusual quietness, always listened to the services.

Dawn of the third day found the *Montague* at the mouth of the Saigon River, where the pilot came aboard. After three hours, the ship would arrive at the capital of South Viet Nam, Saigon.

There, at the debarkation pier, the refugees were unloaded from the vessel which in so short a time had won their love. By this time the sailors were not monsters but "Tot Lam," or "Very nice." The old man who three days before had shrunk from the touch of an American sailor now smiled with his eyes at one who was helping him alight. Both were smoking a Lucky. Many of the children clung to their favorite sailors to the last moment, and several of them went off waving trophies.

Nevertheless, when they left there must have been a feeling of relief in the refugees' hearts and a similar feeling was evident on the sailors' faces. The mass of suckling infants and lively youngsters were gone. The adults who had been sprawling over the decks were gone. But odors of fish, oriental spices and human offal remained. Tied up just behind our AKA was the French luxury liner, *La Marseillaise*. How incongruous it seemed with its decks so clean and white while ours were matted with filth.

At the pier we were met by representatives of the Military Assistance Advisory Group, the American mission assisting in the relocation of the newly arrived refugees. This was my introduction to MAAG and a traumatic one at that.

I was at the bottom of the gangway trying to get some of the coolie-types who were standing around the dock to help the refugees with their bundles. But I wasn't getting anywhere. A tall, lanky, lean, dyspeptic-looking Lieutenant Colonel ambled up to my side and mumbled: "Take it easy, Lieutenant, they won't hurry; it's siesta time." This raised my Irish wrath and, as a consequence, the Navy shouted at the Army and the Army reciprocated. All this afforded the refugees a great show. Later I was properly introduced to Lieutenant Colonel Erwin Jones of the MAAG office in Saigon, a slow-talking, hot-tempered Georgia rebel. Oddly enough our dockside clash led to a relationship which I will always cherish. Erv Jones is now my very good friend, and his presence in Indo-China during that troubled year was decidedly a help.

Just before the debarkation of the refugees was completed, Bishop Pietro Martino Ngô-dinh-Thúc, Vicar Apostolic of Vinh-Long, who was in Saigon, paid a visit to our ship. He is the brother of the defiant Prime Minister, Ngo Dinh Diem, a man who never bowed to the French and who stated emphatically that the Geneva partitioning of Indo-China would lead to a new and more murderous war. The Bishop blessed the refugees and in the name of the Vietnamese Government thanked the officers and the crew of the *Montague* for their mission. He begged God and man to clean the world of its sorrows and blood and despair.

As the refugees filed off, each was given a paper bag with two pounds of rice and two packages of cigarettes, all tagged with the name of our ship and our mission's title, "Passage to Freedom." There were large open trucks at the pier which transported the people to the resettlement areas then under construction, thanks to American Aid.

After the debarkation the ship was given a direly needed clean-up. Clamoring over the side came a gang of coolies MAAG had scraped up. Under the direction of the sailors they manned salt-water hoses and washed the ship fore and aft as thoroughly as possible. Then at 1600 came Liberty Call—relief from shipboard duties and freedom to go ashore in Saigon, the Paris of the East. It was a Cinderella liberty; we had orders to return to the ship by midnight.

In spite of the anaesthetic effect of good French alcohol, on our return we found that the peculiar musty human odor remained.

Captain Cox posted the official record of the voyage. We had transported 2,061 people. There had been two deaths, two burials at sea. Doctor Dooley had officiated at four births, mothers and babies all doing well—including one little guy who faces life bearing the burden of a name dreamed up by his proud parents, Think Van AKA Montague 98 Ngham.

Before turning in, I stood on the deck congratulating myself on being a Navy doctor. "Dooley," I said to myself, "you've seen and done things that are out of this world—but you'll never have another experience to top this one in your whole lifetime."

That's what *I* thought.

FIVE ·

DR. AMBERSON'S TEAM

We returned to Haiphong, picked up another load of refugees, and made another round-trip, which was to be the last of my "cargo runs." By now the anchorage in the Baie d'Along was filled with ships—four APAs (troop transports) and three more AKAs like our own.

The *Montague* was now famous. We had the best health and sanitation record. We were equipped with the biggest and best latrines, the most massive chow lines, the stoutest ladders, and the most mammoth waste-disposal unit. All the other ships were designing and building their own facilities for the evacuation, so our advice was much in demand.

One day I was invited aboard a newly-arrived transport to give a medical and sanitation briefing. While on deck I heard the ship's captain yelling orders in English to a French landing-craft alongside. The French crew obviously knew no English and the situation was beautifully fouled up. I speak French fluently so I decided to go up on the bridge and make myself useful.

The skipper glared at me and said, "Later, doctor!"

I cleared my throat. "Beg pardon, sir, but—"

"I told you—later!"

"Captain," I said quietly, "I speak French. I thought I might help."

"Hell's bells, why didn't you say so?" he roared. "Tell that idiot to pull away and come alongside Chinese-fashion."

I shouted the orders in French, and the landing-craft came around smoothly with its bow to the transport's stern. I got a grateful salute from the Frenchman and a gruff "Thank-you" from the skipper. But as I left the bridge I noticed the predatory look in his eye.

That started it. Word got around that young Dooley could speak French, an advantage not to be overlooked in dealing with the people of a French colony. Soon I was performing all sorts of extra duties that had nothing to do with the practice of medicine.

It was at this time that the flagship of Rear Admiral Lorenzo S. Sabin pulled into the bay. The Admiral was in command of Task Force 90, to whom this evacuation task had fallen. In the rough months to come, I would often invoke his name and authority, sometimes a little recklessly, to get things done. But I did not meet the Admiral until close to the wind-up of the new operation on which I was to be engaged. Then I was to learn that he had been aware of my unorthodox conduct and had given me unreserved support.

I was ordered now to report aboard the flagship to the Force Medical Officer, Captain James Grindell, Medical Corps, U. S. Navy. He told me that he was going to organize a Preventive Medicine and Sanitation Unit in the port city of Haiphong. Later I learned that Admiral Sabin had requested permission from the French to send a party of 1,800 men ashore to build reception-centers. He was allowed to send only 18. The place was inundated with refugees and would soon be infested with all sorts of diseases, including the fancier tropical varieties. The local population would be exposed to plagues and epidemics, and there was a strong possibility that the diseases would spread to American crews aboard the evacuation ships and also to Saigon, where we were depositing our uprooted humanity.

Then Captain Grindell laid it on the line.

"Doctor," he said, "I am considering attaching you to this unit as a medical officer and—well, as a sort of interpreter, let's say. You understand, of course, that this is a voluntary duty. Strictly voluntary. So make up your own mind."

When a man with four gold stripes on his arm, and speaking for the Admiral, says that he is considering a junior lieutenant for something, well, the job is as good as done. Of course, I volunteered. And that is how I became part of the shore-based medical and sanitation unit that soon dwindled into Operation Cockroach under my command.

I hated to leave the *Montague*. It had been my own ship for the past month. Its officers and crew were a great lot of guys, genuine and good. I felt a strong bond to the sailors who had obeyed my slave-driving orders while performing all the loathsome details of the first passage. I never knew what they thought of Dooley until the night we said good-bye.

Then they surprised me with a little ceremony on deck. Traditionally, the *Montague's* enlisted men select from among their own company a Shipmate of the Month. He is given a scroll and his name is listed in the ship's archives. The crew elected me as the Shipmate of the Month and I was the only officer they had ever selected. Having served my hitch as an enlisted man, I could appreciate better than most officers the unusual nature of this tribute, and I had a hard time controlling the tears that come so easily to an Irishman's eyes. If my luck holds out, I may collect other honors in the course of my Navy career. But none can ever occupy quite the same spot in my heart as the honor bestowed upon me by the men of the *Montague*. During the presentation all I could think of was how many times I had raised hell with the men as I ordered them into unappetizing sanitation details, how I had shouted at many, and become angry with a few.

In official theory I was on permanent station duty at the Naval Hospital in Yokosuka, Japan, just loaned to the *Montague* on TAD. The arrangement seems favored in the Far East. It keeps ships supplied with medical service without tying one man down to long-term duty on relatively small ships.

When Captain Grindell decided that I would be sent to the newly formed Preventive Medicine Unit in Haiphong, it involved a lot of administrative red-tape. However, it was worked out without too much sweat; in fact, Captain "Rusty" Ball, the Commanding Officer of my hospital in Japan did not seem to express any particular interest in getting me back. For the first but not the last time, my TAD orders were extended, this time for an additional three months.

On the *Estes*, Admiral Sabin's flagship, I met the officers of the newly minted PMS unit: Captain Julius Amberson, a distinguished medical officer, who would be in command; Lt. Comdr. Edmund Gleason from the Medical Service Corps who knows more about hygiene and sanitation than any contender of his weight; Lt. Richard Kaufman of the Fleet Epidemiological Control Unit, and Lt. David Davis, another doctor, who would be with us for less than fifteen days. Captain Amberson had brought along a dozen enlisted men from Korea and Dick Kaufman had a staff of laboratory technicians in tow. Ed Gleason and Dooley were strictly on their own.

Captain Grindell read the mission's orders: "To prevent epidemics in our personnel, and to provide humanitarian care and medical attention for the refugees as they come within the orbit of our operations." At the time I wondered if we weren't a rather small company for such an ambitious undertaking. But even if I hadn't been as green as I was, I couldn't have foreseen the shape of things to come.

"All right, gentlemen, that's it," Captain Grindell concluded. "Lots of luck to you." The meeting stood adjourned.

And now a word about Doctor Amberson. In all the branches of the service one will meet individuals to whom a cross-eyed baboon would not want to claim relationship. But you also meet men of the moral and intellectual caliber of Dr. Amberson. He was a superb leader and had a wonderful quality of immediately winning the loyalty of all who worked for, or rather, as he would say, with him. He was one of the most honestly patriotic men I have ever met. He had that important command ability to delegate his authority when he deemed it necessary. Dr. Amberson, whether he knows it or not (and I don't believe he does), was one reason why I chose the regular Navy for my career. To work for men like him, men who know and practice the lofty qualities cited in every officer's commission, will always be a pleasure and an honorable duty.

We left the *Estes* one afternoon, took a trip ashore in an open boat and hitched a ride into Haiphong. There a French truck drove us to the best hotel, which was damned miserable—Gleason to perform miracles of sanitation; Kaufman to comb fleas from rats and beg stool specimens from astonished refugees; and Captain Amberson to command and also to stiffen the spine of a junior lieutenant who still didn't realize the "humanitarian care and medical attention" of half a million or so refugees was soon to be his responsibility alone.

SIX ·
THE CITY OF HAIPHONG

At the mouth of the delta on the Gulf of Tonkin, only about 100 miles from the southern frontier of the Chinese province of Kwangsi, Haiphong rates as the best port south of Hong Kong. Yet even in its best days Haiphong was a city of slums, muck and squalor, a rat-infested city inured to swarms of flies and clouds of mosquitoes.

Most large seaport towns have a definite pattern. There are business areas with buildings ranging from skyscrapers on down. There are residential areas and the lowest fringe is usually the waterfront, home of thugs, juvenile delinquents, blaring juke boxes and flop houses. So it is in New York, Marseilles, Saigon and elsewhere.

It was not so in Haiphong. There the docks were almost beautiful, large, built out over the water, wide and sturdy. On the other side of the railroad tracks which ran within a few feet of the piers, there were warehouses, each large enough to house a baseball field. These were built of concrete and had swinging doors wide enough to accommodate three trucks driven abreast. Next came rows of roomy supply depots with huge storage areas, some of them under tin roofs. All this was to be a rich plum for the hungry Communists in less than a year.

The first two or three blocks beyond the piers had some gracious homes, requisitioned during my stay there by the French High Command, consisting of General René Cogny and his staff. There were parks, complete with fountains, statues and the inevitable pigeons.

The Governor's palace, a pink stucco mansion three stories high, stood just beyond the docks, along with the City Hall and the Mayor's residence. These buildings had broad lawns and majestic mahogany trees. Beyond this point the city rapidly deteriorated.

The main street, Rue Paul Bert, ran parallel to the docks, four blocks away. Everything beyond was squalor. Here were the slums, bazaars, flea market, native quarters, Indian quarters, dilapidated pagodas, grimy river waterways, fifth-hand shopping districts, the city jail and, in an adjoining building, the city hospital.

The French Naval Base, on the harbor, was composed of several good-sized buildings and dozens of American-made Quonset huts. Admiral Jean Marie Querville, the French Navy's Commanding Officer during the evacuation of the Tonkin, managed to dismantle a good deal of the base. All the Quonset huts were taken down and shipped south, everything was removed that could be removed without violating clauses of the treaty relating to the destruction of permanent buildings. On many of the buildings the letters "MF" (Marine Francaise) were emblazoned into the concrete façades. Admiral Querville had them chipped out before the buildings were turned over to the Communist Viet Minh.

Neither of the city's two hotels, the Continental and the Paris, had American-type plumbing or running water. But both had the largest cockroaches and rats I have ever seen. When you stepped toward the cockroaches, instead of running away, they ran *toward* you. The rats were large enough to saddle, and they loved to fight.

The rooms were big, with ancient beds under mosquito netting and a couple of aged, musty, velvet-covered chairs. There was a small dance hall on the first of my hotel's two floors, and the cheap music sounded until midnight. It boasted some taxi girls that you could rent for a dance, or for a few hours. Such dance halls were the only places in town, save for a few bawdy bars, that played Western music for the entertainment of the French troops. By Western I mean not Eastern.

We Americans lived for awhile in the Paris and then moved to the Continental. When the others left in October, I stayed on there alone. After a few weeks, I knew every song the orchestra played and I knew what time it was by listening. When "Blues in the Night" started, it was 9:30. At 10:00 it was "Tea for Two." At 11:30 "Love for Sale" was the tops on the pops. The shop always closed with a stirring rendition of the "Marseillaise."

The main street and some of the side streets had the Indian stores to be found all over the Orient. Here one could buy spices, French perfume, cheap woolens and cheaper silks. There were a few good but dirty restaurants where you could buy Indian curry so hot that you did not dare to light a cigarette after you ate for fear of blowing up.

In the early months of the evacuation, French wines and canned foods were available at the military cooperatives. They did not last long, however, as the French were evacuating their military forces as fast as possible. During the last few months, no western foods or wines or even bottled waters were available anywhere in the Tonkin.

The shoeshine boys, who roamed the streets like herds of small cattle, were one pleasant facet of the city to me. They were just little tramps—accomplished thieves—but they were good little tramps and good thieves. They shined my rough combat boots—the inside-out leather type. They rubbed and spat and grinned, and did it again. I would ask them, "Ong di nam Viet khomp?" "Are you going to become a refugee and leave this Communist land?" It was the first expression I learned in Vietnamese. "Yes," they would reply, "we are going south, sometime."

These kids couldn't quite get out the absurd word "Dooley." They called me "Bac Sy My," which, I soon discovered, meant "American Naval Doctor." Later on, when our work got more involved, the kids became a good junior intelligence network. Someone once called them "little Dooleys." I was flattered.

The part of Haiphong that I loved most was really the worst. It was that squirming Oriental bazaar—a real one, not a Cecil B. De Mille reproduction. The bazaar covered an enormous square on one side of the Rue Paul Bert.

Normally the population of Haiphong was about 100,000, but when we arrived in August, 1954 it had been doubled at least by the grey tides of refugees sweeping into the city. With baskets and bundles, they sprawled in the streets, gutters and alleys around the bazaar, and covered the parks like swarming ant-heaps. Through this filth and confusion moved detachments of French sailors and Foreign Legionnaires, busily evacuating French military and civilian property from the doomed city.

Around the fringes of the bazaar were the less revolting displays—fruit, flowers, vegetables, tennis shoes, stolen cameras and binoculars; but deep in the dark recesses, under straw roofs, were the stalls selling rancid butter and fish oils, flyblown pastries and pies, nauseating soft drinks, native beer designed to take a coat from the lining of your stomach, and red meat that could be seen only when the vendor waved away the solid covering of black flies.

Other meats—including cows' heads, birds' eyes, bat wings, dog entrails, dried cockroaches—were dispensed on knee-high platforms. The medicine stall displayed big glass jars of water in which snakes had been allowed to decay; taken daily, with a side-dose of dog liver, this was an all-purpose Tonkinese wonder drug.

Everywhere was the sharp, staccato sound of dried mahogany sticks clapped together. It meant soup for sale. Children wielded the sticks, while their parents sat over blackened pots incessantly stirring the half-congealed brews. Fat yellow dogs and sickly infants with the shining potbellies of famine wandered through the din.

Vegetables? You could buy mouldy potatoes, bright carrots, lettuce, watercress and fantastically large radishes, all guaranteed to give a Western stomach a good case of worms. Tuberculosis milk (from cows, goats and humans)—very cheap this week. And there were areas inside the bazaar where the sun never shone. There you could buy "nuoc mom," the chili sauce of the Orient, the oil from decaying fish mixed with salt. That was the stuff I had ordered thrown overboard that first day on the *Montague*.

While walking you were softly slugged with the heavy hanging cloud of caramel fragrance, sweet opium, drifting hashish. The mournful chants of beggars clashed with the shrieking of children, the shrill cries of hawkers and shoppers, the haggling and barking and bickering. Everything pushed, swayed, moved and, above all, smelled.

Women were bent double, with babies strapped to their backs, and there were others with bellies heavy with their unborn. There were women with their hair meticulously wrapped around their heads and perfumed with oil, carrying children whose hair was covered with a cradle cap and secondarily scabbed with pus. Abruptly one broke out into the daylight on the other side of this Oriental emporium. Here was another flower market, in all its beauty, a heaven next to a hell. There was a spot on the corner that would sell the things that are used in the Buddhist pagodas—paper idols, multi-colored dolls and animals, and slow-burning, sweet-smelling joss sticks. There were constant mournful chants from the mouths of the beggars, the shrieking of the children, the shrill cries of the women, the hawkers and the shoppers.

This was Haiphong, my home until the middle of the following May.

In front of most native homes, whether hovels or mansions, there were usually small red ribbons of paper with drawings of grimacing faces on them. There was an old legend about two brothers who could spot demons even in daylight and could frighten them away. Heaven therefore gave them the mission of barring the way of evil spirits, which were so terrified of the brothers that even their faces on red paper sent them flying.

Perhaps the people of Viet Nam should have hung these wonder-working ribbons all around their country. Then the legendary brothers might have barred the way to the demons of Communism stalking outside, and now holding the upper half of the country in their strangling grip.

Looking at the refugee-overrun city of Haiphong, one did not need to be a doctor to recognize that it was rotten ripe for the outbreak of typhus, smallpox, cholera and other plagues. We said little about it; words were unnecessary.

Depending on your nature, you either yielded to a sense of helplessness or you plunged into work, to reduce the suffering even a little and so help save an edge of dignity for Man—who is supposed to be only a little lower than the angels.

We did not have a single epidemic in Haiphong, in our camps outside the city or on our naval transports, in the entire period of the evacuation. That was to be the final measure of our work.

SEVEN ·

HOW DID IT ALL COME ABOUT?

Now that this was to be my new job, I wanted to find out a little about its background. I understood that the three countries of Laos, Cambodia and Viet Nam combined to make up Indo-China, richest colony of France. I also vaguely remembered that it was the Emperor of Laos who offered President Truman a division of Combat Elephants to help the war effort in Korea.

Doctor Amberson was able to assist me with some general background material; Ed Gleason, Dave Davis and Dick Kaufman didn't know much more than I did. But we learned.

After eight years of war, the Geneva treaty, signed six weeks earlier, had divided Viet Nam at the 17th Parallel into two "temporary zones of political influence" until things could be settled by a national plebiscite in July 1956. Viet Nam herself, the country which was divided, did not even sign the treaty which divided her. Meanwhile her southern half, with a population of 11 million, was to be ruled by the National government in Saigon, and the northern half, with a population of 10 million, was to be controlled by the Viet Minh Communists under the leadership of Ho Chi Minh.

An important clause in the cease-fire agreement provided that a crescent-shaped area around Haiphong was to remain an "open zone to both parties." This was to serve as a staging area for the evacuation of those people in the north who preferred exile in South Viet Nam to life under the Communists. The agreement was that these people were not only to be *allowed* but *assisted* to move south; and a mixed neutral commission, composed of representatives of Canada, Poland and India, was created to supervise the evacuation.

But this small "open zone" around Haiphong was scheduled to shrink gradually, and on specified dates, until in the middle of May 1955 the entire area, including the city of Haiphong, would be given to the Communists. Obviously this was a tricky agreement—just how tricky we would soon learn.

But why were the French so hated by the natives? And what had France done here that was good and had won her continuing American support? I wrote home and asked a friend to send me some books on this baffling country. It will suggest how confusing the subject was to the average American if I tell you that he sent to Indo-China a book entitled "Problems of Indonesia."

After some weeks I felt that I had at least a slight grasp on the situation, so I wrote it all down, with carbons, for anyone who might be interested.

Viet Nam is located in the highly strategic area of Southeast Asia. She lies directly south of China, whose province of Kwangsi is less than a hundred miles north of Haiphong. The China Sea washes Viet Nam's east coast and on the western border is the Kingdom of Laos with its elephants and tigers. The southwest border is formed by the equally ancient kingdom of Cambodia, one of the most rapidly developing nations of Asia.

Japan conquered Viet Nam in 1940. Within three months, by using Viet Nam's raw materials, airfields and seaports, Japan was able to overthrow Cambodia, Laos, Formosa, Thailand, Burma, Indonesia and Malaya. She became a threat to Australia and marched to the very gates of India.

Utilizing such seaports as Haiphong and Saigon, Japan shipped weapons and materials east which led to the defeat of MacArthur's forces and the conquest of the Philippines in 1942.

Economically, Viet Nam is important as the world's fourth largest producer of natural rubber. Her two deltas of the Tonkin in the north and the Cochin in the south produce a rich surplus of exportable rice. Her mountains abound in ores.

In the eighteenth and nineteenth centuries, Europe discovered the wealth of the Orient and all too eagerly shouldered the "white man's burden." England mastered the subcontinent of India. Holland seized the Pacific islands now called Indonesia, the Dutch East Indies. And France, in the 1860's and 1870's, achieved dominion over the three fabulous, storybook kingdoms of Indo-China. From then, until August 1954, Indo-China was a colony of France.

France did many fine things in Indo-China. She brought in the first rubber tree. She developed mines and minerals and built a system of roadways and waterways. Thousands of French families settled in the colony permanently, coming to think of it as their rightful home.

But France did not put into Viet Nam the equivalent of what she took out. She had a political and economic stake in keeping the native masses backward, submissive and ignorant of the arts of government. In a nation of 23-odd million, she built only one university. She was no more selfish than other colonial powers. She was simply following the patterns of the period.

In 1940, France yielded Indo-China to Japan without a real struggle. She set up a provisional government to protect her interests and managed to do "business as usual" with the invaders. It is ironic to note that an important member of that provisional government, Jean Sainteny, at this writing is in the Red capital of Hanoi as head of a French mission seeking to do "business as usual" with the Communist Viet Minh.

In 1945 Viet Nam, Laos and Cambodia were liberated, not by the French, but by the English and Americans.

At this time a man who had become well-known and beloved in the underground during the Japanese occupation came into additional prominence. He would say: "We have gained our independence from the Japanese and I see no reason why we should again yield it to France. We are a strong nation and we will be our own rulers." He set himself up in Hanoi as the president of the "Democratic Republic of Viet Nam." He was Ho Chi Minh, which means Ho, the Enlightened One.

The French sent Ho Chi Minh into exile but on December 19, 1946, his forces started a war for independence—started it by disemboweling more than 1,000 native women in Hanoi because they had been working for, married to, or living with the French.

Many Americans, though they shuddered at such obscene methods, sympathized with his ultimate goals, considering him a patriotic Vietnamese Nationalist. Such nationalists were winning the struggle with colonial powers all over Asia.

During this time, I was a student in college in Paris and I can remember the campaigns for collections of clothes and money to send to the forces of Ho Chi Minh, now called the Viet Minh. I can recall contributing a few dollars to this organization.

But in 1949, after the Communists had conquered China, Ho showed his true colors by proclaiming the Democratic Republic of Viet Nam— which was promptly recognized by the U.S.S.R., Communist China, and other satellite states of the Soviet bloc. Ho Chi Minh had been a Moscow-trained puppet from the start.

After 1949, the United States supplied military and economic aid in the struggle to save Viet Nam from the Communists. But again we failed to make our objectives clear to the people. After the fall of Dien Bien Phu and the tragedy at Geneva, there were Vietnamese who hated the Viet Minh and the French with equal fervor, but who hated the Americans too because the French had fought with American aid. So again the job of winning friends and influencing people was left to a few men in uniform who, officially, had other fish to fry.

However, to the rice-paddy-worker and the coolie there was no difference between 1948 and 1950. One could not speak to such men of dialectical materialism and the new Red imperialism. They had no grasp of the complexities of Communism because these concepts related to nothing within their own traditions or experiences. The rice-paddy-worker knew only that the underground hero and his soldiers, many of them from their own villages, were fighting and often defeating the French. To him this was "Viet Minh Nationalism." He did not know he was placing himself in the bondage of Communism; he only wanted to be free of the yoke of colonialism.

Only when and where the Viet Minh took and held power did the people begin to savor the abstraction called Communism, and for the most part they did not relish the flavor. Slowly, under beguiling slogans and promises, the new masters were taking away their lands, undermining the family loyalty of their children, conscripting their bodies and—especially for the two million Christians—outraging their souls.

And so the war continued until 1954. It did not directly affect Americans living in Kansas City and Decatur and Jacksonville. However, when the battle of Dien Bien Phu began, the eyes of the world focussed on this far-away post. This was our awakening.

By the time the complex struggle came to a head at Dien Bien Phu, the free world no longer had any illusions. It was aware that the life-and-death interests of Washington and London were at stake on one side as surely as those of Moscow and Peiping were on the other. Catastrophe stalked the Tonkin.

Many of us remember Dien Bien Phu, remember how fifteen thousand men fought there. We remember that the number of French dead was fantastic and that most of them died knowing that the fortress was doomed but continuing to fight nonetheless, for the honor of France.

Dien Bien Phu really marked the end of the war in Indo-China. That isolated outpost fell to the Viet Minh in May, 1954. On July 21st of the same year the Treaty of Geneva was signed and officially ended the war. Secretary of State John Foster Dulles walked out of that conference saying that the United States would not sign the treaty because we would not be a party to an agreement that handed over half a country to totalitarian tyranny.

Geneva's promises were many. Most important was the clause that said that the country of Viet Nam was to be divided into two "zones of political influence." The one north of the 17th parallel, the large Tonkin delta with 10 million people would be given to the Viet Minh, the Communist government of Ho Chi Minh; the 11 million people south of the 17th parallel would live under the rule of Premier, now President, Ngo Dinh Diem.

The second important clause stated that anyone living in one zone who wished to go to the other would be allowed to make, and aided in making, this transfer. If they were in the Tonkin of the north and wished to go south, they were to proceed to the port city of Haiphong, where ships would transport them. The small crescent-shaped area around Hanoi and Haiphong was to remain "free" until May 19, 1955. This area was to shrink on successive dates. On May 19, 1955 all the area north of the 17th parallel would be handed over to the Viet Minh.

Early in August there was a trickle of refugees into Hanoi and Haiphong, which are about forty miles apart. In that same month, Vietnamese and French officials asked the U.S. to assist their own forces to evacuate from the Tonkin all the refugees who might want to leave. The United States instantly agreed, Task Force 90 received its orders and within a few days the great exodus was in swing. Neither the French nor the Communists, least of all the Americans, could foresee that it would assume the dimensions it did. In Viet Nam a proud and noble race paid a staggering price in human misery for the issues of freedom. The deal was closed now; Viet Nam had not won.

That was the background as we settled down in the musty, dusty Hotels Paris and Continental.

EIGHT ·
CAMP DE LA PAGODE

Through years of college and medical school I had taken courses in everything from Aristotle to Zoology. Unhappily none of this education included a course in refugee camp building. Dr. Amberson did not indicate that he was aware of this gap in my store of knowledge.

It was obvious that the first problem we would have with the refugees would be that of housing. There were perhaps 150,000 living in the most squalid conditions, sprawling out over the city streets and gutters. There was no sanitation of any kind. The refugees were living under shelters improvised from rice mats, cloth or plastic rain covers.

On our second day in Haiphong, Captain Amberson tossed a sheaf of notes and sketches at me. "Dooley," he said, "your job will be to build refugee camps. There's the general idea. Now get going. And don't bother me about the details." Aye, aye, sir. But at that moment I didn't know the difference between a refugee camp and a playground for girls.

You can't build a refugee camp in the middle of a city; therefore, we looked around on the outskirts. Most of the outskirts consisted of rice paddies or bogs along the edges of the Red River. Finally we found a reasonably dry spot about four miles from town, on the road leading from Hanoi into Haiphong. "Highway" in Viet Nam describes a barely navigable dirt road. At this time, the site was about 40 miles from the Bamboo Curtain, which gave us a little elbow-room. By October 11, under the Geneva schedule, the town of Haiduong would be swallowed, bringing the outposts of Communism within fifteen miles of us, and in January the Curtain would be visible from the camp itself.

Many unkind things have been said about how slowly the cogs of American agencies move. Yet within a few days after he had been informed of our plans, Mike Adler, head of the U.S. Foreign Operations Administration (USOM) in Haiphong, had 400 large tents flown in from Japan. "Army Sixty-Man Tents" they were called; for us they often sheltered 120 people or more.

To help us set up the tents the French Union Forces furnished us some Moroccan soldiers and we found a few hundred coolies. The design of the camp was there in Dr. Amberson's sketch. He was the brain and we were his hands. I was learning how to build tent camps.

After several days of work, the first camp was completed. The tents were arranged in twelve rows. All told, we erected 149 tents, with a broad road-way through the middle of the camp. An elaborate set of drainage ditches kept the place from floating away during the monsoon season, though the ditches did form something of an obstacle course. If you didn't walk with one eye on the ground, you were liable to find yourself knee-deep in a ditch.

Certain broad paddies surrounding the camp were used as latrines. I pulled a few prize boners, which Dr. Amberson caught in time, like locating the latrine area on the windward side. One problem required continuous effort on our part—to educate the refugees not to take their soapless baths in the same paddy they were using as a flushless toilet. About once a month we would spray these fields with a strong insecticide solution. This would kill the bugs and throw into spasms any poor refugee who happened to get caught with his pants down when we were spraying.

Later, in some of the other camps, we dug Marine-type slit trenches and straddle trenches to be used as toilets. A circular windbreak was put around them. The refugees always stayed dutifully within the windbreak but were not in the least anxious to use the trenches themselves. My corpsmen, with the ingenuity of enlisted men, gradually moved the windbreak closer and closer to the trenches until the refugees were finally forced to use them; there was nowhere else to go.

One time, in the early months, we borrowed Commodore Walter Winn's helicopter, hovered over the area and dumped DDT powder through a hose in the bottom of the plane. A great deal of it fell to the earth, but an equally large amount blew back up in our faces. The refugees on the ground watched this astonishing procedure and shouted with glee the equivalent of "What bizarre people, these Americans! They have a fixation on excrement and strange white powder." The helicopter-dusting plan went up in a cloud of DDT.

The colony was scarcely a lovely sight to the eyes and certainly no treat to the nose. Nevertheless, we were pleased, even elated. A beginning had been made. The first row of tents I reserved for my hospital area—a tent for sick-call, a "nursery" for newborn babies, several supply tents and five or six tents for sick patients. I also set aside tents for the elders or mandarins who would act as camp leaders.

We had one large tent in which we stored rice and straw mats. The rice had a private scent all its own (boll weevils, I believe), while the straw mats had a musty odor, especially in the monsoon season. The canvas had a scent and the pungent insecticides we used had theirs. Corpsmen Baker and Harris had a pet baboon, Jasmine, who made her home in this tent too. Blend all these aromas together and add the draft from the washrooms and you will see why visitors never had any difficulty in locating our headquarters.

We christened our first camp "Refugee Camp de la Pagode." The name seemed Oriental and melodious, despite the fact that the area was fresh out of pagodas.

This was just the first camp. Others were to come: Camp Cement, Camp Shell, Camp Lach Tray, Jardin des Enfants, to mention a few. We were obliged to move fairly frequently, when the mud would no longer support us, or when the Red frontier came uncomfortably close, or in one instance when we were driven out by rats, four-legged variety. Like old circus hands, my meagre staff and volunteer refugees were soon adept in tearing 'em down and putting 'em up.

The Vietnamese Refugee Evacuation Committee of Haiphong was directed by Mr. Mai Van Ham, who became one of my best friends. He gave me everything I asked for, from extra coolies to some insight into the Oriental mind. He was frequently at odds with the French and occasionally with an impatient doctor. Sometimes we almost came to blows, but the situation would always resolve itself when we both realized that, each in his own fashion, we were endeavoring to do our utmost for Viet Nam's oppressed. Mai Van Ham is a true patriot. His tireless devotion to his overwhelming task was magnificent.

Now we began to round up the refugees and move them in with us. In the Medical Tent we held daily sick-call. Here, with our American Aid medicines, we saw three to four hundred refugees every day. Respiratory diseases were common, as were trachoma, worm infestations, fungus infections, tinea and tuberculosis. These were just everyday run-of-the-mill complaints. Every corpsman I ever had could soon identify a case of yaws at ten feet.

The Navy supplied our unit with every piece of machinery, a truck, water tanks, a jeep and insecticides. However, it didn't seem quite fair to the Navy that we should ask it, officially, for soap, vitamin pills, dressings and aspirin for the hundreds of thousands of people who eventually were to pass through our area.

During the months of August through October, we acquired most of our pharmacy for the camp's sick-call through that time-honored, slightly illegitimate, Oriental custom known as cumshaw. My corpsmen and I would take turns running out to the bay in boats or hitch-hiking on the Commodore's helicopter. Any nearby U.S. ship was our target. We would bum a dozen bottles of vitamins, half a dozen vials of penicillin, a handful of band-aids, some antibiotics, a few hemostats—we would accept anything they were willing to give. Through the unbounded generosity of the Navy, unbeknownst to the Navy, we amassed a formidable armamentarium of drugs.

In return for these gifts to cumshaw we would give lectures to the crews on just what was happening and describe what most of the refugees had to endure to escape. We often carried a large plastic-covered map of French Indo-China with us to dramatize the 17th parallel. The talks were always well received.

And so, through this quasi-honorable means, we kept our pharmacy stocked. However, by December most of the ships had left and only four or five transports remained. We couldn't keep going back to them, so we devised another system.

I decided to write home for medicines. Terramycin was the most important drug, so I wrote first to the Pfizer Laboratories Division of Charles Pfizer and Company, Brooklyn, N. Y. I told them of our job, of our people, our camp and our problems. I even sent some photos. My letter closed with a request for a "small contribution—of, say, 25,000 capsules—of terramycin."

The Pfizer Company responded immediately with 50,000 capsules. Later they sent some penicillin, streptomycin, and magnamycin. The total commercial value must have been tens of thousands of dollars. Its real value to us was incalculable.

In response to my letter, Mead Johnson of Evansville, Indiana, sent us many gallons of liquid vitamin preparation; Pan American Airways sent 10,000 bars of soap, and other companies sent many other things. This was the "decadent capitalistic system of America" responding.

Rest assured, we continually explained to thousands of refugees, as individuals and in groups, that only in a country which permits companies to grow large could such fabulous charity be found. With every one of the thousands of capsules of terramycin and with every dose of vitamins on a baby's tongue, these words were said: "Dai La My-Quoc Vien-Tro" (This is American Aid).

These companies performed a great service; I am sure not their first. They didn't send regrets, they didn't promise to "investigate" my claim; they responded with the enthusiasm of great corporations in a great country. When I wrote to thank them, telling them of the impact their contributions had made, they responded with letters thanking *me*. Imagine that! Every person from whom I requested aid responded wholeheartedly. It gave me a feeling of nearness to all the people in my country. It was as if all the wealth of America were in my own medicine chest. All I had to do was reach and ask, and reach and ask I did. Camp de la Pagode became a corner drugstore. About all we lacked were comic books and ice cream.

Mike Adler had a small warehouse of medicines flown up from U.S.O.M. supplies. These were sent to the Viet Nam Public Health Office in Haiphong, which in turn sent them to us—always with a smile. It was American Aid reversing itself. "From U.S.O.M. to Viet Nam to the American doctor."

At Camp de la Pagode we processed potable water. Our aim was a gallon per refugee per day and sometimes, daily, this was as much as 12,000 gallons. If medals could be awarded to machines, I would recommend the highest honors for our water-purifying equipment. We used a gasoline-engined water purification unit which is standard in the Marine Corps Supply Catalogue. Except for minor, though of course exasperating, complaints, that spunky little unit, rigged up by Lieutenant Commander Ed Gleason, ran for nearly 300 days with a minimum of faltering. The water was drawn from a rice paddy, passed through a sand-filter and two chemical feed tanks, and finally through a chlorination gyzmo before passing into the big 3000-gallon rubber storage tanks. This was *nouc my* (American water) which the refugees drank with obvious distaste. They much preferred the typhoid flavor of the water in certain forbidden paddies.

The particular paddy from which our water was lifted had to be barbed-wired off because the refugees would wash their feet, food and livestock in it. One morning all the water in that rice paddy was black. We investigated and discovered that the cause was vegetable dye that a peasant had used to color her clothes for the summer Viet Nam fashions. She had dumped the concentrated solution into the rice paddy when she had finished with it. We had to put the camp on water rations until the stuff had cleared.

On several occasions our rubber tanks were slashed, probably maliciously and by pro-Communists. And then again inquisitive kids would climb up the sides of the tanks and drop wooden boats, or occasionally drop themselves, into the water. Great sport! We finally erected a barbed-wire fence around the water tanks.

While we are on the subject of *nouc my*, let me tell you of two of my corpsmen, one of whom was not really a corpsman but an Aviation Boatswain's Mate, Third Class, who was utilized in everything we did. That's Norman M. Baker, at the moment of this writing stationed on the U.S.S. *Philippine Sea.* The other lad was a six-foot-six-inch, two-hundred-pound Swede named Edward Maugre, a Hospital Corpsman, Second Class. The refugees loved them. You would see them walking around the camp, probably with sprayers on their backs, surrounded by a mob of shrieking kids. The conventional idea—it's a sound idea—that the children of Viet Nam are irresistible was put in reverse, the children found my corpsmen irresistible.

One day I heard more than the usual uproar of screaming and yelling at the water plant, so I went over to see what was up. Baker and Maugre had decided that the water sediment tanks needed cleaning so they took six of the Vietnamese children, removed their clothes and threw them into the tank, waist deep in water. They handed them brushes and soap and told them to scrub the bottom and side walls. The children were jubilant over the job, and the corpsmen ended by fighting a small war to keep all the other children in the camp from climbing into the tank and joining the soapy six.

Lieutenant Commander Ed Gleason was the sanitation and hygiene expert and at first he was the only man who knew how to solve the occasional maladies of the water-plant equipment. In fact, he constructed the units and nursed them from burping infancy to belching adolescence. When he left, he succeeded in passing on his magic to Baker and Maugre.

The water units were always rather frightening to me. Every time I laid a hand on a lever, either sand would fly out of a hose or the engine would groan and die. So, though I admired the unit from a distance, I left it pretty much to the corpsmen.

When Admiral Sabin visited us on an inspection tour, he asked Maugre what the water tasted like. Maugre replied respectfully, "Dunno, sir, I never touch my own product."

Whenever something went wrong with the unit, I gave Baker my jeep and a carton of cigarettes, and in the voice-of-command I had learned from Dr. Amberson, I'd say: "Baker, get that damned thing fixed—and don't bother me with the details." Hours later, Baker would return with a couple of Legionnaires, all full of cheap brandy and smoking American cigarettes. I never knew where the Frenchmen or the spare parts came from, but the water-machine always became as good as new. And Baker always had an awful hangover which, alas, I am unable to doctor effectively, except in the usual fruitless ways. But he never bothered me with details.

Our first refugee camp became the center of attraction for visiting dignitaries. Admiral Sabin and Commodore Walter Winn, who relieved the Admiral as Commander of the Task Force; General J. Lawton Collins, the former U. S. Army Chief of Staff, who was serving as the President's personal trouble-shooter in Viet Nam, General "Iron Mike" O'Daniel, the Chief of Military Assistance Advisory Group of Saigon, and many other visiting firemen were taken on usually muddy tours of the usually very muddy camp.

The Viet Nam governor of our small area was a patriot by the name of Nguyen Luat. He had been educated in France and chose to return to his own nation of Viet Nam. Before the war, he had been the editor of a newspaper in Hanoi. During the war he had fought with the French as an officer. The Governor came out almost every week and tramped through the camp speaking to his people and lifting their hearts and their spirits.

The Mayor of the city of Haiphong was Mai Van Bot. He would come to the camp often, though without the entourage of the Governor. He was a simple man and a fine one, well loved by the Americans who knew him.

Less well-loved visitors to the camp were Viet Minh Communist agents. They visited us daily. The refugees would point the first finger of suspicion. They would tell us: "There is a man in Camp de la Pagode Tent 5B who is saying that we have made a great mistake by coming here. He is saying that we should return immediately to fight for the true nationalists, the Viet Minh. He is very strange, this one." The police would find such agents in the camp every couple of days.

The people of Haiphong would come out on their rickshaws and take a look at us to see if living conditions might be better than those in town. I am sure that many moved out to this new housing project.

Vietnamese Public Health, who were desperately short-handed, gave us some native nurses when they could. Like all natives, these girls were so anxious to get to the safety of the south that none of them stayed with us very long. We would find some relatively clean-looking refugees and persuade them to stay on in the camp a month or two, instead of the usual ten days. We would teach them to wash their hands and other basic things; they learned quickly and were always anxious to help. Then we crowned them "nurses." Along with running a camp, being interpreters, father-confessors, American images, doctors, corpsmen, water-plant operators, and the like we thus served as professors of a school of nursing.

After a few weeks the camp was going full force and we were a thriving little community all our own. We had our own name; we had our own government; we had our own hospital, complete with corpsmen and black-toothed, betel-chewing nurses, and we had our own groceries. The daily ration was six hundred grams of rice, meticulously weighed, a couple of fish and such extras as were available.

I have left for the last the most important center in the camp, our church. It was not a great and noble structure—just another tent with its sides rolled up. There was a wooden altar there, and the Blessed Sacrament was reserved by day and night. Every morning, in the shy and early dawn, Mass was said for the camp's fifteen thousand inhabitants. I feel sure God heard the prayers of these poor refugees. They sought no favors. They did not ask God where their children would roam beyond tomorrow's arch, but they thanked Him with strong voices in prayer and in song. They thanked Him for having given them their freedom.

And they turned to the Mother of God, to the Blessed Virgin of Fatima, and said, "Remember, O most gracious Virgin Mary, that never was it known that anyone who fled to Thy protection, implored Thy help, or sought Thy intercession has been left unaided, and we thank Thee, O Queen of Queens."

NINE ·

OUR "TASK FORCE" SHRINKS

With refugees streaming in and others being evacuated, giving the camps a continuing population that ran as high as 15,000, our primary job was to delouse, vaccinate, inoculate them, and screen out those who had communicable diseases. But there was more to it than that. At the sick-call tent I was now seeing between 300 and 400 people every day who were desperately in need of medical treatment. What was I to do? Leave them in the camp to die? Send them back behind the Bamboo Curtain?

There is a motto in every service that says (approximately) that a man should keep his mouth shut and his internal system in order and *never* volunteer. Fortunately it is a rule that Americans talk about but seldom observe when things get tough. And I guess I have a special tendency to stick my neck out.

Captain Amberson was worried by my impulsiveness, which was increasing the work-load of the camps. I had argued that the spraying and vaccinating being done in town was haphazard and dangerous; hence no one should be allowed aboard ship without being processed by us. Now I brought the Captain another headache.

"Doctor," I said, "we've got to do something for these sick people. Rules are rules, but we can't surrender a woman and child to the Communists just because the kid has smallpox. We've got to treat the smallpox so that the family can get aboard a ship."

He looked at me wearily, but with obvious understanding. As a doctor he agreed with me heartily. He just felt sorry for a young eager-beaver who thought he could lick every problem in sight.

"All right, Dooley," he said. "Treat the smallpox. You know the limitations as well as I do. Go ahead and do the best you can."

Thus therapy on a vast scale was added to the delousing, vaccination and camp sanitation—at least doubling the dimensions of the medical effort. We stepped up sick-call and I enlarged my hospital tent for surgery.

Captain Amberson was suddenly called to Washington, D.C. He was ordered to leave immediately, which meant in twenty-four hours. We scared up a seat on a CAT plane that was taking Chinese Nationals out to Taipeh. Usually I can watch Commanding Officers leave without any emotion whatsoever. When this one left, however, there was the definite feeling of loss— both of an excellent boss, and a good friend. He was replaced by Dr. Britten, who wanted to set up a laboratory for the Fleet Epidemiological Disease Control Unit. We couldn't put it out in the camp, because the microscopes and other equipment were very expensive and there was too much chance of theft.

The French Navy Base was the solution. Admiral Querville was most cooperative and gave us an empty warehouse. Here we established our portable lab and brought the specimens that we collected in the camps to be analyzed and catalogued.

The laboratory didn't look much like Bethesda Naval Medical Center but it was functional. We had large wooden tables, several hard folding chairs. For the boss, we stole a large velvet-covered couch which looked as if it had come from Emperor Gia Long's throne room.

Commander Sidney Britten, Dr. Amberson's successor, was a lab man from way back; his main interest was in the epidemiological end of the work, just as Captain Amberson's main interest was in field work, such as teaching JG's how to build refugee tent camps. Dr. Britten took over the lab at the Navy base and left sick-call and the running of the camp pretty much to me.

I spent most of the day holding sick-call, except for a couple of hours during the heat of the afternoon. It was during this breathing spell that the mandarin who was Chief of the Camp gave me my Vietnamese lessons. He spoke impeccable French and this was our common denominator. With some concerted effort over a couple of months, I was able to speak Vietnamese as well as I needed to, with an adequate Tonkin accent. It is a very easy, monosyllabic language. I even learned some Vietnamese songs.

At this time our days had a persisting and often amusing pattern. Dr. Britten would head a group who would drive out to the camp with determined jaws set. He would sit in the sick-call tent, in the 105 degrees of humid heat, wearing a jungle cap, green Marine fatigues, and with boots and trousers tucked in the tops in an attempt to escape being eaten alive by the malarial mosquitoes, which were about as large and deadly as small jet fighters.

He would direct his corpsmen, James Cobb, of Los Angeles, Joseph Milo, of Lynn, Massachusetts, Donald Whitlock, of La Sunta, California, Walt Hoban of Philadelphia, Art Prichett and Robert Prusso—I am not sure where they hailed from—while they collected venous and peripheral blood smears. They would use these for studies and send hundreds of the answers back to fill the shopping lists of National Naval Medical School. I understand that this work resulted in at least two medical discoveries, one of considerable importance.

Meanwhile I would stand out in the camp and, with candy, try to entice the children to give us stool specimens. In this sometimes ludicrous job I was assisted by my corpsman, Dennis D. Shepard, a Salem, Oregon, boy, and a very fine one too.

My Vietnamese was then pretty poor. I knew how to say "stool" and "sample" and "give me" and, of course, "please." But when I combined these words into a sentence, I would evoke howls of laughter. I would just have to repeat the words, point and grunt, and then go through the process all over again. Shepard would nod, point, smile and pass out candy and small paper boxes. Some of the children would take these containers, given for another purpose, and put the candy into them. Others would take aim and spit into them. "No, no," I would say. "Stool specimens."

Then some would disappear with the boxes and return them with either microscopic or overflowing contents. But most of the refugees would just disappear, boxes and all. I am afraid that Dr. Britten was disappointed with my end of the collection operation.

Lieutenant Richard Kaufman, of Pittsburgh, also of the Medical Service Corps, was in Dr. Britten's unit. He and Lt. Comdr. Gleason spent a good deal of time crawling along the pipes of the city's inadequate water and sewage systems. Dick also placed rat traps all over the place, even in the hotel we lived in. He would catch the pony-sized rats alive, then comb their luxurious coats for fleas which might indicate the presence of plague.

Chief Cobb and Hospital Corpsman First Class Joe Milo were deeply interested in mosquitoes, both in the malaria-bearing kind and in those that carried yellow fever. They set up mosquito traps around the latrines, the water plant, the sick-call tent, our hotel rooms and other choice spots.

Don Whitlock, Hospitalman Second Class, spent hours peering into his microscope at blood smears, cataloguing percentages and so on.

So we were a strange lot, we Americans; Shepard and I armed with our stool specimen cups, Cobb and Milo with their bottles of mosquitoes,

Whitlock with his slides, Dr. Britten with vials of blood, Ed Gleason with maps of the city's sewers, Dick Kaufman with his live rats. At this moment there is probably some refugee in Saigon writing a book about his experiences with those amazing inhabitants of the United States who came to Haiphong with their incredible customs and even more incredible collection mania.

By the end of October we had collected thousands of specimens of every nature and kind—fully enough, Dr. Britten decided. At this time the French Navy informed Admiral Sabin that the situation with the Communists in this still-free zone was getting very sticky, and that it might be better if there were fewer Americans in Haiphong, though we only numbered about twenty all told. The French, and we too for that matter, lived in a vague but constant dread that the Viet Minh would "liberate" this port any day and take us captive. The Viet Minh had already taken over the Tonkin's capital, Hanoi, less than an hour away, shrinking the free zone to just a few miles around Haiphong. General René Cogny called Haiphong into a state of "guarded emergency."

Ed Gleason left a few weeks after Dr. Amberson flew to Washington. Commander Britten and Lieutenant Kaufman returned to Japan in October and took with them all of the corpsmen who were part of the FEDCU unit.

I was left with only three corpsmen to help me—Dennis Shepard, a new arrival, Peter Kessey, who was superb, and noble Norman Baker who was to be with me to the bitter end. Now a Naval medical officer of one year's vintage was in sole command of the refugee camp and related functions. He was subject to the directives of superiors, but in practice he was left almost wholly to his own devices. By guess and by God, I kept the unit running for the remaining eight months.

Daily I expected new brass to arrive and take over, but no one came. Much later I heard from Admiral Sabin himself what had happened. Captain Amberson had told him: "The situation in Haiphong is extremely dangerous and the fewer men we have ashore the better. Young Dooley has the situation well in hand and can carry on."

Sure enough, in mid-November orders came through designating me "Commander, Task Unit 90. 8. 6." The decimal points indicated I was far down the line, but I was pretty proud. Then some lunkhead, undoubtedly a line Lieut. Commander, decided that for security reasons our mission would be known as Operation Cockroach. Damn!

TEN ·

THE POWER OF PROPAGANDA

Often in the early evening when the day's work was done, I would go to the tents with the mandarin Chief of the Camp and talk to the people who had just arrived from the Communist zone. The refugees, really escapees, were just as interested in me as I was in them. I asked them what their life had been like under the Viet Minh rule.

Thus I was able to learn a good deal about the people of the Tonkin, who had come under the heel of Communist oppression. I was able to understand the confusion in their minds and in their nation. They scarcely knew friends from enemies. Natural pride in their own country had been exploited until it became hate for any other nation, especially for France and for the United States, since the U.S. supplied the French with tanks and guns and planes used in the colonial war.

Perhaps some of these natives had helped to bring the new Communist police state into being, but their hope and faith had turned to suspicion and disillusionment. To them, Ho Chi Minh and his forces had represented nationalism. The "Benevolent Aid" that the Viet Minh had accepted from Red China had seemed benevolent indeed. Hadn't China accepted similar aid from Russia and hadn't this helped to create the new and glorious Red China? At least, the Viet Minh radio always said that Red China was glorious.

The Communists knew just how to handle the average Tonkinese rice-delta family. They played upon the pride of such families in their fields. They promised agrarian reforms. They promised to divide lands belonging to the colonial rich among the native poor. And this was done. However, the poor were soon burdened with such a tax that their pocket money at the end of the harvest was less than it had been before.

The Viet Minh promised the water wheel. This was to be a great thing for the land. The Tonkin is divided into small paddies, each about the size of a football field. Small mud dikes around the fields separate one from another. During the life of a rice crop, there are times when it must be in water and times when it must be dry. So at various times the water must be transferred from one field to another. If the receiving field is lower than the other, there is not much difficulty. But if it is level or higher, the water must be transferred by hand, with buckets. The transfer goes on for hours at a time, and it has been going on for centuries.

Ho Chi Minh said: "I will give you a water wheel. This will ease your labors. It will lift the water for you." And when he took over he did give water wheels to thousands of farmers. There was one metaphorical flaw in them. As they belonged to the state, it was only simple justice for the state to ask the farmer, as his end of the bargain, to pay the state a certain percentage of his crops. As can well be imagined, that percentage was not small.

And so, as more and more of the promised "reforms" were put into effect, more and more of the Tonkinese began to dream of escape. The so-called guarantee of free and unmolested passage was now clearly a farce and ours were probably the only camps in history that people had to escape *into*.

Meanwhile, the Communists bombarded the people with stories of the imperialistic French and Americans who were kidnapping Tonkinese citizens. They hammered the stories home, hour after hour, month after month. All young men and women were required to attend "re-education" classes every morning. Here the political commissars reiterated again and again their stories about the American barbarians.

To rice-paddy peasants, some of the stories sounded pretty plausible. Americans are known to be obsessed with the subject of cleanliness, so perhaps they do cut the hands from those who vomit on their ships. America is a land of tremendous manufacturing operations, so perhaps Americans do need coolies for slave labor. It fits the picture—the boot fits the foot.

Their propaganda campaign was next to agrarian reform in importance. To be efficacious propaganda must be onesided. Those exposed to its fiery tongue must never be allowed to hear any other tongue. The curtain which crashed down on Asia had the same impact, though of bamboo, as the Iron Curtain had in Europe.

One thing did pierce this curtain. The refugees told me of secret battery radios, smuggled in to them just lately, on which they would listen to the Voice of America. By this means they learned of the evacuation, and of the promises of Geneva. When they arrived at our camps they eyed us cautiously, and sometimes with active dislike. They were probably thinking, "Look at that sailor the young Doctor calls Baker. See him going around with that spraying—maybe disease-spraying—machine on his back. What deviltry is he capable of?"

He wasn't capable of much. Norman Baker, Aviation Boatswain's Mate, Third Class, is first-class in my book, or maybe first-class plus. He was sent to me early in the game as, of all things, my French interpreter. The person who sent him must have been the only one in the line of command who did not realize that my facility in French was the main reason I was here in the first place.

Baker and I decided it was the obligation of neither of us to set matters straight. "All right, so I won't interpret," he said in substance, "but I think I might be useful in other ways." It was the understatement of the year. Baker is the American sailor who was the real hero of Haiphong.

All my corpsmen felt the people's unrest and fear. We might be holding sick-call and see an old woman, perhaps a leper, squatting on her haunches watching us closely. She might stay for hours, watching us clean, inject, treat and dress the refugees. After some time and with much hesitancy, she might come up and ask for something for her "dao mat," or trachomatous eyes. Even then, she was full of doubt.

However, the "miraculousness" of our drugs was a great persuader. I had never thought much about the power of antibiotics, vitamins, soap, cleanliness and the rest of it. They have power unbridled.

Vaccination afforded a special problem, as the people had been told that we would inject diseases into them if they came into our camps. American bacteriological warfare! We were reported to be carrying out large-scale medical experiments and using the Tonkinese as guinea pigs. That was also one reason why it was so hard to collect specimens for FEDCU. Specimens, for Heaven's sake, for what?

They were so wary of us that it was often difficult to get them into the sick-call tent for treatment. So we would hold sick-call in *front* of the tent. Then some ten thousand refugees could squat on their haunches all around us and observe "What will he do?" "Watch him . . ." "Be careful . . ."

As for those stories about ships with huge mouths that spewed people overboard—well, no wonder that, when the refugees first sighted the LCTs and LSMs opening their bow doors to embark them, they would surge back in a wave of fear.

A priest would stand on a truck with a loudspeaker and talk and talk, sometimes for hours, during embarkations, telling the people to go aboard and not to be afraid. He would often get down and walk aboard for a moment himself in order to set an example. So the refugees would go aboard too, but fearfully, every step of the way.

Often they had leaflets that they had been issued behind the Curtain. The leaflets were downright absurd, but still . . .

One showed the American ship *Marine Adder*, a transport. It showed violently seasick refugees leaning over the rail vomiting. They had their hands braced on the rail. Sailors with white hats, the devils, were cutting the hands off the people as they braced themselves on the rail. Things are tough all over.

Even the refugees who did not literally believe this nonsense were never quite sure. Some of the younger ones, who might loosely be termed intellectuals, would quiz me about the atomic bomb. They had heard that the Atomic Control Commission had completely destroyed the State of Nevada. Then it had annihilated Bikini and other islands in the Pacific. Was it true that the next explosion was to be in the Tonkin? They just wondered. "Why did they ask?" They held up a leaflet. A piece of Viet Minh propaganda showing an aerial view of their ancient, and beloved capital of Hanoi. Over it were the three concentric circles of Atomic destruction. Printed on this was just one word that all could read—"My" which means "American."

They even felt suspicious about the simple white Navy skivvy undershirt. I gave a talk downriver on the *U.S.S. Askari*, a repair ship. Partially to thank me, but mostly because of a sailor's eager willingness to help, the crew of the ship sent me a coffin-sized locker box stuffed with Navy cotton T-shirts and underpants.

The refugees certainly needed them, the shirts at least and, if not so badly, the shorts also. The box reached the camp and the refugees gathered around. I handed one of them an undershirt. He took it in his hands and looked at it, mute. He didn't feel the material. He didn't hold it up like an American woman in a department store buying a bra. He just held it in his hands and watched me closely.

Sensing disaster, I tried something. I took my own khaki shirt off in front of the mob and showed them that I was wearing a white T-shirt with my name and service number stenciled across the front. It was just like the ones I was passing out. I said a little prayer, hoping that this would do it, and maybe the prayer did. A boy held his shirt up and another slipped one over his bare torso. Soon the shirts were going like nylons in a bargain sale. Thank God it worked—I had no intentions of showing them my skivvies.

I wish the boys on the *Askari* could have seen the kids, customarily bare bottomed, running around the camp in Navy shorts (usually on backwards, for the sake of efficiency) and the girls in T-shirts with "Sam Goldblatz,

BM3, 278-00-19," or "Jack Flanagan, FN, 339-27-61," stenciled across their bosoms.

Mike Adler's successor, Roger Ackley, arrived from Germany, where he had been dealing with refugee problems. He was a large and jovial man. Much of the joviality left him after he had taken a hard professional look at the abject misery around us. He coined the expression "American Impact." We four of the medical unit, the first Americans most of the refugees had ever seen, were in an excellent position to contribute to the American Impact. My boys and I sat down and figured out a plan. I suppose an Admiral of the Line would say, "We promulgated a feasible policy." The boys were quick to see that every move they made was considered a move by America, that their every action had massive reactions. If they pushed the children roughly away, or splashed women with a jeep's wheels, or blasted its horn at them when they squatted in the road, that was America pushing, splashing, blasting; it would reflect on our nation as a whole. It was hard to be patient with the throngs that followed us everywhere we went, even to the bathroom (that field over there to the left of the camp). Yet I never saw a man lose his temper.

My boys treated the refugees with patience, understanding and a little love. This was a largely negative approach. We had a positive approach as well. We began our own little program of selling America. It began with the expression, in Vietnamese, "This is American Aid." All my boys learned the expression and repeated it every time they did anything from passing out an APC to helping a child pull his pants back up when they fell down. In fact, we used it so often that when the refugees, in turn, would give us a bowl of rice, or help put up a new tent, or push my jeep out of the monsoon mud, they would grin and roar, "This is Vietnamese Aid."

Roger Ackley obtained many small American Aid emblems. They were nailed to boxes, plastered on bottles of medicines, attached to the water tent, fount of that cursed *nouc my*.

You couldn't really say that we were staffed and organized like the Pentagon for a really big educational effort, but I believe our sliver of salesmanship was of prime importance. Rival ideologies are fighting this war now and *not* with guns and hydrogen bombs either. They are competing for the souls of those who are rising in search of a better life. So we have to demonstrate that *our* way of life has qualities that are good.

This the men of the Preventive Medicine Unit understood. And this, to the best of their abilities, they did. I salute them for it.

On a radio broadcast from Hanoi, now the Communist capital, there was a nightly program called Voice of Viet Nam. I remember one broadcast. It was on a so-called "Art and Literary Program," for the rice peasants of the delta. The subject was, "This is an American." I quote its text word for word:

"His head is a blockhouse. His beard is barbed wire. His eyes are bombs. His teeth are dum-dum bullets. His two arms are guns and from his nose flames shoot out. A vampire, he sucks the blood of little children. His forehead is a nest of artillery and his body is an airfield. His fingers are bayonets, his feet tanks. He puts his fangs out in order to threaten, but in his hideous mouth he can only chew scrap iron because he has against him the powerful forces of our people of Viet Nam, who are valiantly fighting. All things considered, the American is a paper giant."

Hey you, out there in Tucson, Kenosha and Des Moines! Do you recognize yourself from this description? Eaten any good babies lately?

Well, the refugees had no radios, so they didn't hear that particular broadcast. I don't believe they would have given much credence to it anyway. Baker's head didn't look like a blockhouse. He is, and looks like, a kindly sort of guy. My nose gives forth no flames. And most of the rest of the medical unit gave up sucking the blood of little children as soon as the Republicans were elected.

The Viet Minh propaganda even began to affect the International Control Committee of Canadians, Poles and Indians, set up by the Geneva treaty. The committeemen visited our camp frequently to investigate Communist claims that we were doing this or that to the detriment of the refugees. They investigated a claim that we were polluting the water with poison (that one left Ed Maugre speechless). They investigated a claim that we were spraying the refugees with a powder that rendered them sterile. We were spraying them with a powder all right—DDT—and perhaps it rendered their body lice a bit sterile.

And then there was that old standby—the Americans and French were forcing the refugees to leave the Tonkin. We were kidnapping them. Here is a quotation from the Viet Nam News Agency broadcast of November 27, 1954:

"The French Union forces and the agents of the U.S. imperialists have been endeavoring to carry out raids and kidnappings in the Haiphong perimeter, forcing the population to evacuate to South Viet Nam. At 9 p.m. last night they mobilized armed police and police agents to encircle Du Hang Street and took away 50 youths. They shamelessly declared that 'the youths must enroll in the army, otherwise they will be drafted to work in the rubber plantations in South Viet Nam.'

"In five days, the imperialists' agents arrested 117 pedicab drivers and brought them to the south. According to still incomplete figures, 551 persons in Haiphong have been caught in 21 raids in one month.

"In Kien An three raids were carried out during the same periods, and 99 persons were arrested, while in Quang Yen others were victims of similar measures.

"The Vietnamese people of the Haiphong perimeter, as well as those throughout the country, strongly protest against these Fascist activities and urge the French Union forces immediately to cease their raids, kidnappings and forcible evacuations that seriously encroach upon the Geneva armistice agreement."

We had many raids and riots in Haiphong, but I don't have to tell you that we never forcefully evacuated anyone. On the contrary; believe me, on the contrary. Many a night, after I had done a fourteen- or fifteen-hour trick in sick-call, I would have been overjoyed to see the evacuation come to an instant stop. I was fed up. If I was an imperialist—how, outside expanding Russia, do you go about being an imperialist nowadays?—I never felt much like one. I felt like a dog-tired, half-baked, rather frightened young doctor.

But the truth, I guess, strange as it sounds even to myself, is that I was enjoying the burden, and more so as it waxed heavier. I enjoyed it in the sense that a cross-channel swimmer enjoys his swim even when his breath labors and his limbs are numb. My growing fear was that a newcomer, no matter how able, might not feel as strongly as I did about the fugitives and the things they were fleeing. What, I asked myself, if he could not see through the rags and sores and stench to the soul of Viet Nam, as I was beginning to glimpse it? The sort of outer force that my Navy orders represented was replaced by my own inner compulsion to finish the job.

Again and again I went to French or the two American officials to complain about something, only to emerge with one more responsibility on my agenda. For example, I thought at one point that the handling of rice was inefficient and unfair. "Give me the job and I'll see to it myself," I said in a flareup. I was taken at my hasty word and thereafter managed the rice rations.

But it is true, as I say, that we did have riots, or near-riots, at Haiphong. The first time we set up the compressed air motors and the DDT dusting machines we had a near-riot on our hands. Ed Gleason was the boss of this operation and he had a dusting-gun in hand to lead his corpsmen, who were lined up behind him with six more. The idea was that as the refugees passed down a line they would be given a good going-over with DDT to help keep down louse-borne epidemics.

In the first group of refugees were several small children. When they got alongside Ed he pushed the trigger on his gun and swirls of white dust flew down on the kids. Their mother had a long balance pole across her shoulder with a basket hanging on each end. When she saw this American blowing powder on her children (she had heard of that particular American atrocity), she took off after Ed, swinging that pole like everything.

I laughed so hard that I lost track of exactly what happened then. I think that after a blow or two Ed managed to get his arms around her, polka fashion, and the chief mandarin and his men helped to break up the fight. Then Ed dusted his corpsmen thoroughly to demonstrate the benign nature of this powder to human beings. The corpsmen didn't dust Ed.

Baker and I also took some beatings, not all of them minor, at the hands of these misguided and hysterical people. But, remembering the importance of "face" in the Orient, we were always careful to take up where we left off.

One day a woman brought me a baby whose body was covered with ulcers. Yaws and ulcers respond miraculously to penicillin and this looked like a routine case. I gave the infant a shot in the buttocks and told the mother to bring it back the next day.

A few hours later, I heard shouts and curses, and saw the woman holding the baby aloft for the people to see. Here was proof that I was an American monster! The child had reacted to the penicillin with an angry-looking, though quite harmless, case of hives. The distraught mother was in no mood for explanations. She handed her baby to a bystander, grabbed a stout stick and called up a dozen sympathizers. When Baker rescued me at last, I had broken ribs, black eyes and miscellaneous bruises.

The next day, with the whole camp watching, I went to the woman's tent alone and unarmed. As I expected, the hives had disappeared and the horrible ulcers were healing nicely. The woman burst into tears, and fell at my feet begging forgiveness. She remained in the camp for weeks, serving as one of my helpers at sick-call, always eager to exhibit her nice clean baby. The effect on the refugees was worth the fractured ribs.

ELEVEN ·

THE STORY OF CUA LO VILLAGE

The French Navy was constantly on the alert for escapees in the waters along the free enclave. They had patrol craft and a seaplane conducting a continuing search for sampans which looked as if they were seeking haven.

In the early months, the refugees floated down the river's many tributaries into Haiphong, but as the Viet Minh controls tightened this became impossible. So the braver people set sail from their coasts in sampans not built for the bold winds of the South China Seas.

Captain Gerald Cauvin of the French Navy was in charge of this particular operation and he kept us informed of his activities. This was a great help to me at the camp because it warned me what to expect.

Early one morning, Cauvin sent a man to our camp to take me to the French Navy pier. He said he had just received a radio message that there were fourteen large junks out in the Baie d'Along.

Cauvin was sending down a French craft, an LSM, to meet the junks and bring them to Haiphong. I alerted the camp to expect five hundred or so very sick people (actually there were more than eleven hundred). Then Captain Cauvin and I went aboard the LSM and sailed four hours down the river to the bay. The seaplane that had spotted the refugees meanwhile had returned to Haiphong.

We arrived in the bay about noon. It was absolutely silent, this strange place with its bare rocks jutting high—no foliage, no vegetation, just barren grey stones. They were like giant stalagmites piercing the water's surface, needling toward the sky.

The sampans had sailed into the bay, one behind the other. They were huddled together. Several of the boats were lashed end to end. As we headed toward them, we observed them closely through our binoculars. The brilliant noonday sun on the clear water made this a storybook fairyland, but what we saw was hardly a storybook sight.

Jammed onto these fourteen sampans were more than a thousand refugees who had sailed an unbelievable two hundred miles in the turbulent South China Seas. They did this in these small fishing junks, risking all dangers, against all odds, accomplishing the near-impossible. Though they were in the warm sun, they were drenched and cold. The sea had made them so deathly sick that they had vomited their stomachs dry. Even from a distance, you could see that the coldness of the night had made them stiffen in every joint and ache in every bone. They moved around the sampans helping one another, yet in the mass they seemed immobile, sprawled over the wooden decks.

It was as if they moved in a slow-motion picture. The constant soaking in salt water during all hours of day and night had made their skins dry, and the blazing sun of noon had cracked it. The continuous immersion of their feet made their ankles swell and bloat. We could feel the misery of their situation even before we touched them.

When our LSM was close enough for the refugees to make out the French flag on our stern, a heart-warming thing happened. Recognizing us as friends and not as foes, they hoisted, on a broken spar their own drenched flag; a flag they had hidden for years . . . their symbol, their emblem, their heraldry.

To the top of their highest mast they hauled the Papal banner, a yellow and gold flag displaying the Pope's tiara and the keys of Saint Peter.

As we pulled alongside, eager French hands reached down to help these people into the well-deck of the LSM. Most of the refugees were transferred to our ship. Some of the healthier men were left aboard a few of the sampans, which were lashed to the sides of the LSM. We headed back to Haiphong with our load.

We handed out tea, water and French rolls to the escapees. Though they were inadequate in amount, they helped. The little LSM with a crew of only two dozen did not carry large food stocks. How I wished I had thought to bring along a hundred sacks of rice.

Cauvin and I found several elders who seemed to be the leaders. These we took to the cabin and asked: "Where did you sail from? What was life like in your village? Why have you come? Who are you?"

They told us their story, in sad and weary voices, as though they had repeated it a thousand times. In a slow monotone, in good French, they told us about their lives. We listened for three hours.

The story was not especially new; we had heard similar stories from other escapees. But there was a poignancy here that was even greater than usual. Their escape was planned and executed entirely without outside aid; with only two ancient tools, faith and hope.

Though at this moment I am thousands of miles and thousands of hours away, I can vividly remember nearly every word. The old men with wrinkled, haggard faces sat across from us, sipping their strong tea, speaking softly, unhesitatingly:

"Cua Lo is our village. It is about 300 kilometers south of here, on the sea coast. It was a happy village years ago. Our landscape is flat, divided into an infinite number of small rice paddies, often brilliant green with the rice crops. Overhead, during the dark grey season of the monsoon, damp clouds scud across the sky. During the hot season the sun shines forth in all her splendor and our skies are clear blue. All day you can see our people working in the fields, irrigating their crops and plowing in the red-brown mud behind squelching water buffaloes.

"Others in our village were fishermen. These junks we have come on belong to them. The junks are strong, have two masts and large mustard-colored sails. But they are crudely built, and are not meant for the high waters of an open sea.

"Our enemies became our rulers in 1951. They gave us a new set of laws, a new history, a new way of life . . . the Communist way of life. Yet the Communists say it is Viet Minh nationalism. This was a dull uncertain peace. It is all very confusing, even for us, the mandarins, who are supposed to be intelligent.

"Now anything at all that had been concerned with the French became tainted. In the eyes of our new historians, everything the whites had done was evil. Even the good they had done was evil, for it had been done only out of sordid self-interest.

"True the French introduced some medical science to Viet Nam, and conducted campaigns against epidemics. But this, we were told, was done only so that they could obtain sound coolies and healthy slaves.

"Our new way of life was supposed to be Utopia. But it did not take long to see that the underlying idea was that the present generation must always be pitilessly sacrificed to the happiness of the one that is to come.

"The new land reforms produced only famine, which now claws at the belly of all our people. Their 'materialism' became an ogre which sucked our land dry. At first the attainments of Viet Minh nationalism seemed to conform to authentic justice. Then it would show itself in true form—a lie. The new sociology has led to family denunciations, self-criticism and distrust. The people of our village have been ruthlessly sacrificed to the idea of economic utility. Never before has there been cruelty of this organized order.

"We all had one thought—to escape—and so for weeks we made preparations. Every day we hid away small balls of rice. There could be no open talk of escape; nothing could be done straightforwardly. All had to be done by stealth, since the village was run by a mandarin who, though he was an old friend of ours, was now a Viet Minh Commissar, and had been made cruel and warped by his new beliefs. Everywhere he had agents stationed, in the market place, in nearly every hut.

"We made plans but could not hold meetings. According to the new laws, there could be no gatherings of more than four people. We passed the word while we bent our backs in the rice fields, or while our fishermen unloaded their catch, or while our women visited in the market place.

"Finally plans and prayers reached a climax. The night had come. There was no moon, the sky was dark and the seas were calm. From eleven o'clock until one the next morning, we slipped down to our boats singly or in twos. Meanwhile a lad named Mai Van Thinh, loudly singing and shouting, was creating a disturbance at one end of the village. This drew the police, the Commissar and many soldiers to see what was going on. Meanwhile our boats loaded.

"These junks were built to handle about twenty-five people each. That night they each carried more than a hundred. As quiet as the night itself, we slipped away from the shore and headed out into the South China Sea.

"Yes, we escaped from the village successfully. However, we were not especially jubilant, because our thoughts were with Mai. Sooner or later his part in our escape would become known. Then what would be his fate?

"Mai's father and mother had been killed in the war, and in 1953 his only brother, Cham, had been burned alive, apparently because he was the head of a Christian youth movement. On the afternoon of January 16, 1953, he was tied to a tree and brutally beaten with short bamboo sticks. Then his blood-soaked body was splashed with gasoline, ignited, and he was burned to death.

"Using both oars and sails, as rapidly as we could we headed straight out to the open sea, eager to get beyond the three-mile limit to international waters. By morning we could not see land and we felt comparatively safe. That is, we were safe from one danger; we had the sea to struggle with now.

"We wanted to sail north and we had no compass nor any extensive knowledge of navigation. However, we turned to put the sun at our right hand and headed for Haiphong, where we knew the French and Americans would be willing to help. They would take us all the way to Saigon.

"Our trip lasted five days and five long nights. We could not have fires, for our wood was too wet. We were forced to eat our rice when it was damp and soggy. Our tea was soaked with salt and only served to increase our illness. We had little drinking water or none. The decks of our small junks were splashed by every wave. We were miserable.

"Early this morning we found ourselves in this strange place and knew we must have reached the legendary Baie d'Along. When we saw your seaplane we were sure. And now we are free. . . ."

Quietly the mandarins told us this story. With awe we listened to this recital of magnificent courage and hope.

And now a chant came from the well-deck of the LSM, a soft hymn that the mass of refugees were singing. We all walked out on deck and listened. I could not make out all the Vietnamese words. The mandarins hummed with the song and then translated it into French for us.

The people were offering their thanks to God for His help during this crisis in their lives. They chanted: "Oh, Lord, we love the beauty of Thy house and the place where Thy glory dwells. Provide that our days be spent in peace with Thee."

TWELVE ·

PHAT DIEM'S LONGEST HOLY DAY

In Haiphong, the port city of Viet Nam's Tonkin delta, the languages to be heard seemed as varied as those on the Tower of Babel. French forces were still present, though not in great numbers. We Americans, although just a handful, managed to make our own voices heard above most of the others. The priests who ran the Catholic Mission—Father Felice, Father Lopez and their assistants—were from the Philippines and spoke Spanish.

Then there were the three-man teams of the International Control Commission, which contained representatives of one democratic country, Canada; one Communist country, Poland; and one supposedly neutral country, India. One day, in a group of twenty people, I heard the following languages spoken: English, French, Vietnamese, Indian, Polish, Sikh and German. No Spanish that morning—Father Felice wasn't there.

The International Control Commission was set up by the signatories of the Geneva treaty in July of 1954. Its long title was usually abbreviated to "CIC." It was to be the responsibility of this commission to enter all the areas of Indo-China during the next two years and report back to Geneva. The Commission was to make observations in both parts of tragically divided Viet Nam, and also to conduct investigations into the countries of Laos and Cambodia. It had no police power or military power but, in theory at least, it had a great deal of diplomatic prestige.

The Commission kept fixed teams of observers in Saigon, Hanoi, the capitals of Cambodia and Laos and other large cities. Then it had mobile teams which would travel from one spot to another on both sides of the parallel to satisfy themselves that the terms of the Geneva treaty were being faithfully carried out. The election planned for Viet Nam in 1956 was to be supervised by the CIC. According to the plan, in casting over 22 million votes the people of North and South Viet Nam would decide whether their country would unite or remain divided. They would also choose the kind of regime under which they wanted to live. There was not the shadow of a doubt that the 10 million in the Communist north would "decide" in favor of a continuation of the Communist regime—the Communist bosses would see to that. What would be decided in the south was another story.

In theory, anyone who wanted to see members of the Commission's teams had the right to do so at any time. So anyone who might have a complaint against either side would be able to air this complaint in the presence of international representatives.

Like so much in Indo-China, this looked extremely good on paper. In practice it left something to be desired. The Commission was highly effective in some ways, but in the field of helping the refugees who wanted to move south, it was inadequate.

The Viet Minh had a healthy respect for the Commission and its teams, since they had the power of appealing to world opinion. If the world is aware that, despite their promises, the Communists did *not* freely release Tonkinese for the refugee evacuation, the Commission must get credit for the fact. In enlightening world opinion, the Commission has done a superb job. Those of us in Haiphong knew at first hand that it was telling the truth because the refugees who escaped would describe their experiences to us and we had to treat many of those who did attempt to escape and were caught and punished.

But all the CIC could do was to find out the facts and report them. It had no power to force the Viet Minh to allow the refugees to leave.

If CIC representatives were visiting a certain village, they might set up a council table in the public square and spread the word that anyone who wished to talk to them could come and do so. But just outside the square the Viet Minh might erect road-blocks to keep out villagers and people from nearby cantons. The Viet Minh would claim that the road-blocks were for the protection of the International Control Commission representatives. But as matters turned out, the representatives could receive complaints and other information only from natives within a very small area.

And those who complained always feared reprisals, which did occur frequently. The CIC representatives might have a truck parked alongside the council table and, after listening to the complaints of the people, might vote to allow them to leave and might tell the Viet Minh heads of the village of their decision. But that was not enough. The only way for a villager to be sure of getting out was to climb on the truck and leave immediately after the decision was reached. There and then. And the CIC could not furnish that much transportation.

Within the CIC committees there arose the same problems that arise in all conference bodies containing representatives of the Communists. The Poles seemed determined to be stumbling-blocks and I personally witnessed their obstructive tactics many times.

I would take a refugee to the CIC, a refugee who had been horribly beaten up by the Viet Minh. There would be a council meeting. The refugee would tell his story. After hours of wrangling, he would be sent back to the camp. It seemed that the Polish representatives always wanted proof that obviously was unobtainable. Certainly this poor peasant had been beaten—that could not be denied—but what hard-and-fast proof did he have that the beating had been administered by the Viet Minh? What proof did he have that the bullets which had torn into his arm were Communist bullets? The peasant would have to present something substantial in the way of proof, which of course he couldn't do, and not just his maimed body and feeble voice.

The movements of the CIC's mobile teams in Viet Minh areas were usually secret. That was so that nothing could be done in any particular village by way of a "fix." But a fix often occurred, nevertheless.

In October one of the mobile teams visited the city of Thai Binh, one of the largest in the Tonkin. The fix was in. There was absolutely no one in the community who had any objections to Communist rule. Every one of those who came to the council hearings had words of praise for the Viet Minh. Life was pleasant and the peasants were happy and the skies were blue. No one wished to leave. "Freedom" in the north was vastly superior to that life of bondage and subjugation in the imperialistic south . . . at least, such were the stories that went around the world about Thai Binh. It just happened that a great many photographers were present on that occasion, which also tied in with the visit of Prime Minister Nehru of India. There was also world-wide coverage by Communist and "neutral" newspapers.

Officers of the French Navy decided that perhaps they could do something in the way of a fix themselves. The French Navy did a great deal to help the refugees and deserves high marks for it. In this case, Captain Gerald Cauvin, the chief of the Deuxieme Bureau (Intelligence) drew up a plan.

Cauvin and I rounded up all the people who, we thought, might be of help, and the French Navy did the rest. The town chosen for our fix was Phat Diem, some fifty miles from Haiphong, behind the Bamboo Curtain. Many of the refugees in my camp had told me that there were thousands upon thousands in and around Phat Diem who wanted to escape to the south, but could not. We chose the bravest and strongest among those in the camp who actually *had* escaped from that area, both men and women. We had them meet with Cauvin, some other French officers and me. It did not take long to gain their confidence. They were told of the plan, accepted their part in it and left Haiphong to cross back behind the Bamboo Curtain. Going behind the Curtain was not nearly as difficult as getting out in front of it.

Via this underground force, word was sent to the people of Phat Diem and the cantons nearby. "If you want to escape, gather in the church of the village of Phat Diem on November 1, the Feast of All Saints. If you go there, representatives of the CIC will visit you. You will be able to make your declarations to them, and perhaps gain your liberty."

The church at Phat Diem had not yet been closed by the Viet Minh. Ostensibly the people were to gather for the Holy Day of Obligation. And so they did.

From all the cantons in the area, thousands came to Phat Diem. People overflowed from the church into the mission yards. (All the missions in Indo-China have large courtyards in front and playyards around them for the inevitable nearby church school.) Here the people came to pray on the first of November.

Simultaneously, in Haiphong, and in other cities of Viet Nam, an intensive campaign got under way to persuade the CIC to go to Phat Diem and investigate the complaints that had "filtered in to us." Admiral Querville, General O'Daniel in Saigon, Admiral Sabin from his flagship at sea, Mayor Bot of Haiphong and many others sent notes and telegrams to the head of this particular mobile team.

But something went amiss. For reasons that I do not know—they were never explained to me—the members of the mobile team were unable to go to Phat Diem immediately. They could not go on the first, or the second or the third of the month.

Word was smuggled to the people of Phat Diem to wait, have patience, stay in the church, wait. Admiral Querville offered his own helicopter to the CIC men, though they had two planes of their own. There were more messages urging them to go to Phat Diem. And there was more delay.

The Viet Minh became suspicious. Why was this one Holy Day of Obligation lengthening into three? The Communists ordered the people to return to their homes. The people would not. The Viet Minh put guards around the church yard and forbade all and sundry to sell or give food or water to those within the mission walls. Let them have no food, no drink, just prayers; that is what the Viet Minh ordered. This starving-out process is a weapon of war dating back to the legions of Carthage, and doubtless to far earlier times. It was applied ruthlessly in Viet Nam in 1954.

Nevertheless, the people stayed. Only a few of the weaker ones left. All the others waited for the representatives of the CIC, for they had faith in the word that had been sent to them. This patient race is not robust. Many are frail and susceptible to a variety of diseases. Yet their faith in their dream of freedom was strong enough to provide the nourishment they needed in this time of stress.

The days stretched out. Four became five, then six, then seven, and the hungry children cried. Mothers who were nursing infants dried up and were no longer able to feed. Hunger and thirst became passions. From lack of sanitation, disease got under way. Many became ill. Yet they waited—and prayed.

Finally, around the tenth of November, the CIC representatives went to Phat Diem. Members of the group told me later that they were nearly overcome with nausea when they got within a hundred yards of the mission. The odor of sickness was that intense. The Canadian members of the group said even the Polish Communists were amazed at the filth and squalor in which the people were huddled.

The CIC people took thousands of declarations, immediately ordered that the natives be allowed to eat and drink and move freely in and out of the mission. They sent vehement protests to the Viet Minh authorities and issued a public statement in Hanoi against the government of Ho Chi Minh and against his treatment of the people in the mission of Phat Diem.

In deference to world opinion, the Viet Minh ordered local authorities to allow the people to leave. But there was a trap even in this.

The Viets set up offices capable of processing one hundred people a day. One office issued passports, but only after sheaves of papers had been filled out by the applicants. Another office sold tickets for the Viet Minh buses, which reputedly would take the people to Haiphong. The tickets cost 8,000 Ho Chi Minh piasters each, the equivalent of about nine American dollars. For a peasant with a family of six, this represented a formidable sum of money.

But to people from different parts of the world who asked about this particular evacuation, the Viet Minh responded: "Yes, we are furnishing the bureaus, passports and transportation for all who—mistakenly, we believe—have decided to go to another zone. No sense of injustice, no hysteria, racks the Democratic Republic of the Viet Minh."

It was not until the 15th of November that the first group of refugees started to leave Phat Diem. Instead of bringing them up the road on a trip that would have required only a few hours, the Viet Minh sent them through a complicated itinerary. They took part of the trip on buses. Then they were stopped and told that the buses must be repaired and that they would have to spend several days waiting. During this period the Viet Minh lectured to them incessantly about the error they were making and about the American and French atrocity camps in Haiphong and Saigon.

Now the refugees were transferred to junks and sampans and floated up the Red River to Hanoi. More delays, more haranguing, more frustration followed. From Hanoi, trains finally took them to Haiphong, where French trucks transported them the few remaining kilometers to our camp.

Thousands of other refugees went through all the delays the Communists could think of, finally to reach a point, far behind the Bamboo Curtain where it was noticed that their 15-day exit permits had expired. So they were sent back to the villages they had come from originally, there to attempt to start the evacuation process all over again.

Luckier refugees were picked up by the French Navy in small craft it had waiting at the very edge of the Bamboo Curtain, at the Bac Cuu. There the French stopped all Communist junks, and with representatives of CIC aboard, demanded that the people be handed over, so that they could be promptly transported to Haiphong.

In spite of the inconvenience and hardships, the maddening lectures, the inadequacies of transportation and the brutality of the Viet Minh, the people persisted. In Phat Diem alone, as was indicated by a final count before the CIC men left the area, about 5,000 of the original 35,000 gained their freedom.

THIRTEEN ·
BUI CHU MEANS VALIANT

Wars give birth to songs of warriors, to Rolands and to Arthurs. Wars give birth to legends of courage and valor, to Bataans and Inchons. Yet the strange new peace that came to the Tonkin brought forth innumerable instances of valor as great as any ever shown in combat.

I know a good many such stories. I have been an eyewitness to dozens and I have been told of hundreds more.

I remember the refugees from the province of Bui Chu who came to my camp in November.

Bui Chu is a province eighty miles from Haiphong. In Bui Chu, as elsewhere, under the "light" of Communism there was only darkness, and the family warmth died in the people's thatched homes. But the spirit of the people did not die, nor their hope.

The Tonkinese of Bui Chu were relatively rich. They had crops and water buffalo and little fields in the familiar green of the delta. Then came eight years of war—first a colonial war, then a war of ideologies. The wars brought desolation. Homes were destroyed, families broken up, crops taken. Water buffalo died and lands were made sterile. For the peasant the calamity was complete. His land, his ancestors and his family make up his whole life. He has nothing else, except his God.

Now new rulers gave the people new laws. They obliged these farmers to attend daily lectures on the evils and errors of capitalism and democracy. They preached hatred against the institutions, traditions and customs of colonial Viet Nam. Everything "feudal" or "reactionary" was to be destroyed. The concept of the all-important family was feudal and reverence for ancestors was reactionary. The whole province came to seem to the people like an immense prison. Their Christian catechisms were burned and they were told that religion is only an opiate. It was a life without comfort, without worship, without even enough food.

The promised agrarian reforms were carried out here as elsewhere. This meant that all who had more than two *mauu* of land (about as much as an athletic field) were considered capitalists and accused of exploiting the laborers who worked with them in the fields. When I asked such laborers if they were not pleased with gaining land, they would often say: "Sometimes it pleased our bellies but it never pleased our hearts because we knew it was wrong."

And, as has been said, because of increased taxes more land did not always mean more food.

The plight of the land owner who had many *mauu* of land was drastic. If he had a great deal of land, that meant he was comparatively wealthy and powerful, and if a man is wealthy and powerful he cannot exist in the Communist state, unless, of course, he is a member of the Party. Such people were sometimes given the choice of becoming members of the Party. If they did not consent, if they did not agree to give up their land and their religion and send their sons to serve in the "People's Army," they were apt to be beheaded. Do I exaggerate? The sons of such men have told me that they had witnessed the beheading of their own parents. I do not believe they lied.

For the people of Bui Chu there was only one answer, escape. Which was easy to hope for and dream about but very difficult to achieve.

There were more than 30,000 Catholics in Bui Chu province alone. In the Vietnamese underground, and in the French and U. S. Navies, a plan was laid. Date and hour and place were decided upon. The date was November 30, and the place was a spot off the shores of the province near the fishing village of Van Ly, a village known for its long, broad beaches.

A large French repair ship, the *Jules Verne*, stood off the shore just outside the three-mile limit. Then four LSMs pulled alongside the *Jules Verne* for imaginary repairs. By planned coincidence one of the United States Navy's large transports, the *General Brewster*, was passing empty from Saigon on her return trip to Haiphong. At this spot, she too stopped for a little while.

The Vietnamese underground had spread the word to the people. At the escape hour minus ten, the sea was uneasy. On the three-mile stretch of churning water from the ships to the shore there was nothing to be seen but the moonlight, and that was too bright . . . too dangerous. Then the escape hour arrived, eight o'clock. Within minutes the sea was a veritable mass of bumboats, barks, and bamboo rafts.

Thousands of escapees appeared on the beach and dragged their boats across the sands into the tide. They headed out to the small French craft which were speedily spreading in toward them.

French and Vietnamese met and the French craft opened their bow doors wide and silently engulfed the refugees, many times raft and all. Then the French craft turned around and raced out to the *Verne* and the *Brewster*. They disgorged their loads of pitiful people and returned to pick up more.

On a small bamboo raft lashed together with rope and perhaps only a few feet square, there might be as many as ten members of a family in their brown cotton garb, drab, quiet, frightened. If the weight of the load made the raft submerge, sometimes until the sea was around their knees, they would hold their children up high.

The moon was bright. Would it give them away? The sea was rough. Would it capsize their boats? The big ships were but two. Would they be enough? Did the enemy yet suspect? Would machine gun fire soon cut loose and give frenzy and terror to the night?

These fears gnawed at the Vietnamese as they aimed their crude boats toward the open sea. But they were truly valiant and all risks were taken, including the risk of death. By dawn there were 6,000 escapees on the U.S. and French ships, which then set out for Haiphong. There they discharged their loads into our camps and returned to Bui Chu for more.

Operations continued for two days and nights until the number of escapees numbered more than 18,000. On the third day no refugees appeared on the beaches, save for a small group stranded on a sand spit. Soldiers appeared and the escape from Van Ly halted.

But not the dreams of those who remained imprisoned there. Another time would come; there would be another chance. They would try again.

When the ships came to Haiphong bearing these particular refugees, they were unloaded at the piers by night and day. We would transport them to the entrance road of the refugee camp. It is a half-mile walk from there to the tents. The first night when the refugees arrived the trucks let them off just at the entrance. Lining each side of the entrance road, shoulder to shoulder, stood thousands of refugees who had arrived on earlier nights and days. Most of them held lanterns or candles. The newly arrived would walk between these lines of flickering lights in a poignant parade of pathos.

They were scanned by other refugees seeking word of relatives, perhaps of sons or daughters, and they were bombarded with weary and usually hopeless questions.

"Have you seen any of the Duc Ly family?"

"Did you see anyone swim away from the capsized Quan boat?"

"Have you heard what happened to the village of Thanh Hoa?"

"Have you seen my son? He is seven."

Some did find relatives and friends. Most did not.

In days and weeks following, while people from Bui Chu lived in the camp, they required constant medical care. Many of the children were hideously scarred from bouts of smallpox. Others had the new pustules of the epidemic form. Perhaps secondary infection had set in. Their fevers raged. Dehydration racked their small bodies, and I lost three or four a day to this one disease alone.

Beri-beri and scurvy were common. In part, at least, these vitamin deficiency diseases owed their existence to the Communists' so-called land reforms. They brought starvation to many, though not enough to kill, just enough to maim.

Beri-beri would make their ankles puff and swell until their feet became so tender it was impossible for them to walk. The skin would pull tightly over the swollen ankles and would tear with the slightest shock. Many could not wear their sandals or walk on even the softest ground.

Scurvy made their bones brittle and fractures were seen at every sick-call. Gums became rotten and teeth decayed and broke off.

My corpsmen often walked through the tents at night giving injections of morphine to those in the most excruciating pain. But when thousands of such cases came upon us suddenly, we had to ration relief from pain; there were just not enough morphine-like drugs in all Haiphong for us to do otherwise. Penicillin is the drug of choice for yaws, and fortunately America had sent me plenty of this. We treated more than 200 cases every day, 200 bodies disfigured with stinking sores on the hands and feet and face.

Starvation left many scars, for example on the babies with their swollen bellies. All who had escaped had become seasick and this enfeebled them the more. These miserable people who had fled to our camp were now my patients.

The people of Bui Chu, I found, are not unlike my fellow Americans. Americans never fail to like the Vietnamese when they get to know them. It is impossible not to respect their driving compulsion for freedom, impossible not to admire the story of such a valiant people as those of Bui Chu. The main difference between them and us is that we have our freedom and our hearts command us to keep it. The Vietnamese does not possess it and his heart's command is to struggle against all odds to achieve it.

And so the escapees continued to flood into our camps like the monsoon rains, spilled and overflowed into the adjoining roads and fields. As soon as possible we processed them to the transports. Every day we embarked four to five thousand, but they often came into the camps faster than that.

This was my camp's population. My city of sprawling tents staked out in knee-deep mire and mud. We were thriving—with vermin, filth, disease, and death. Yet ours was a camp of hope and pride, and a camp rich in tales of heroism.

FOURTEEN ·

THE ORPHANAGE OF
MADAME NGAI

Although daily life at the camp was far from dull, there was a certain monotony, born of repetition, in our existence in Viet Nam. Day after day, week after week, month after month, we saw the same diseases, the same misery. We experienced the same shortages of materials, the same lack of help.

Worst of all, we had the same sense of inadequacy, the feeling of being unable even to scratch the surface of the despondency all around us. Combine this with the personal discomforts, the lack of hot water and clean clothes, the withering heat, the continuous sweating, the necessity of speaking always in a foreign language—and you get some idea of the continuous effort that each day's task demanded.

There was no place to go and say, "The devil with it," no place to put your feet on a table, drink some gin and tonic and read the funny papers. Our constant companion was misery. If we did knock off for an afternoon, a sense of guilt would fill us and the afternoon's pleasure would be gone.

Sometimes, when there was a U. S. Navy ship down in the river, we would go out, bum some hot water for a shave and pass an hour or two with our own people. The men on those ships will never know what it meant to my boys and to me when they let us use their quarters as our temporary home.

Towards the final months of the evacuation, these occasional visits to U.S. ships became real highlights. The *Cook*, the *Diachenko*, the *Bass*, the *Begor*, the *Balduck*—these small APDs looked as grand and glorious as the *Queen Mary* to those of us who worked ashore. Their sailors and officers with their friendship helped me keep some level of sanity.

However, there was another highlight in our Haiphong life. This was the orphanage of Madame Vu Thi Ngai, the orphanage of An Lac.

This orphanage and its hundreds of smiling children became *our* orphanage and *our* children. We really sort of adopted them, as they adopted us. Madame Ngai was the head of the place and my corpsmen and I became the Orphanage Medical Department. The U. S. Navy became the Orphanage Trust Fund. If this sounds a bit involved, I can only say that it became more so as the months went by. Whenever there was an opportunity, the kids would be taken out to one of the ships, where they would be given an American-type party.

Madame Ngai was a proud Tonkinese woman who had once been wealthy. She was lovely, with fine-textured skin, jet black hair, brilliant white teeth and an olive coloring that was exquisite. Her eyes were broad and wide, with that charming Oriental slant that quickly captivates so many.

She was large. Like many women who run orphanages, she had and needed room for a capacious heart. Nature had designed her bosom bountifully so that she might the better accomplish her essential task—that of loving children. Madame Ngai succeeded in capturing the hearts—and the wallets—of all she met, and she succeeded in meeting not a few. Especially Americans with large hearts or large wallets, or preferably both.

There was only one other person in all of Viet Nam who was charming as Madame Ngai, and that was one of her wards, little Lia. Let me tell you about Lia. Lia was a seven-year-old girl who was as delicate and as pretty as only the perfect doll-sized Oriental can become. She had fine little features and a complexion that seemed almost transparent. She was shy, but not too shy. And when she grew fond of you, how very fond she grew!

Lia was one of the older girls of the orphanage and busied herself caring for the infants as well as she could. But there was one thing wrong with Lia. She had one leg, and where the other had been she had a short stump. Her right leg had been blown off at the thigh when she stepped on a land mine in January of 1954 near the town of Phuly. The explosion made her an orphan as well as a cripple.

For a right leg, she used a rough-hewn wooden crutch. I met Lia when I first went to the orphanage in August. After some time, she let me examine her stump. It had healed poorly and there were raw granulating surfaces on it even six months after the traumatic amputation. I asked Lia if she didn't want to let me take care of the stump for her. She replied that she did, because she loved the "Bac Sy My." So we started a little campaign. With some minor surgical procedures, secondary closure of the wound was obtained. Then Lia did all the things I asked. She stretched the stump, exercised it, soaked it, kept the dressings on and kept it clean. As a result, she had a good functional stump by Christmas.

I wrote to Henry Sherck of the A. S. Aloe Company of St. Louis, told them Lia's story and asked for help. Their response was refreshing. Although they could not themselves supply the artificial limb that I had asked for, they did consult with the Hanger Limb Company, which is in St. Louis also. The two outfits decided that the man to manufacture this new leg was at the Cosmevo Ambulator Company of Paterson, New Jersey. They told me the measurements they wanted and we sent the information along. And so a limb was made that would be suitable for this little girl, a limb that could be adjusted to her growing. Some time later, the limb arrived in Haiphong.

Lia now had a new leg, an American leg. Her eyes glowed when she put it on and walked for the first time. She cried and smiled and then cried again (and so did Baker, and Madame Ngai, and so, I confess, did I). Gratitude spilled out of Lia's eyes until she couldn't say thanks—and didn't have to.

Alas, Lia's leg brought moral problems to the orphanage. The little girls of Viet Nam ordinarily wear long black pants down to their ankles but, to show off her new leg, Lia most of the time went around pantless. Though the children were mostly very young, this still proved to be embarrassing, and we had a devil of a time trying to get Lia's pants on. She was so enamoured with her leg that she even slept with it. When we asked her not to, she was puzzled. She did not take off her Vietnamese leg when she slept, she said, so why should she take off her American leg?

Mr. Cosmo Invidiato, head of the Cosmevo Company, recently wrote to tell me that, in effect, his company had recently "adopted" Lia. "To judge from your letter," he wrote, "and from what can be read between the lines, conditions must be horrible for the inhabitants of that faraway country. Somehow it is difficult for us back home to understand the sacrifices and hardships that other people are continuously undergoing. Sometimes we fall to musing on our uselessness." I can tell him his firm wasn't useless to little Lia.

Another child we all loved very much was Nguyen. We never knew his last name. Madame Ngai said she found him, when he was four, in the village of Thai Binh. Nguyen was now six, had a winning smile and a caressing face. Nguyen had tuberculosis of the spine and was a misshapen hunchback. It was difficult for him to walk, so he waddled. He could not sit down comfortably and would lie down to eat his meals. When he laughed very hard, which he did wonderfully and frequently, he would fall to the ground on his back and roll. Nothing seemed to stop him from keeping up with the others; when it came to visiting an American vessel, he was by all odds the best man about the ship. I believe he has a collection of some fifteen sailor hats which were given to him or, more often, swiped by him.

There was a two-year-old child whose name I do not remember. He had had trachoma infections in both eyes as an infant and now, at the advanced age of two, was totally blind. If he had had a minimum of medical care during infancy, he would now be able to see. But this he was denied, and so he will live in darkness forever.

There were other children who had the bony deformities of congenital syphilis, others who were cerebral palsy cases, or spastics, or otherwise diseased. Some were really pitiful to behold, even for a case-hardened doctor. They had seen death in hideous forms, and had felt its shock and horror. They had witnessed villages pillaged, fields destroyed, and had known the stink of decaying dead. But, to the young, God gives the blessed clouds of forgetfulness and soon the bestiality of their background faded. So the children of the orphanage smiled, and they loved, and they made life seem good and complete.

The way Madame Ngai would thank those of us who were fortunate enough to have the chance to help her was to invite us over for dinner, which for some of us greenhorns sometimes was a secretly frightening experience. It was always a true Vietnamese dinner. Please have some more bat-wing soup, rice, of course, in all its forms, fish heads, chicken served with the head on, sparrow eyes crushed and made into a paste, raw pork with sauces, that damn oil made from decaying fish, salad—where from, Oh Lord, and how well washed?—and other foods which were, surprisingly enough, pretty tasty even to American palates. (I ask you not to consider their origin and development.)

During dinner we would squat on our haunches or sit on pillows on the decks. Buddhist joss sticks always smoldered in colored jars of sand. There were usually a few Vietnamese and French officers present. But politics and war were barred from the conversation. The differences between colony and mother country, between America and France, between white man and yellow man, between JGs and, let's say, Lieutenant Commanders—all were excluded from or dissolved at Madame Ngai's fluid parties. At one of the parties we asked her to tell us how the orphanage was born. Where did she find all these children? Where did she get the money to feed them? Who were they?

Like many of the people of her race, when recounting a story Madame would speak as though retelling an ancient legend. She spoke as if in a dream:

"In 1946, in the village of Thanh Hoa in southern Tonkin, there were many great battles. Families were split. Dead littered the village. Children were abandoned on the roadways to die alongside the bodies of their parents. Wars do not have time to stop to take care of the infants.

"I lived in Thanh Hoa. In fact, at one time my family was the wealthiest of all in the canton. I had a lovely large house with many *mauu* of fields around it. Although much of my home was destroyed in battle, I was still able to live there. I went along the roadways and took the children who, I found, were still alive, and brought them from the ditches to my house. My servants and I took care of them.

"But when another battle started in Thanh Hoa, we knew we would have to escape. So, with my brood, I left. I took my jewelry and the gold cubes that I had and went to the nearby village of Nam Dinh. Here I bought a new house and continued to care for the children, whose numbers had now swollen to six hundred.

"When Nam Dinh fell to the Viet Minh in 1949, I was forced to move again, only this time with a thousand children. Those moves I repeated five times, finally settling here in Haiphong.

"The Mayor of the city gave me a fine building to house my children and the city helped to support them. But at the beginning of this year, the year of Dien Bien Phu, the French needed my building for a hospital, so I was obliged to move to the house we occupy now. I should be ashamed to entertain you in such a common house, and yet it is my home, and so I am not ashamed. This is how I came to be the mother of a thousand children.

"My own husband was killed in the first month of the war, and my two children are living in France. I have never really left Tonkin, and many say that I am so French I am almost colonial. I do not hate the French. I know they have done many good things for my country. The language that we are speaking now is French.

"But my people are confused. They do not know the value of things, of friends, of foes. And that is how I came to be."

After she told us her story, we understood more than we had understood before. Yet there was so much, so difficult to understand, in this land. The buildings she had were inferior and, by our standards, inadequate. The main house was a small, perfectly square building, with two rooms on the first floor and two on the second. Although it did have electricity (one bulb in each room), it had no plumbing or any other modern fixtures. Behind the house there were two other buildings which were sleeping quarters for the children. There were four rooms on each floor and about twenty children slept in every room. Then there were several large open areas with tin roofs over them and with many hard wooden beds. Here the other hundreds slept, and during the monsoon rains, canvas was dropped over the sides to prevent wind and water from entering.

The funds Madame used to run her orphanage were her own or were acquired mysteriously. The clothes she gave to the children were sometimes those she was able to charm from some French Admiral or General—for example, Admiral Querville.

Admiral Querville, the Commanding Officer of the French Navy, at one time in 1954 had a surplus of navy blue uniforms. At a large French dinner party, with a surplus of good wine, Madame Ngai, with a surplus of bosom, beguiled Admiral Querville out of some of his surplus uniforms. They were then cut up and down and made into small suits for her children.

When General René Cogny, Commanding Officer of the French ground forces, captured a Viet Minh warehouse full of Communist uniforms, Madame Ngai heard of it. At the next dinner party, General Cogny was put to the same test undergone by Admiral Querville, and again Madame Ngai's orphanage came out the winner.

The orphanage was prospering. Madame Ngai loved every child, and smothered them all with great tenderness and devotion. Her children were good and well-behaved Buddhists.

The Americans entered her life in August of '54 when the small landing force arrived in Haiphong to set up the funnel's mouth for the evacuation of the refugees. The Military Assistance and Advisory Group (MAAG) had several officers there under Colonel Hamelin, USA, and Colonel Victor Crowziat, USMC. Mike Adler was there as head of the United States Overseas Mission. My boss, Dr. Amberson, and I were on hand too. It did not take long for Madame Ngai to find us—or perhaps for us to find Madame Ngai; I don't remember which it was—and we were soon completely conquered by her goodness and by the smiles of her herd of kids.

Madame Ngai had never met another American save one—a flier downed during the Japanese occupation, whom she had hidden in her home. Although she spoke exquisite French, the only words she knew in English were "Yes, thank you very much." When we told her that this expression lacked variety and might even be dangerous at times, she would smile and say in French, "There is no need to say anything else."

When Captain Amberson left Haiphong, his last words to me were: "Don't neglect those kids at Madame Ngai's." That was one of Captain Amberson's orders that Dooley tried to obey to the letter.

Dr. Amberson had started sick-call at the orphanage and I was able to continue it until April 1955, when the outfit moved to the south. Sometimes, after dinner, while the Frenchmen regaled their hostess with tall tales, I would take my bag and make the rounds in the big house of the orphanage and in the outlying sheds. Many of the children were undernourished, though desperately well cared for and well scrubbed. In fact, there was enough disease and infirmity among these kids to give a man a complete residency in pediatrics, and they made my professional visits busy ones. But there was always time for a romp or two, particularly with my pal Nguyen.

I bummed a lot of things off the ships for the kids, and the ships gave a lot spontaneously. But I couldn't keep using Navy funds earmarked by Congress for whitehats in order to help orphans in Viet Nam. Medicines had to be acquired in some other way.

I wrote again to the Mead-Johnson Company of Evansville, Indiana. I told its executives of the orphanage and reminded them how, during my years in medical school, they had sent me samples of their various vitamin products at least once a month. I asked them if they would now send me enough vitamin "samples" to provide adequate daily doses for six hundred children for six months. They responded by sending me enough vitamins for about a thousand children for a year.

The children took this medicine as they were asked to, though I do not believe that the fish taste and the sour aftertaste in their mouths contributed much to their love of America. But, whatever the taste, their health improved a great deal.

At the University of Notre Dame, at South Bend, Indiana, there is a lady whom many students have come to know and love. I was one. She is my second favorite lady at the University of Notre Dame—Notre Dame herself is first. I wrote Erma Konya, telling of the orphanage of An Lac, this time begging for clothes. As a result of that letter, Erma began sending a package of clothes a month and is continuing the practice now that the orphanage is in Saigon. Each package contains fifteen or twenty small, colorful T-shirts, some small socks, shorts, some combs, perhaps some lollipops. One time there were a few pairs of bright colored suspenders. The kids wore these around the waist like belts; they didn't like them the other way.

Often when a U.S. ship would come up the river we would ask the captain if he were agreeable to a children's party. If the answer was "Yes," at two o'clock in the afternoon we would pile thirty or forty children into a truck, drive them to a pier and load them on a crash boat which would take them out to the ship.

By the time they arrived, the children were usually a little wet and always very noisy. They would have an hour of comic movies, then cookies and ice cream (this usually gave them diarrhea). A sailor would be assigned to each child and it was a tossup as to which of the pair had the better time. After the movies and the banquet, the children would entertain the sailors. They would sing Vietnamese folk songs or do ancient Tonkin dances. The older boys would demonstrate judo. A single crew member would find ten up-roarious children all attempting to throw him at once. Obligingly, he always ended up on the mat. The kids completely captured the hearts of the sailors, and when they left the ship their hands and pockets were full of candies and cookies, their stomachs were full of ice cream, their hearts and eyes full of love and wonder—and they usually wore the sailors' white caps.

Many of the sailors had bought colorful scarves in Japan to take home to their girls in America. Mysteriously, these began to appear on the heads of the Vietnamese orphans of Madame Ngai.

One LST which gave the kids a party was used as a heliport for the Commodore's helicopter. The Commodore intended to take the helicopter out to the Baie d'Along on official business. He had planned to hop off at 1330, but since the children would not arrive on ship until 1430, the Commodore was easily persuaded to wait until then. That would enable the children to see the helicopter take off—a most thrilling and memorable sight indeed to these Vietnamese orphans. The children enjoyed it tremendously, and the dignified Commodore seemed to enjoy their enjoyment. At any rate, he waved so frantically he almost fell out of his helicopter.

Mornings, when we would load refugees at the embarkation zone, Madame Ngai would come and bring half a dozen of the older children. They would help the refugee children of Viet Nam to carry their bundles and sometimes carry the refugee children themselves. They would help the mothers with their baskets and their balance poles. Madame Ngai would pass out bread to the refugees, bread that had been bought with American Aid money and cut up to make small sandwiches. Madame Ngai, and Madame Querville, wife of the French Admiral, passed out more than 700,000 loaves of bread to embarking refugees while I was in Haiphong, which is a formidable number of loaves in any language.

Whenever something was needed at the orphanage that could not be found in the city, which was dying a little more every day, we would turn to the USN. We could always ask whatever Navy ship happened to be in the area for whatever was needed, from nails to napkins, food to floorboards.

Some ships contributed canned and powdered milk. Others contributed cuts of meat. Many took up collections. On the *Balduck,* with her crew of fewer than 120 men, more than $200 was collected and given to the orphanage as a Christmas present. The *Cook* collected over $200 also, in addition to contributing the usual sundries, including pencils and toothbrushes. The sailors would buy such articles in the PX and send them to the children as gifts.

Commodore St. Angelo, who was the Navy "boss" in the middle months of the Evacuation, took an interest in the orphanage and decided that the children should learn some American sport. Somehow or other he hit upon ping-pong, and he had the ship's carpenters build a table for the kids. One of the junior officers on his staff, Lieutenant Al Moses, wrote to his wife in the States and had her send paddles, balls, and a net. Soon the orphanage resounded with children howling and scurrying after the ping-pong ball. And it wasn't long at all before Madame Ngai could beat all comers.

When things were not going too well at the refugee camp, when the mandarin in charge wasn't getting things done as well as could be expected, I would go to Madame Ngai and tell her my troubles. She would jump into my jeep, ride out to the camp, and in no uncertain terms straighten things and people out.

I remember one time when we had just completed a big clean-up campaign, getting the refugees to clean and burn and in general to shine up the camp a little. Now the chief mandarin and some of the lesser officials were getting difficult, as we all did from time to time. Madame Ngai cornered some of them and began ranting: "This camp is filthy. Never saw it look so bad. Why aren't you helping the American doctor to keep your own camp clean?" I thought the camp looked cleaner than it had looked for months, but decided to hold my tongue.

Madame Ngai had the spirit and fight of a girl of sixteen, though she looked to be about thirty and was actually nearer sixty.

When was the orphanage going south? We kept raising the question, fearing that she and the children might be trapped. "Not yet, not yet!" was her answer, week after week. There were still children coming into her home who needed her. She would hold on until the last minute. This caused concern among the French and Americans, who never lost apprehension that Ho Chi Minh might "liberate" Haiphong before the official date in May of 1955.

By the middle of April, however, the city was plagued with Communist riots and demonstrations, and Madame Ngai at long last made up her mind that the time had come for her to move on. Arrangements had already been made in Saigon by the United States Overseas Mission. A building had been found and the American Wives Club of Saigon was waiting for this fabulous woman to appear. They had heard of her and her kids from every acquaintance of their husbands, who had ever visited Haiphong.

So, in the middle of April, the orphanage moved, in toto—beds, mats, planking, pierced steel plating used for floors, desks, bassinets, barrels of chopsticks and rice bowls, small sewing machines, coolie hats, blankets, rice, vitamin pills, artificial leg, ping-pong table and everything else. At that time it sheltered about eight hundred children.

Commodore St. Angelo had me send Baker south with the orphans to make sure they were well treated on all sides. He returned to me a week later; during his absence it was a rough week for me. Admiral Querville personally supervised proceedings when they went aboard an LSM early in the morning, and, before the sun rose over the Red River, the children were on their way down to the bay to be transferred to the *General Brewster* for their Passage to Freedom. After the two-day, three-night voyage, they were met by the American Wives Club and taken to their new home in Saigon's shaky safety. Meanwhile, Madame Ngai's American "orphans" in Haiphong sighed with relief for her sake—and suddenly felt very lonely.

Madame Ngai had never before been out of her beloved Delta. The fact that she had to abandon it represented a personal loss as well as a national tragedy to her. She often spoke of her belief that the Tonkin would be regained.

"We Tonkinese are a militant people," she used to say, "much like those Texans you have told us about. We know that we will some day wrench our land back from the Viet Minh. Of this there is no doubt."

With women like this in a nation, faith and hope in it will persist, whatever the temporary chaos.

The determination of the men of Viet Nam: determined to worship their God, determined to be free, determined to escape to be so.

Determined men have escaped on rafts, hurriedly made by lashing together bamboo poles.

Here is a transfer, four miles out to sea. Over 15,000 have sailed from the coast of Bui Chu.

They reached the eerie, fairyland-like Baie d'Along, four hours down river from Haiphong, the portal to their freedom.

Fatigue after escape . . . with the ever-present symbol of Jesus Christ.

When they arrived in Haiphong, they came to my huge camps, deep in the monsoon mud.

Flooding of the camp was our constant plague. Epidemics were imminent. Yet

It was never hard to find water to bathe a child in. The monsoons furnished enough. Norman Baker's chlorinated-water-plant made more.

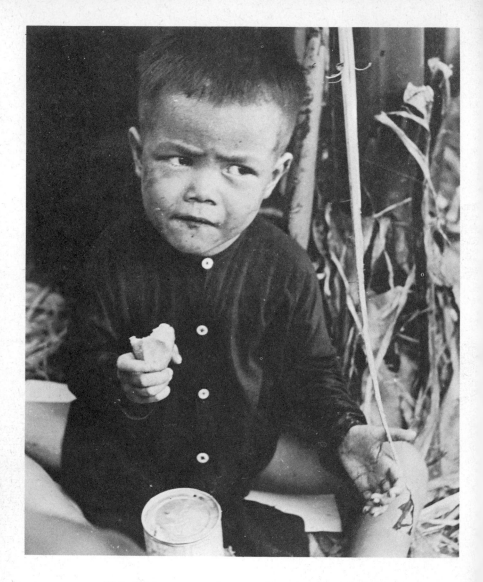

This lad is not sure about anything just yet, especially that canned American milk.

Every refugee carried some heraldry of his belief in God. This belief gave him strength to escape.

The shuttle service . . . small French craft for the four-hour trip from Haiphong to the anchorage of the American ship.

This man had been so badly beaten he could not walk. Refusing to be carried, he crawled out with shoes on his hands.

Saigon, May, 1955: President Ngo Dinh Diem awarding me his nation's highest award, "Officier de l'Ordre National de Viet Nam." It is I who am grateful.

Often we just opened the boxes on the back of the jeep, and treated from the tailgate.

Mead Johnson's Deca-Vi-Sol doing its job for a soft-skinned jungle child.

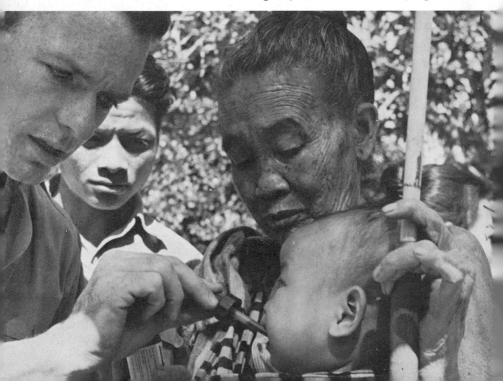

FIFTEEN ·

COMMUNIST RE-EDUCATION

The children of Viet Nam become old very young. They are mature and grave while still in early adolescence, and they are often very brave.

A number of them worked for us in the camps, staying on for months. They did adult work, accepted adult responsibilities; when they could bum cigarettes, they even smoked like adults. Yet they were only eight, or ten or twelve years old.

Each of my corpsmen had six or seven such young assistants. The badge of honor was a white sailor hat. A retinue of them followed me around day and night, sometimes to my embarrassment. They might come to me and lead me to a feeble old woman who could not leave her tent, or take me to see a man who was crippled. They would run errands for me, fetch things I wanted, boil water for the sick-call tent. Sometimes they did my laundry, but on such occasions they were apt to wash the clothes in a rice paddy, and the *wrong* paddy at that, so I discouraged this. And sometimes they would ride my truck just for the fun of it, as children should.

During the months when I was living in Haiphong hotels, they would sleep outside my door. They were often the go-betweens when newly arrived escapees needed help immediately.

Whenever Mr. Ham or any other Vietnamese official wanted to see me, he would spot one of these kids with the sailor hats, or one of the shoeshine boys, and tell him to "find the Bac Sy My."

When one of my assistants would leave for the south we would hold a little ceremony. Various ships' officers had given me their Ensigns' bars. So, on the official day, the Quan Hi, or Lieutenant, would commission his assistant a Quan Mot or Ensign in the U. S. Navy. A bar was pinned on him and his sense of self-importance increased so you could notice it. I hope the

Personnel Department of the Navy will be understanding when it hears about my unusual recruiting service.

The Viet Minh directed much of their propaganda at the children and adolescents of the nation, and they went to unbelievable lengths to drive the propaganda home. The first time I ever saw the results of a Communist "re-education" class was during the month of December. What had been done to these children one December afternoon was the most heinous thing I had ever heard of.

Having set up their controls in the village of Haiduong, Communists visited the village schoolhouse and took seven children out of class and into the courtyard. All were ordered to sit on the ground, and their hands and arms were tied behind their backs. Then they brought out one of the young teachers, with hands also tied. Now the new class began.

In a voice loud enough for the other children still in the classroom to hear, the Viet Minh accused these children of treason. A "patriot" had informed the police that this teacher was holding classes secretly, at night, and that the subject of these classes was *religion*. They had even been reading the catechism.

The Viet Minh accused the seven of "conspiring" because they had listened to the teachings of this instructor. As a punishment they were to be deprived of their hearing. Never again would they be able to listen to the teachings of evil men.

Now two Viet Minh guards went to each child and one of them firmly grasped the head between his hands. The other then rammed a wooden chopped chopstick into each ear. He jammed it in with all his force. The stick split the ear canal wide and tore the ear drum. The shrieking of the children was heard all over the village.

Both ears were stabbed in this fashion. The children screamed and wrestled and suffered horribly. Since their hands were tied behind them, they could not pull the wood out of their ears. They shook their heads and squirmed about, trying to make the sticks fall out. Finally they were able to dislodge them by scraping their heads against the ground.

As for the teacher, he must be prevented from teaching again. Having been forced to witness the atrocity performed on his pupils, he endured a more horrible one himself. One soldier held his head while another grasped the victim's tongue with a crude pair of pliers and pulled it far out. A third guard cut off the tip of the teacher's tongue with his bayonet. Blood spurted into the man's mouth and gushed from his nostrils onto the ground. He could not scream; blood ran into his throat. When the soldiers let him loose he fell to the ground vomiting blood; the scent of blood was all over the courtyard.

Yet neither the teacher nor any of the pupils died.

When news of this atrocity came across the Bamboo Curtain, arrangements were made for escape, and soon teacher and pupils were in Tent 130 at Camp de la Pagode.

We treated the victims as well as we could, though this was not very well. I was able to pull the superior and inferior surfaces of the tongue together and close over the raw portions. The victim had lost a great deal of blood and, as we had no transfusion setup, all I could do was to give him fluids by mouth. He could not eat anything solid, not even rice. For the children, prevention of infection was the important thing. Penicillin took care of this, but nothing could give them back their hearing.

The purpose of this book is not to sicken anyone or to dwell upon the horror of Oriental tortures, which we recall from World War II and from Korea. But I do want to show what has come upon these people of the Delta. And justice demands that some of the atrocities we learned of in Haiphong be put on record.

One midnight, shortly before Christmas, I was awakened by knocking on my hotel door. Two young boys asked if Bac Sy My would please go with them right away. I thought they were from the camp, and that there was something there that needed my attention. So I quickly dressed and went out to the truck. As we were heading out the road, the children motioned for me to turn off onto a path running between two rice paddies. I didn't understand, but they were so earnest that I followed their directions. We turned and drove several hundred yards to a straw paillote, or round hut-like building.

I bent, entered the low door, and then noticed first how dark it was and secondly how unexpectedly large it was inside. There was a kerosene lamp burning in one part of the hut and near it were several kneeling figures—an old man, an old woman, several boys—chanting prayers in a quiet monotone.

They greeted me with "Chao ong, Bac Sy My," clasping their hands before them and bowing their heads, in the Oriental fashion. Then I saw that there was a man lying on a straw mattress which in turn was atop eight or nine long pieces of bamboo, making a crude stretcher. His face was twisted in agony and his lips moved silently as though he were praying, as indeed he was.

When I pulled back the dirty blanket that was over him, I found that his body was a mass of blackened flesh from the shoulders to the knees. The belly was hard and distended and the scrotum swollen to the size of a football. The thighs were monstrously distorted. It was one of the most grisly sights I had ever seen. The idea of merely touching this man was repugnant.

I felt queasy, knew I was going to be sick and rushed outside. Inside that hut I had just seen a masterpiece of systematic torture. Under the sky, I retched and vomited my insides out. I was grateful that no one followed me; they understood and were patient.

I am not sure how long it took for me to get hold of myself, but I finally regained enough nerve and stability to go back and care for this human nightmare. But what could I do? For his pain I could give him morphine. For the belly I could do little, as the skin was not broken in more than four or five spots. All the bleeding was subcutaneous, in bruises which were turning a purple-yellow. I put a large needle into the scrotum in an attempt to drain out some of the fluid. Later I would insert a catheter into the bladder so that the patient could urinate. What else could I do?

I asked the old woman what on God's earth had happened to this poor human being. She told me.

He was her brother, a priest, from the parish of Vinh Bao, just on the other side of the Bamboo Curtain. Vinh Bao was not more than ten kilometers away from Haiphong.

The area had been in Viet Minh hands for only about seven months and the Viets had not yet completely changed the pattern of village life. The priest was permitted to continue celebrating Mass, but only between six and seven o'clock in the morning. This was the time when most of the peasants were just ready to start the morning's work and, under Communist rule, this was the hour when people had to gather in the village square for a daily lecture on the glories of the "new life."

This meant that they were unable to attend the parish priest's Mass either daily or on Sunday. So, for the few who dared to risk his services, the valiant 57-year-old priest held them in the evening. The Communists decided that he needed re-education.

Late the night before, Communist soldiers had called at the priest's chapel, accused him of holding secret meetings and ordered him to stop. Defiantly he replied that nothing could stop him from preaching the word of God. And so this is what they did: they hung him by his feet from one of the crude wooden beams under the ceiling. His head was so close to the ground that he later said, "Frequently I would place my hands on the ground to try to take the pressure off my feet."

With short, stout bamboo rods they proceeded to beat the "evil" out of him. They went on for hours; he did not know just how long. They concentrated on the most sensitive parts of the anatomy. "The pain was great," the priest said. It must have been very great indeed.

He was left hanging in the church and early the next morning his altar boys found him there and managed to cut him down. They were only eight to ten years old, and they ran to their parents, attending compulsory classes in the square, and sobbed out the news.

The parents told them what to do and then said good-bye to them, knowing that it might be good-bye forever. The children lashed together an arrangement of bamboo poles that could be carried as a litter and floated as a raft. They put the priest on this and carried him down the back lanes of the village. They hid him near the bank of the river, which formed one of the boundaries of the free zone. After dark, they lowered the raft gently to the water and, with three on each side, paddled to the middle of the river where they were swept into the down-river current. The coolness of the water probably did more for the priest than most of my medicines. They managed to get him across the river to the free zone without being seen. Arriving late at night, they carried the man to the hut of his sister. Then they came to find me.

I made daily visits to him thereafter and gave him antibiotics and more morphine. Miraculously, he survived; his own strong constitution and no doubt his faith brought about a cure.

Sooner than I would have considered likely he was sufficiently recovered to be taken to Camp de la Pagode. Although he was still crippled, he was soon saying daily Mass and teaching the children their Catechism; in fact, for a time he served as the camp's more or less regular chaplain.

Perhaps I should have let him do it when he insisted that he must return to the village. Perhaps the world needs martyrs, although Tonkin, I thought, had an oversupply already. Next time the Communists would have killed him for sure.

I know that it is not just to judge a whole system from the conduct of a few. However, this was Communism to me. This was the ghoulish thing which had conquered most of the Orient and with it nearly half of all mankind. From December until the last day, there were two or three atrocities a week that came within my orbit. My night calls took me to one horror after another.

Early in my Haiphong stay I was puzzled not only by the growing number but by the character of Communist atrocities. So many seemed to have religious significance. More and more, I was learning that these punishments were linked to man's belief in God.

Priests were by far the most common objects of Communist terror. It seemed that the priests never learned their "Hoc-Tap Dan-Chu," their "Democratic Studies and Exercises," as well as they were expected to. This meant that they had to be "re-educated" more severely than others. It is difficult to take men whose lives had been dedicated to belief in God and straighten them out so that they no longer believe in God. In fact, most of them proved unconquerable.

Catholics have many pious ejaculations which they utter frequently—"Jesus, Mary and Joseph," for example, and "Lord have mercy on us." The Communists ordered the priests to substitute new slogans for them, for example, "Tang gai san u xuat" (Increased Production), and "Chien tranh nhan" (The People's War). Perhaps the expression most often heard in the conquered north was "Com Thu" (Hatred).

The Communists have perfected the techniques of torture, inflicting in one moment pain on the body and in the next pain on the mind. When Tonkin spring came and the monsoon ended, I thought perhaps nature might bring a change in the tenor of things. I was wrong. On the first Sunday of March, I was asked by Father Lopez of the Philippine Catholic Mission to come visit a "sick man," a priest who had just escaped from the Viet Minh.

We walked across the huge sprawling courtyard to the living quarters. In a back room there was an old man lying on straw on the floor. His head was matted with pus and there were eight large pus-filled swellings around his temples and forehead.

Even before I asked what had happened, I knew the answer. This particular priest had also been punished for teaching "treason." His sentence was a Communist version of the Crown of Thorns, once forced on the Saviour of Whom he preached.

Eight nails had been driven into his head, three across the forehead, two in the back of the skull and three across the dome. The nails were large enough to embed themselves in the skull bone. When the unbelievable act was completed, the priest was left alone. He walked from his church to a neighboring hut, where a family jerked the nails from his head. Then he was brought to Haiphong for medical help. By the time of his arrival, two days later, secondary infection had set in.

I washed the scalp, dislodged the clots, and opened the pockets to let the pus escape. I gave the priest massive doses of penicillin and tetanus oxide and went back to the mission every day. The old man pulled through. One day when I went to treat him, he had disappeared. Father Lopez told me that he had gone back to that world of silence behind the Bamboo Curtain. This meant that he had gone back to his torturers. I wonder what they have done to him by now.

Priests were not the only victims of brutality. One day an old woman came to sick-call in the camp. She was wearing a cloth bound tightly around her shoulders in a figure-of-eight. We removed the cloth and found that both the collar bones had been fractured. En route to the camp, she told us, she had been stopped by a Viet Minh guard who, for the crime of attempting to "leave her land," had struck her across the shoulders with the butt of his rifle, ordering her to go back home. This fractured the bones, making her shoulders slump forward and causing excruciating pain. Nevertheless, she managed to escape. In time, with medical care and a regimen of vitamins, she healed.

Always there was the painful thought: "My God! For every one of these who come here, there must be hundreds or even thousands who could not escape."

One day a young man came to sick-call with a marked discoloration of the thumbs. They were black from the first joint to the tips. He was suffering from gangrene, of the dry type, called mummification. There was no great pain, no blood, just raw necrosis of tissue.

He said he had been hung by his thumbs to "re-educate" him. This had happened about a week earlier, and since then his thumbs had been getting a little darker every day. Now they were beginning to smell.

During the course of the examination, while I was manipulating the left thumb, a piece of it actually broke off. There was no bleeding, no pain; there was just a chunk of his thumb that stayed in my hand. This dried piece of flesh, like that of a mummy, had crumbled away with the slightest pressure. The circulation had been cut off for so long—he said he had been left hanging for days—that permanent damage had been done, and all the cells and tissue had died distal to the point where his thumbs had been tied with cord.

"But remember, my friend," one of the elders said to me, "these people might never have left the north if the Communists had not done these cruel deeds against those who preached and practiced their religion."

I feel sure he was right. There were many Buddhists among the refugees, but when I thought of the attendance at daily Mass I had no doubt that 75 or 80 per cent of them were Catholics. Of the 2,000,000 Catholics in Viet Nam, about 1,750,000 lived in the north. Then came the Communists and inevitable disillusionment with the promised reforms. Perhaps they could have borne up under the oppressive taxes, the crop quotas, the forced labor and the loss of freedom. But when the right to worship God was taken from them—often by the most brutal means—they knew it was time to go.

"What fools they are, these Viet Minh," the elder said. "They coax the people to stay, tell them lies, and even try to stop them at the perimeter.

Then they do the very things that will drive the people into exile! Perhaps it is the will of God!"

To say that the Communists tried to stop the refugees at the perimeter was to put it mildly. Though under the Geneva agreement anyone had a right to leave the north who wanted to, the Communists began to violate the agreement on this point from the day it was signed.

As I have indicated earlier, they employed trickery, threats, violence and even murder to stop the southward rush of their subjects. "It is my duty," said Premier Diem in Saigon on January 22, 1955, "to denounce before the free world and before Christendom the inhuman acts of repression and coercion taken by the Viet Minh against the populations wanting to leave the Communist zone, acts which are flagrant violations of the Geneva agreement."

The Premier later estimated that a quarter of a million more would have left if there had been no harassments. My own belief is that this figure is not half large enough. The unbroken flow of the luckier, and of the wounded and mangled who made it to the American camps, was a clue to how many failed to make it. Besides, it is reasonable to assume that thousands who thirsted for freedom lacked the courage or the vitality to take the risks.

Many and various were the Communist devices to keep the people in the north. They made it illegal for more than one member of a family to travel on a bus or train in the affected area at the same time; or for more than two persons to go on foot together on the roads pointing to the evacuation zone. This made it difficult for would-be refugees, whose families were large and held by powerful bonds of unity, to break away.

Nevertheless, desperate parents often sent their children ahead, two today, two tomorrow, with instructions to get to the American camp. By the dozens and the hundreds I saw youngsters, alone, exhausted and sorrowful, arrive and settle down on the fringes of my camp to wait for their elders. Many a time they waited in vain.

In many parts of the Tonkin the Communists ruled that special passports would be required—not to leave the country; that would have flouted Geneva too crudely—but to cross from one canton into another. Obtaining the passports involved steep fees and fantastic red tape. But only with such documents were the refugees permitted to travel as family groups.

Having at long last received its passport, a family might set out on foot on the long road to Haiphong. Fifteen or sixteen days later, their food almost gone, sore and perhaps sick, they would reach a canton line. They would run into that old dodge of the expired passport.

The Communist guard would examine their hard-won document and laugh. "Comrades, this passport is good for only fourteen days. Didn't you know that? Oh, you can't read? Well, anyhow, go back and get a new one."

As a leftover of the war, many roads were sown with mines and booby traps. The victorious Communists dug them up. But often they did not detonate them. Instead they tossed them with designed casualness into rice paddies, swamps, and bushes close to the perimeter of our evacuation area. If citizens trying to crawl to freedom at night were blown to bits, it only served them right.

Yet here are the terms of the agreement: "Any civilians residing in a district controlled by one party who wish to go and live in the zone assigned to the other party shall be permitted *and helped to do so* by the authorities in that district." Those italics, of course, are mine.

SIXTEEN ·

LEADING THE LIFE OF DOOLEY

Reveille for Dr. Dooley and his small band in Haiphong was 5 A.M. I shaved in a basin of cold water, brushed my teeth with chlorinated water brought from the camp and dressed, all in a matter of minutes. My standard working clothes—and every day was a working day—consisted of khaki trousers or shorts, a T-shirt and a uniform shirt with the sleeves cut off.

Never did I neglect to wear my collar insignia and my Navy hat. These, especially the hat, were important. Symbols mean a lot in the Orient. To the hundreds of thousands who passed through my hands, the bars on the collar and the eagle on the hat stood for authority, true, but also for friendship and for that whole far-off nation called the United States. My corpsmen and I were determined to impress upon the people that what we were doing for them was being done through the generosity and love of the American people.

"Yes, the gloves on your hands are good," a refugee might say. "But the eagle on your cap is bad."

"No, the eagle on my cap is good," I would answer. "Without the eagle there would be no doctor-gloves. The eagle stands for America. America sends the Navy, which brings you the American Navy doctor. And the American Navy itself takes you to safety in Saigon."

These arguments went on interminably at sick-call. Sometimes I wished it were possible just to work without talking. But this job had to be done.

Almost always I found one or two boys sleeping in the corridor outside my door and a few more sprawled in my jeep. There would be a few of these "little Dooleys" at my heels when I appeared, at a little after five, either at the camp or in the village church, for Mass.

After Mass, breakfast. Usually I returned to my quarters, where I made instant coffee on a hot-plate and drank it, with crackers. (In the earlier months, in the few remaining shabby restaurants, French and Indian, I sometimes treated myself to more substantial fare.)

By six o'clock or a little later, I was in the Medical Tent for the day's first assortment of tropical ailments, fractured limbs and suppurating wounds. Patients queued up before my arrival, and there was still a line by the time I knocked off for lunch.

For that, I might head for the orphanage, where Madame Ngai was sure to fix me a hot meal. Wherever I went, I usually brought my own water, since I couldn't afford to be too sick too often.

By one o'clock I tried to be back in camp for the serious business of learning Vietnamese.

At three, when the temperature dropped to a more tolerable 100 or so degrees, I resumed sick-call. However long the lines, I had to crowd in visits to the hospital tents for checking, treatments and sometimes surgery. This carried me to 5:30 or 6 P.M., at which time I drove my jeep to other areas where our people were quartered, including a warehouse in town which housed thousands of them.

Dinner, too, might be contributed by the orphanage. Then, by eight or thereabouts, I was back in my room for a cold sponging and bed. There was a prayer in my heart that I might be allowed to sleep through until morning. But often my young guardian angels would be obliged to waken me. Someone's condition had taken a bad turn, or new atrocity victims had arrived for patching.

Such was the basic pattern. This, of course with many variations, was the life that I led from the end of August till the middle of May. It melted off fully a third of the 180 pounds I had arrived with. The routine went on despite several bouts of malaria, four different types of intestinal worms, and a mild but uncomfortable case of acne. My hands were dyed red, because I did not have much alcohol to use as a cleansing solution but did have plenty of tincture of merthiolate. After I left Viet Nam, it took a week to bring my hands to near normal.

The drain on my energies never really bothered me profoundly. I was young, had a sound constitution and was a sound sleeper. The psychological strains were harder to manage. Try as I would not to let the sorrow and savagery bother me, the goad of conscience drove me to do more and more, and the stabs of guilt reminded me that I could not do enough.

Toward the end of my assignment, I seldom went out to the ships in the bay. It was a four hour trip by small boat. With the Viet Minh itching for trouble, our launches made no trips after dark and the daylight hours were my busiest. But the lure of a hot shower and a decent meal often seemed irresistible. Once I succumbed to the lure, and sent a message, via my walkie-talkie, requesting the command ship's helicopter.

When the skipper asked me what was up, I answered boldly: "Sir, I am in desperate need of a hot bath and a decent meal." He merely chuckled.

Actually the whole task force knew about Dooley's bathing difficulties, having heard about the time I went aboard the flagship and was invited to luncheon in Admiral Sabin's cabin.

I was wearing a battered khaki shirt and trousers, my hands were stained red with merthiolate, and I needed a bath. Nevertheless, with all those high-ranking officers present, the Admiral seated me at the foot of the long table, directly facing him. I was obviously flattered, but he brought me up short.

"Don't get any ideas, Doctor," said the Admiral. "You just smell so bad I want you as far away as possible."

I would soon see a time when my heart was so heavy that I grasped like a child at anything that was good for a laugh. I even began to look kindly on Baker's clownish pet baboon, despite the fact that he was chewing the seat covers off our truck.

SEVENTEEN ·
THE DYING CITY

The months passed but the refugees continued to pour in week after week from all the provinces of north Indo-China. Some days we would get fewer than a hundred; other days there would be thousands. They came by boat, by land, by foot, by junks and sampans.

Camp de la Pagode was taken down in March and other camps were erected. During January and February, we had three huge camps with a total capacity of over 30,000.

Eventually all of my Navy corpsmen left except Norman Baker, the dauntless interpreter who did everything else but interpret.

It was at that luncheon given by Admiral Sabin that I made a clean breast of the Baker affair. "You see, sir," I said, "I speak French, and now I speak Vietnamese, so I hardly need an interpreter. But Baker is a wonderful all-around assistant. So I've been holding on to him under false pretenses."

"Well, well," the Admiral said, assuming a mock-serious expression. "I hate to disappoint you, but you weren't fooling us. I knew all along you were pulling a fast one."

It turned out there were a lot of other fast ones that he hadn't minded either. There had been complaints about my habit of lifting supplies from ships in the area. "Look what Dooley's done now—60 drums of oil and he just signed his name for it! Who the devil does that boy think he is?"

"Well," the Admiral would say, "I'm sure he wouldn't have taken the stuff if he hadn't needed it urgently."

Also, he had become inured to my rare but high-handed raids on ship personnel. For example, at a time when I was acutely short-handed, I requested that four volunteer corpsmen be given TAD (Temporary Additional Duty) with me. Since their Captain had no desire to release them, I sent a message directly to the Admiral. It must have reached him, for the four men were soon at work in my camps.   •

Many months after our talk on his flagship, I received a letter from Admiral Sabin commending me on having been awarded the Legion of Merit. In it he wrote: "The Book says the Lord will help those who help themselves and it seems to me that, in the evacuation of Indo-China, you, Dr. Dooley, several times managed to give the Lord a nudge."

Not once did the Admiral fail to endorse my nudging. I had superb support from on high, and without it I would have been licked.

By April the push began to slow up. Evidently the new masters of North Viet Nam had plugged most of the remaining holes in their Curtain. The French Army was almost gone, along with its equipment, Quonset huts, tanks, office furniture. Only a few hundred French soldiers were still encamped on the nail of the finger-like projection of Haiphong. Operation Cockroach, my end of the more elegantly named Passage to Freedom, was entering its final stage. Once, when a helicopter was sent from a ship for me, the Communist perimeter was already so choking-close that the plane had to land on a small lot in town.

Haiphong was dying. Every day more shops and houses were deserted. Only a few civilian vehicles remained of the thick motor traffic we had found on arrival. The reeking bazaar which had fascinated me was burned "by accident." There was little doubt that it was the work of Viet Minh infiltrators.

The few officers of MAAG left, except an Air Force Major, Ralph Walker. Roger Ackley, replacing Mike Adler toward the end, brought some new ideas and the camp administration was revamped.

Major John McGowan, U. S. Army, was the Military Attaché who stayed on until the very last day. He was another excellent type of career officer who did his job with all his heart, withstood all discomforts and managed to retain his sense of humor. I was lucky to have men to work with like John McGowan. They were a constant inspiration—and a constant gig in the rear. When I felt myself slipping, becoming lazy, I would see other Americans in Haiphong doing their jobs well, and then guilt would get me. "Up and at 'em."

By now my evenings were spent either at the camps, talking to the refugees, by this time in their own language, or in town, at the abandoned bank building (the coolest place in town) where John and I would argue big subjects like Army versus Navy and bigger ones like wine and women. We would consider it a treat when relatives would get mail through to us and we would have a copy of *Time* or *Newsweek*. The Embassy in Saigon sent a plane up with our mail once or twice a month. This was always a great day.

We had used an amazing tonnage of DDT, plus thousands of gallons of Lindane, and other insecticide solutions. The water systems had worked overtime and now I believed they should be put out to pasture in the green fields of North Carolina.

All the city people who intended to leave were leaving or had left. By this time, most of those remaining in the city could be assumed to be pro-Viet Minh, if not actually full-fledged Communists. It was now that real trouble began.

The Governor's staff and the Mayor's staff left, with only skeleton crews remaining. All was grim and silent on the streets. Violence became common in the "new society" about to install itself on the ruins of Haiphong. The first riots exploded in the second week of April.

It seems that several hundred Viet Minh trucks arrived with so-called refugees piled high in back. These refugees did not want to live in the camps; they wanted to move into the city, where there were hundreds of empty buildings.

As the trucks tried to drive across the Ha Ly Bridge leading to the city, the French stopped them and forbade them to enter, saying that the Viet Minh were not to take over completely until May 19, and that this was beating the Geneva deadline. The truck occupants argued that as refugees they could enter at any time.

Tempers became short on both sides. The bogus refugees pushed across the bridge and the French soldiers poured out tear-gas bombs. Hand-to-hand fights developed. Several of the "refugees" were killed, hundreds were wounded, including many soldiers; and the Red radio broadcasters in Hanoi had themselves another propaganda holiday. Such clashes became ever more frequent.

I had one more difficult task to perform. The shoeshine kids were still in the city, and still my friends and protectors. One time my camera was stolen when I foolishly left it in my truck, parked on a side street. I told the artful dodgers of my loss. They were furious to think that anyone would steal from their American doctor. I think they were also furious to think that other people were horning in on their own purloining territory. Within a few hours my camera was returned. They said they had found it. I wondered whether one of the lovable, larcenous kids had probably stolen it himself without knowing to whom it belonged.

The time had come for the shoeshine kids to go. I consoled them with assurances that the shoeshine business was certain to be lush in Saigon and that a good thief, like a religious man, finds it hard to survive in a police state.

What convinced them finally, I think, was the matter of shoes. The idea came to me in a flash one day. "Well," I said, "you might as well throw those kits away. There will be no more shoe-shining when the Viet Minh arrive. Or do you think you can shine canvas shoes?"

They looked at me suspiciously, and then at one another. I wasn't kidding! From their frequent forays behind the Bamboo Curtain, they had learned that canvas sneakers were standard equipment among the Viet Minh.

At that point they agreed to be vaccinated and dusted with DDT. One April morning, Baker and I boosted a few of them into a truck and went downtown to gather up the rest from the street corners. We gave them each a loaf of bread and a final delousing and watched them shoulder their shoe-shine kits and file sullenly aboard the landing craft. They arrived safely in Saigon, and I'm sure that city hasn't been the same since.

On May 10 the Viet Minh staged another proof that the American doctor and Americans in general were hated by the population. Our green truck was stolen. It was a one-ton truck Doctor Amberson had gotten from the Haiphong Public Health people. They had received it from the French, who got it from the U.S.A. through American Aid. I used it for ten months, for every conceivable mission. It had been turned on its side in a riot and, in another demonstration, had had all its windows broken. The spare tire, the cap of the gasoline tank, the windshield and the light bulbs were missing towards the end. Baker's baboon had eaten most of the interior, yet the spunky little truck still ran. The monsoon rains had done their best to make it moldy. You couldn't sit down in it with clean trousers and come out looking the same. Yet the little chariot could go anywhere, haul anything, and was well known throughout the city. To make sure that no one forgot it, Mike Adler had the big American Aid insignia painted on its side.

On the tenth of May it was stolen from a parking space near the bank building. Late that night we found its charred and blackened chassis in the town square. The Viet Minh apparently had burned it in a public demonstration to illustrate to the Americans that they were despised and to the Vietnamese that the new Democratic Republic of Viet Minh would have nothing to do with anything "made in the U.S.A."

I was as depressed as if a friend had been murdered, and for a moment thought of having what was left of the chassis buried with military honors.

USOM officials in Saigon probably are still filling out chits to account for ONE TRUCK, DODGE, ONE-TON, GREEN.

The Catholic Mission was now about empty. The nuns, the school children and all the priests except one very old native had been sent south. Sun-burned Father Lopez had packed up his bicycle and departed on the *General Brewster,* taking his one clean cassock and his intestinal worms with him. Father Felice, who always looked so jaundiced in spite of my vitamin pills, antibiotics and phenobarbitol, left on an embassy plane in the last week of April.

I hated to see them go; they had become good friends. They were made with hearts of that proverbial precious metal and they had been wonderful to our small tribe of Americans. It was Father Felice who offered early Mass every morning in the Mission Church, usually full of barefoot chanting natives. He tells me he could usually determine when I arrived because of the way my boots squeaked as I made my way to the very front row.

The old native priest who was left in charge would say Mass until Haiphong fell, and intended to try to continue even after the Viet Minh took over. He knew that he might be made to suffer but he said that he was old and that a martyr's crown might ensure his entry into Heaven. Haiphong's last weeks found his Masses attended by a dwindling handful of the devout.

The pride of the Mission was their statue of Our Lady of Fatima. Several decades before, when Haiphong Catholics were in Rome on a pilgrimage, His Holiness the Pope had given it to them with his blessing. It stood on an altar of its own just to the left of the main altar. It was an object of popular reverence, with flowers and burning candles always around it. Day and night peasants prayed before it.

There were many discussions about the advisability of removing the statue of Our Lady of Fatima. Should it be taken south when Father Lopez and Father Felice left Haiphong? Should it be kept until the very last possible day? Or should it be left to give comfort to the few who might, for one reason or another, remain behind?

In the end, the decision about the statue was made by an American, Norman Poulin. Roger Ackley was called back to Germany toward the very end and our embassy flew Norman up to succeed him. Norman spoke impeccable French. His job was to help wind up the final details of the evacuation. He was charged especially with getting out the American equipment that remained north, the tents, the few vehicles, some American Aid rice, and other products which USOM was determined not to leave behind for the use of the Viet Minh.

The last American embassy plane flew in on the eleventh of May, the main airport had gone to the enemy, so it landed on an abandoned military airstrip. The pilot of the plane had a message from Father Felice. He asked: "Is the statue of Fatima all right or have the Viet Minh defiled it?"

Norman met the plane and received this message. I was there hoping there would be a message for me to get on this plane and get the hell out of Indo-China. (There wasn't.) We held a short conference and made a quick decision. We sped to the Mission in the jeep, which was on its last legs. We buttonholed the poor old priest and tried to bamboozle him. "We want the statue. We want to send it south on the embassy plane."

The old priest shook his head. "Oh no, it must stay."

We failed to convince him and at last we pretended to agree. "Very well, perhaps it must stay."

Then, as he tottered back to his cubicle, we went into the church on the double. We climbed up on the little altar and literally kidnapped the statue. We wrapped it in an American Aid blanket which was on the jeep's floor and whisked it out to the airport. At this writing it is standing in a church built especially for the refugees, just outside Saigon. And that's how Our Blessed Lady of Fatima, with a boost from American Aid, made the Passage to Freedom.

When people ask when the heart of Haiphong stopped beating, the date I give them is the fourth of May. It was on the fourth of May that, according to the treaty, an advance echelon, the Viet Minh Committee of Experts, was allowed to enter the city. They were to go to the City Hall, the Governor's office, the public utilities plants and so on and learn how to take them over from the Vietnamese, the last of whom would leave on the sixteenth of May on the last boat out. Thus there would be no sudden cessation of water or electricity and, in theory at least, the turnover of the city would be smooth.

The Committee arrived, 480 strong, in brand-new, Russian-made Molotova trucks. They were impeccably dressed in high-collared grey uniforms, pith helmets and canvas shoes, and most of them spoke French very well.

They stopped me about four times daily, when I was trying to cross a street, or drive out to the camp or go down to the docks, but they were always polite and respectful. They said I was the only American they had ever met who could speak their language. Why had I learned it? Did I intend to stay on and try to help the "true people of Viet Nam" when the Democratic Republic established its offices? I replied that my job was just about over and that I expected to be leaving soon.

They sent a delegation out to the camp and gave me a bit of dialectical materialism.

"When you treat people in America," the leader asked, "do you make any distinction between Democrats and Republicans?"

"Certainly not!"

"Very well," he said. "There must be no distinction here between capitalistic dupes and the loyal people of Viet Nam."

Then the cheeky bastard ordered his men to divide up my pharmaceuticals and surgical supplies—half for me and half for the Democratic Republic of Viet Nam. And there wasn't a thing I could do about it.

I tried to be polite with the newcomers but perhaps I merely gave them the impression that I was afraid of them. And I was. I was constantly afraid that they would lock me up somewhere and hold me for investigation. Investigations can stretch out for years in Communist states, as many an American knows to his cost. And we were only four Americans in all of North Viet Nam.

The arrival of the Committee of Experts was not bad in itself. But trouble arose because, when they arrived, they brought several thousand armed bodyguards with them.

The bodyguards raised hell in the village. When they arrived, riots, fires, "spontaneous" anti-foreign demonstrations, and beatings of men and women who had been friendly to us became common. The newcomers cynically blamed all these things on the French.

There was a riot in front of the City Jail and the Committee of Experts demanded that all prisoners be released immediately. The French replied that they would be released on the sixteenth of May, according to the agreement, and not until then. This demonstration ended up in tear gas and firing on the crowd.

I climbed up in the steeple of the Mission one afternoon and looked all around the city. You could see little puffs and clouds of smoke in seven or eight parts of town, where demonstrations were being broken up with tear gas. The French used it frequently as the last violent method of dispersing mobs.

The forces of General Cogny, keeping cool heads, did a good job at keeping some semblance of order during these last weeks. As for me, I spent most of my time dodging riots, driving blocks out of my way to get to my objectives, so that I would not be stopped and questioned. A good deal of the time I spent just being afraid.

By the 10th of May we had taken down the tents of our camps and moved the remaining refugees into empty buildings in the city. It was on the twelfth of May that I saw my last grisly atrocity.

By this time the Viet Minh legally had all but a very small area on one side of Haiphong, but illegally they had just about all of it. Their strength was visible everywhere. They patrolled the main streets and waterways, and there were sentries at every intersection. They captured a young Vietnamese boy, a wild type of lad, who still wanted to escape from Viet Minh territory and dared to try.

He attempted to duck through back streets across the line of demarcation, known as the DMZ or Demilitarized Zone. Here he was apprehended by the Viets. They formed a circle around him and beat on his feet with the butts of their rifles. They continued this until the victim collapsed, then added more blows for good measure, all on the feet and ankles. This was what was to happen to runaways in the future!

The Viets stopped beating the boy only after he was unconscious. When he regained his senses, he found that he had been left alone and that the road was abandoned. He dragged his shattered, mangled feet into a nearby alley. There a rickshaw driver found him and somehow got him across to us on the free side.

I had no X-ray equipment but it was obvious that the damage was beyond repair. The feet and ankles felt like moist bags of marbles and were already gangrenous. I had only a few instruments left and a little procaine and penicillin. I did the best I could by disarticulating the ankles where they connect with the lower leg. Someone else would have to do a more thorough amputation job later. We managed to get the boy into a crash boat which took him out to a French LSM, waiting to sail for the south. He was crippled for life, but at least he was free.

Our last loading day was the twelfth of May, a dry hot morning. The shuffling of thousands of bare feet made acrid dust rise off the ground at the loading area. One could taste the dust. It made the tongue feel thick and the teeth gritty. There was little sound except for the chugging of the LST motors. We were still spraying the refugees with DDT.

A May morning in America means spring, softness, sweet odors, perhaps a cool misty rain. But here the heat of the Indo-China sun was intense, the glare of the river was blinding and the smell of the refugees was overpowering.

This was the last day of the last loading. Some 3,600 refugees would take the trip, first to the bay and then on to Saigon, huddled together with their cloth bags, their balance poles with household possessions at each end, their babies on mothers' hips. They were as desolate a slice of the human race as any that had preceded them. They walked slowly in line to be dusted with DDT, to accept a loaf of bread, or perhaps a few diapers and small bags of clothing. But to me they were not a mere mass of wretchedness. I had come to know their valiant hearts and stout spirit. Somehow, over the bitter months, without knowing how it happened, I had identified myself with their dream of life in freedom and their tragic destiny. They had become my suffering brothers.

Of course these last refugees were not really the last. There were still a couple of million behind the Bamboo Curtain who never had a chance. But we had done the best we could. And I hope the men who made the deal at that lovely Geneva lakeside are happy with the results.

I had been taught to believe in and do believe in God's love, His goodness, His mercy. And I knew that in some small degree at least these qualities can be shared by man. But I had seen very little of them in the last year.

"I must remember the things I have seen," I said to myself. "I must keep them fresh in memory, see them again in my mind's eye, live through them again and again in my thoughts. And most of all I must make good use of them in tomorrow's life."

I watched the last LCT pull away from the dock and, as I came to the full realization that it was all over, a quiet grief engulfed me. The boat headed downriver and an enormous sun was sinking in a burst of splendor.

EIGHTEEN ·
AFTERWORD

Why did the refugees feel about us, America, as they did in the years before Dien Bien Phu?

It should be remembered that every rumbling tank that overran the villages of the Tonkin, every blazing napalm bomb that seared the huts of the natives, every gun and jeep and truck and uniform that brought havoc upon the people in what they considered a "colonial" war—all these were "made in the U.S.A." The people of North Viet Nam considered the United States as a vast warehouse and supply depot for France's colonialism, as indeed we were. I don't know the exact figure, but it was in the hundreds of millions of dollars of aid, in military materials, to France for the war in Indo-China.

This equipment from us was laden with propaganda potential on both sides of the Bamboo Curtain. But only the Viet Minh Communists took the initiative. Perhaps it was because many Americans consider the word "propaganda" a dirty word. ("Information" is more acceptable.) Perhaps it was because, by its very nature, the cogs of a democracy turn slowly. In any event, the Communists didn't lose a moment.

The Viet Minh had a well-staffed and extremely effective psychological warfare department, under the leadership of General Giap, the man whose army conquered Dien Bien Phu. The propaganda was directed not at the leaders, not at the mandarins, not at the government heads, but it was directed at the common laborer of the delta. And the propaganda succeeded horribly well.

In the areas that had been under the Viet Minh control for five, six and seven years, the propaganda did little good. These people knew by the emptiness of their bellies that the Viet Minh was a fraud. The illness of the minds of their Communist re-educated children proved to them that the new system was evil—much more evil than France had ever been. But to those in the areas that had only been recently conquered, or turned over to the Viet Minh through the Geneva Treaty, Communism still held a fascination.

They were attracted by many of its ideas, especially the promise of land reforms. The people of Viet Nam had borne the burdens of colonialism for over eighty years and they were weary of them. The Communists offered the allurements of a "new way of life." The Democracies offered nothing, though they had the greatest things to offer—justice and freedom. I do not mean to imply that Communism was "voted" into power, but it did not meet with intelligent, or indeed any other kind of opposition.

The people from the two zones never met face to face. One of the first rules of the conquering Communists was to restrict travel. As a consequence it was difficult to spread the truth about the "new way of life." And to those disillusioned people from the old zones who got through to unconquered ones the response would often be, "Well, when the Viet Minh liberate *our* areas it will be different. We shall work harder to produce the paradise that they have promised. The reason your province is in anguish is because you are too slow, you cannot work long hours, you take siestas, you do not toil the fields long enough. Things will be different when *our* province is rid of the French yoke. . . ."

One might ask why, if they were so much in favor of the new rule, and if they so hated Americans as an extension of their French colonial rulers, did so many of them attempt to escape to Haiphong? The answer is simple. For the greatest majority of the refugees, utilizing American ships was just the lesser of two very imminent evils. The first evil was the suppression of their religion. The second was that of risking one's life on an imperialist American ship.

The Viet Minh suppressed their religion. The Viet Minh closed their churches. The Viet Minh put priests and ministers to the fields to work, or killed them. All outward manifestations of religion were destroyed. Because of this, and not because of anything we did, they decided that it would even be worth the risk of contact with the Americans, in order to gain what they knew was religious freedom in the South under Ngo Dinh Diem.

As I have tried to show, when the Tonkinese arrived at our camps their emotions ranged from deep hate to mild distrust. Very few refugees arrived wholeheartedly joyful that they had reached the threshold to their passage. Instead they arrived fearful, apprehensive, and sometimes absolutely antagonistic. At first they accepted everything, from penicillin to their daily bowl of rice, with marked reluctance.

At the start the refugees associated only terror with a uniform. However, they were soon learning to associate help and love with our work. I wanted to be sure they realized that our love and help were available just because we were in the uniforms of the U. S. Navy. The reason we were there to help them was because we were in the service. That is why Baker saluted me, and called me Quan Hi, which means Lieutenant, rather than Doctor. Everything we did was done because the American Navy made it possible for us to do it. Soon we began to feel a quiet pride in our hearts at being Americans. We had come with ships to take them to freedom, with medical aid to heal their ills and bind up their wounds, with large supplies of life-saving drugs freely donated by American firms merely on my say-so. We had come late to Viet Nam, but we had come. And we brought not bombs and guns, but help and love.

The two groups that inspired me to write this book were at diametrically opposite poles of civilization. That stinking mass of humanity under foreign skies, those miserable and diseased people who in the depths of anguish had hearts so splendid and a faith so powerful, were my first inspiration. The other group were my friends in the Navy—the fifteen thousand sailors and officers who gave such touching and tender care to the wretched of Viet Nam. They did this without orders, simply because they wanted to help people who "didn't have it so good."

A finer lot of men cannot be found anywhere on this earth. When they encountered the problem, they asked for an explanation. When it was explained, they understood. When they understood the suffering, they decided to alleviate it. And they *did* alleviate it. They conquered the hearts of every one of the refugees who sailed on our ships. They did this with an enthusiasm and wholesomeness that defies description.

Certain ships stand out in my memory as superb. First the *Montague*, AKA 98; then the little APDs, the *Balduck*, 132; the *Cook*, 130; and the *Diachenko*, 123. Lastly the gawky LSTs, 885 and 1096. Certain men, Pete Kessey HM3, Norman Baker ABM3, Dennis Shepard HM3, Commander Le Forge, and Lt. Johnny Fusco, Lt. Johnny Walker and Lt. H. S. Hayden, and the inseparable Lts. Ted Torok and Hal Zimmerman, the excellent Commodores, especially Captain Walter Winn—these I remember.

My understanding and very patient boss, Admiral Lorenzo S. Sabin, USN, who must have spent many hours wondering just what the devil his Lieutenant (junior grade) was doing in Haiphong that was a little legal.

I was always borrowing equipment, demanding supplies, and acting as though I had four more stripes than I wore. I was usually illegitimate and out of channels. But the Admiral backed me all the way. His staff men—Lt. Floyd Allen, Major N. R. Smith, and cigar-chewing Major John Kelly—helped me with everything from logistics to chow.

Lt. Pat Ledwidge, Ensign Charlie Rush and Lt. Bob Athout put up with me, lent me clean clothes, and gave me plenty of boosts when my morale was sagging. Lt. Don Stibich, in spite of his youthful face and soul, was a truly fine man, and a constant inspiration to me to become as good as he seemed to think I already was. Lt. Al Moses, one of the most genuine men I have known, gave me stability when I needed it; I needed it frequently.

Commander Wendell Mackey quietly infused some patience into my Irish breeding which I needed when my mob required a touch of "diplomacy." Lt. Tom Avertt I remembered especially because he loved the children of Madame Ngai, and did so much in their behalf. Some civilians too gave me intangibles, Mike Adler and Roger Ackley especially. Air Force Major Ralph Walker, a confrere of Haiphong, gave me more than he received from me.

One other name shines forth—Army Major John McGowan. A military man through and through, a true Christian and a real philosopher, he spent many a night explaining principles and military ethics to me. He took vague concepts which I could not catalogue and helped me with them, gently probing me to think further, examine and analyze. He could define terms like Communism, war, dialectical materialism, death. He would knead and mould my mind, and mature my reasoning. He would always lead me to a just decision. We seldom talked that he wasn't really teaching, without ever seeming to do so. To him I owe a great debt. If there is anything creditable in this book, to him goes much of the credit; thanks, John.

When I returned to the hospital in Japan at the end of the Indo-China experience, I weighed less than 120 pounds, and with a six-foot frame this looked rather lean. Commander Charles Mann of the Medical Service Corps took one glance at me, and offered me two weeks leave. He gave me something else—two orders: (1) eat plenty of raw steak, and (2) write a book. With tongue in cheek he *ordered* me to write. Charlie, here is the book I promised.

To the typists with their ceaseless work goes my gratitude, especially to Elmo Mims and to Joe Polifrone.

Passing through Hawaii on my way home, Captain W. Lederer, USN, well-known in the editorial and publishing worlds, gave me a real boost.

He pushed the appropriate buttons, and found my publisher, and therefore gave me the platform from which to tell my Viet Nam story.

Silas Spengler and Joe Albanese, though never in Viet Nam, had an understanding of the situation down there, and an understanding of this doctor's work. And they knew my sadness. They spent long hours helping me to form this manuscript, advising me on it, and never losing confidence in me, even when I direly lacked it myself. Being with them I felt as though my head was in the sky, high and clear, but my feet firmly planted on God's earth, staunch and sure. And for them my heart has much gratitude.

And finally and perhaps the most important of all, Lt. Norton Stevens, USNR, deserves my deepest thanks. He who served with me in Indo-China, and again with me in Japan during that rocky period when all was over, and so much seemed confusion. Nort sat with me many a night and would say, "O.K. Tom, just slow down, take it in your stride, you'll be fine. Soon you will see the splendor of the thing again. Now there is only depression from what you have witnessed. In time you will see the glory of it." Thanks to you, Nort, now I do see what you spoke of those foggy nights in Japan.

The best that I can say of all those men is that they are good Americans. The best that I can say of myself is that I can call them my friends. If apologies are due for some of my erratic ways, then I ask them to remember that

> "The woods are lovely, dark and deep,
> But I have promises to keep,
> And miles to go before I sleep."

U.S. Naval Hospital
Bethesda, Md.

THE
EDGE
OF
TOMORROW

FOREWORD

This, the true story of six young Americans, takes place in an exotic land of tinkling wind bells and clashing cymbals, half a world away—the Royal Kingdom of Laos.

This is not a document of figures and facts, nor is it to be taken as a historical narrative. It is not a generalization, nor is it fiction. It is a true story of six Americans who formed a fellowship with the people of Laos, and indeed with many other people throughout the world, as you will soon see. At the start I would like to tell you about the concept of this fellowship, and about the man who conceived it.

Since my earliest days in medical school the work of Doctor Albert Schweitzer has been one of the great inspirations of my life. To enter into correspondence with him was a cause of great satisfaction to me. And the biggest thrill of all occurred recently when I visited the great old gentleman himself. It is difficult to describe him. He has sensitiveness and forcefulness at one and the same time. He is both tender and majestic. His grizzly old face is wonderful to see.

One of Doctor Schweitzer's most important concepts is that of the Fellowship of Those Who Bear the Mark of Pain. I and my men have found this Fellowship wherever we have gone. Who are its members? Doctor Schweitzer believes the members are those who have learned by experience what physical pain and bodily anguish mean. These people, all over the world, are united by a secret bond. He who has been delivered from pain must not think he is now free, at liberty to continue his life and forget his sickness. He is a man whose eyes are opened. He now has a duty to help others in their battles with pain and anguish. He must help to bring to others the deliverance which he himself knows.

Under this Fellowship come not only those who were formerly sick, but those who are related to sufferers, and whom does this not include? On the members of this Fellowship rests the humanitarian task of providing medical help to the "have-nots" of the world. Dr. Schweitzer believes that men of medicine should go forth among the miserable in faroff lands and do what has to be done, in the name of God and Man.

In a very small way, because of my profession, I have found entrance into this Fellowship. I have discovered hundreds of others in it, too. Many people all over the world heard of our mission to Laos. Thousands wrote to us, many offered gifts, and some offered useful suggestions. Others volunteered to come and work with us. One man even sent me a detailed outline of a Community Development Plan that he had used in South Africa forty years before. These people were all members of that Fellowship, even though they didn't realize it.

The list of things that were sent to me would bring tears and smiles. There were a few foolish things, some useless ones. But the greatest part were wonderful, and desperately needed. The only repayment I can think of is the simple utterance of gratitude.

The help of the schools was perhaps the warmest of all. Dozens of schools wrote and asked what they could do, so we tried to give each a project. Franklin School Three, in Passaic, New Jersey, sent hundreds of bars of soap that they had collected. Their teacher, Miss Mary Kennedy, suggested that each student write me a letter. My mail was already hitting about two hundred and fifty letters per month, but the grade-school children's letters were most appreciated. One little fellow wrote that he stayed with his father at a New York hotel and while there he talked the maid out of a "whole suitcase full of hotel soap." The soap was important because in the mountains of Laos there is none, nor is there any kind of substitute. We would give a couple of bars of "sabu" to each skin case that came to sick-call.

Freemont Junior High in Anaheim, California, sent me nearly five hundred pounds of soap, every ounce of which was put to use. Many doctors and nurses sent me sample-size medicines that the pharmaceutical houses pass out. I had plenty of the basic antibiotics, but these assortments were just the thing for an odd case here and there.

The Irish nuns of St. John's Hospital in St. Louis, Missouri, have no idea of how much one nurse "borrowed" from them. She even sent me a spinal anesthesia tray that I needed, with a note saying that the anesthesiologist helped her make up the tray. Another nurse, Clare McCartney of Santa Barbara, sent me over thirty boxes of medicines, samples of drugs for everything from nausea to nose-bleeds. To have people so far away take such a personal interest in my mission reminded us that we were not alone.

A few days after the little boy Ion was operated on (see Chapter VI), I received a letter from Chaplain K. I. Rewick of Punahoe School in Honolulu. His high school students had taken up a collection and sent me several hundred dollars. We decided that this was just about the cost of the medicines and bandages that we would need for this boy, so we wrote and told them that Ion was "their" patient. We sent pictures as he progressed, and tried to keep Punahoe School up to date on his condition. Ion could not pronounce the name of the school, but he did understand that hundreds of young American boys and girls were taking care of him.

An old shipmate of mine, Larry Aggens, went on a regular Chicago Roundup program. He gave talks to raise money for us. The only time Larry took off from this program was while he was in the hospital having an injured eye treated. As soon as he got out, with a plaid eye-patch and a Hathaway shirt, he returned to his task of being beggar-in-chief of the Dooley mission.

A doctor in England sent us books on the medical problems of the tropics. Several doctors in America also sent me medical texts. Mr. Brayton Lewis of the Holliday Bookshop in New York made a point of keeping the Dooley mission up to date on new books. Monthly we received a book or two, and along with *The Saturday Review* that the Helperns sent, we were fairly *au courant* with the world of letters.

Assistant Secretary of Defense, E. Perkins McGuire, sent me several hundred dollars specifically tagged "for liquid cough medicine."

When my boys came through Hawaii on their way to Laos in September 1956, they stopped at one of the luxurious hotels on Waikiki. One evening they were greeted by three ladies who had read of our mission and of the boys' arrival, and had decided to entertain them. The boys had a great time. When they said good night, one woman offered to send the daily newspaper to Laos. The boys smiled but gave the address, and from that day until our departure "Mis" Spring sent the daily Honolulu *Star Bulletin*. It always arrived in bunches of eight or ten, but we were pretty much up to date on the news. Thanks, Mom Spring!

On a plane a few years ago, I met a Bill C. White. He was going to Mexico for a vacation from the hard labor of acquiring a college education. We talked about my planned mission and he was intensely interested. Months later, in Laos, I received a letter from him along with a box of chocolate bars. The letter was welcome, but the candy bars were true manna. I wrote and thanked him, and he kept the boxes coming for the rest of my time. Bad for the complexion, but good for the heart.

It seems that the depth of goodness and responsibility in Americans is often more apparent abroad than it is at home. This thoughtfulness quickened our pulse. A lot of good-will for America was born when we explained to the Lao the origin of the candies, baby clothes, pencils and T-shirts which we gave them.

One day we found in the mail sack a large crate which was badly beaten up. We opened it and found inside stuffed animals, drawing books, sheets of colored paper, a wild assortment of ribbons, safety pins, hair barettes and just about everything that you might find on the mezzanine floor of Macy's. We also found a note saying that this was a gift of the Morning and Afternoon Kindergartens of McKinley School, Harrisburg, Illinois. After we thanked them by mail, their teacher, Miss Mildred Walden, explained how she had heard of our work, and decided that Kindergarten was not too young for her students to begin to learn of their responsibility to other lands—a responsibility that comes to them as birthright because they had the great fortune to be born free men. I admire this woman for her desire to teach internationality to even the youngest. There is no need to worry about the quality of education with teachers like her.

We sent some polaroid pictures of her children's box-in-action. She said that one little girl commented: "Look, Miss Walden, that child has the stuffed horse I brought to school for the Box for Laos." If this is not foreign aid on a person-to-person basis, what is?

One day I received a dollar bill in the mail. It was from a blind girl, Aurora Lee, who lived in Thailand. She had read The Reader's Digest Braille edition of my book, Deliver Us From Evil. Later she heard that we were in Laos and wanted to help. Somehow she found an American dollar and sent it on to us. Mrs. Iva Gordon of Timberville, Virginia, saw a picture of us in a newspaper and thought we looked crummy. She sent us two pairs of khakis and shirts per person. They were well received; I guess we did look crummy.

The Rotarians of Hong Kong sent us a check, as did the Rotarians of Honolulu. The Hawaiian Residents' Association sent us 475 pounds of roller bandages. Admiral Stump transported them to Saigon for us. In cubic measurement this load was the equivalent content of about one box car. Gestures like this illustrate to Asians that Americans can project beyond national boundaries the generous and kindly impulses which are so characteristic of them.

The Basilians, a Catholic Youth Organization in Los Angeles, wrote that they wanted to send something for the four of us. I explained how I would have given an arm and a leg for some U.S. pancakes with maple syrup.

Every week for the remaining sixteen months we received a box of pancake mix and a jar of syrup.

I attended Notre Dame University in the middle forties, and a good friend of mine on the staff there was Erma Koyna. When I was in Viet Nam, she sent things to my refugee camp. In Laos, hardly a month passed that I did not receive something from her. If she did not directly buy the gifts, then she bamboozled the poor salesmen who came to the University. The salesmen ended up sending a crate of lollypops, soap, candy bars, and the like.

I was able to extend my mission beyond the planned six months because my money was holding out through the kindness of my friends. And how many hundreds of hours of prayers were offered around the world for Dooley and his boys? This was an everflowing fountain of encouragement for us. I knew my mother's prayers were the most powerful, for her love is closest to God's. And there were teachers, friends, brothers and others who were always sneaking our names into their prayers. I thought of my beloved Irish nuns at St. John's Hospital in St. Louis. While saying their prayers, brogue and all, at the feet of Our Lady, I'm sure they added: "Please take care of Doctor Tom, he's such a hothead . . ." Out on Clayton Road the Dutch nuns at St. Mary's and Desloge Hospital also wrote that I was remembered in their prayers. I once asked them to "pray like hell" for me. They wrote back that they were "praying like heaven." I have spent years working with nuns, but never really learned much about them and their singular and secret way of life. Yet I remember their goodness, the sweetness of their soap and starch, and the softness of their reprimands. Now I am learning the power of their prayers.

I received a note from a priest who had just been released from a Communist torture cell in Red China, where his hands had been crushed between two stones. He was offering a daily *Memorare* for the blessings of Jesus on us.

A little Jewish girl in school in New Jersey says that she prays for me "frequently." A priest in Cincinnati offers our name during each day's Mass. In how many churches around the world have people lighted small flickering candle flames for us? With the candles they uttered: "God, grant safety, peace and success to Tom Dooley and his boys." How grateful we are to them and to Him.

I wish I could make personal acknowledgment in these pages to each and every individual and organization (see Chapter One for an important group of these) whose help we have received. Unfortunately, I do not have enough space for that, and have only been able to cite a few examples of the many generous acts, both material and spiritual, for which we are indebted. Instead I will close with the prayer which served as our inspiration in Laos and may well stand as the epigraph of this book:

> Give us, Thy worthy children,
>   The blessings of wisdom and speech,
> And the hands and hearts of healing
>   And the lips and tongues that teach.

THOMAS A. DOOLEY, M.D.

Box 2
Times Square
New York, N. Y.

CONTENTS

ONE ·

"BUT I HAVE PROMISES TO KEEP"

High above the Pacific, flying westward in a luxury airliner, the night passes swiftly. Passengers put away their books and briefcases; one by one, the reading lights wink out. Lulled by the monotonous beat of the engines, the Honolulu-bound vacationers and the businessmen bound for Tokyo and Manila slumber peacefully.

But I am the sleepless traveler, my mind filled with memories that are more captivating than dreams. I close my eyes and recall that wretched refugee camp in Haiphong in the Spring of '55. Operation Cockroach the Navy called us—one young Navy doctor, still professionally wet-behind-the-ears; four young enlisted men who had only a few months' training as hospital corpsmen; and a half-million filthy, diseased, mutilated Asians fleeing from the godless cruelties of Communism.

That was North Viet Nam during what was ironically called the "Passage to Freedom." That was where Dooley really came of age.

How many times have I told that story? I told it not only in the pages of *Deliver Us from Evil*, but whenever and wherever I could find Americans who were willing to listen. But, at least, it was never told in vainglory. For what we *did* in dying Haiphong was far less important than what we *learned* there.

We had seen simple, tender, loving care—the crudest kind of medicine inexpertly practiced by mere boys—change a people's fear and hatred into friendship and understanding. We had witnessed the power of medical aid to reach the hearts and souls of a nation. We had seen it transform the brotherhood of man from an ideal into a reality that plain people could understand.

To me that experience was like the white light of revelation. It made me proud to be a doctor. Proud to be an American doctor who had been privileged to witness the enormous possibilities of *medical aid* in all its Christlike power and simplicity. Was that why the foreign-aid planners, with their billion-dollar projects, found it difficult to understand?

I preached so ardently that my folks began to worry. "Look, Dooley," my friends would say, "you've had adventure enough. When are you going to settle down?" My mother reminded me of all the things I had always wanted, and now might have. A home, a wife, kids, a nice medical practice, maybe a few fine hunting horses. My old medical mentor told me I'd better get on with my postgraduate training if I hoped to be a good orthopedic surgeon.

How could I make them see that things would never be the same?

I remember those lines by Robert Frost that kept echoing in my mind during those fretful days:

> The woods are lovely, dark and deep,
> But I have promises to keep,
> And miles to go before I sleep.

I knew the promises I had to keep. I knew that the keeping of them would take me many miles, back to Southeast Asia, to the very edge of tomorrow, where the future might be made—or lost.

One evening in February 1956, after I had been home from Asia only a few months, I went to a dinner at the Vietnamese Embassy in Washington, D.C. This night I had a premonition that all hope of returning to Indo-China with a medical team of my own would hinge on whatever happened at that dinner.

Regretfully, I was aware that I could not go back to Viet Nam. The north was now locked behind the Bamboo Curtain. I was not needed in the south where the medical teams of the Filipinos' Operation Brotherhood were already doing a wonderful job. Where else could I operate and utilize my knowledge of Indo-China? Cambodia? Laos? Would I, as an American, be welcome there in view of the ticklish political situation?

To help me find an answer to these questions, my good friend, Ambassador Tran Van Chuong of Viet Nam, had arranged a dinner party for me to which he had invited a number of Cambodian and Laotian diplomats. Late that evening I was still talking about the kind of medical mission I had in mind—small, privately financed (mostly out of my own pocket), without any government or church sponsorship or obligations. The team would consist only of myself and a few of the young Americans who had served with me in North Viet Nam.

We would be plain Americans working among the plain people of the country, wherever we were needed, in paddy fields and villages, in jungles and mountains. Perhaps, if we did a good job, we might inspire other Americans, doctors and laymen, to follow our example of international cooperation on a people-to-people basis.

The Cambodians listened, politely non-committal. But I saw that the Laotian ambassador, the Hon. Ourot Souvannavong, was following me with keen interest.

"But, Dr. Dooley," he asked, "why should you, a young man just released from your naval duty, with a career before you, choose to make this sacrifice? Obviously, you have much to offer. But what do you stand to gain?"

Once more, I tried to explain my deep conviction that medical aid, offered on a people-to-people basis, could form lasting bonds of friendship between East and West. If this was true, we American doctors had a duty to perform. Since I had served in Southeast Asia and had seen the need, the duty for me as an individual was inescapable. Besides, I was young, unattached, free to go wherever I was needed.

Suddenly, I remembered something that big, hardboiled Boatswain's Mate Norman Baker had once said in answer to a somewhat similar question. Gambling on my ability to translate Baker's homespun American into French, I explained how Baker had groped for words to explain our motives, and then blurted out:

"Aw, hell, sir, we just want to do what we can for people who ain't got it so good!"

The Cambodians raised their eyebrows and smiled—Baker's words had hit the mark. But Ambassador Souvannavong beamed, and from the way he shook his head in frank admiration I could practically read his mind: These incredible Americans!

"Dr. Dooley," he said, "my country would be honored to receive your mission. Will you come to see me at the Embassy in the morning?"

The following day, seated in his study, the Ambassador gave me a briefing on social and political conditions in the Kingdom of Laos. He began by telling me why medical teams like mine were needed there. For the entire population of about two million, he said, Laos had only *one* doctor who was a medical graduate by western standards. He watched my astonishment with a sad smile.

"Oh, we have a few young men we call *médecins indochinois*," he added.

"They are graduates of the *lycée* who have had a little medical training. But for the vast majority of our sick people there are only the witch doctors and the sorceress." (The *lycée* is roughly equivalent to an American junior high school.)

Then the Ambassador explained that the one doctor in Laos was his nephew, Dr. Oudom Souvannavong, who was also the Minister of Health. "I am sure he will welcome you, and give you all the help you need," he said. "And I must warn you, Doctor, that you will need help and guidance. You will find everything in my country difficult, possibly dangerous."

We stood before a huge wall map, and the landlocked Kingdom of Laos, which extends down the middle of the Indo-China peninsula, reminded me of a long bony finger, with the huge knuckle attached to the red hand of China and the fingertip poking into Cambodia and South Viet Nam.

Ambassador Souvannavong pointed to the northwest province bordering on China and Burma. For the first time I noticed a name that was to haunt me—Nam Tha.

"If you go up here, where you will be needed most," he said, "you may face considerable danger. Nam Tha is isolated, the people are poor, disease is rampant. The political situation is delicate—very difficult for a Westerner to understand."

I looked at the map, and was struck by the fact that Nam Tha lies almost on a straight line due west of the tragic city of Haiphong in North Viet Nam —perhaps 500 miles as the vulture flies. The two adjoining provinces had become the temporary haven of the Communist-led Pathet Lao under the terms laid down by the Geneva Conference of 1954—the same conference that had partitioned Viet Nam and committed Cambodia and Laos to a "neutralized" status in Indo-China.

I said we were willing to take our chances, but I also promised to be discreet. Ambassador Souvannavong shook my hand warmly, and assured me that he had confidence in me.

"Many times before," he said, "white men have come to help us. But always they had other motives—colonization, trade, even our religious conversion. I really believe your motive is purely humanitarian. That will make your mission unique in my country," he said. Then, with a twinkle in his eye, he added: "And, also, for some of my people, a trifle hard to believe."

To give my mission legal status, Angier Biddle Duke, president of the International Rescue Committee, arranged to have us taken under the aegis of the IRC, which enjoys worldwide respect. I took another look at the bank account in which I had been salting away the proceeds from my book and lecture tour, and said a prayer. Then, profiting by my experience in Viet Nam, I again made the rounds of the pharmaceutical companies and surgical supply houses with my hat in hand.

Their understanding and generosity overwhelmed me. The Charles Pfizer Company gave me over $100,000 worth of antibiotics. Johnson & Johnson supplied bandages and surgical dressings. The A. S. Aloe Company of St. Louis, Mo., donated a complete line of surgical instruments and equipment, and the Aloe employees passed the hat and presented me with a handsome check!

The Mead Johnson Company gave me a bill of lading for a huge supply of vitamins and protein extract, and Mr. Johnson wrote out his personal check for $5,000. Walt Disney presented us with a sound projector and a collection of Disney movies for the children of Laos. The Willys Company presented us with a jeep, especially constructed for rough-country operations. (We later named the vehicle Agnes, after my mother.)

I went to Abercrombie & Fitch in New York and ordered a lot of essential equipment—cookstoves, lanterns, sleeping bags, etc. The bill was staggering. When the salesman learned the nature of my mission, he excused himself and disappeared into a vice-president's office. He came back with the bill slashed to a fraction of the original amount.

One day in Washington, D.C., I was waiting to testify at a hearing of the International Rescue Committee concerning free Viet Nam's role in Asia today. A dynamic little woman, who was very late, sat down beside me in the last row and whispered, "Has Doctor Dooley given his speech yet?" I smiled and said, "No, but he should be great." She nodded and said, "I have been chasing that man halfway around the country." "Why?" "I want to give him five thousand pounds of protein." At that moment I was called as the next speaker. We met afterwards in the corridor and it turned out that she was the affable Miss Florence Rose, executive secretary of the Meals for Millions Foundation. She did give me five thousand pounds of their multi-purpose food, which was directly responsible for saving hundreds of lives in my mountain hospital during the following year.

The U. S. Navy did not let me down. They agreed to transport the tons of medicines, food and equipment that I had accumulated, even though I was now a civilian. They transferred this for me to South Viet Nam, at a tremendous saving to my mission.

I spent several weeks going in and out of the various American agencies in Washington concerned with work in Asia. The International Cooperation Administration promised me a great deal, sincerely and genuinely, but the end result coming from their men-on-the-scene in Laos, turned out to be very little. However, I.C.A. in Washington helped me greatly in the earlier planning stages. So did the United States Information Agency, which pledged a battery-run tape recorder.

During this period I met Mrs. Raymond Clapper, widow of the famous war correspondent killed in Korea. Mrs. Clapper is the head of the CARE offices in Washington, D.C. By guiding my steps, introducing me to people, and just being a good friend, Mrs. Clapper became a sort of midwife to the birth of Operation Laos of the International Rescue Committee. (Incidentally, CARE has an excellent midwife kit, in appearance much like the flight bags which air travelers carry; it was Mrs. Clapper's idea that CARE donate about fifty kits to the graduates of the midwife classes that I planned to inaugurate. Later in my story you will learn the good use to which they were put.)

But I had left the most difficult phase of the plan—lining up my men— until the last. All along I had been counting on Norman Baker, Peter Kessey, and Dennis Shepard, the most devoted and dependable of the enlisted men who had been with me in North Viet Nam. This wasn't going to be easy. Denny Shepard, newly married, was taking his pre-med at the University of Oregon. Pete Kessey was attending pharmacy school in Austin, Texas. Baker, also a bridegroom, was still in the Navy. Would they as civilians return to that part of Asia where they had seen such wretchedness?

However, Pete and Denny responded to my call promptly and enthusiastically. Baker's ship was somewhere at sea; several weeks passed before I could get in touch with him. Then one day, in Washington, I received a long-distance call from Baker in San Diego. When I told him about Operation Laos, his roar could be heard from coast to coast, even without the help of AT&T.

"What! Back to Indo-China? Are you crazy? Why, you slave-driving fool —sir—you couldn't pay me to go back into that hellhole! Besides, my wife wouldn't stand for it! Hell, no—not a chance!"

There was an awkward silence. I just let him simmer down. Then. . . .

"Hello . . . You still there, Doc? Listen, you don't really need *me*, do you? What makes you think we can do any real good out there? And there's something you seem to have forgotten. (*Hearty chuckle.*) Little Old Baker is still the pride and joy of Uncle Sam's Navy!"

I assured him that I needed him, that Operation Laos was one helluva big challenge, and that I was pretty sure I could get him out of the Navy on an early discharge. I could hear him grumbling and moaning.

"Aw, whatthehell, Doc, sure, I *volunteer!* But Priscilla's going to divorce me for this, sure as shootin'!"

(Bless her heart, Priscilla Baker did nothing of the sort. She went right ahead with a project I didn't know about at the time—having their baby.)

In July, 1956, after a short seven months in America, I started on my return trip to Asia. I lectured in Hawaii, Japan, Hong Kong, and then flew to the Philippines to speak with the founders of Operation Brotherhood. From them I could glean much for my own mission, for we had really borrowed the whole idea of non-governmental, non-sectarian medical service to foreign nations from this Filipino endeavor.

My men followed behind me, and we were to meet in the Philippines. On a sweltering day in August I stood in the Manila airport watching a plane glide down through the heat haze rising from the runway. It taxied around, and the door swung open. Out stepped Pete Kessey, our lean and hungry looking Texan, followed by 200-pound barrel-chested Baker (flexing his muscles, as always), and then quiet, serious Denny Shepard. How very young they looked! Pete and Denny were 25. Baker was still only 21. Yet they were more mature and dependable than most men twice their age.

We had about an hour's wait before leaving for Saigon, which was to be our "staging area." The boys plied me with questions. What kind of gear did we have? How had I ever high-pressured the Navy into hauling the four tons of stuff to Saigon? Where did we go from there? What kind of place was Laos? ("Yeah, man," groaned Baker. "I can see now that this means living on C-rations and holding 24-hour sick-call!")

When we were back aboard the plane, the talk turned serious. I got out my map and explained that, if my plans went through, we would operate up north in the province of Nam Tha. Denny gave a long, low whistle of surprise. He had a bundle of notes and clippings, and knew as much about Laos as I did.

I told them about the flying trip I had made to Hong Kong to meet Oden Meeker, a dynamic young American, who had served in Laos with CARE during the famine of 1954. Oden strongly favored the plan to operate in Nam Tha. It was a critical area, he said, the most isolated part of Laos, and politically the most vulnerable. "Those mountain people have rarely seen a white man," said Oden. "They have no allegiance to the central government. They're just ripe for the Commie treatment."

The boys listened solemnly. Then Baker said: "Look, Doc, you've got to level with us. What are the odds on this setup? I'm a married man now. So is Denny. Fact is, Priscilla's going to have a baby. Besides, I never did like the sound of those Chinese prison camps!"

Well, I said, the odds were about standard for that part of the world.

No better, no worse. We'd been in tough spots before, but we had done our jobs, and come through with our hides intact. Baker hooted.

"Oh, we sure did—only you forget that we had the U. S. Navy back of us last time!"

I let that pass, and switched to the kind of job we had to do. We wouldn't be "showing the flag" so much this time, as we had in Haiphong; we'd be showing American face to a lot of Asians who had been told that American white-men didn't give a damn. I reminded them of what we had learned in Haiphong, and invited them to think of what we could accomplish by working among people on the village level in Laos.

Pete Kessey spoke up. "Doc, it looks to me like you expect to accomplish an awful lot in a short time. You know we only signed on for six months. You think we can do a job by then? And what happens to you when we pull out?"

That was the one part of the plan that had me worried, but I couldn't admit it. After six months, I said, I'd be able to play it by ear. I told them about the *médecins indochinois*. Maybe I could train a few young Lao to serve as assistants. And I also had a scheme in mind for getting a few replacements from the States.

They sensed that I was whistling in the dark. Baker declared that this was the screwiest part of the whole setup. Pete just shook his head. I was glad when Denny Shepard broke it up.

"This is one devil of a time to be talking about going home," he said. "We're not even there yet!"

TWO ·

ARRIVAL IN LAOS

The huge Vietnamese cargo plane made three trips from Saigon to Vientiane with our four tons of crates and packing cases. We went in on the last flight, made a perilous landing on the steel-mat runway, and climbed down bone-tired after six hours perched atop packing cases. While a small army of coolies unloaded, we piled our essential gear into an antiquated truck and headed into town. The jeep named Agnes was driven across Cambodia, Thailand, and north to Laos on an unbelievable ten-day trip. It was floated across the river on a sampan, and finally arrived at Vientiane.

Vientiane, laid out by the French as the colonial capital of Laos, has broad avenues lined with huge teak and acacia trees. But when we arrived the monsoon rains had turned these unpaved boulevards into rivers of mud, crowded with ancient automobiles, oxcarts, pedestrians, wandering buffalo and sleepy dogs. Signs of the ending of the French colonial period were everywhere. Paint peeled from buildings in huge patches, there were buffalo wallows on the lawns of the National Assembly, and the caretaker's wife had hung out her laundry along the elaborate colonnades.

When we pulled up before the new Samboun Hotel we had a minor but revealing mishap. The brand new concrete pavement collapsed under the truck's weight, and the front and rear wheels on the right side sank hub-deep in the ditch, pitching everything to starboard.

We climbed out and surveyed the damage; the Laotian driver just shrugged and said, "Bau pinh yanh." We soon learned that this is a common expression in Laos. It means something between "Well, never mind" and "The hell with it." Two days later the broken-down truck still stood in front of the hotel, listing to starboard in the ditch. *Bau pinh yanh!*

The first and second class rooms of the hotel were not yet ready for occupancy, so we were lodged in the "slave quarters." These servants' rooms were small but clean, and of course they had never been occupied by slaves!

While the boys supervised the warehousing of supplies, I hustled over to the U. S. Embassy to pay my respects to Ambassador J. Graham Parsons. The visit was brief and formal. I detected a coolness in Ambassador Parsons' manner. Dooley's "unofficial" mission, apparently, wasn't very popular in official circles! In fact I was later to learn that in the eyes of most Americans in Laos Dooley was "annoyingly autonomous."

Then I went to the Ministry of Health and gave my name to the receptionist. A few minutes later a handsome, energetic young man, about 35 years old, popped into the reception room and came toward me with hands outstretched. This was Dr. Oudom Souvannavong, the only doctor of medicine in Laos, and certainly the most unministerial Minister of Health I have ever met.

He escorted me into his private office, spoke glowingly of my book, and told me of the high esteem in which I was held by his uncle, the Ambassador to the U.S. Then, with these pleasantries out of the way, his manner changed suddenly.

"Tell me, *mon docteur*," he asked suspiciously, "why have you *really* come to Laos?"

For the next ten minutes he questioned me sharply. What was my connection with the U. S. Government? Was I still a naval officer? Why had the Navy transported my supplies to Saigon? Was I an agent of the CIA or any other intelligence service? What was my religion? Did I represent any Catholic missionary society?

At first I was flabbergasted, then I struggled to keep my Irish temper under control. (Much later, I learned that suspicion of foreigners was prevalent in Laos at the time.) I answered his questions candidly, perhaps a trifle sharply. At last, he began to smile again, apparently satisfied that I was neither a spy nor a Jesuit in disguise.

He knew that I was interested in the north, and I enlarged upon this. As I told him, "From a medical point of view there are tribes in the mountains whose health is wretched. From a political point of view, these people have no real allegiance to the central government of your country. From my personal point of view, there are sick people there and furthermore people who had been flooded with potent draughts of anti-Western propaganda from Red China."

I told the Minister that in conversations with his uncle in America it was thought that the place most in need was the northern Province of Nam Tha. I re-emphasized that I wished to work for the Lao government and any allegiance that I might win through medicine would be directed to the Royal Lao Government. I wished to be part of their Ministry of Health. Dr. Oudom replied: "I have heard of your wishes to go to the north. There are many hazards there, isolation, the precariousness of border life, Communist banditry, the monsoon rain's fury, the lack of transportation." He reminded me how unknown the white man was, and how superstitious and sometimes hostile the primitive people of this foothill world of the Himalayas could be. But the Minister had cleared his conscience with necessary warnings, and now realized our determination to work where we felt the need was greatest in spite of risks.

"Frankly, *mon docteur*," he said at last, "it pleases me greatly that you are willing to take your medicine to these most wretched of our people. You have our complete approval. But, first, I must ask you to get the approval of the American Ambassador."

This request, after all the emphasis on my independent status, amazed me. But Dr. Oudom was adamant. Reluctantly, I headed for the American Embassy, feeling pretty sure that I was in for trouble.

Ambassador Parsons was emphatic in opposing my plan to go to Nam Tha. Indeed, he wanted my team to stay as far away from the China border as possible. The political situation in Laos was touchy; conditions in the north might even become explosive. No matter what I did or said or even could prove, it was inevitable that people would suspect me of being an American espionage agent. (How true, I thought—remembering Dr. Oudom.) Certainly, in the north the Communists would do everything possible to spread the word that I was a spy. While he conceded my right to go anywhere in the country that the Lao government would permit, he pointed out that if I or any of my men became involved in an "incident," the entire American position in Laos would be jeopardized.

"To go into the north at this time," he insisted, "would be extremely unwise, Dr. Dooley. I must ask you to reconsider the matter."

So, that was that! Ambassador Parsons did not forbid me to go to Nam Tha, but he certainly would not approve my going. By withholding his approval, he vetoed the plan, in view of Dr. Oudom's terms. I completely disagreed with him. In retrospect, I'm afraid I disagreed with him vehemently and somewhat brashly.

I asked him where he thought my team might operate. Without a moment's hesitation, he replied that there was scarcely any part of the Kingdom of Laos where medical aid was not needed. We went over to the map, and he indicated the area around Vang Vieng, about 120 miles north of the capital but still far south of the China border. During the Indo-China war, he said, Vang Vieng had been captured by the Communists; conditions there were still pretty bad.

Crestfallen, I went back to the Ministry of Health and told Dr. Oudom that Nam Tha was out—for the time being, at least. To my amazement, he agreed completely with the American Ambassador! He also concurred in Ambassador Parsons' choice of Vang Vieng. Health conditions were deplorable there, he said. The town had a medical aid station, but no doctor, nurse, drugs or equipment.

"You can perform a real service in Vang Vieng," he assured me.

So Vang Vieng it was. Back in the slave quarters of the Samboun Hotel, the boys heard the news with dismay. I had other things to worry about. This change of plans was going to cut deeply into my slim bankroll. Most of our equipment was designed for the mountainous north, rather than for the jungles and lowlands of Vang Vieng. Even our pharmaceuticals were intended primarily for diseases we would encounter up north.

Baker listened to my lamentations and said: "Oh, well, Doc—*bau pinh yanh!*" (Actually, when we finally did get to Nam Tha many months later, I was humbly grateful to Ambassador Parsons and Dr. Oudom for insisting upon a "shakedown cruise" in Vang Vieng.)

I now thought of Oden Meeker. Through Mrs. Clapper's introduction I had had a chance to meet the dynamic Meeker in Hong Kong. He is the young author of *The Little World of Laos*, a Lao veteran, having spent time there during the famine of 1954. Oden Meeker knows misery well. Through CARE, thousands of pounds of rice and salt were dropped from airplanes over the famine area bringing relief to thousands. While at lunch with Oden, the name of the province of Nam Tha had come up. Oden was one of the few to have ever been there and he corroborated all the Ambassador said about white men rarely being seen there. This added to my determination to take my team to Nam Tha. Incidentally, from Hong Kong I had flown on to the Philippines, where I was met by Oscar Arellano, and Amelito Mutuc. They are the founders of Operation Brotherhood, the Filipino Medical Unit whose teams are scattered throughout South Viet Nam. It is easy to understand why the Filipinos hold their heads so highly. They seem doubly proud to walk as free men. These people are on the "offensive" for democracy. They do not just sit around denying what the Communists say of us but rather they get out there and do something about it. Oscar Arellano says that each of his team members are "walkie-talkies for democracy." He said to me one afternoon, "When a man's head is empty and his stomach empty, his democracy will also be empty." To do their part as men born in freedom to help their fellow Asians, Operation Brotherhood was inaugurated as a vast medical relief program in South Viet Nam. The Philippines are the first of the nations of Asia to extend help to other nations.

Now at the Samboun Hotel in Laos, I had the first chance to glance over some of the papers that Oscar Arellano had given me on the history of Operation Brotherhood. In them I found this wonderful statement by Amelito Mutuc: "I would like to rally all young men who are earnest about life. I should like to arouse civic consciousness amongst people. I should like to instill in them the acceptance of the responsibility to work for the common whole, to free them from bias and prejudice and create in them the sincere desire to understand and to cooperate with people of other creeds and other loyalties . . . I am sure that there is a vast reservoir of talent and zeal in the region of Asia in the persons of young men of action whose devotion and dedication to service, to the community, nation and world, I can avail of without reservation."

That night in Vientiane, to get away from our worries, the boys and I went sightseeing. Strolling through the city we found a Laotian "love court" going on and squatted down in the audience. I had often heard of this unique Lao entertainment which chants of the art of courtship. It is sheer poetry, improvised on the spot. The boy extols the beauty, grace, virtue of the courted maiden; the girl sings of the boy's nobility, charm, bravery. The audience listens raptly, applauding an inspired passage with an enthusiasm that Americans reserve for touchdowns or home runs.

But I had something else in mind. We needed an interpreter. Baker and I both spoke French fluently, and Pete and Denny had a working knowledge of it. What I wanted was a dependable man or boy who understood the Laotian dialects and could translate into French. Squatting in the love-court audience, I decided to begin the search then and there.

"What is this performance?" I asked loudly in French. "What is the meaning of these words and gestures?"

The people turned and stared at me. Then a voice said: *"Moi parler français, monsieur."* He introduced himself as Chai, and proceeded to interpret the love poetry into passable French.

Chai was a short, husky lad with beautifully modeled features, wide-set eyes, clear bronze skin, and jet-black hair. He wore the native sarong, knotted at the waist, an immaculate white shirt with French cuffs (the colonial influence) and, of course, no shoes. I remember noticing his short, stubby fingers. I didn't realize that they would one day serve me expertly across the surgical table.

When the love court ended, we introduced ourselves more formally. Chai was a graduate of the Vientiane *lycée*, and apparently had a natural flair for languages. I explained that I was a doctor, and that we were going to Vang Vieng. When I said we needed an interpreter, he accepted the job enthusiastically. He claimed to know all about Vang Vieng where he had *parentage*—which we would call kinfolk or kissin' cousins.

A few days later we piled into jeeps and started to make a reconnoitering trip to Vang Vieng, 120 miles north. I asked Chai if he knew the trail. *"Oui, mon docteur."* Did he think it would be passable? *"Oui, mon docteur."* Later, I discovered that Chai was not a liar; he was just congenitally unable to say no.

For the next five hours, under blazing sun, we crept and crawled through dense jungle, plowed through monsoon mud, and hit long stretches of suffocating dust. But we also saw some of the most fantastically beautiful scenery on earth.

When we reached the cool, swift, inviting Nam Lick River, we parked the jeeps, shucked our clothes, and soon were splashing in the green water. Everyone, that is, but Chai. We looked around, and saw him sitting forlornly on the river bank.

Baker went over to the embankment, had a long conversation with the kid, and then came back grinning from ear to ear.

"For Pete's sake, don't laugh, Doc," he said. "He can swim all right. But he just ain't been checked out by the phantom that runs this river!"

I thought Baker must be kidding. But when I had dried myself and dressed, I sat down beside Chai and learned that it was all true. Buddhism in Laos has a strong admixture of ancient animism; and for people like Chai there are more spirits and phantoms in Laos than there are fairies and leprechauns in Ireland.

"This phantom of Nam Lick has taken many lives," Chai assured me. "But when we return to Vientiane I shall make an offering, then I can swim in the Nam Lick without fear."

Sure enough, a few days later, Chai plunged into the river and swam and splashed with the rest of us. He had gone to the Buddhist temple in Vientiane, made his offering, and had been "checked out" by the monk for swimming in the Nam Lick. Chai even had a talisman or charm, which he now wore tied to his wrist with a cotton string, to prove it.

We learned something else about Chai: he would not kill anything. Later when patients paid me for an operation with a live chicken or duck, Chai could not kill the birds for our dinner. However, he was resourceful in many ways and he solved the problem neatly by finding a pagan, a Kha tribesman or a villager, who was delighted to twist the bird's neck for a few cents! What about fishing, a sport which Chai loved? Wasn't this killing, we asked him. "Non, mon docteur, I merely take the fish out of water. If it dies, that is not my fault. I have not killed it." We were aware that Chai represented a fairly high standard of life in Laos. Though born a peasant, he had received a lycée education, spoke fair French, and was a bright lad in all respects. If Chai was so bound by the world of spirits and phantoms, how strongly must the totally ignorant people of the kingdom be dominated by them. What obstacles would this create in our practice of medicine?

That first night was spent in the hut of the chief of a village half way along the road. Here was the first chance that we had to sit around a villager's house and converse. We were amazed and frightened at the tenacity with which these primitive people clung to their world of phantoms. How bound they were by the despotism of good and evil spirits, white and black magic.

The next day we drove through more staggering, luxuriant jungle until nightfall.

We had seen absolutely no sign of life along this trail for several hours, and the sight of the sleepy village of Vang Vieng seemed to us a haven.

The setting for Vang Vieng must have been selected by a master artist. It is spectacular. The village rests at the foot of stupendous walls of rock, rising two thousand and three thousand feet into the sky. These mountains have no foothills. There's no gradual rise or slope. Just an absolutely flat plain; then suddenly, abruptly, a staggering wall of rock. The tops of these mountains are covered with pine and on the side walls stubby trees grow out of the rock at painful angles and reach upwards for light. The tributary of the Mekong River winds around the mountains in search of lowlands. There are many stories of this river's perils, stories of deadly leeches, parasites, huge fish, rays and snakes, as well as Chai's stories of spirits and dragons.

The broad river pays no attention to the road. There were several places along this trail where large bridges were necessary and hundreds of places where smaller ones were needed. In the dry season floating bridges or small planks suffice, but when the rains come these are all washed away. Hence, the road is unusable for six months of the year. Even during the dry season, which starts in September, the 120 miles from Vientiane to Vang Vieng took two days.

THREE ·
SICK-CALL AT VANG VIENG

Thanks chiefly to one elderly member of Chai's *parentage*, whom the boys irreverently named Ojisan (Japanese for "old man"), about half the people of Vang Vieng were out to meet us when the trucks and jeeps of Operation Laos arrived in town. Ojisan had spread the word that we were white medicine-men bringing powerful remedies to the people. Hence many of the women and children came with gifts of flowers, cucumbers and oranges.

We found the Lao dispensary at one end of the square (actually the area surrounding the town well) directly across from the home of the Chao Muong or mayor. It was a low, whitewashed building of three rooms. Since it had no living quarters, Ojisan gave us a house which he owned at the southern end of the town.

Norman Baker was our chief construction man, in the best Seabee tradition; and under his direction the boys went to work converting the dispensary into a small hospital. They swept, swabbed, disinfected, and then whitewashed. With the aid of a half-dozen coolies, we cleared the surrounding yard (which was to serve as our "reception room") of debris, cow dung, and heaps of foul bandages and dressings. Then we built a fence to keep out the wandering water buffalo.

The medical supplies were uncrated, and the boys did an ingenious job of converting the empty boxes into tables and benches, and cabinets in which to store our pharmaceuticals. Then we borrowed some cots from the local detachment of the Royal Lao army. When these had been deloused and repaired, we set them up in one room which was to serve as the ward.

Our living quarters presented a tougher problem. Ojisan's house was a typical Lao hut perched six feet above the ground on stout poles surrounded by a "porch" and reached by a steep ladder. We climbed up, took one look inside, and came out shuddering. The place was filthy.

The boys tore out everything inside the hut including the bamboo partition between the two rooms. They swept the ceiling clear of soot, cobwebs, and rats' nests, then went to work on the walls. When this accumulation of ancient crud had been swept out, they hauled up buckets of river water, broke out boxes of soap-powder and bleach, and swabbed the deck Navy-style.

The villagers presented us with woven bamboo mats for floor covering, and we laid out our bedrolls and hung mosquito netting. Then we installed all the packing-crate bookcases, benches and tables, and placed two cots against the wall as lounges. This would be our "living room."

Pete Kessey insisted that even the poorest white trash back in Texas wouldn't live in such a place. Maybe so. But, at least, no one could ever say that the men of Operation Laos lived apart from the natives in an air-conditioned "American compound."

We never announced sick-call, and we needed no publicity. Only a few days after our arrival we were awakened one morning by sounds that were to become a familiar part of every dawn—the howls of sickly babies, the hacking coughs of tubercular mothers. Why wait on line at the hospital, when you can camp on the doctor's front porch!

Frankly, I was overwhelmed by the horrible health conditions we found in Vang Vieng. These were yaws, tuberculosis, pneumonia, malaria and diseases far more heartrending. I was appalled by the sight of so many women mutilated and crippled in childbirth, and by the many traumatic injuries long neglected and horribly infected.

The hideous yaws we could cure with the "1-2-3 treatment"—one shot of penicillin, two bars of soap, and three days! There was little we could do about the tuberculosis, except to control the paroxysms of coughing with cough syrup; for it is the wracking cough that frequently causes pneumonia and hastens the tubercular's death.

One of the most horrible diseases for us to treat was leprosy. Here the patients who gaped at us were just remnants of human beings, rotted and bloated beyond ordinary shape. In dealing with this loathsome disease I had constantly to suppress the strong urge of nausea.

More than 50 per cent of the patients we saw had malaria. Usually these people had survived many attacks of the disease, and achieved a certain immunity; but they were left with greatly enlarged spleens. When the spleen is diseased, the blood loses some of its ability to coagulate, and the slightest cut or bruise can cause a serious hemorrhage. So we pumped vitamins into almost every patient we saw.

One morning at sick-call a poor woman pushed a huge, smelly bundle of rags into my arms. I peeled away the layers of clothing and uncovered a baby about a year old. It was a hideous sight. The abdomen looked like an overblown balloon that was about to burst, the chest looked like a miniature birdcage. There was a tiny monkey face with wild, unseeing eyes. Kwashiorkor's disease! And this was only the first of countless cases we were to encounter in Laos.

Kwashiorkor's disease, fairly common among backward people in the tropics, is not caused by infection but by ignorance. It is the grotesque result of malnutrition. Metabolism fails, muscles waste away, liver and spleen are enlarged, the abdomen swells, and the heart and circulation are damaged. The end result is death.

But this horrible process is reversible if caught in time. This was an extreme case. The mother had fallen ill and was unable to nurse her baby; so, from the age of about six months, the child was fed only rice and water.

Successful treatment of Kwashiorkor's disease depends upon extremely cautious feeding so as not to overtax the weakened system. We injected vitamins, and then used the wonderful protein powder called MPF (Multi-Purpose Food) supplied to us by Meals for Millions. MPF can be used in many ways. Two ounces of the powder made into a broth, for example, provide proteins equivalent to a steak dinner.

We put the baby on a diet of MPF solution and fruit juices and got remarkable results. The damage to the heart and eyes, unfortunately, was irreversible. But the child lived.

That night I told the boys that we were adding another project to our overloaded schedule. We were starting regular classes, open to all comers, in nutrition, hygiene and similar matters. There was entirely too much disease caused by ignorance in "our town." We might as well get after it now.

Every day, from dawn to high noon, we held sick-call at the hospital. In the afternoons we loaded our faithful Agnes (already showing signs of age) and held "jeep-call" in the surrounding countryside, often with Pete and Denny in charge when I was doing surgery. Then, in the evenings, the crowds would gather in front of our house for Walt Disney movies—and for our lectures on the facts of living, delivered *via* our proud interpreter, Chai.

Chai decided that he would have all the earmarks of his new position as interpreter for the Americans. He bought himself a pair of shoes while in Vientiane, and now was a man of station. But he walked with such a painful gait that it only lasted a few days, and he was barefoot again on the soft sod of Laos. For special occasions he put them on again, but these were rare and painful moments.

Sick-call was always an ordeal; for, aside from disease and ignorance, we had to contend with the quaint customs of the people. The line would form sometimes double, in the crowded courtyard and file into the dispensary. I would sit on a chair, with Chai beside me, and try to get the patient to sit on the bench facing me. That wasn't as easy as it sounds.

To the people, the American doctor was a "mandarin"—high on the social totem pole. (Even Chai acquired a certain nobility by association and was always addressed as *Thanh,* an honorific reserved for more important personages.) But the trouble was that, according to long established custom, the humble Laotian's head could never be higher than the mandarin's. Consequently, when examining a patient, I was forced to bend or squat lower and lower. Sometimes I had to grovel on the dirt floor in order to listen to a heartbeat!

We also had difficulty with the Lao nurses we were trying to train. These earnest, intelligent boys and girls would perform the most distasteful duties, handle any part of a filthy and diseased body. But at first we could not get them to clean a head wound, or even hold a patient's head while I stitched the scalp or pulled a tooth. The Lao believe that the spirit of Buddha resides in the head, hence even touching it is like defiling the tabernacle.

Obstetrics, if I may call it that, was our biggest problem from the outset. We estimated that about 50 per cent of the babies were lost before or during delivery. One out of every five mothers died in childbirth, and many of those who survived were left horribly mutilated.

To the Laotian midwife, the job is over once the baby is born. The child is wrapped and placed in a basket, ashes are rubbed on its forehead, and the grandfather blows into the infant's ear to impart wisdom. Meanwhile, the mother, who has given birth to her baby squatting upright on a stool, lies neglected and often hemorrhaging critically.

The care of the child's umbilical cord was another frightening spectacle. As scissors are not available, the cord is cut with two sharp pieces of bamboo. This cleanly severs the cord, but the bamboo is usually filthy. The midwife then rubs into the open end of the cord a powder made of earth and ashes. It is believed that when this is rubbed into the cord the child will absorb some of the power and strength of the trees, and the spirits of the ancestors who are buried in the soil. Ghastly as this seems from the standpoint of sterility, it is astonishing that we never saw a single case of an infected umbilicus.

Hence, we gave high priority to our midwife training program. There were about four practicing midwives in Vang Vieng when we arrived, and perhaps as many more young girls who aspired to the calling. We won them over to our side, had them help around the hospital, and made them promise to call us for each childbirth. When we went on a call, we would take along one or two of the younger girls. And, always, we carried a bag containing the wonderful midwife's kit prepared and distributed by CARE. Each of these kits contains gowns, gloves, cord ties, basins, bowls, dressings, soaps, towels, etc.,—all the essentials for the delivery of 25 babies.

We taught the girls the principles of modern, aseptic midwifery, and the importance of post-partum care of the mother, including removal of the placenta. Then, after each one had delivered 25 babies under supervision, and had proved her proficiency and dedication, she was "graduated" with appropriate ceremony, climaxed by the presentation of the CARE kit— always the bag that I personally had carried and used. (This was extremely important for "face.")

Just as in America nurses are "capped" at graduation, we "bagged" our midwives in Vang Vieng. And it worked. Those wonderful young women, armed with their CARE kits and somewhat dedicated to the aseptic principles we taught them, have removed many of the old horrors from maternity in that part of Laos.

Our practice of medicine was not confined to humans alone. One day a man came to Pete and presented the symptomatology of his friend. This friend lacked pep, was unable to hold his head up, had bad feet, and was losing weight. The man said that this syndrome came upon the friend a few weeks after he had been badly mauled by a tiger. Peter registered astonishment and inquired further, "How old is your friend?" The man had no idea. Nor could you ask how much weight he had lost, because in Laos there is no system of measurements for anything of this size. Peter asked many more questions and finally said that the man would have to bring his friend to the clinic. The man said that he had done this already; his friend was tied up outside the hospital. Peter went outside and found the friend, a small Tibetan pony, tethered to a tree. Pete called to me and I went and joined in the consultation. Indeed, the pony was in bad shape. The tiger had torn the throat and chest considerably and had slashed the forehead open. Each claw mark was infested with maggots. I sent for water, soap and cotton and proceeded to wash and clean the sores. We put some antiseptic over the wounds and then wrapped a large dressing around the horse's neck to prevent further maggot infestation. Pete rotated around each end of the horse injecting penicillin, none of us knowing the exact dosage of the antibiotic for horses. This patient came back every day looking a little better each time. Finally we discharged him from the active treatment list. It was now too late to save ourselves; the word spread and hardly a week passed that someone did not bring a horse or a water buffalo to us for treatment. The complaints were as myriad as those of the two-legged patients—bad eyes, cough, loss of weight, fever, or just senility.

One dawn we were sitting around our not-yet-completed house eating C-rations and coffee for breakfast. I glanced at the gathering of women on the front porch and was commenting to Pete about it. There were usually people there every morning, but this day there were so many they had overflowed to the front lawn. Among them was a small young lad of about twelve years old, who was not a member of the Lao race but rather was a Kha tribesman. All of the people looked bad, but this lad looked worse than any. He was squatting, shivering in the early morning coolness, draped in filthy rags. When I left the house to walk down the lane to the hospital, he got off of his haunches and said, *"Koi chep ken kenoi,"* which means, "I have a sore leg."

When I looked at the massive infection from an old cut on his leg, I wondered how on earth he could even walk. I asked him through Chai, the interpreter, how he had come to us. He said he had walked two days and two nights and had arrived at our house around midnight last night. Why did a feverish lad spend a cold and dismal night squatting outside my house? "I did not think it would be right to disturb the American mandarins while they slept."

We started immediate treatment. Under anesthesia, we slashed open the pus pockets of his legs and drained them. We gave him penicillin and antipyretics. We did not put on any dressings but let him lie in bed on clean sheets, allowing the pus to drain out of the open tracts. Several days later we convinced him of the attractiveness and the importance of a bath in the river, which was just down the road a bit. Even with his fever, a bath was imperative.

We gave him soap and a brush and he hobbled on down and scrubbed like he has never scrubbed before in his life. He wanted to please us. My boys rewarded him by giving him one of their clean T-shirts and a pair of khaki pants, and they then gave him a fine new CARE blanket that he could keep. The Kha boy was overwhelmed. Rarely have I seen a happier boy. He spent the next ten days in our new hospital receiving antibiotics, vitamins and what American nurses call "T.L.C.," tender loving care. This is what he devoured more than anything. He liked being liked. He loved being cared for. This wistful lad had suffered a lot and deserved some happiness. He had the right to disturb us whenever he wanted to. We explained this to him repeatedly. When we discharged him he was cured of the staphyloccus infection of his leg; and cured of the more insidious poison, fear.

While we were in Laos I had a small battery-run tape recorder. I made recordings on this every week and sent them to a St. Louis radio station, KMOX. The station played them in St. Louis in hopes that people there would understand a little bit of what we were up to. I tried to tell the people who listened something of this little Kingdom of Laos, of the sadness, the chaos, the disease. I tried to tell the people in St. Louis of the children in the area of my world. I know many people in St. Louis listened to me, because they responded. One time I commented, "I certainly wish I had some hot chocolate." I should have known better; the response by mail, air freight, and other modes of transportation was overwhelming and we received hundreds upon hundreds of cans of hot chocolate. My boys commented that I should have said, "I certainly wish I had a steak sandwich and some french-fried potatoes."

The Basilian Club sent me weekly boxes of pancake mix. This started an increase in our standard of living but a decline in the lining of our stomachs. Peter decided that he would fatten the boss up and perhaps improve his disposition, so he began to prepare pancakes for our morning's breakfast. I am sure that he had never cooked a pancake before in his life. No matter how large, how small, how long or how quickly he worked, Peter's pancakes always had that same consistency—putty. Once he had some batter left over, so he decided to keep it until the next day. But on the following morning, he found he could not use it—the stuff had solidified.

Never in the thousands of hours that I had devoted to thinking about and planning for this mission in Laos did I anticipate the depths of misery in which we would have to work and eat and sleep and live. Never did anybody in the Washington briefings, in the Lao Embassy, at the Hong Kong lunch or in the refugee camps of Viet Nam adequately indicate what life would be like for us four Americans in the tropical jungles of Central Laos. I had done considerable research on Laos; back in America I scoured the public libraries, the National Geographical Society, the State Department, the United States Information Agency, and every other source that might have on hand some information on the conditions of the country in which we had chosen to work. I tried to plan my mission around the facts that I acquired in this manner. However, I was completely stunned by the conditions that existed in the village of Vang Vieng.

After a few weeks in Laos a twenty-year-old lad named "Si" joined our team. He became our housekeeper, cook, bottle-washer and handyman. Si had the features of an eleven-year-old boy and took great pride in his two gold teeth, a mark of wealth to these people. He took very loving, tender care of his Americans. Having a coolie, a cook, a houseboy, interpreters and other servants in Laos is a different thing than it is in America. We considered these people an integral part of our team, not employees. They dined with us, bathed with us, swam with us, worked with us, and came out on night-calls with us. Later they became extremely devoted to us, caring for every aspect of our life, easing the strain whenever they could. We grew to love them all very much.

Our domestic life was a life of monotony. It was the same every day—long lines of sick at the hospital, worrisome diseases, stink, and misery. The food we ate was also monotonous. Our meals were the least attractive part of our day. During our time in North Viet Nam we were lucky never to have had any serious intestinal problems except an occasional bout of dysentery. This was partly due to caution on our part and partly due to luck. Not being so sure of the latter this year, we decided to be doubly cautious. The Navy gave us a large supply of C-rations to help us in our dietary problems. How can one ever get diarrhea on C-rations? Aside from the first day, when sheer agony forced us to eat Chinese soup, we lived on C-rations for many, many months. Pete, whose job it was to supervise the cooking done by Ojisan's wife, was a man with a magnificently large imagination. Without any chef's training whatsoever, Peter was able to concoct a masterpiece for each meal. The only complaint was it was always the same damn masterpiece.

C-rations come in varied cans, not in the multi-colored attractive cans of the American super-market but dull, green, grey cans that make you feel bilious just to look at them. The food consists of can one, beans and meat; can two, beef stew; can three, pork sausage without gravy; can four, beef and peas; can five, chicken and noodles. Peter would alternate these and mix the food with locally cooked rice, skilfully blending into this glorious mess just the right amount of B-1. What is B-1? This is another C-ration nightmare consisting of crackers, cocoa and jam. So that we could have breaded rice and meat, Peter cooked this mélange. Port Arthur, Texas' gift to Doctor Dooley was Peter Sherrer Kessey and his culinary masterpieces.

It was easy enough to joke about our food and extremely important that we do so. The maniacal monotony of our diet and the constant problems of digestion became terrible things. It is strange how large and overwhelming such small things as this can become when you're living in a jungle on the edge of the world. In order to maintain our mental equilibrium, it was important to keep high our sense of humor.

As the weeks progressed we became more renowned throughout the area.

We always urged the villagers to pay us in barter for our medicines and for the treatment that we were giving. This was important for their own pride and was important for us too. It was expensive running this mission and I had made all my plans for Northern Laos and had brought most of my equipment prepared for cool or cold weather. As a consequence of not being allowed to go to the North, I had to buy a lot of different equipment. I was constantly worried that my money would run out before I ever would get to my destination, the North of Laos. Any saving of money became important to us and the simple idea of having our patients pay us in produce assumed great importance. At the end of a day in the clinic we would have a dozen eggs, several coconuts, perhaps a bottle of the local whiskey and, if the day was good, a scrawny chicken.

Every morning we would hold sick-call at our hospital. Then after lunch we would load the jeep up with medicines and hold a "jeep-call" in the afternoon. A jeep-call consisted of two members of the team driving to one of the dozens of outlying villages around Vang Vieng. The jeep would be driven into the village with the horn blaring. We would park, drop the tailgate, send someone for a bucket of water, and open the boxes of medicines. At once our portable clinic would be plunged into its flourishing practice. The people we would care for in the afternoons were those who were either too sick or not sick enough to make it to Vang Vieng, perhaps a four-hour walk away.

On jeep-call there was not the nerve-wracking pressure of misery and confinement that we felt in the crowded room at the clinic. At least we had mobility and a measure of fresh air. We knew the importance of going into the huts of these people. Never had they seen an American. Never had they received white men in their homes, and they were just as proud of their homes as we are. I would estimate that we have been in over three thousand Asian homes. Often the insides of these huts were oppressively sultry and humid. Most of them by our standards were filthy, and they were plagued with lice, fleas, gnats and insects. Always in the darkest corners there were the pot-bellied children, the undernourished, the malnourished, and the miserable.

We always carried a black bag, a must for M.D.'s in America and a good idea in Laos, too. In the jeep we would bring extra boxes of combiotic, terramycin, Meals for Millions, sterile solutions, T-shirts and perhaps some candy as distractions and bribes for the young and old. A stateside friend sent me a boxful of small American flags. We had one huge flag flying over our house and others tacked to medical bags, kits and boxes. Denny rigged a fine little symbol of our country's splendor on the fender of our jeep. It was frequently torn by the brambles along the jungle trail and splattered by mud, but it nevertheless served proudly as our symbol of home.

We did not bleat about the glories of stateside plumbing; we spoke not at all of the beauties of Mount Vernon; we offered no praise for the democratic system; we did not proselytize. There were just two things that we identified ourselves by. The first was the American flag. And the second was the words with which we instructed our interpreters to precede every statement: *"Thanh mo America pun va . . .* The American doctor says." We wanted eloquence in deeds, not words.

In late winter I received a letter that made me feel like a village priest elevated to the Cardinalate. It informed me that the Junior Chamber of Commerce of the United States had voted me as one of their ten outstanding young men of 1956. This brought many blessings. One of them was that I was asked to become an honorary member of the Jaycees of Laos. This outfit was in its formative stage and was composed of leading young men of the capital. I joined and, at the only meeting I was ever able to attend, the Jaycees asked what they could do to help my mission. I had come here to help the Lao and the Lao in turn were offering their help to me.

Every couple of weeks two members of my team would take the drive through the jungle to get to Vientiane. They would pick up the mail, send ours out, buy whatever supplies were needed, load all into the trailer and return the next day to Vang Vieng. Every month we would have to buy another barrel of gasoline and gingerly carry it to our village on the tired back of Agnes.

Though it was always a break to get away from the clinic, the jeep drive was a frightening experience. If the vehicle should break down, it was certain that the two men would have to have a hike of several days in order to get to the capital. There was rarely any traffic on the road during these months. In spite of Baker's administerings, Agnes was limping and lugging herself around, showing the result of her arduous and frequent jeep-calls.

Once in Vientiane, our spirits would climb. Buoyancy and humor are requirements for men in my kind of work. To us the best part of Vientiane was the house of Howard and Martha Kaufman. Howard was certainly the best friend we had in the kingdom. He is an anthropologist and, to my knowledge, the only government-employed American in the kingdom who has taken time out to learn to speak the native Lao. He is with Community Development Programs of the United States Operations Mission but unfortunately due to "the exigencies of a large mission" he is not given opportunity to leave the capital to get to the communities. His wife Martha, though only about twenty-five years old, was almost a mother to us all. Martha never batted an eye when we would arrive filthy from a many-hour drive, timing our entry with their dinner hour. Water would be ready and we would have a hot shower and clean up. We always kept some fresh clothes in Howard's dresser. Martha would have more food prepared and we would sit around a table (instead of a crate) and sit on chairs (instead of the floor) and eat a dinner (instead of C-ration).

Months later, when my University of Notre Dame men joined us and we frequently said the family rosary aloud at night, I heard Protestant Pete Kessey complaining to Howard about it: "Seems you can hardly get to sleep at night, up there in the jungle, what with the Catholics clicking their beads all the time."

I cannot give full praise to these three men of mine and the two who later joined us. These men did the dirty work, seldom grumbling and usually joking a bit. They were excellent men in every sense of the word. Peter Kessey had a willing heart and a gentle hand; he spoke to the people in a Texas-American accent, and somehow they always seemed to understand. Norman Baker, my French-speaking mechanic and general man around the place, could slap on a dressing that was guaranteed never to come off; he would sweat and grunt but he got it on and it stayed on. Denny Shepard, who was going on to medical school, was brilliant and practiced a high caliber of medicine. I am afraid Dooley was a hard taskmaster; I frequently lost my temper, but the boys persisted. I believe that my men showed heroism, sacrifice and guts, not in any one great dramatic action, but rather in constancy.

FOUR ·

"PHASING OUT;" THE CEREMONY OF BACI

We kept a $20 bill tacked upon the wall. The understanding was that anyone who got mad, or homesick, or just fed up with the job could take it and head for home. No one ever touched that money. But I am sure there were many times that the boys were tempted during those endless days and nights of dealing with misery, filth and disease.

Denny, the newlywed, missed his wife terribly, and spent his odd moments composing lengthy letters. Norman Baker became increasingly jittery as the time for the baby's arrival drew near. (Fortunately, my mother kept in close touch with Priscilla; and when Master Arthur Thomas Baker showed up one day in November, the excited father got the good news in less than 72 hours, thanks to the Embassy mail-room in Vientiane!)

All of us developed a sort of compulsive fear of contamination. We were always conscious of the contagiousness of everything we touched. No matter how many times we scrubbed up during the day, washing our hands in alcohol until the skin became dry and brittle, we felt a mad desire toward evening to burn our clothes and literally bathe in alcohol.

Instead, someone would yell: *"Ab nam Nam Song!"* ("Let's head for the river!") We'd shuck our clothes on the embankment, plunge in, and spend the next half-hour soaping ourselves. Still, we never felt entirely clean.

That was what gave Pete the idea for the shower. To start with he had only a shower-head which he had swiped from the hotel in Vientiane. But he dreamed up a weird arrangement which involved a 55-gallon gasoline drum rigged on a tripod about 18 feet high. With the help of Ojisan and a few coolies he set out in search of lumber. The only hardwood available was teak—it took four strong men to lift one five-foot beam. That never fazed Pete.

After two weeks and much sweating and swearing the shower was finished. It looked like a cross between a Texas oil derrick and the Leaning Tower of Pisa. The big barrel was lowered on a block and tackle, and filled with water. Then the line was hitched to Agnes. The jeep drove down the road and raised the 400-pound load. When the barrel was secure in its supporting cradle, someone would climb the rig and light the little kerosene lamp placed on a shelf beneath it.

It took about two hours to heat the 55 gallons of water to ideal temperature. The whole operation was fantastic; but everyone who scrubbed himself under that steaming water agreed that *la douche de Pierre* (Pete's Shower) was a huge success. At least we all felt a bit cleaner.

One day in November we were busy as usual, and at midday we just bolted our food and went back to work. While nobody mentioned it, we were all aware that the day was Thanksgiving. We were just a little more homesick than usual. Then, along toward dusk, we heard the roar of a jeep. A cloud of dust boiled up the road to our house and out stepped a short, chubby young man with a wonderful smile—Jefferson Davis Cheek of Comanche, Texas.

Jeff Cheek, who was attached to the USOM in Vientiane, was one of our few and infrequent visitors. Now he announced that he was dirty, tired and hungry after the long trek from Vientiane. He demanded to know what we had to eat.

"C-rations, brother!" said Pete. "Today it's beef and peas plus rice." Jeff laughed and hauled a dusty bag out of the back of his jeep. It contained a complete Thanksgiving dinner—roast turkey, cranberry sauce, mashed potatoes, pumpkin pie. He had even brought along the alcoholic trimmings, which we enjoyed while the food was heating in the hospital sterilizer.

After we had feasted royally, we sat out on the porch and talked about Savong, the little girl Jeff once had brought to us from Ban Tsieng.

We had been in Vang Vieng only a few weeks when Jeff Cheek came to visit us for the first time. He was driving along the jungle trail, when a group of natives stopped his jeep and appealed for help. They showed him a little girl, about 14 years old, lying on a mat, semi-conscious and obviously near death.

This was Savong. Some time earlier, no one knew how long ago, she had scratched her leg in the jungle and it became infected. Ignorant and helpless, Savong's people just left her lying in the hut. Eventually, the entire leg became horribly bloated and the infection spread up into the groin. That was the way Jeff found her.

This poor sailor made the mistake of growing a beard — an object of fascination to the kids.

Norman Baker, a fine sailor, a good American, my constant companion, my helping hand, and my friend.

Finally on the U.S. transports, the refugees look through a hawse-hole at the uncertain future.

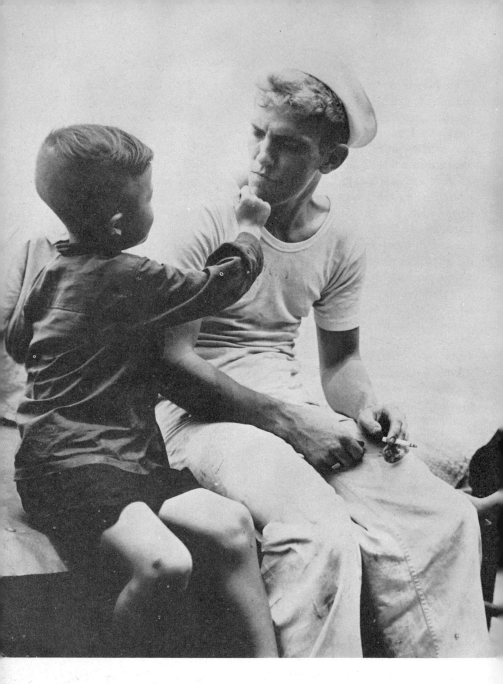

This child had been told that American sailors would roast him alive. Now he doesn't believe it. But he did.

He placed her gently in the back of the jeep, and drove slowly through the jungle, reaching Vang Vieng after dark. We opened up the hospital, but after one look I had my doubts about saving her. Yet there was something about this child that touched us deeply. She seemed symbolic of all the miserable, neglected kids in Laos—Southeast Asia is full of Savongs. So we were determined to save her.

Of course, she was filthy after such long neglect. We literally had to scrub the nearly lifeless little body with soap and brush before proceeding. Then, when she was clean, we gave her a minimum of anesthesia, and I began to operate.

I had to incise the bloated leg from knee to groin. The horrible green pus filled several containers. When the drainage stopped, I saw the cellulitis, which can best be described as a mass of boils involving the muscles and underlying tissues. When we got through, there was nothing left of that massive leg but bone and a few soggy muscles.

She had lain for so many months in one position, that her "good" side was covered with massive, weeping pressure sores which we cleaned and dressed. Then we revived her and administered infusions of saline and glucose.

Pete, Denny, Baker and even Chai took turns hovering over Savong all through that night and the next day. The fever dropped, she brightened, and then began to cry. Not from pain now, but because her anguish was over. Between sobs we heard her mumbling "*Cop chai, cop chai, cop chai.* . . ." Over and over—"Thank you, thank you, thank you. . . ."

Weeks passed and Savong grew stronger. First she sat up, then she walked a few steps. The boys trimmed her hair in a sort of feather-bob, gave her a toothbrush and taught her how to use it. Somehow they even obtained female clothes. Then Jeff Cheek came with presents of hair-ribbons and combs. We decided that Savong really looked beautiful.

Months later we discharged her. She was strong and well, although she limped a bit on that frail little leg. Her people came to take her back to Ban Tsieng.

Before she left we took a picture of her. We gave one print to Jeff Cheek because, we said teasingly, Savong was "his girl." The other print we kept for ourselves. Whenever we felt homesick or disheartened we would look at that picture of Savong. It served to remind us that, for some people, things might have been different had we stayed comfortably at home.

Toward dusk one evening, early in December, I watched the crowd gather in front of our house for movies. Peter and Denny hung the screen from our front porch. Baker, timing his entrance like a professional, picked up the 130-pound generator and carried it through the crowd to its place near the projector—his strongman act was an unfailing hit at every performance.

When the picture began I took my favorite seat on the porch, above and behind the screen. From there I could study these wonderful faces, young and old, glowing in the light reflected from the screen, captivated by the colorful magic of Walt Disney's *Fantasia*. I remembered how we had once considered dubbing in a Lao sound-track on these movies, and then abandoned the scheme as too costly. Now I was glad we had left them as they were. Walt Disney's creations have a universal language of their own.

I thought: How many times had I been told that the Lao were lazy people, ignorant, backward, indifferent to their own betterment? How many times has that canard been uttered by cynical westerners against neglected people everywhere who never had a chance? Here in Vang Vieng I had living proof of its falsity. Never have I seen people respond so readily to encouragement, or to make so much from so little help.

Our classes in sanitation, hygiene, food and nutrition, infant and child care were popular and paying off handsomely. We had "bagged" many midwives, and these girls had achieved an *esprit de corps* that had elevated midwifery to a proud profession that attracted other candidates. The Lao nurses were increasing in number and proficiency. Each fortnight, by arrangement, when the boys made the trip to Vientiane for mail and supplies, they brought back a senior from the *lycée* for a week. We hoped to inspire these young men to study medicine. Already we had trained a dozen "practical" nurses, more than were needed in Vang Vieng.

Now, I knew, the time was approaching when we would have to "phase out" of Vang Vieng. My mission was not to set up a permanent American outpost, but to establish something that the Lao themselves could carry on. True, it would be primitive by western standards; but it would be better than what these people had before.

I believe that those of us who attempt to aid in a foreign land must be content with small achievements. Americans in the capital said that I practiced 19th-century medicine. They are correct, I did practice 19th-century medicine, and this was just fine. Upon my departure our indigenous personnel would practice 18th-century medicine. Good, this is progress, since most of the villagers live in the 15th century.

So that phase of the plan was settled in my own mind. Kam Lak, the senior nurse, would take charge. He was a conscientious, highly intelligent young man who already could be entrusted with minor surgery. Kam Ba, his wife, who was probably the best of our midwives, could serve as his assistant. We left them a few surgical instruments and about $10,000 worth of drugs. The Ministry promised them further supplies.

My boys were scheduled to depart for home within the next month or so. Baker was anxious to get back to his wife and baby; Denny Shepard, who also had a bride waiting, had to get back to the university, as did Pete Kessey. I had two replacements lined up; I was just waiting for one more letter from South Bend, Indiana, which would clinch the deal. Then. . . .

The movies ended, and the crowd began to drift away. The boys took down the movie screen, stowed the gear, and began to bat around our living room before turning in.

"Gentlemen," I said, "I have news for you." Baker groaned loudly, and rolled over on the cot. (He claimed that whenever I addressed them that way another dirty job was coming up.) "For a job well done you get shore leave from—I hope—December 22nd, reporting back to Vientiane on January 2nd, 1957. Expenses paid—within reason. I would suggest you spend the holidays in Hong Kong."

Of course, they were jubilant. But I felt this was a small reward for all they had done. When they worked for me, they had no Saturdays or Sundays off. Denny wanted to know where I would be.

"I'm going to Manila," I said. "But I'll be back in Vientiane the day after New Year's. It's time for me to see the high brass. I've got to know what the score is."

I spent the holidays in Manila where I delivered some lectures. Then, on January 2nd, I arrived in Vientiane and went directly to see Dr. Oudom at the Ministry of Health. He greeted me enthusiastically, and told me that the Premier wished to see me. This was quite a surprise, but Dr. Oudom smilingly refused to elaborate. We went over to the Ministry where, after a short wait, we were ushered into the Premier's office.

Prince SouvannaPhouma spoke glowingly of my mission in Vang Vieng. Much to my amazement, he seemed to be familiar with every detail of our operations, the nurse and midwife training programs, the hygiene and sanitation classes, the jeep-call system, etc. Then he inquired about my plans for the future.

When I explained that my funds were running low, and that I could remain in Laos only about four months more, it was his turn to register surprise. Apparently, he hadn't fully realized that Dooley, and not rich old Uncle Sam, was footing the bills!

It was then that he made his magnanimous offer. Beginning immediately, he said, the Royal Lao Government would provide *toutes les facilités*. The army would furnish transportation and supplies. The Ministry of Education would furnish anything I needed for an educational program. I would have free access to the government's medical supplies. The government would even pay the salaries of my Lao personnel.

This was almost too good to be true. But I decided I might as well shoot for the moon—*Bau pinh yanh!*

"Your Excellency," I said, "don't you think my medical mission could accomplish more for the Royal Government if you sent me into one of the northern provinces?"

"I most certainly do!" he said emphatically. I looked over and saw Dr. Oudom's beaming smile.

The Premier then mentioned two possible areas of operation, Muong Sing, a town near the Burma border, and—Nam Tha! He explained that both villages now had operational landing strips. He would put a small plane at my disposal and he would keep a supply line open. Of course, there were still certain dangers in the north, he added. But there were police and soldiers from the local garrison who would be assigned to me as bodyguards.

I thanked him sincerely. Aglow with the good news, I went to the American Embassy, and asked to see Ambassador Parsons. Again, I had a pleasant surprise. This time the Ambassador greeted me warmly, and congratulated me for the fine job we were doing in Vang Vieng. When I told him about my conversation with the Premier, he seemed delighted.

"Yes, Dr. Dooley," he said, "I really think it would be a splendid idea for you to go north now."

Ambassador Parsons explained that conditions in Laos were much more stable now. Border incidents were less likely. With the opening of the airstrip at Nam Tha, closer and speedier contact was now possible. Moreover, he said, our work in Vang Vieng had won the confidence and respect of the Lao Government. We were less likely to be taken for spies or *agents provocateurs.*

Now I faced the difficult task of "closing out" of Vang Vieng. Fortunately, I still had my three veterans, Baker, Pete and Denny, to help me. I met them at the Samboun Hotel, and they heard the good news with mixed feelings.

Baker already had booked his passage on a flight leaving in mid-January. Denny Shepard decided to go up to Nam Tha and spend a few weeks helping me get settled. Pete Kessey, the lone bachelor of the trio, scratched his head thoughtfully. He was due back in Austin for the Spring term of pharmacy school. "Well, shucks," he said, "they can get along without me, Doc. Guess I'll string along with you for a few months more."

We piled our bags in the jeep, and for the last time Agnes made the rugged trip through the jungle to Vang Vieng. Poor Agnes! She wouldn't be going north with us. The Premier and Dr. Oudom had warned me that there were no roads in Nam Tha.

In Vang Vieng we told Chai and Si that we were leaving for the North soon and of course we wanted them to come with us. They just uttered a low moan. But when we said that they could quit if they were fearful of the North, they looked insulted and said, "Where you go, we will come always."

Ojisan was unhappy to see us leave as we had become good friends. We assured him that Vang Vieng would always be our first love but that the people of Vang Vieng had taught us many things. One of the things they had taught us was the care and responsibility of our neighbors. Ojisan himself had so frequently pointed out the importance of driving to the surrounding villages for jeep-calls. Now we were going to do the same thing, but we were just going very far away. We also told him that we hoped the United States Operations Mission would come to Vang Vieng with some programs, either in education or perhaps even in medicine or agriculture. Ojisan hoped they would, too. Later, they did.

We held our last class in the local school and asked the children to remember what we had taught them. They replied that they would not forget their Americans. We graduated and "bagged" some more girls from the midwife training course and began to plan out days in January.

We were timing this phase out. We did not wish to offend the village by leaving abruptly so we planned to spend four or five weeks doing our work as usual, explaining to each day's sick-call that we would soon be leaving and that the Lao nurse and midwives would continue our work. We told all the villages that these people were very capable and that we would leave the white man's miraculous medicines behind for the villagers. They were sad to see us go but pleased that we were leaving things behind.

The town of Vang Vieng gave us an elaborate *baci*, a ritualistic ceremony, climaxed by a grand feast, which the Lao hold to celebrate a birth, a marriage, a soldier's return from the wars, or the departure of cherished friends. The women of the village built a small pyramid from palm leaves, and decorated it with flowers, candles, baubles, and bangles. The finished product stood about two feet high. It was then placed in a beautiful hand-made silver bowl. From the top of the pyramid to the bottom of the bowl long streamers of white cotton were hung. Around the base of the bowl the women placed, with great precision, succulent pieces of pork, rice, sweet-meats and other delicacies.

All the participants in the *baci* then sat in a large circle on new mats or blankets around the center pyramid of flowers, close enough to lean forward and touch the bowl with an outstretched hand.

An old sorcerer then chanted the Invocation to the Spirits. We sat on the floor with our long legs tucked beside us, our left hand held up as if in prayer, and our right palm extended upwards touching the bowl. In his chant, the sorcerer asked Sakke, who lives in the Paradise of Sixteen Floors, to come join us. He called on Kame, who lives in Kamaphob; and on Charoupe, who lives in the Divine Spheres. He begged Khirisi, who dwells in the mountains and the rivers to come with Attarikhe, who abounds in Sweet Air. He begged all the divinities of Dawn and Dusk, the spirits of Night and Day, and the nymphs of the Mountains and Flowers to come to this *baci* and partake of the food which is laid out for them.

After the sorcerer felt that all the spirits were present, he called on the souls of those for whom the *baci* was being given. The Lao tribes feel that the soul is a vagabond, and must be recalled to the body from time to time. In a sing-song fashion he incanted words which meant "Come, be with us, Souls, return to your home of flesh, fear not the tiger nor the phantoms, come to us here now where the good divinities and spirits have come; fear not, return to your bodies. . . ." According to the Lao belief, there are thirty-two parts of the human body and each possesses a soul. So the sorcerer had to implore each of the thirty-two parts; this took a little time. When both the spirits and the souls had finally arrived, we sat back and rested a moment. The second part of the *baci* then began.

The sorcerer first took a piece of cotton string from the center pyramid of blossoms and knelt in front of those for whom the *baci* was being offered. He made a wish for me, and while chanting his wish he tied a string around my wrist, and very meticulously twirled the ends lest the wish fall out of the string. When he finished with me, a second person tied another cotton on my wrist, and a third and so on. This was repeated for each of us. By the time the ceremony was finished, we had more than a dozen cotton strings around our wrists. Each offered a wish, and each was a bit more bizarre than the former:

"May you always be strong against the tusks of elephants."
"May you be safe from the jaws of the wild boar."
"May you be rich."

"May you have many wives."

"May you possess all wisdom and health."

"May you be blessed with prosperity and strength."

"May your jeep not fall off the road nor your airplane from the sky."

"May you always carry with you our love."

"May you return to us, your friends."

The old betel-chewing women, the wise elders of the village, the giggling girls, the mayor, all tied on us the cotton strings of friendship and called on the presiding spirits to witness the sincerity of their wishes.

Chai had told us that the person receiving the *baci*, to show his gratitude and understanding, must do his part. So after each string was tied, we clasped our hands together in praying attitude and said, "Cop chai liiiiii, ɔɔɔɔɔ."

After the *baci* was finished, the sorcerer again thanked the spirits and told them they might leave, and the souls that they might return to their life of roaming. Then everyone started to eat the rice balls, sweetmeats and the other food that the spirits didn't eat. And of course we drank lots of "choum," the local rice alcohol.

Finally the day came for our leaving. We had everything crated up and were sitting on the front porch of our now-empty house. The army trucks that the Minister was sending up to us were due in an hour.

Hundreds of people had gathered in the square to bid us farewell. We had *baci* strings tied around our wrists almost up to the elbow. The villagers brought many going-away gifts—flowers, corn, chicken, the local whiskey; gifts of good wishes. We said many farewells to Ojisan, the nurse, the mayor, the kids. We were all sitting around feeling melancholy; but soon the trucks would be here and our melancholy would dissolve in the sweat of loading.

We waited all morning, all afternoon. We unrolled our sleeping bags and slept all night. Next day the trucks arrived. The army drivers had no explanation whatever nor did we demand any. We were used to this sort of thing and did not let it bother us anymore. Again there were many farewells, more flowers, more corn, more gifts. We even felt bad saying goodbye to the betel-chewing oldsters. They had become our friends.

The last glimpse we had of the villagers of Vang Vieng was from the back of an army truck as it jolted along toward the jungle road. They looked like a lot of little bears, pawing the air as they waved their arms *toward themselves* in the parting gesture that means "come back soon."

FIVE ·

NAM THA AT LAST

When we arrived in Vientiane, there was the inevitable foul-up. The airline had advanced the departure of Baker's flight by one hour without bothering to give us more than 15 minutes notice. We barely made it. Cussing air travel like a true sailor, Baker managed to dash through customs and heave his own bags aboard the plane just before the door closed. As the plane took off, I suddenly realized that my friend and assistant, Norman Baker had left before I could adequately thank him for his work and his kindly fellowship.

Denny took charge of preparations for the move to Nam Tha, while Pete Kessey and I made the two-hour flight to Bangkok to meet our two new men. On the way, I told Pete what little I knew about these boys.

Among the scores of letters I had received from volunteers, there was one from John deVitry, an undergraduate at Notre Dame, my alma mater. He was the son of French parents, now American citizens; and his reasons for wanting to serve a stretch with us in Laos impressed me. I wrote to my old friend, Miss Erma Konya, who is on the administrative staff of the University, and asked her to investigate him. Her report on John deVitry was highly favorable, and she recommended another boy, Robert E. Waters. We corresponded, and the deal was settled.

We saw them get off the plane at the Bangkok airport, two typical crew-cut college boys, somewhat bedraggled after the 45-hour flight. Pete Kessey groaned: "O Lord, Joe College and his roommate. I'll bet they even brought their hi-fi gear and recording albums with them!"

John deVitry was a tall, slender, sensitive and serious-minded fellow, 21 years old. Bob Waters was only 20, but tall, well built, and obviously the extrovert type. They both looked pretty soft and green for the part of the world where we would be operating.

If I shared Pete's original misgivings, I am happy to report that we were both dead wrong. "Joe College" is a common masquerade; beneath those campus-cut clothes lie the heart and sinews of our nation. Both boys turned out to be prodigious workers. John was a born diplomat, something the Dooley mission needed badly. Within thirty days they were both crusty and uncomplaining veterans taking life on the China border in their stride. I guess we all have to start somewhere.

Now that the rainy season was finished, and a landing strip ready for us at Nam Tha, we prepared to go north. Denny had purchased all the things on the list, and we brought many new supplies from Bangkok, plus two new men. We were to fly in two trips. The first one would be a Bristol airplane, the second a DC-3. Before loading we estimated our weight on paper and divided the gear accordingly. When the trucks got to the airport we were able to weigh the boxes exactly. To Pete's horror we found that it would be impossible to transport all the lumber. He had meticulously dissected the Vang Vieng shower and brought it along with hopes of reconstructing it in Nam Tha. We loaded the aircraft and with a feeling of poignancy left *la douche de Pierre* behind us.

We left Vientiane in a huge, obsolete Bristol cargo plane with a belly like a landing craft, tremendous wings, and a pair of undersized propellers. For the next three hours we flew north over a cloud layer pierced occasionally by jagged mountain peaks. Then we descended and saw the vast rain-forest of the Nam Tha valley. It looked like a rich green carpet decorated with the scarlet of flame-trees and the soft blossoms of frangipani.

The rain-forest trees are devoured by clinging, tenacious tendrils and trailers, saprohytes, clawing into the fleshy bark trying to consume the very core of the tree. One might draw a corollary with the techniques of Communist conquest in Asia.

The French pilot made several passes at the little landing strip. Then we began to climb again, and the co-pilot came back and said, "Trop petite!" The muddy strip was too short for the cumbersome, overloaded Bristol. I went up to the cockpit and persuaded the pilot to try again. He looked at me pityingly, and shrugged with Gallic indifference. We swooped in and skidded to a stop with only a few feet of the runway to spare.

When we opened the doors of the plane, we found a large crowd of villagers gathered around. We jumped down to the ground and knew that at last we were on the soil of the north. Two years ago, straight east of here, we had worked in North Viet Nam. For years I had dreamed of working here. For a year I had planned it, and for the past five months we had been proving ourselves and our mission. And now we had arrived. We were in the northernmost fingertip of freedom jammed into the underbelly of Communist China. This was a dramatic moment for us all. None of us said very much. We knew that halfway up that first range of hills just north of us was the rim of hell.

Despite its isolation, Nam Tha proved to be a bigger and more progressive village than Vang Vieng. We traveled afoot from the airstrip into town. Our tons of supplies and equipment had to be moved by sheer coolie-power. The trail led directly into the apex of the triangular area which is Nam Tha's public "square," lined with houses and shops, an elaborate Buddhist temple, the police headquarters and local jail, and the "mansion" of the Chao Khuong, or Governor of the province.

Halfway along the base of the triangle we found the house that we were to occupy. It was a solidly constructed building formerly occupied by the Chao Khuong itself. In one part was a telegraph office and the living quarters of Pavie, the operator, and his large family. Another room was occupied by a couple of young school teachers. We asked everyone to stay put. Chai, Si, our houseboy, and Kieu, our new interpreter (who spoke English and once had worked for the American Embassy), took the room near the school teachers. Bob, John, Denny and I took over two large rooms. Pete Kessey, yearning for privacy, found a small, dark closet which he named "The Black Hole" and converted it into a bedroom. We did not close any part of the house off; doors were always open and Pavie, the teachers, and just about anyone who wished to could meander in and out of our living room. Their naked babies were just as much at home in our part of the house as in any other part.

Only a short walk from the house we found the recently completed (on the Premier's orders) dispensary building. We went to work on the hospital as soon as we could. The main dispensary building was transformed to the main hospital building. It did not take too much to do this. The building was about thirty-five feet long, divided into three rooms. We left one room entirely in the hands of the Lao dispensary nurses, changed the second one to be used as an office, and the third one became the Sick-Call Room.

We built a large table, covered it with linoleum, and placed it in the Sick-Call Room. At the house we had a small generator that we used for the movie projector. In Vientiane we had purchased a very bright desk lamp, and hooked this to the operating room table and onto the generator. Now we had an operating room.

We kept the small pressure sterilizer in our house, and carried the sterile goods back and forth on our bicycles. The hospital compound was about a five-minute ride from the house. The generator was slung under a pole when it had to be transported, or from time to time we could use the Chao Khuong's jeep.

An abandoned bamboo building next to the Clinic was cleaned up and painted. We had to wait several weeks until they found enough lime in the mountains. When mixed with water this made a pretty good whitewash. John, Bob and the coolies built fifteen beds from teak wood and old army metal cots. We spent several days cutting out pictures from the old magazines that we had, and pasted these to the walls to brighten up the place. When the ward was finished it looked fine, by anyone's standards.

A third building was fixed up as a sort of "isolation ward" for leprosy cases. This was not up on stilts like the ward, but was a small thatched hut. We built nine bamboo cots here. Thus it did not take long to have a three-building hospital in good shape.

True to his word, the Premier had prepared the way for us. The Chao Khuong and the local representative of the Ministry of Public Works did everything possible to help us. Nguyen Cauvin, the public works official, was an amusing and pathetic character, half French, half Vietnamese. He had done a good job on the schools and had built our hospital. But his great ambition was to build a road across the province from Nam Tha to the Burma border. Lacking modern road-building equipment, and depending solely on the hand labor of coolies, he had never been able to progress farther than the muddy trail that ran about 10 miles past the airstrip and was washed away each year during the monsoon season. Cauvin became one of our best friends.

The Chao Khuong was a curious but likable fellow. He spoke rapid-fire French, but always through a cloud of cigarette smoke, and without ever removing the butt from his lips except to light another. Only John, our diplomat, could completely understand him, so they became bosom pals.

The first time I asked the Governor to dine with us, he accepted with a grave bow—and never showed up. When we went after him, he explained that he had not received the proper invitation in writing, as was customary in France. I explained that, in America, a verbal invitation was considered correct for informal occasions. He nodded smilingly, and seemed satisfied. However, when we invited him after that he would always raise his eyebrows and inquire: "—à la français, ou à l'américaine?"

Denny Shepard decided to devote the short time he would be with us in Nam Tha to setting up a clean, efficient, adequately stocked surgery. So he went right to work installing equipment and sterilizing instruments, and making our sterile packs and surgical drapes. It was a good thing he did. For surgery started sooner than we expected.

On our second day in Nam Tha we heard a great commotion in the village. Escorted by the Chao Khuong himself, some natives appeared at the compound carrying two "sedan chairs" crudely fashioned from bamboo and slung on long poles. I went out and took a look at the occupants, and yelled to the boys to get the operating room ready for an emergency.

But this was more than an emergency. It was our first evidence of Communist "banditry" on the northern frontier. While Denny and I scrubbed up, the Chao Khuong told us the story. Apparently the bandits had swooped down on this Yao tribesman's hut in a little village near the border. They had hacked at the occupants with long swords, literally quartering the grandmother and a small child, and critically wounding the tribesman and his wife. The carnage did not last long. When neighbors, attracted by the screams, reached the hut the bandits had fled—stealing nothing.

The villagers placed the wounded couple in the improvised sling-chairs and made the arduous journey down the valley to Nam Tha. It had taken a day and a night, and how the victims survived the ordeal I will never know.

The woman's head, face, and breasts were severely slashed, and the wounds were already infected. She had a raging fever, and was in excruciating pain. We gave her antibiotics and morphine, and turned our attention to the husband, who was in worse shape.

Half his scalp had been neatly lifted from the skull, apparently by one sweep of a sharp knife or sword. His jawbone was broken in several places, and one side of his face was slashed away from the eyelid down to the lips. He had a fractured arm and a lot of gashes.

Cleaning and suturing the scalp was comparatively simple. The maddening task was repairing the multiple fractures of the jaw. Because all the teeth had been knocked out, there was no way to hold all the fractured ends in approximation, so I had to remove a large section of the broken jaw and part of the dental structure. Then I sutured the gum, and repaired the face, lip and eyelid, and went to work on the fractured arm.

With the help of antibiotics, anti-tetanus shots, and a lot of intravenous feeding, the unfortunate fellow eventually pulled through. But he will never be a pretty sight.

The woman's head was such a mass of infections that nothing could be sutured immediately. I was able to repair the face and the mutilated breasts without too much trouble. Our main job was to keep her alive, clear up the infections, and finish the surgical work later.

The Chao Khuong and one of his officers had remained in the operating room during the entire bloody procedure. When it was over the Governor wandered outside and lit the inevitable cigarette. After I had washed up, and wandered outside, he was still there, puffing away pensively.

"That's the way it goes," he said sadly. "We'll send out a patrol, and find—nothing. For a while that village can sleep in peace. Next time the devils will strike elsewhere."

There were a lot of questions I hesitated to ask him. Who were these border bandits? Did they come from Red China? Or did they belong to the Pathet Lao? But I had been warned in Vientiane not to pry deeply into such matters. And, on such short acquaintance, I knew I had to watch my step with the Chao Khuong. The Governor pointed out that this beating was just another indication that "peace" did not exist in this part of Asia, even though this was the year of a million blossoms. The hideousness of Communism is much in evidence here. Ambassador Parsons was justified in his fears for us and our work in this area.

The Chao Khuong invited me to visit his residence the following evening for a good talk. Unfortunately, I had to break that engagement. For the next night we were busy with another "basket case" which taught us that we had to cope with a different kind of enemy: witch doctors.

SIX ·

THE STORY OF ION; WITCH DOCTORS

Along toward nightfall a man came to our house begging us to save his 10-year-old son who lay near death in the mountain village of Ban Pareng. What was wrong? The boy had been burned, the man said, "black like a chicken or pig." When had this happened? The man stopped to calculate time.

"Fourteen nights ago," he said. "The night was very cold. Ion, my son, wore three extra shirts to keep warm. He backed closer and closer to the fire. Then his shirts burst into flame."

The soldier from the constabulary who brought the man to us urged us to wait until morning. The trail to Ban Pareng, he said, was treacherous. Besides, if the boy had lived for fourteen nights and days, he would probably keep until tomorrow. (*Bau pinh yanh!*)

But the father was frantic; the case sounded both serious and puzzling; and, besides, we would be busy with sick-call in the morning. Pete, Denny, and Chai found flashlights, and I checked the contents of my bag. Then we told the man to lead the way. We took the road leading out beyond the airstrip—Cauvin's "road." Now we learned why jeep-calls were impossible in Nam Tha.

Walking in single file, we made our way through the jungle. Then we found the mountain trail and started to climb. For the next hour or more we clambered up steep rocks, and crossed several rope-and-bamboo bridges that swayed perilously over torrential rivers. An old man of 30, I was exhausted when we reached the little village of Ban Pareng.

We were ushered into a large, gloomy hut, perched high on stilts. The room reeked with the acrid odor of burnt flesh. The father led us to what looked like a pile of filthy rags lying in one corner. In the flashlight beam I saw a wisp of a boy sprawled on his stomach.

The lad was charred black from shoulders to buttocks. He was barely conscious, and lay motionless in the most distorted posture. Yet the boy's entire back seemed alive with motion. I pushed the light closer. The back was swarming with maggots feasting on the charred flesh.

The father explained that after the accident the local witch doctor had smeared the burns with a paste which I later learned was compounded of pig grease, betel-nut juice, and cow-dung. The deep third-degree burns were bad enough. But this grotesque treatment, probably repeated several times over the fortnight, had helped to produce this horrible living death.

There was nothing we could do under the circumstances. If the boy remained in the hut much longer he would certainly be dead. Getting him down the mountain and into Nam Tha seemed almost impossible, but it was our only chance. We told the father to find a large basket, some rope and a strong pole. Pete and Chai remained behind to supervise the perilous "ambulance" operation. Denny and I found a guide and started back to Nam Tha.

We were scrubbed up and ready when our basket case arrived at the hospital some hours later. We put Ion on the table, sprawled on his belly, and Pete took over the tricky job of administering the open-drip anesthesia. Our generator had not yet been hooked up; and, because of the dangerous ether fumes, we couldn't light the oil lamps. Fortunately, we had several battery-powered "miner's lamps" that could be strapped on our heads. They served perfectly in this emergency.

We flooded the boy's back with soap and water, and gently scrubbed away the filth. I began to debride the dead tissue, and soon found myself down to the bones of the rib cage. It was much worse than I had anticipated. The muscles of the shoulder girdle had been severely damaged, and huge areas of the buttocks completely destroyed.

Finally, Ion was bundled in antiseptic ointment and fluff gauze, and gently carried to a bed. After weeks of neglect, with little food or water, the pathetic little body was weak and dehydrated. We tried to administer fluids intravenously, but we couldn't find a vein that hadn't collapsed. We even had difficulty finding muscles on the emaciated body that would take a penicillin injection.

Denny and Pete spent what was left of that night pushing fluids subcutaneously into Ion's abdomen and legs. At best, he was what could be described as an "extremely poor surgical risk." (By some miracle, he survived and got well, a terribly deformed little boy.)

We had seen some severe burns and injuries in Vang Vieng. I knew that we probably would see even worse cases in the isolated north. But how often, I wondered, would our troubles be compounded, as in Ion's case, by the weird practices of primitive "witch doctors"?

I was not sure that a child like this could live even in all the sterile magnificence of an American hospital. Here we were, half a world away, working with flashlights, a minimum of equipment, and on a case most doctors would declare futile. But the children of Laos seem weathered to hardship and pain, and Ion had the guts he needed. With the power of medicine, blended with the power of prayer, and sprinkled with a little sweat, Ion pulled through. When he awoke he found his bed brightly decorated with multi-colored balloons and he found his day-and-night corpsmen very happy. How much we have learned here in Asia. There is a oneness in this world.

After the operation I walked slowly back to our hut. My boys all voted to sit up the rest of the night with Ion. Seeing these young men devoting their most tired hours to that child seared something into me. It is the simple clear-cut realization that the brotherhood of man does exist, as surely as does the Fatherhood of God. Indeed, we are our brothers' keepers.

Before we came to Nam Tha, and perhaps from time immemorial, the witch doctors had ruled supreme. No one ever questioned their wisdom or the power of their nostrums or incantations. But now the wretched people were torn between the magic of the traditional sorcerers and the new ways of the white medicine-men.

Finally the witch doctors put a "hex" on our hospital. They surrounded the compound with little mats of woven bamboo mounted on short posts stuck in the ground. That may sound silly. But, for all practical purposes, that hex worked like the proverbial charm. No one, no matter how desperately ill, would come near our hospital for help.

These witch doctors were all respected village elders. But our two most formidable adversaries were Old Joe and a crone we called Maggie.

So we decided to adopt an old American stratagem—"if you can't lick 'em, join 'em." Instead of antagonizing the witch doctors, (and this may raise the hackles of the American Medical Association), we began to treat them as "colleagues in the healing arts" who practiced a somewhat different discipline of medicine with which we disagreed and yet respected.

One afternoon I returned from an emergency call in the jungle to find Pete holding an earnest professional conference with Old Joe. Pete gave me the eye, and I squatted down and listened respectfully.

Old Joe had spread out before him a weird assortment of sticks, bamboo slivers, betel nuts, boiled leaves, pig grease, cow dung, and was explaining the theory behind his *materia medica*. Most of it was fantastic. But here and there I recognized fragments of the universal folk remedies (like the use of spiderwebs in open wounds), the effectiveness of which are acknowledged by modern medicine.

"Well," said Pete, "we just belong to different schools of medicine. We use different drugs, different methods, but we are both working for the same thing—to free the people from the evils of disease and suffering. The important thing is for us to work together. We'll teach you what we know, and you will teach us." That sounded fair enough to Old Joe.

From that time on Old Joe rarely missed a sick-call. We would administer a shot of penicillin, Joe would invoke the proper spirits. We would splint a fracture, then permit Old Joe to tie the indispensable red, white and black strings around the splints. If we were paid two coconuts for fee, Old Joe received one. (In America this practice is held in a bad light; they call it "fee splitting.")

His recovery rate had never been so high, so Old Joe was happy—and became our staunch friend. (However, he never acquired much faith in antibiotics. It was absurd, he said, to stick a needle in someone's backside when the infection was in the patient's head!)

Maggie was my own special problem, but whenever I held sick-call she rarely left my side. She was a snaggle-toothed old crone, and the dirtiest woman in the village, dressed in a ragged western-style blouse and skirt with a filthy towel wrapped around her head. Maggie shaved her head regularly, but she never washed her hands.

After handling each filthy patient, I would carefully wash my hands in soap and water, then hold them out while an assistant poured alcohol over them. Maggie was fascinated. I patiently explained that soap and water plus some of this powerful liquid banished any "evil spirits" that clung to my hands from the dirty wound. Maggie nodded knowingly. The germ theory, explained that way, made sense to her.

One day I had a small child whose head was covered with horrible green sores. The scalp was alive with lice, but had hardly any hair at all. A drastic clean-up job had to be done before I could treat the scalp, so I handed Maggie a bottle of strong shampoo and told her to take the child down to the river and wash him thoroughly.

When she returned the child's scalp was bleeding in places, but it was immaculately clean. Then I glanced at Maggie's hands. In the process, they too had been washed cleaner than they had been in many years. But that wasn't enough for Maggie! I saw her go over to Chai and hold out her cupped hands. He poured alcohol over them, and she scrubbed vigorously. Maggie was learning!

As you can see Old Joe and the other witch doctors believed in the more natural drugs, like betel nuts, slivers of wood, boiled leaves, cow dung, baboon's blood, spittle, pig grease and incantations to the proper spirits. Old Joe had a most unique treatment for a compound fractured arm. I believe this tip should be recorded by the American Academy of Orthopedic Surgeons: The man with a broken arm is laid on his mat with his head facing to the south. The special deities of the orthopedic service are invoked in a loud prayer. Red, black, and white strings are tied around the fractured limb. The open wound is stuffed with cobwebs. The arm is then bound in bark. Roots are placed around this and a small bamboo cage is woven directly on the arm. The patient wears this for several weeks, if he lives. He rarely does. But if the patient dies, the loss is directly proportional to the position of the sun or the moon, or the number of evil spirits hanging around the neighborhood. The spirits and phantoms of these simple people cling to the cloak of night and fly on the wings of day.

One morning a lad came running to the hospital. He begged us to hurry to his village to see his little brother. We went, brought the child back and spent the remainder of the day trying to keep him alive. Cholera had struck. The child was a healthy, pink-cheeked lad at sunrise. A few hours later he had diarrhea. Soon it became severe. Then vomiting began. By noon his salt loss flung his limbs into painful spastic contractions. Never developing a fever, the evacuation continued in unbelievable amounts, the child writhing in muscle spasms due to salt loss. By evening, in spite of the intravenous and subcutaneous infusions of fluids, he had lost nearly half his body weight. He died at sunset. This was our first cholera case. Unhappily, it was not our last. We are veterans now. The Lao call this the "water death" because it comes with the first monsoon rains. It ends in a month or so, but the number of deaths in the interval is staggering. Because of vaccinations, the numbers slaughtered diminished just a bit. Imagine the horror of cholera if it would tear loose in downtown New York. Yet "there is only one child in the world, and that child's name is All Children." The Minister of Health heard of the cholera cases that we were having. He sent up several thousand vials of cholera vaccine. Our native nurses and midwives went out throughout all of the valley and vaccinated the people. The natives did the vaccinations so the simple villagers were quick to accept it.

The sick-call in Nam Tha was similar to Vang Vieng, though we had more surgical cases and during the early months the lines were a lot longer.

However, in Vang Vieng all the cases were Lao, with an occasional Kha, while in Nam Tha there were many different tribes, each with their own ethnic characteristics. We now met such people as Yao, Thai Dam, Thai Neua, Lolo, Lan Ten, Meo, Lu, Chinese and Kha. We had to get interpreters for each dialect. Maggie could handle a couple of them. Our Kha coolies could speak Yao and Lao. Chai claimed that he understood the Meo, but I doubt it. The Thai Dam and Thai Neua speak a dialect similar to Lao. We all learned the Lao dialect with a mountain drawl.

Frequently a patient would have to go through four interpreters before she got her problem across to the doctor. It was not uncommon for an old gal to sit down and give her complaint to an interpreter in Meo. He would translate it to Maggie in Yao who would tell the coolie in Kha who in turn translated it to Kieu in Lao, who would tell me in French. I would ask Bob in English to give the lady something for her constipation.

Each tribe had its own costume. Many of them were brilliant with colors. In the morning when we would go to the clinic we would find clusters of these people, many who had traveled by foot or Tibetan pony for four or five days. Some had come to us from deep within Red China. The Yao tribes wear a dark blue headdress folded like a turban, such as exist in Arabia. Around this they wrap a large silver chain. At the end of the chain dangled the personal necessities like a silver toothpick, silver ear cleaners, a spatula for their betel-nut preparation and perhaps a tiger tooth or bear claw for good luck. In their ear lobes the Yao wear huge loops of silver, and around their necks a solid silver necklace about the thickness of your thumb. If they are wealthy, they frequently wear two or three of these heavy necklaces.

The Yao coats looked like the full-dress tails that we wear for formal occasions. But instead of lapels they had long rolls of tufted red material, not unlike yarn. This coat is worn next to the skin, without a shirt. It has solid silver buckles. Their pants are heavily embroidered with cotton in intricate designs. They are held up by taking the coat tails and wrapping them around the waist to form a thick belt. The pants come to just below the knees. Of course, they were barefoot.

The Thai Dam girls were the prettiest of them all. They wear their black hair in a tight bun. Into this they frequently stick large silver pins with bells and bangles on them. These pins also serve as ear picks. They wear a tight-fitting blouse buttoned all the way from neck to waist with beautiful squares of silver. Their long tight skirts are gracefully folded around their slim hips. At the bottom of the skirt there is a wide band of heavy embroidery, sometimes done with gold and silver threads.

The Kha Kho tribal women wear heavy rings in their ears, too; more often, their ear lobes were only yawning holes circled by a string of stretched flesh. These support huge, egg-sized knobs of gold or silver, their life savings. The Kha Kho men, like the Thai Dam and Yao men, frequently have a wispy black mustache, no more than a hundred hairs. These droop from the corners of their mouths. They look like Tartar tribesmen, but their soft eyes bespeak the mysticism of Asian holy men.

The Thai Neua dress like the Chinese with high mandarin collars, except that they added a white turban. The men of the Yao, Thai, and Chinese races wear the long classic pigtail of hair. It is said that the origin of the pigtail dates to the time of the conquest of this part of the world by Kublai Khan, who ordered all the men to grow long pigtails. With a cord of hair like this, a passing horseman could grasp it and lop off the man's head with his sword easier than if there was no pigtail to grasp.

All these mountain tribes are good and gentle people. Perhaps they sometimes hid a vicious spirit, but rarely did we see it. They are infinitely patient and possess qualities of devotion to family that are magnificent.

The new boys were improving each day, learning the things that needed to be learned and frequently things that should not have been learned. Of this last genre was the ability to start the "village symphony". Pete and Chai were the members of this late show. Late at night while all the village was in bed, Chai would beat his arms against his body and cackle like a flapping rooster. Pete, in another bedroom, would cock his ear, listen attentively and cackle back like a not-very-ladylike hen. Then Chai would call again and in a few minutes all the roosters and hens in the village would join in. The success of this symphony was directly proportional to the number of chickens singing. Unfortunately, this happened too successfully and too often for my sleep.

We had a great deal of livestock around our house at various times. At intervals we had monkeys, gibbons, parakeets, anteaters, a baby wildcat, a baby panther, a baby bear and other less easily identifiable pets. Our house also boasted free-roaming and not too pleasant rats and bats. The rats were the largest I have ever seen. You could slip a saddle on these animals and enter them into the Kentucky Derby. On the middle of the dining-room table we had a large tray on which we kept salt, pepper, catsup and other condiments. At night the rats would climb up on this table and raid the tray. We found it necessary to build a large wire-mesh to keep this tray covered up. Another time a rat fell into the water barrel and drowned; we found him there in the morning.

The bats were equally bad. They would circle our living room at night while we were trying to write letters. Though not vampires or biting bats, they certainly were a sickening nuisance. John decided one time to try to trap them with the wire-mesh cover that was used on the dining-room table. He did catch one, but this did not alleviate the condition very much.

One of the most trying things to endure was the inability ever to get away from each other. There was absolutely nothing to do but work and sleep. It was difficult to read by the bleating kerosene lamps, and the heat was too enervating. There was no local movie house, bowling alley, or bar. The boys usually spent the evenings making up surgical packs or writing letters. I always had a great deal of correspondence. I never knew that letter writing could become such a pleasure. I found myself becoming more intimate at a distance than I did or would become when I met friends face to face. In the quiet of a jungle night one can write of deeper hopes and fears, and perhaps bind friends with a tough fiber of understanding than at close hand. I am afraid my letters were not always pleasant. They, like the land of Asia, were full of misery and wretchedness and nobility. Our life and my letters told of hideous death and the magnificence of a simple people. To those who had to endure these long epistles I can only beg them to "be to my virtues very kind, to my faults a little blind."

Along with numerous night calls another thing that prevented uninterrupted sleep was the frequent nocturnal visit of some huge water buffalo. We had a fence around our place and a wooden gate to boot. But the gate was seldom closed and during the night the meandering water buffaloes would frequently drop in for a snack of green grass. If a calf would stray away from the mother, the old lady would bellow and order it to return. A plaintive wail would burst forth from Junior, and that would start the chickens up, which would make the dogs start barking, and on and on. These sound like trivial things, but they become mammoth when you're trying to get some rest. As long as we could continue to laugh at these things, we could continue to do our work, though sometimes it took dogged perseverance.

Whenever an airplane came to Nam Tha we became as excited as the mountain people. We would always run over to the airstrip. The French pilots who flew these small craft would swoop low over our house to indicate that they had something for us. Sometimes these pilots would bring French bread—a real treat. Their wheezing little planes were miraculous. They always managed to make it safely from Vientiane to Nam Tha and back, though it was difficult to think of one mechanical reason why they should; one plane was appropriately called "Le Peut-être" or "The Maybe". Once the pilots handed us a small bag but told us not to open it until we went back to the house. We were delighted to find bread, cognac and canned butter, and laughed at their note: "French Aid for the Underprivileged Americans of Nam Tha."

I can think of no event in Lao life surrounded by more superstition and tradition than the simple birth of a child. This is not unique with the Lao; in all primitive societies the birth of a baby is usually surrounded with a great deal of necromancy and custom. This combination makes very difficult any advancement into a more modern world.

The Lao calendar is not the same as that of the West. As a consequence, I could never take the woman's word on just when the baby would be born. Rarely did anyone know. In Laos the people believe that "when the fruit is ripe, it will drop."

All of my boys became good midwives, for them a talent of debatable value. I believe even Boatswain's Mate Baker could handle a delivery if he had to. Just a week after the new men arrived, I had to leave them alone in Nam Tha for a few days. Pete was breaking them in well. In Vientiane I received this cable: "All's fine, spent last night in labor, a boy for Bob and a girl for me."

John said that he was nervous enough during a delivery, but those sorcerers beating drums nearly drove him mad. Bob once spent twelve hours sitting and waiting, but after all, the woman had waited nine months.

When we were called at night, we hitched our miner's lights to our heads and bicycled to a nearby village. These lamps were like headlights that strapped on and had a long cord attached to eight batteries that we carried in a case in our pocket. The light was strong and ideal for the trail. During the delivery they worked well too, leaving our hands free. Sometimes we almost blinded each other.

There was an Oriental "reticence" to a delivery in Laos. It was as natural as God meant it to be. There was modesty, but much less than there would be in the States. All during the delivery, the family walks around the house, cooking soup for the other children, chewing betel-nut, drinking hot tea and wailing occasionally to show their empathy for the woman in labor. The other family members were just shadows, but we could smell their presence and feel their body heat.

No statistics exist on fetal mortality for Laos but I would estimate them to be about like this: Fifty per cent of pregnancies do not go to completion. Of one hundred babies conceived, only fifty will be born alive. Of these fifty, twenty will die during infancy, from smallpox, cholera, malnutrition, whooping cough, or pneumonia. Of the thirty left, ten will die during childhood from malaria, trauma or dysentery. The twenty remaining will live to be ninety years old.

During a pregnancy there were many regulations that the mother must follow. Some were sensible, many were not. For example, an expectant mother may never eat bananas, honey or egg plant. From the time pregnancy begins she may not put on jewelry or participate in any Love Courts, Lam Vongs or Bacis. She was forbidden to sit on the top step of any staircase. (This last is not so foolish, as the staircases leading into Lao houses are usually just an inclined ladder, with bamboo rungs. Even I have fallen off these.) Every day when the woman bathes in the river she was supposed to brush her hair with eels if any were available. This is to facilitate delivery.

The Lao skirt is hemmed on the bottom with a wide band of beautifully woven designs, sometimes intricately ladened with silver and gold threads. The rest of the skirt is just a cloth tube. During her pregnancy the Lao woman must never hang her skirt up to dry in any but the "normal position." If the skirt is hung upside down the child may present itself in the wrong position. There are certain invocations that a good Buddhist girl must recite during her pregnancy. Simply because she is pregnant is no excuse for her to avoid her work.

I have delivered after the women had spent the day decorticating rice, weaving, or working in the fields. This is good. Hard work keeps the child small, and with the mother being on her feet continuously, the baby is in a head-down position. The squatting posture of Asians also helps the pelvic musculature, facilitating deliveries. Primitive women have their children easier than others. There is no mixing of races here; no Swedish girl with a French mother and married to an Irishman with Scotch ancestry. Because it is a Lao married to a Lao, the child is fitted well to the pelvis from which he must make his exit.

When it was obvious that delivery will soon ensue the father called for all family members to come to the house and help. A birth was a family affair. The mother was put over in a corner, in a certain part of the house, facing the south, towards the religious capital, Luang Prabang. Some old snag-tooth sorceress was the midwife. When she entered the house she was given, as an offering, a small silver bowl with three fruits. Later, when we Americans became assistants to the sorceress, we got the fruits.

The first thing the witch doctor did was to rub betel nut oil, perfumes, orange rinds, and other "medicaments" onto the mother's abdomen and forehead in hopes of helping the obstetrical procedure. All the neighboring women came and sat in one part of the house chatting, and occasionally moaning, groaning, grunting and gasping, in order to help the poor mother.

The men sat outside the house around a huge fire. The only men allowed inside were the wise men of the village who set up musical instruments in a corner. They lit candles, and banged on the drums throughout the whole delivery. The hut was packed to suffocation. The stifling odors that arose from the sweating bodies blended with the smoke from the indoor fire. Therefore the primary requirement for a newborn child, oxygen, was a rare commodity. The mother's misery was augmented by the kindness of her friends.

The young woman was squatting on a small stool, clinging to a loop of rope hanging from the ceiling. In this strung-up position, she labored. The fact that she was sitting on the baby's head did not seem to register with them.

The Lao woman tried to breathe deeply through her mouth as she had been told that this will bring air to her child. The intention involved was better than the physiology. The crowd of family wailing and crying stole any stray bit of air that might have been laying around the hut.

The first thing we did when we were called was to greet the relatives and villagers outside the house, chat a moment, then go inside and empty the house. Only a few members of the immediate family, about fifteen, were allowed to remain. Then, with a minimum of kibitzing we could do our work.

We bowed toward the sorcerers over in the corner who were still beating their drums. Then we went to the woman in labor. It was absolutely impossible for me to lie on the floor to deliver a child. So we had the woman lie down. This always caused much consternation, but a grunt of approval from the sorceress doubling as midwife, accomplished the transfer of position. Again, much fuss about the direction of the head, the side of the house, and presence or absence of more relatives.

Chai took up his post with a large flashlight at the foot of the mat, issuing orders like Admiral Stump. And the people obeyed. We examined the girl to find out how things were coming along. We then struggled for a few moments with two or three skirts that the woman had snugly wrapped around her. Fine, shouldn't be much of a wait. So the sorceress and I discussed techniques. It was very dangerous if we did anything to offend these sorceresses. They have an important place in their community, and we could bring all hell down upon us if we made them lose face.

I would mention that the head was in this position and about this much dilation. Chai always explained that having a baby while lying down is the American way, and much less painful. (It is because we have given the woman a Demerol tablet.) Also some penicillin pills, and plenty of vitamins and iron.

As we had some time to spare, this was the opportune moment to talk to all the women in the house about various factors important to clean deliveries. But first there was a custom that must now be observed. On the woman's pelvis, over the baby's head, the sorceress had to sprinkle a little dirt from the earth. This is to infuse into the baby the spirits that live in the earth; the good earth wherein are the bones of their ancestors, wherein are the genii who shall come to the baby's life. I did not object to this practice. It would make little difference if I did. But I asked that they dump the dirt early. After they finished, I scrubbed the woman with soap and water, with as much splashing and commenting as possible. I pointed out that because the dirt of the centuries was the more important, it was sprinkled on first. Then my soap.

In our CARE midwife kits we have packets which contained a small triangular piece of muslin to be used as a baby cloth, some gauze and a cord tie. This was laid out, with as much sterility as possible, always explaining what we were doing, and asking if the sorceress did not approve of the American technique. She nodded her head in solemn agreement. We sometimes had the sorceress scrub her hands and assist us (after she spat out her wad of betel nut). Over in the corner the friends were still beating on the drums, the fire still burned, smoke was as thick as in a Manhattan nightclub and the odors overpowering. But we are beginning to stink by this time ourselves, so "Bau pinh yanh".

Anesthesia was unheard of. The mother was given a few bamboo jiggers of local rice wine and I added a mild narcotic. Various leaves and herbs were applied to the mother's nostrils because it was felt that a fit of sneezing helps labor. It certainly adds to the discomfort, though oddly enough it has certain therapeutic value. During all this time the husband was sitting at the head of the mat holding the wife's face in his hands, and blowing into her ear. Don't forget, the baby needs air.

During the last few minutes of labor all the women in the hut (and me too) would begin to shout "bing bing bing!" And the woman bings and bings, "pushing" as hard as she can. The child was born, to the great relief of the family, doctor, husband and oh yes, mother too.

When the delivery was complete, the newborn baby was immediately handed over to the sorceress who was holding the sterile muslin. The hemostat clip was left on the umbilical cord.

In Laos it is felt that after the baby is delivered, all is finished. The mother is wrapped up in a clean skirt and put to bed. The placenta is ignored. As a consequence, hemorrhage is extremely common. We explained the error in this, and demonstrated the proper delivery of the placenta *"à l'americaine."* Then according to the Lao custom, we called for the bamboo. We placed the placenta in this hollow piece of bamboo and it was later buried under the front steps of the house. This is to bring brothers and sisters for the newborn child. The mother is fine, so attention is turned to junior.

Now custom demands the village elder to cut the baby's cord with two pieces of sharp bamboo. I did not object to this at all. We had learned by now. I first clipped the cord and tied it off with sterile ligature. From that point outward, the village elder can do all he wants. After he cut it with bamboo, he then rubbed ashes on the end of the umbilical cord. All this of course is distal to my sterile knot. Black, red and white cotton cords were tied around the wrists of the mother and child, invoking specific phantoms to come with their blessings.

There were then other rites of birth. A small ball of rice and pork was put behind each ear of the child. This was so that he shall never be hungry. The father wrapped the child in his *pakamo*, the sarong-like skirt. If the child was a boy, the father put into this swaddling bundle an article of labor. He wished him to be courageous, so he placed a small knife there too. If he had wished him to be studious he would have placed a writing brush; if a hunter, a crossbow and arrow. If the child had been a girl, a small gourd, or article of the loom, would have been placed in the bundle. The rice alcohol was then passed around, and everyone rejoiced. The husband gave us four coconuts as our payments. We kept two and gave two to our "assistant" the sorceress. This husband, as at home, managed to look as exhausted as his wife, but I think it was only show (in both instances). It is said that there are some tribes over in Burma that get the husband into the act in a more meaningful way. During the wife's labor, the husband is hung by his feet, outside of the house.

SEVEN ·

THE FELLOWSHIP OF PAIN

Each morning I walked into the hospital compound with the feeling that I was traveling backward in time to a disease-ridden world that had ceased to exist long before I was born.

Ironically, I was always reminded of what the profs had told us in medical school: "We can now look upon leprosy, gentlemen, as a disease belonging to the Biblical era. . . . These yaws, dysenteries, and worm infestations you will probably never encounter in civilian practice. . . . We may say that the terrors of diphtheria, typhoid, smallpox vanished with the advent of modern vaccine therapy. . . ."

Ah, yes! But here they are—with others even more terrible—crowded into my own "waiting room"—the commonplace problems of any average day. True, this is Asia in the 20th Century. But not the 20th Century that western man knows!

Sick-call in Nam Tha was much more difficult than in Vang Vieng. Our patients were more numerous. The diseases were more varied, more severe. Ignorance and superstition were more prevalent. Traumatic injuries, often neglected or mistreated, made surgery a 'round the clock nightmare. Usually the symptoms were of the kind which are apparent to the naked eye. There were pregnant mothers, frequently tuberculars, carrying small children foul with smallpox or covered with sores. There were doddering oldsters with yaws, or swollen spleens, or wasting with leprosy. Then there were always the pathetic kids with skinny arms and legs, pinched faces, and enormous bellies.

We were often dealing with critical health problems born of colossal ignorance. These people have become so inured to disease, which is simply a part of their existence, that they speak of *kia tamada*, "normal fever."

Malaria, for example, is a normal fever. You just live with it until, eventually, the spleen and liver are greatly enlarged and as hot as stones left out in the noonday sun.

They have lived on the edge of starvation for so long (despite the availability of natural nourishment) that their bodies have lost the capacity to store vitamins, fats, proteins. Only a few days' illness can throw the system into negative balance.

We pumped them full of vitamins, and passed out huge quantities of that heaven-sent MPF provided by Meals for Millions. I was often tempted to start hygiene classes, such as we held so successfully in Vang Vieng. But in Nam Tha there wasn't time. Sometimes it seemed that every other case I saw at sick-call required some kind of surgery, and my schedule grew top-heavy.

So we did the best we could. Sick-call itself became the classroom, and each case served as a lesson. Naturally a garrulous Irishman, I talked incessantly, but as simply as possible, for hours on end. Chai and Si, Maggie and Old Joe, the nurses and the coolies would jabber away in the various dialects. Thus, we tried to make the crowd in the yard understand why this woman or child was suffering, and how the suffering could have been avoided.

The people listened with wide-eyed attention. They were eager to learn. I could see in their faces what I am convinced is universal truth: No one really *wants* to be sick and miserable. Even the most "backward" people, given half a chance, will follow simple rules in order to be healthier and stronger.

So I think our sick-call "lectures" really did some good. Of course, the multi-lingual bedlam made those hours that much harder on our frazzled nerves. Fortunately, none of us had ever expected them to be easy.

One morning early in March a small plane swooped low over our compound and then headed for the landing strip. We knew it had come to take Denny Shepard on the first leg of his long journey home, back to the States and his long-suffering little bride.

With a lump in my throat, I asked one of the Lao nurses to take over and went outside. Denny had made us promise that there would be no farewell ceremonies. We were to carry on as usual. He just shook hands all 'round, and picked up his gear which was tied to both ends of a native balance-pole. We watched him trudge down the Main Drag, then he turned and waved before taking the trail to the airstrip. I would miss Denny Shepard sorely. He was a born doctor, and I always felt better when he was working across the surgical table from me. Now things were going to be different.

Pete Kessey was now the only one left of the original three, and his time was running out fast. Chai, fortunately, had developed into a dependable assistant. Thanks to Denny's tutelage he was now almost as good as any trained hospital corpsman. John deVitry and Bob Waters were catching on fast, and made good "circulating nurses" in the operating room. We had seven Lao nurses in training, four men and three girls. They were now familiar with my requirements. But I always had to watch myself in dealing with them, particularly when we were working under stress.

"Face" is a sensitive thing in the East. It means more than pride, personal dignity, or self-respect. With my taut nerves and terrible Irish temper, I was inclined to say things that would not only offend but cause the Lao to "lose face." And now I needed all the help I could get.

Surgery had become my heaviest burden. Scarcely a day passed without its quota of emergencies—a man who had been mauled by a bear; a kid whose hand had been blown off while playing with a live cartridge left over from the war; a worker who had virtually chopped a foot off while cutting bamboo in the jungle. But the cases that really taxed my skill as a young and inexperienced surgeon simply turned up in the line at sick-call. Some I would have to send away as hopeless. More often, and against my better judgment, I would say to Chai or Bob, "Put it down for surgery—first date open." Thus, instead of diminishing, my operating schedule grew longer by the day.

On the day Denny left, for example, a dignified Thai Dam tribesman came escorting his young daughter, a lovely girl with exquisite features, dark eyes, and perfectly groomed black hair in a chignon worn at the nape of the neck (indicating, according to Thai Dam custom, that she had not yet found her man). With an apprehensive look in his eye, the father explained that for years her feet and legs had been covered with sores that never healed. He lifted the ankle-length skirt, and on the legs were raised bronze plaques of tissue. When I saw the huge, bloated, ulcerous legs my heart sank.

There were no knee or ankle reflexes. I took a scalpel and jabbed it into the foot, the ankle, then keep into the calf of the leg. She never winced. I needed no laboratory test to confirm the diagnosis. It was leprosy. We got at least a half-dozen new cases every month. There was little I could do for this lovely girl except clean up the secondary infections and administer palliatives. We didn't have the facilities for long-term disulfone therapy.

Then a man appeared with a wife who had an enormous purple tumor, about the size of a tangerine, hanging from her lower lip. The husband begged me to remove the horrible thing. They were both unmoved when I explained that the operation was difficult and dangerous. Actually, I had never performed such an operation, and had only a vague recollection of the procedure described in the textbooks. But the growth was already corrupt, and infection on the face is extremely dangerous. I decided to take a chance.

After several days on antibiotics to clear up the infection, the woman was given heavy sedation and a local anesthetic. I made what I hoped was the "classic" V-shaped incision, removed the tumor, and did as neat a job as possible of reconstructing the vermillion border of the lip. Since I had no laboratory for pathology, I had to assume that the tumor was malignant and trust to God that I had got it all.

Some weeks later we discharged the woman, healed and happy. The lower face was taut and crooked; but then I hadn't hoped for any masterpiece of plastic surgery. The husband looked upon it as a miracle. Later, I learned that he was mayor of a village some miles distant and quite an influential fellow in the valley. He did a lot to spread the word that the white medicine-men in Nam Tha were to be counted among Buddha's blessings.

I am sure that Denny will remember "Harriet." He has no way of knowing, however, that after his departure she became part of a beautiful and compassionate episode which the rest of us will always remember as the story of Harriet and Paul.

Harriet was not her real name. The boys had a habit of Anglicizing unpronounceable Lao names, and of bestowing entirely new names when that was difficult or impossible. This pathetic young mother, about 20 years old, was a Kha, a people who once were slaves and now comprise the Lao servant class—the humblest "hewers of wood and drawers of water." So they called her Harriet.

She came to us on a litter, delirious and in a condition too horrible to describe. I had seen women before who had been mutilated in childbirth, but none like Harriet. Even her bladder had been torn and her bowels ruptured. She needed many weeks of emergency treatment and pre-operative care. After that came a series of operations extending over many months.

When Denny left in March Harriet seemed more like a human being. She was still in bed, suffering considerable pain and discomfort, with a catheter in her bladder and a rubber tube connecting it with a container on the floor. But she was on the mend when we placed Paul in the ward across from her.

Paul was a terminal cancer case. The disease had eaten away his pelvis and extended up into the abdomen. We could do no more than excise the tumors, and give him sedatives. He would improve some, then, in a few weeks, the malignant process would light up again with even greater fury.

Harriet and Paul required much more nursing care than we were able to give them. But we could do just so much and no more. However, out of the pain and suffering of these two miserable strangers, a beautiful and compassionate relationship was born. When the sedation wore off, Paul would moan and writhe in agony. Harriet would struggle out of bed, sling the catheter tube over her shoulder, and come to fix Paul's pillows, and comfort and feed him.

Then Paul would have his "good days." He would insist upon taking care of Harriet. Once, when he felt particularly strong, he was missing from the ward. The Lao nurse found him down at the river's edge laboriously washing out some of Harriet's soiled garments.

At last, Harriet was well enough to be discharged. She went to work as a laundress in the village. But she was unable to pay anything for all the care she had received. So, remembering that pride is strong even among the lowly Kha, we accepted her offer to work in the hospital as part-time cleaning woman and attendant. There she spent most of her evenings. Paul, who now needed constant care, became her special charge.

I was in the distant mountain village of Ban Phu Van when death brought a merciful end to Paul's suffering. The Lao nurses told me later that Harriet was at his bedside to the very end. They were as deeply moved as I was by the devotion of these two people. We had been privileged to glimpse the true nobility of what Albert Schweitzer calls "The Fellowship of Those Who Bear the Mark of Pain."

Wild animals created constant havoc in the surrounding jungles. Everyone had been talking about tigers lately, and the boys wanted a day off to go tiger-hunting. We had no time for days off. I would have liked a tiger rug, but I could picture a Dooley-skin rug in some tiger's lair. One day about dawn we were shaken from our cots by a boy jabbering something in machine-gun Lao. We heard just one word, "sua" which means "tiger." (In different tones it also means "shirt," and "buy.") We had visions of some horribly mauled child lying in a pool of blood. After Chai cleared his head enough to interpret for us, we found that the boy's father had just shot a tiger, and he wished to give it to us. With much joy we went to the man's village. He had bagged a splendid three-hundred-pound tiger measuring seven feet from tail to nose. The villagers pointed out to us that there were many nicks in the tiger's ears; they claimed that this was proof that at some time this animal had eaten a human being. I could see no physiological relationship between a nicked ear and a digested human being, but I did not argue.

Another extremely dangerous animal is the wild boar. When the animal sees a person, instead of running away he will always lunge at the individual. To hunt them the Lao find a narrow clear strip like a trail or a path. Then villagers form a line and, almost shoulder to shoulder, walk through the jungle beating their drums and yelling. The boar runs ahead, finally crossing the cleared path. There, up in a tree, the hunter sits with an old musket or flintlock.

One man had not yet climbed up the tree when a boar lumbered out of the jungle into the clearing. As soon as he saw the man, he attacked. The boar is the size of a very large hog and has two vicious curled teeth, sometimes eight inches in length. The animal immediately downed the native and turned and sank his teeth into the flesh of the man's thigh. The leg was impaled on the curled fangs and as the boar shook his head he threw the man about, ripping the flesh off of the leg. Finally the screaming man tore loose. The boar kept slashing with his teeth until he was finally driven away by the other villagers. They sent a runner to us immediately and told us he was being carried to Nam Tha. Finally he arrived, a mangled man who was almost exsanguinated by this time.

We had to tie off the femoral vein at the knee, so severe was the hemorrhaging. The man's right hand was mutilated beyond all hope of repair. We just cleaned it, cut away the dead tissue and closed it. No consideration could be given to any later function. It was just a glob of tissue and tendon. Antibiotics, anti-gangrene and antitetanus syrum prevented too much infection. Many, many weeks later the young fellow could walk though we had a difficult time coaxing him to extend his leg. It was still painful and there was some tendon shortening. Months later he returned to visit us and was walking with only a slight limp. His right hand had healed all right, but it was completely useless, a limp appendage hooked to a forearm.

Such is life for the people of the jungle. I personally lived to a certain extent in a state of fear all the time I was in Laos. Fear of isolation, fear of loneliness, and fear of the great and ominous rain-forest. I believe that only a stupid man is bold in the jungle. The snakes, leeches, bloodsuckers, tigers, wild boar, bats, mosquitoes malignant with malaria—the presence of these quickly abolishes any primitive thrill of adventure and replaces it with an alarming dread.

As the months passed, there was an occasional evening when sickness and death seemed to take a respite, although never for long. Then I liked to wander around the town of Nam Tha, greeting friends and neighbors, and nursing in my heart a secret joy. We were Americans, our skins were white, our speech and manners and habits were different. But we weren't strangers or curiosities any more. We "belonged."

At the base of the big triangle which was the "town square" (or the Main Drag, as the boys called it), we hung a huge sheet, 180 square feet overall, between the trees. This served as our movie screen. Directly behind it, the projector was on the front porch of our house, and the amplifiers placed on a tree stump. Thus, on an average evening, as many as 1000 people, squatting on both sides of the screen, could enjoy the movies.

The peddlers set up their stands, lighted by flaming torches and kerosene lamps, along the road and did a thriving business selling Lao sweetmeats, soft drinks, rice-balls with chopped pork, and the strange bugs, bats, and little fishes that are rare delicacies to the Asian taste. Our movies had been a tremendous boon to the trade, and John and Bob grumbled that we ought to get a cut of the profits.

When the show starts, I stroll leisurely down the Main Drag. I pass the Police Headquarters, home of our bodyguards, and greet the weary, mud-caked cops lounging on the porch after a hard day of jungle patrol. I stop before the Buddhist temple, a magnificent pagoda covered with gilt and porcelain, and admire the two angels, exquisitely carved from jade, that flank the steps. Beyond the Buddhist temple is the abode and shop of Mrs. PhoumaSassady, weaver, seamstress, merchant of sorts, and our benefactor and friend.

Mrs. Sassady has another distinction, which Denny Shepard discovered the day we arrived in Nam Tha. She owns the only Singer Sewing Machine in town—an ancient, pedal-operated model, but capable of wonders. Denny brought Mrs. Sassady bolts of linen from our stores, and she hemmed and sewed them for surgical drapes. She has been sewing for us ever since, mending our clothes, and making new garments patterned on the old. She refuses to accept payment. But, knowing that even Americans must "save face," she does accept an occasional chocolate bar. Bless you, Mrs. Sassady!

Across the way there is a line of non-descript and shabby shops, most of them lodged between the stilts of the elevated houses. But halfway down the street we come to the clean and well-stocked "general store" of Sisavath, which is attended by his young son, a student at the lycée in Vientiane, who is now home for the holidays. Young Sisavath, a handsome lad of 15 with a keen mind, speaks excellent French and a few words of American like "Okay," "Thank you very much" and (inevitably) "Atom Bomb."

Next comes the shop of Khuna, the village jeweler, a craftsman who works wonders with silver and gold. Money has little meaning in Nam Tha, and paper money none at all. Gold and silver, yes! But in this land of barter, even precious metal loses some of its basic value. So, instead of hoarding it, the people bring their gold and silver to Khuna, and he converts it into beautiful chains, necklaces, earrings, blouse buttons, and such practical ornaments as toothpicks and ear-cleaners.

A few months ago Khuna fell and sprained his ankle. In addition to the usual strapping, the use of novacain injections is optional in such cases. For some reason, I shot Khuna's painful, swollen ankle with novocain—the long-lasting variety. The immediate cessation of pain astonished him. He showed his appreciation by showering us with beautiful silver chains, bracelets, and ornaments. The boys were delighted. Then I saw a worried look on Bob Water's face. "How about that?" he asked. "Will the novocain wear off before the ankle heals?"

Near the apex of our triangle, where the trail to the airstrip starts, are the houses and shops of our Pakistani community. Jacob, Abdullah, and Ismail wandered across through north Burma, settled in Nam Tha, married Lao women, and fathered huge families of the cutest kids in town. But they cling strictly to their Moslem beliefs. When the rest of the town indulges in the frequent Lao festivals, drinking the local alcohol and eating succulent pork, the Pakistani remain aloof and adhere strictly to their own code. Yet they are congenial and respected members of the community.

Jacob, father of many sons, has a bald head and the long beard of a patriarch. Abdullah is a huge man with an enormous belly; I removed a fibroid tumor from his rear-end and he became my devoted friend. Ismail, a good man, has the dubious honor of running the biggest opium parlor in Nam Tha. Some of my patients are among his best customers—but they are also my most wretched and incurable cases. Probably they enjoy the pipe more than they do my morphine. Under these tragic circumstances I find it hard to blame them.

On the Saturday before Easter, we were busy with sick-call when two tall, rugged characters, obviously Americans, appeared at the hospital and saluted us with a hearty Hello. They introduced themselves as Pastor H. Carl Currie, a slim, balding man of about 40, and Pastor R. C. Hall, a smiling, crew-cut chap in his early thirties. They were both missionaries, of the Seventh Day Adventist Church. Pastor Hall said that when they landed at the airstrip some native had simply picked up their baggage and brought them to us. Where else would a couple of white men be going in Nam Tha?

We found two empty boxes and asked them to sit by while we finished with sick-call. Then we took them over to our house and started a conversation that continued far into that night. With only a break for sleep, chow, chores, and our prayers, we continued talking well into the Easter day.

The Adventists have a fine medical center in Bangkok, and several medical missions in Northern Thailand. Pastor Currie, one of the keenest and most devoted men I've ever met, told me they were exploring the possibilities of setting up a mission in Laos. He kept plying me with questions, and I told him all I knew about conditions in the central and northern parts of the country.

On Easter Sunday while we were eating lunch, we suddenly remembered a promise we had made several days previously, to circumcise a few of the Pakistani boys in our village. According to the Islam calendar this particular Sunday was a "felicitous" one for them, and we had been requested to perform the ceremony on each child whose age was on the even year. We expected to nip through this procedure in a few minutes. Then we discovered how prolific the Pakistani really were. I have forgotten the number but we did over seven circumcisions that afternoon. They were not all infants, so complete surgical procedures had to be done. Far after dark we crawled back to the house and just collapsed. Only to hear Pastor Currie laughing loudly. "Think of it," he said, "Irish Catholics eating lunch with Seventh Day Adventists, on Easter Sunday, performing an ancient Hebrew rite on Moslem children in the Buddhist Kingdom of Laos!"

The more I saw of Pastors Currie and Hall, the more I was convinced that they could perform a wonderful service for Laos, and I encouraged them to try it. Pastor Currie was puzzled by the Lao Government's attitude toward missionaries. I am happy to report that the attitude has officially changed.

One of the greatest festivals during the Buddhist calendar year is the feast of Songkran. This is held on their New Year's Eve. On this day all refuse in the village is burned, and each house is given a thorough cleaning. There is a belief that anything belonging to the previous year must not be carried over to the New Year. This would be unlucky. It is a sort of Public Health Department Cleaning Day, backed by a strong traditional belief. This belief is much more effective than prosaic reasoning would ever be.

Every morning at dawn the Buddhist *bonzes* (priests) bang on the Pagoda gongs. This indicates that they will soon wrap their golden mantles of invisibility around themselves and go into the streets to beg for their food.

With humility that somehow looks haughty, they hold their bowls in the crook of their arm and walk in long lines through the winding lanes of the village. In front of each house, kneeling on one knee, is a member of the family who puts some rice or some cakes into the bowl, and then says "Thank you." The *bonze* says nothing, indeed, if it is a woman who puts the food into his bowl, he cannot even look at her. The belief is that if one gives food to a *bonze* one is storing it for his own life after death. The *bonzes* are only the intermediaries.

But on the feast of Songkran the *bonzes* do not go out into the village. Rather, the food is brought to them in the Pagoda. In 1957 the Buddhist New Year's Day celebration fell on the 12th of April. Early on the 13th several days of feasting began. The long tables built at the Pagoda were loaded with food, rice, fruits, meats and a local orchestra played the khenes, cymbals, and of course the drums.

All the Buddha images were bathed, and the Abbot of the Pagoda was given a ceremonial bath. The young people of the village poured scented water into the palms of the older people, then presenting them with a towel. Chai tells me that in the former days the young people actually assisted the elders in their bath and to change their clothes. But this was too old-fashioned for the Buddhist year 2500.

The rest of the day, and for several after, the holiday spirit ran amuck. The strangest things are done on these days. For example, if you are liked, and someone wishes to express their liking, they throw a large gourd of water over you. Unfortunately we found we were well-beloved. As we would walk down the road a heretofore shy little girl would come out of her house and thoroughly douse us with water. But this is magic; the girl is hoping that we will have an abundant rain in the ensuing monsoon season, and this rain will bring a good season of cultivation. The pouring of water so abundantly over each other is a sort of wet prayer that we will have much water for our fields.

During this season many stories are told to the village children. Most of them have to do with water. The ancient legend I remember best concerns the mythical serpents, called Nagas, who lived in a lake in the Himalaya fairyland of Anavatapta. Their main source of sport was to float around on the lake's surface and spout water through their long snouts. This water would then rise to the heavens and fall to the earth as rain. On feast days these serpents were fed in hopes that they would be happy, spout a lot, and bring much rain for the season. So the New Year's celebrations in both America and Laos are Wet Feasts.

During all the various Buddhist feasts, great festivals were held. These gentle people love a party. They would have boat races, Lam Vongs, love courts, *bacis,* and the orchestras would play until late in the night. The balladeers would chant their sing-song themes of love, heroism, history, and fantastic stories of ancient legends. And I've a sneaking suspicion, judging from their grimaces, that they sometimes sang about the American medical team that had come to their land.

We noticed that many trees in the village had been gaily decorated for Songkran, while others were ignored. It was explained that the trees that were covered with spangles and baubles were "bo" trees. This tree is the symbol of the Lord Buddha's enlightenment, for it was under a "bo" tree that Buddha sat in meditation, and received his third eye of inner vision.

During this season of the year many love courts are held, and this was a place where we could always find our interpreters and nurses, just as we first found Chai.

The supplies were still holding out, though I did write to Pfizer for some refills. They sent me all the more I needed. Meals for Millions sent me some more protein powder. Here this powder was referred to as *"Ya mi henh."* The vitamins, being a solution, were called *"Ya mi henh nam"* while the powder did not get the word "nam" added to it. *"Ya"* means medicine. *"Mi"* is "to have." *"Henh"* means "great strength."

The people of this country live on the edge of starvation. They seem to have no storage element for vitamins, fats or proteins. Only a few days of illness throws them into negative balance. Beri beri, a vitamin B-1 deficiency, was our most frequent complaint. Vitamin deficiencies were also the cause of much of our eye problems. Deca-Vi-Sol was given to nearly every patient who came to our sick-call. Meals for Millions was given to all who seemed to need "strength." This included the naked, shining, pot-bellied children, the pregnant tubercular women, and the oldsters plagued with yaws, malaria or other sicknesses.

I tried to get the parents to bring the children to me as soon as they became sick or developed a fever. But they did not understand this. As I have explained, they considered many fevers as "normal" and it was almost impossible to convince them that there was no such thing as *kia tamada.* By the time we would get the child he would be plunged into beri beri, if not something even more serious. The basic fight in Laos is ignorance, not disease.

In Vang Vieng we had formal classes in the village school three times a week. We taught the rudiments of hygiene and sanitation. In Nam Tha, as the lines were longer and surgery more time-consuming, we could not have these formal classes. But we held sick-call in such a way that each case we discussed became a class. All the waiting line would be huddled on the porch. When a child would be placed before us with this or that malady, we would instruct the mother on the care or prevention of such a sickness. All of the crowd sitting before the open doors on the porch would listen attentively to what we would say. They were eager to learn. They do not wish to be miserable. They want to progress and be healthier. They fully realize that they need not always be sick.

The best way to teach an Asian is through another Asian. We did this through our nurses and midwives. We taught them the use of our equipment, bandages and solutions. We taught them the way to deliver children without lacerations, infections or blindness. Then we gave them the CARE midwife kits to use themselves. We instructed the Army corpsmen with the small military group at Nam Tha. We then gave them the medical kits needed. Occasionally village chieftains would send someone down to us for a few days to learn a few facts about treating fevers or whatever was plaguing the village that week. We would teach, give the implements and medicines and send them back. In importance, teaching ranks next to surgery. In time consumption, it was about fifty per cent of the day. But rarely was it the lecture such as you visualize in America. We would often take a homemade blackboard to a village and gather all around for a talk about deliveries, or malaria, or the relationship between dirt and disease. But far more effective was the living illustration of a pathetic little child, followed by explanation to all in the clinic (and there would be over a hundred daily).

We once had a Thai Neua come to us from North Burma. This tribe live on the Western China-Burma frontier. He had a puncture wound of the foot which had been longstanding, and now most of his foot was one gaping red-crusted cavern. It exuded the worse stink I have ever known. All the tendons of his toes and ankle were scarred and shortened, and he could walk only with the help of a strong cane. If he had been a wizened old man, he could not have walked at all. We asked him how many days it took to travel to us. He said, "A great many." He said that our work was known even that far up in the western hills. Evidently our candle was giving a good light.

Every week Chinese came down from the Yunnan and Canton. They were really political refugees. They were living under the new Chinese Communist land reforms, and were being taxed accordingly. Much as they might not have liked the former regime, the new "agrarian reformers" were not living up to their promises. Though they had no religious quarrel with

Communism, as the Catholics of North Viet Nam had, nevertheless they wanted to move out of that part of the world. Many had *parentage* in North Laos, and they would trickle down to this village.

The refugees I remember with the most tenderness is an old couple who came all the way from Canton. We took care of them, gave them blankets, medicines, and *"Ya mi henh."* The Governor gave them a small hut not too far from his. Weeks later this old Chinese came to our house and gave me a gift. As I was a mandarin, for my size 11-C feet he had made a pair of black cloth Chinese shoes about size seven.

A very rich Chinese once came down from Muong Sing, on the Burma border. He brought his attractive fifteen-year-old daughter who was cursed with a huge harelip. We repaired her and after her discharge from the ward, they disappeared into the underbelly of China. The Chao Khuong claims that he was a Red Chinese Army Officer. All we know is that he was very cooperative and most appreciative of what the Americans had done for his daughter. We transformed her from a somewhat hideous little girl to a very acceptable one. I think it will be more difficult for him to hate us now.

The constant escape of these people in China is symptomatic of the ulcer of unrest that is eating into China. Perhaps some day the sadistic murder, fury and fear of Communism will flood the land with too much blood. Perhaps the blueprint for terror which now wracks the land of China will be tossed aside and the people will revolt, demanding their freedom. Without pontificating, I pray that America will stand up and help such people in China as the relatives of the old shoemaker. We must. History teaches that we must. The cynic might say that the only lesson which history teaches is that mankind learns nothing from it.

Our surgery was just about as busy as any operating room of comparable size in the states. We once had a young man who had been hacking bamboo from the jungle to be used in building his home. His large machete-like knife hit a green bamboo and skewered off it, slicing deeply into his ankle. He severed most of his Achilles' tendon, with only a little bleeding. He was brought to us, and we were able to approximate the tendon ends and the sheath, and cast him in an extended position. Many months later we saw him, and he had regained nearly complete control of his leg.

Late one afternoon in May we saw two young people running across the compound to our building. Breathlessly they said that a child was coming with his hand blown off. Within a few minutes he was at the hospital. There was very little bleeding, but the whole face, abdomen and hand were peppered with black powder. And where the hand should have been was just a blasted blob of tissue. The boy had found an old cartridge in the jungle, probably something left over from the war. Just like boys in America, wondering what it was, he banged it on a rock. The explosion tore off much of his right hand, put out his right eye, and powder-burned all his belly. He was in the operating-room within hours after the accident. Because of the proper medicines, he did not develop gas gangrene, one of our most hideous visitors.

With Bob and John assisting, and Chai circulating, we amputated the finger stumps and disarticulated the small bones of the hand. We injected novocain into the nerve roots and double ligated the larger vessels. After a thorough cleansing we were able to close four-fifths of the wound, allowing just a small tube for drainage. Function was not even hoped for. We were able to get good results, and the hand healed well. For the eye there was nothing we could do. He lost an eye and a hand, but he was grateful for his life.

Just a few days later we had had a mail delivery from America and I had received one of the most touching letters I believe ever written. It was from a woman who said that she was "dying" from bone cancer but "no one tells me so." She said that the excruciating deep agony in her leg and arm bones was a great cross for her to endure. But she said that she was glad she had pain because she wanted to offer it to God in order to gain grace for "people like you boys." To me it was the power of her prayers that gave us sufficient talent, time and medicines to effect a cure for a little lad with shattered bones.

We repaired a lot of harelips. It is not any more common in Laos than anywhere else, but the problem is that the word spread around the mountains that the white medical team could cure this congenital defect. Sometimes we would get as many as five and six each week. Most of them were young adults, and we could operate under regional anesthesia, mobilize all the tissue of the cheek, and get a good closure. An adult patient is usually cooperative and cosmetic results are excellent. However, with kids it was really a fight. With the howling children we had to use open drip ether along with novocain. After the child was deep in anesthesia the mask would be removed and I'd operate as fast as I could, before the youngster began to awaken. Every few minutes I'd stop cutting while my assistants would put a sterile towel over the child's face and give some more ether. The children sputtered and spouted from time to time, but the majority of the repairs came out remarkably well.

Chai once told me that he had been in the market place and heard a child describing an operation. This child was born with a hideous harelip.

He was thirteen before the white doctor came to his village. The parents brought him to us immediately, and we scheduled him for surgery. The operation had good results and the only remains of the huge defect was a small line scar. With much ado he was telling his companions of the procedure. "The white witch doctor, the tall one who talks so fast, told his assistants to pick me up. The two assistant witch doctors put me on that long table that they have over in their hospital hut. Then one of the assistants put some sort of charm over my face that looked like a piece of cloth. Then they dripped some horrible sweet smelling magical liquid on my nose. I almost vomited but was soon transported somewhere else, like in a dream. I don't remember anything, but later I woke up in another one of their huts. My family was around, and they had a small piece of metal for me to look in. I saw my face like I can see it reflected in the clear river. The white doctor had pulled my upper lip shut and sewed it up like my mother stitches her sarong. Mother says that she watched them through the window and that I bled all over the place. They collected it in pieces of material and put it all in buckets on the floor. My face was no longer my old face, but a new face just as you see it now. Strange, these white men."

We had no electricity, therefore no X-ray was available. Fractured arms and legs were set by the touch alone. Plenty of plaster and buckets of prayers, and these fractures healed adequately. Gangrene was a constant threat. I remember one man who had been working in the field, and somehow his water buffalo trampled on him. His left arm was fractured, with both bone-ends piercing the skin. This happened in the morning. All that afternoon and the next morning the distant witch doctor did her best, with herbs, cages, cow dung, and incantations. During the night a foul odor exuded from him and dusky irregular dark blotches appeared on the skin.

That next afternoon she sent him to us. By this time gas gangrene had set in. The hand was completely cold, bloated and full of bullae. The forearm and arm were crepitant with subcutaneous gas. Amputation was the only answer. But before this could be done we had to attack the gangrene, and get the man out of the semicomatose condition he was in. The first injection of massive amounts of anti-gangrene serum caused no trouble, but the second dose caused a terrible allergic reaction, nearly resulting in his death. Again plenty of antibiotics, good nursing and adequate amputation, and he returned to his village alive.

We did have happier times in Nam Tha. One of the greatest occasions for us is the day that we introduced something astonishing into the lives of the village kids. We held a track meet. We laid all our plans through the head of the village school. And then dug up prizes. We held three-legged races, fifty-meter dashes, tug-of-wars, and other "advancements" of our civilization. For prizes we distributed every Hershey bar, pencil and calendar that we had. We even had some propaganda photos of the King of Laos. These we gave to the top winners. Then each winning child also had his picture taken with our polaroid camera. This was a permanent memento of his day of glory.

The anti-whiteman propaganda that the Communists so deftly injected into these villages along the China border was partially dissolved in our solutions of terramycin and Deca-Vi-Sol. But I believe track meets, village parties, movies, and rough-housing with the children helped as much.

John, Bob and I are Catholics. In the isolation of the north there are no priests, though on two occasions during our time at work, an Oblate missionary came to visit us. It was good to have our hut of a house transformed into a church of God during the thirty minutes that the priest offered holy Mass. I have attended Masses in the most magnificent cathedrals of the world, in many of the nations on the earth. I've heard sermons in most of the languages of Europe, and several of Asia. But never did the words seem to take on such a meaning, never was there such a profound depth to this meaning as when a small French missionary genuflected before our table-transformed-into-an-altar, and said: "I shall go unto the altar, to the altar of my God. . . ."

The physical layout of our living in Nam Tha was better than Vang Vieng. But it had to be because the circumstances in which we lived were ten times worse. Nam Tha was a village in medieval times. It was a constant task to keep our house in "livable condition." We had constantly to repaint, rescrub and rebuild. One afternoon a whole lower side of the wall fell out. These walls are made from woven bamboo, then a mixture like wattle is made from cow dung, rice straw, betel juice, lime, and some other ingredients known only to God and the natives. This paste is then spread on each side of the bamboo. The overall effect is sort of a smelly adobe.

Many say that the Lao are a lazy people. From my experience of living like a Lao, in a hut like his own, I am of the opinion that this is not true. Let me mention a few things a man must do. He must forge the iron, and make and repair his plow, carving the shaft and yoke himself. He must constantly rebuild a new harrow and blade. He must repair his house, weave new walls, cut thatch for the roof, repair the tools of the kitchen. He must keep his cart, feed his oxen, make rope and fiber. He must make hemp and weave the nets, then fish for his meals. He must build his loom so his wife and daughter can weave. But first he must grow, gin, mill and dye the cotton. He must care for the sick buffalo, cultivate his fields, practice his religion, and raise chickens, ducks, and grow a garden. This man is not lazy.

He may be ignorant, but a merely well-informed man is the most useless bore on God's earth. The Lao man has culture and expert knowledge in a specific direction; narrow to be sure, but nevertheless, deep.

If an American feels as though he is slowing down, he has many stimulants that he can turn to. Bourbon and water before dinner, extra caffeine in his coffee, perhaps a dexedrine or thyroid pill. The Lao does not have these. His food is humdrum and not especially nutritious. Glutinous rice is the staple of their diet. This is steamed and eaten with many sauces. There are condiments made from fish, pimento and other spices. The most popular is called "padek." This awful puree of salt and fish is the Chili Sauce of the Orient. In Viet Nam the same lousy stuff was called Nuoc Mom. Eggs are important in the diet. The word in Lao for chicken is *cai* and the word for the egg of a chicken is simply *cai cai*. Dairy products are not eaten. Beef, pork and fowl are killed only on feast days. On these occasions a local rice alcohol is drunk. To my buds this stuff tastes like kerosene.

Tobacco is grown, along with opium. When the mountain people are low on rice they go to a neighboring village and barter tobacco or opium for more rice. It is not uncommon to see a child of five or six smoking a huge cigar. Both sexes, at practically all ages, smoke their own tobacco, which is rolled in a small banana leaf.

Our diet was a mixture of East and West. We ate their scrawny chickens and fertilized eggs with our C-rations. We ate our canned meats with their fish sauce. Once we tried tiger steaks, but they tasted like old tennis shoes.

One of the most constant sources of entertainment to us was the ever present group of dirty brown kids. They were around all through the day and most of the night, staring at us. Especially they loved to watch those bizarre Americans eat. They were sometimes sullen, sometimes bright, always curious. Some of the splashes of children would glare at our glossy white faces and hands, and jabber amongst themselves, while others would just sit and look. The Dooley carnival tent was not restricted to just children. Frequently the shy little kids would sit with their mothers and alternate their glance from her to us, and back to her for reassurance.

For a while we had a Meo lad who spent some evenings with us. This tribe lived at high altitudes; it is said that they cannot survive at lower than 3300 feet. I asked the boy why his people always lived on the mountain tops. He didn't know but said he would ask his father. When he returned in a few days he said he had asked, but his father said he had not the answer, but would ask his grandfather. The old man said that his own grand-father had lived on that mountain top, and his ancestors were buried there, and he could see no reason for moving.

These Meo look much like the Tibetans, and come from the ancient Mongol Kingdom of Su-ch'uan. Their language is related to the Yao dialect. The Meo wear baggy light blue pants and a short, loosely fitting shirt that ends at the bottom of their rib cage. They wrap a brilliant scarlet sash around their waists and loop large hoops of silver around their necks, wrists and ankles. The men are solid and firm, and their bare midriff reveals a thick abdominal musculature. The French claim the Meo are the best soldiers of Laos. Every Meo you see is carrying a long gun. These guns are the old flintlock, and they carry a water buffalo's horn filled with gun-powder. The barrels are about three feet long, and the handle is shaped like a pistol. The whole gun is laboriously hand-made. It has been said that these guns are modeled from some guns given to the Chinese centuries ago by the Jesuit missionaries.

We passed many a long evening with youngsters like this sad-eyed Meo lad. We always loved to open packages and everyone, especially visitors, en-joyed watching us. It took hours to open all we might receive at one mail call. We would go over the medical samples, the instruments, vitamin pills, Hershey bars, and magazines. We learned that it is not necessary to have a bar or movie or a TV set nearby. The simple things of life can give us happiness.

One of the most maddening furies of Nam Tha were the teeming swarms of bugs that would infest the air. It was impossible to do surgery at night. When emergencies demanded that we did, the bugs would swirl around the light, climb into our hair and faces, and even onto the wound. Nets, screens, nothing we could contrive would keep them out. The atmosphere would be absolutely solid with insects. We had to turn our kerosene lamps out on some nights because these bugs would make any living unbearable. We would just give up the fight, get under a mosquito net and try to fall asleep.

Pavie and his friends, who shared our house, were constantly ambling in, sitting on the couch, talking with us, looking at the magazines, or just star-ing. They frequently pitched in when we were knocking out parts of the wall, collecting rain water, redesigning the house, or abolishing some of the room's drabness with picture-hanging, or catching bats. Pavie's babies would crawl into our part of the house, micturate a little, then crawl out.

One of the few visitors we ever had in Nam Tha was a woman. Her name was Marion Dix, a lecturer and photographer from Hollywood. She had heard of our work and had done documentary films on Operation Brotherhood, on Viet Nam, and other parts of Southeast Asia. She wrote and asked if she could come to our place. Months later she received the answer in the affirmative, and it took her only a few weeks to arrive in Nam Tha.

Most people were fearful of visiting Dooley. Many fluttering females would never have thought of boon-doggling it into Nam Tha. Many American men would take no chance on being so close to the Chinese border, with a chance of becoming marooned. But plucky Marion Dix left her chromeplated Hollywood and, in slacks and a halter, arrived at the airstrip with a hundred pounds of cameras.

She stayed with us over a week, lived in our house and even used our shower (first and last female to do so). I told Marion that we thought she was a great gal. To come all the way to Nam Tha was risky enough, but to come during the monsoon season was doubly dangerous. We apologized for her being forced to live in a houseful of men. She answered, "Why this is what every woman dreams of!" She said that while cooking our dinner, so you see 'twas good to have a woman around the house.

Another event happened in May. Rarely did we ever get visitors, and the occasion was always bright for us. Even with the sense of humor that we tried to maintain, loneliness gnawed on us considerably. But before this visitor came, something else happened. We delivered Mrs. Cauvin's fourth baby. There was a minor scandal in the village because the child had slate blue eyes. The Chao Khuong was first to discover it and loudest to announce it. In honor of the occasion Cauvin gave us a bottle of champagne that he had hidden for months. This bottle of champagne had quite a story to it. He had a friend in the capital send it up months before and planned to present this to us on the auspicious occasion of his fourth child's birth. But more came of this bottle, too.

I must first explain that we lived close to the earth, close to the level of the humanity with whom we worked. We had no fancy things like big electrical generators, running water, hi-fi record players, or plumbing. But we did have enough to make life bearable and somewhat enjoyable by the new standards that we were forced to adopt. To be sure, we often yearned for stateside life. What was ordinary, now became a luxury. But while in the forest primeval, in a dirty little village, we lived as graciously as we could. We were clean, changed clothes for dinner, shaved every day, used decent language save for an occasional work-a-day word, and were a happy family. Of course, no champagne.

Mr. Bill Davies, a friend who worked for the Squibb Pharmaceutical Company in the Philippines, wrote that he was going to tour the distributors in Asia. He would be in Vientiane and he asked if there was any chance that he could get to Nam Tha. He was interested in the work that we were doing. Obviously we were interested in Squibb Pharmaceutical Company. I wrote all the explanations of how he could charter a small plane and fly to us if he came here before the rains and I told him of how much we wanted him to come. We loved visitors and so few ever came. This letter got out on one of the infrequent plane trips and many months later he arrived in Nam Tha. Bill stepped from the plane a rather ashen grey. His foot landed on the muddy airstrip and we immediately burst out in smiles. Here was our visitor dressed in an impeccable Brooks Brothers suit, silk tie and, as he said, "twenty-eight dollar shoes." Slogging through the mud he reached our house and collapsed from nervous exhaustion. He said he had never endured such a hazardous nor harrowing flight in all of his life. He said the pilot kept flying further north, and he was sure that he was deep over Red China. He claimed that if his insurance company had ever seen that airplane, they would immediately have canceled all policies. When the pilot finally pointed out the landing strip at Nam Tha, Bill Davies said that it looked no bigger "than my children's playpen."

We suggested that before dinner Bill take a good hot shower with some soft rain water. This would soothe him a bit. He was amazed that we had this accoutrement of civilization, but he quickly accepted and thoroughly enjoyed it. He then switched to some of our clean khakis and was in a mellow mood for dinner. We turned on the battery-run tape recorder and listened to some classical music sent to us by our friend Bill Donovan from USIS-Saigon. There were no commercials, no canned flap-doodle, just music. In honor of the occasion John and Si had prepared an exceptionally good chow. After dinner we drank the Cauvin delivery fee, that rare bottle of champagne. Although it wasn't very cool, Davies was astounded to find that we had such high caliber "luxurious" living here in the jungle. Several days later not without some concern the plane returned him to Vientiane. Many months later he sent us a thank-you note. He apologized for his tardiness in writing but said that he was busy composing an article for Confidential magazine. Its title was to be "Hot Showers and Cold Champagne, or The Truth Behind the Dooley Mission."

We were always being thrown from one extreme to the other. We would behave for a few minutes like stateside Americans and this was fun. Then suddenly some horror would make us again painfully aware of the rim of hell upon which we were balanced. Only a few days after Bill's letter came and we were bathed in chuckles, a boy was brought to our clinic and we were thrust into the stink of it all again.

That afternoon four Thai Dam men arrived in Nam Tha in near exhaustion. They had two stout bamboo poles on their shoulders between them and hanging from this was a roughly made litter. On top was a thin mattress and nearly hidden beneath cotton blankets was a headful of hair and the haggard gaunt face of a young boy. His friends and his brother had carried this boy down from a village several days away. They managed to get this crude-looking stretcher across the mountains and through the valley. They set the pitiful load before the hospital and we went out to examine the child. The first thing we noticed was how horribly infested he was with lice. He had head lice in his hair and scabies over all of his body. As we pulled the cloth blankets off of him, we saw a horrible sight. This boy looked like a man recently released from Dachau. His whole body was contorted with pain and frozen in this twisted position. He had a deep muscle infection of the left leg and had had this for a long time. Because he lay on his mat of a bed and never moved, all the rest of his body wasted away, atrophied. His left leg, the good leg, was no bigger around in the thigh than my wrist is. His knee was swollen and infected and the thigh and calf muscles looked like the meat on frog legs. He had several huge bed sores on his spine and back. He was so filthy that even as he lay there the ever-present flies started to crawl over his face, around his lips and into his eyes and ears. His brother kept constantly brushing these hideous creatures off him.

We agreed to keep the boy, Nai, in the hospital but the first thing we demanded was that he go down to the river and be thoroughly scrubbed up. Reed Carnrick Pharmaceutical House in New Jersey had sent us a shampoo called Kwell which kills body lice immediately. They also sent some ointment which, upon one application, will clear up a severe case of scabies. After a thorough washing with soap for the first time in his life, we finally admitted him into the ward.

The next morning my boys constructed an orthopedic bed. This consisted of a stout bed with teakwood posts around it and a frame overhead. From this frame a trapeze bar was hung. The antibiotics along with surgical incision and drainage cleared up the infection in a few days. The fight was now physiotherapy. Nai had many months of exercise ahead of him. We taught him how to do various exercises which would help to restore his muscle strength. His heel tendons were almost frozen in a position which made his toe point straight out, and he could not flex his foot upwards. His younger brother stayed at the hospital and cared for him. This youngster learned how to do all of the exercises and spent most of his day passively moving his brother's arms and legs. He also kept urging Nai to do it himself, actively. I believe it would behoove divorce-ridden America to learn of the devotion to family that exists amongst the primitive people.

Months later on a cane that his brother had made for him, Nai could stand at the side of his bed. Soon he walked around the bed though clutching at the wooden frame. Later he could get across the ward, and one day he called to me. He had walked across the compound and stood before us at the main building as proud as any boy in the world could be. And we were proud of him, too. Nai had conquered his disease and with his own guts he overcame his muscle atrophy. A few weeks later the boy who had come to us near death returned to his village. He held his head high, walked straight and well, and was dressed in American khakis wearing blooming good health.

The force of kindness and love exhibited by my boys and by his brother redeemed Nai from ugliness and tragedy. The greatest bond among nations is faith in this force. An Asian brother and some American helpers, both taking care of a stricken lad, taught him how to walk again. Kindness is close to God and disarms man the quickest. You will never find this boy nor his brothers fighting against an American. They will remember us, with love.

We had hundreds of patients like Nai, boys we could cure. And we had patients like the girl with leprosy, to whom we could offer not even a breath of a chance.

All of our life was not fetid, however. We had some wonderfully happy moments, aside from the joy that came to us from our work. Some of our happiest times in our life in Nam Tha came from "Dammit." This was a pet gibbon that the boys had acquired. He was jet black all over save for his bottom exposure which was red, and his white muttonchop whiskers. Even the whites of his eyes were nearly black and in my opinion his personality was certainly so. There was much debate on what name should be given to this two-foot tall creature that had been chosen as our permanent house guest. We drew straws and Pete won. On his not-so-very-broad-shoulders fell the responsibility of naming and caring for this thing. "Dom" means black in Lao. This thing could not have been any blacker. Dom can easily be debouched into dam. The "it" just comes naturally. The thing was named "Dammit" and will remain so forever.

His arm span was three feet, while his height from his toe to his head was only a hairy two feet. Yes, this gave him a slightly ungainly look, and the strangest gait I've ever seen. He walked upright on his legs, like certain Americans, but to maintain his balance he held his arms over his head, the elbows bent, with the forearms and hands dangling behind him. He leaned forward and tottered much like those little toys you used to buy from salesmen on the street. You set them on an inclined board, and they would waddle down it. Besides his gait Dammit had several other facets of personality that I believe worthy of mention. One was his great love. The other his detestation. His love was for Peter Sherrer Kessey, John deVitry and Robert Waters and anyone else who happened to walk past. All my men basked in the warm sunlight of Dammit's love. As for Tom Dooley, Dammit could not stand him. Rarely could he get near him, and when he did, Dammit would always micturate with uncanny accuracy.

Being beloved, Dammit was pampered. After caring for the Lao all day the boys would lower themselves to pampering this thing at night. The greatest treat was the weekly bath. I liked to see the gibbon being bathed because I knew that if the boys would only turn their backs a moment I could so easily have drowned him. No luck!

This bath water is not just ordinary water. Rain water was preferred, but sometimes the "harsher" river waters had to be used. The porcelain basin that we shaved in became the royal tub for delicate Dammit. The water was specially prepared, suds with the softest soaps, temperature tested on the flexor surface of Pete's alabaster forearm, and scented with someone's after shaving lotion (probably mine). As his highness' unshod feet would be submerged in the water he would give a noble kick or two, and then would allow himself to be slowly dangled into the basin, lowered ever so gently, ever so slowly. Finally when all the suds came over his shoulders, and his hands were under water too, Dammit would adopt a look of kingly disdain and contentment. After soaking, and several rinses in pre-tested waters, Dammit would be wrapped in someone's best terrycloth towel and rubbed down thoroughly. He loved it. Who wouldn't? After that he got a touch of after shaving lotion (too much water dries the skin) and a cloud of perfumed Cashmere Bouquet (which we imported from Hong Kong) powder to give him that safe feeling so important to growing gibbons. Of course such a cleansed and fastidious gibbon could not be sent back outside to be chained to the tree where he lived. Not after all that effort. So he was kept inside the house for a few days. Only at my insisting (and I *was* the Commanding Officer of this outfit) did they put a diaper on Dammit. They carried Dammit around with them in their free time. He would be immaculately clad in diaper, baby undershirt and looked all the world like some humans I know.

Pete had Dammit with him one time when we were on a village housecall. A huge snake about seven feet in length, and the size of my forearm, slithered across the road in front of us. I do not know the species, but probably a python. Pete jumped away, pulled out his pistol and aimed with the intent to kill. Dammit was in his usual position on Peter's stomach, with his arms around Pete's chest, and legs around his belly. Dammit screamed like a frightened virgin and clasped all the tighter. Pete stood there trying to shoot the python while firmly holding Dammit against his chest. I could not help thinking of those moldy paintings inside State capitol buildings depicting the early West. Especially the one with the staunch pioneer woman with her child clutched to her breast, her chin thrust out defiantly ready to battle the bitter winds and wilds of the West.

In Nam Tha we often used bicycles to get around in our village. The boys had built a wooden platform on the back of my bicycle so that I could carry my ubiquitous black medicine bag. On evenings when the weather was just right, Pete would take Dammit for a ride. Dammit would squat on this wooden board on the top of the back fender, wrap his lengthy arms around Pete's nearly non-existent waist and ride around town, with his chauffeur, majestically surveying all he commanded.

The boys built a house for Dammit in a large tree in front of our place. He had a long enough chain so he could leap all around the tree like his stupid ancestors did. There he would sit and glare at the "humanity" that might be passing through the village square. There was always a handful of people looking at him, for he was a sight indeed. I am glad the blasted thing did some good. He was a source of entertainment to everyone in the village as well as to Operation Laos of the International Rescue Committee. So deeply immersed in a sea of misery all around us, a stupid little thing like a pet can wield tremendous power to keep us in good spirits. It is pathetic that a man gets into such a position, but oddly enough, a gibbon can get him out.

In the jungles of Asia there are two types of gibbons, the golden ones called "Chanee" and the black ones called "Kang." Although they live in the same jungle together they never mate (looking at Dammit I could understand how the Chanee felt about it all). But this is a peculiar situation. They are the same animal in every respect save for their colors. Yet they would never mate.

The reason is understandable to the Lao. An ancient legend explains it.

It is because of the good Prince Chantabun and his fickle wife, Chalernsri. You see, many years ago Prince Chantabun was the greatest Prince of the Kingdom. He was brave, stalwart and honest and all his people loved him very much. He was a great hunter and frequently fought tigers with his bare hands. The unfortunate thing about Prince Chantabun was that he was not handsome. In fact, he was very ugly. On a hunting trip the Prince met and fell in love with Chalernsri. She was a beautiful woman, but a commoner. They were married immediately and lived many months in happiness. They would frequently hunt together and on one such hunting trip they were stopped by a bandit. This bandit was masked, but he was tall and very straight and had about the same physique as the Prince. The bandit demanded that the Prince give him all his money. The Prince did. Then he demanded that the Prince give him his jewels. He did. Then the bandit demanded the Prince's wife, but the Prince refused and at such an insult attacked the bandit. They were evenly matched. The terrible fight lasted many hours. The bandit's mask was torn off and the wife noticed that the bandit was a most handsome fellow. The Prince nearly won and if his wife had helped him a little he could have been the victor. But the princess could not force herself to strike the beautiful bandit even though he was an evil man. At last the bandit hurled the good Prince to the ground and with a powerful thrust lunged his bloody knife through the Prince's chest. He then turned to take his pleasure with the fickle wife, who had sat idly by while the fight was going on, and while her husband was bleeding to death. But as he reached for her, the arm that went out was that of a black hairy ape, a gibbon. The gods were so angry at the bandit for killing the good and gentle Prince Chantabun that they had turned him into a black gibbon called "Kang." The gods were equally angry with the Princess, and they turned her into a golden gibbon called "Chanee."

The Chanee live all over the jungles of Southeast Asia and they can be recognized by their cry of "poo ahh," "poo ahh." This word means "husband." This is the punishment meted out by the gods for all the descendants of the Princess who would not come to the aid of her dying Prince. And for both Kang and Chanee the bliss of marriage can never be theirs.

The kids of Asia are wonderful. Here in northern Laos the families seem to vie with each other for the most fancy and different hair styles for their children. Some shave the head completely save for the cowlick, letting this grow like a pony tail. The Cantonese element in the north do this and then braid the cowlick. Other parents shave the boy's head, leaving a forelock which makes the fellow look a bit like a shetland pony. Some cut all the hair save a ring around the head, like a Franciscan tonsure.

The girls in the mountains never cut their hair. They let it grow long, and deftly knot it in the back, putting various ornaments into the knot. They wear long silver needles, decorative chopsticks, silver sticks with bells on them, silver knots and other delicate filigree chains. The effect is beautiful. Most of these girls have hair that falls close to their knees. When they bathe in the river, they untie this knot and it is a graceful and beautiful sight. They have no beauty parlors, permanents, settings or oils. In the North the Thai Dam girls wear their knots either in the back of the neck, or on the top of the head. If they do not have a husband, the knot is at the nape of the neck. If they have already found a man, the knot is on the top of the head.

While in Laos we all learned to speak the language of the land. Not fluently, to be sure, but adequately. Medical Lao is very simple. The word *chep* means pain. *Li* means lots of, or the superlative of anything. The longer the word is dragged out, and the higher the pitch of the voice, the more intense the meaning. All one has to do is learn the words for the parts of the body, or just watch the patient point to the head and listen to *chep hua liiiiii*. Although we all advanced to a point where we could understand most medical problems and express ourselves in the clinic, we still had a difficult time at dinner with the governor. Always the wrong intonation. For example the word *cai* can mean "chicken," "egg," "fever," "faraway," or "nearby," depending on the tone used, and the length or the brevity of the word. You can see how embarrassing this can get.

There were many clinical problems that I had not planned for. One of these was dentistry. I brought no dental instruments; little good they would have done, for I know nothing of this profession anyway. When people would come with loose teeth, like a term-pregnancy, the solution was obvious. For the first couple of weeks the Baker's tool chest was an adequate supply of instruments. At least for extracting. On one of our early visits to Vientiane we went to the Minister of Health who had given us free entry to his well-stocked warehouse. Most of his medicines and equipment were given to the Lao Government as American aid. As there is only one doctor by international standards in the kingdom, the majority of the aid medicines just sit in the warehouse. I was amazed as I walked down the halls of this building to find all the best antibiotics, medicines and instruments stored and not being utilized. We found the dental shelf, and stocked ourselves up with what we needed. Most of the instruments seemed unwieldly and all definitely unknown to me. Which one do I use where?

I wrote of this problem to a dentist, Dr. Karl Strobach, in Saint Louis. He sent back detailed diagrams and articles on just how to pull a tooth, when to, and when not to. He indicated the treatment for some basic dental problems. He later sent me some more delicate instruments which replaced the ones that we were using.

Dentistry then consumed about ten per cent of sick-call. No matter what the problem was we had only one Rx, extraction. Before each extraction we would give an injection of penicillin to protect the patient (though he could never understand why we gave him a shot in his bottom when it was his tooth that hurt). I believe one of the hardest tasks that we all had to become accustomed to was tooth-pulling. Afterwards, the boys scrubbed their hands with alcohol for several minutes each. I hated to do this job, so thoughtfully sloughed it off to the boys.

Our nights and days went on. Our weeks and months passed. The hideous skin diseases, the ringworm, the filth, the itch, the diarrhea, the leprosy, these became everyday visitors from hell to Nam Tha. The monotony of misery. The children with their pus-filled eyes, wearing rags for clothes, tattered and pitiful, these became "our" children; their problems, "our" problems. And when they improved, we too felt better. And when they thanked us here was our pay. This rich sense of satisfaction with even a small accomplishment. This is the way in which God sometimes said that He was pleased with our work.

In college we were taught the ubiquity of God. But to see God in all things when you are plunged into bleating materialism is sometimes hard. I certainly cannot see God when I look at a Mercedes Benz convertible. But in the jungle it is easier. Here we can know God a little better. Perhaps it is because of solitude. We can see God in the tropic rain, in the monsoon mud, in the tangy sweet smell of the earth that comes upon us as we walk amongst the mountains. The mimosa, the frangipani, the tamarind trees, the thatched roof, the quiet peace of the hills and valleys, the cool refreshment of the river, the surge of the night, the bustling of the market place. God is more intimately present in us than we realize. We ought to shut up a few minutes and seek Him. Life can signify much. We must just listen to the voices which are inside each of us. All we need to do is listen more acutely, rub our eyes and see things a bit better. If the light is seen, if the sweet odor is grasped, if the sound is heard, then a man's whole being is caught up in soul-satisfying contentment.

A man working in this world without tapping his own reservoir of spiritual strength is like a twin-engined plane flying with only one motor. He may get there, but it will be mighty difficult. Often, late at night, Bob, John and I would kneel beside our cots and pray the family rosary out loud. Our whole job took on a new meaning when we remembered the words, "Inasmuch as ye have done it unto the least of these, my brethren, ye have done it unto Me."

EIGHT ·
A ROYAL VISIT

After ten months in Laos, I realized that I knew little more about the political situation than I did when I arrived. It was like living in a political Never-Never Land peopled by phantoms. You were aware of conflicting forces and of ever-present dangers. Yet it was impossible to identify them clearly.

This was due partly to the curious internal situation. The Royal Kingdom of Laos was a house divided against itself. The old King SisavangVong, ruler of the "independent kingdom within the French Union," lived in retirement in the ancient capital of Luang Prabang, but he had three nephews who were potent forces in Lao politics.

One brother, Prince SouvannaPhouma, the Premier, was striving to preserve Laos as a sort of constitutional monarchy friendly to the West. Another brother, Prince SouphanouVong, leaned strongly toward the Communists of China and North Viet Nam. The third and oldest of the half-brothers, Prince Phetserath, sometimes called the "George Washington of Laos," had withdrawn from active politics and was serving as a curious sort of peacemaker. All three brothers, however, insisted that their political differences were strictly a "family affair" which would be settled amicably and in due time.

In 1940, when Vichy France consented to the Japanese occupation of Indo-China, Prince Phetserath took the position that France thereby lost all claim to Laos as colony or protectorate. Then, in 1945, before withdrawing in defeat, the Japanese declared Laos an independent kingdom. King SisavangVong went into exile in Thailand, and Prince Phetserath became head of the shortlived (1945-46) Republic of Laos.

However, in 1946, France reconquered Laos, restored King SisavangVong to the throne. The three princes and about 10,000 members of the Free Lao party fled to Bangkok. Later that year the French-Indochina war began. Three years later, the embattled French declared Laos a free nation on July 19, 1949, within the French Union. The three princes and their followers returned, but were unable to agree politically. Prince SouvannaPhouma became Premier of the Royal Kingdom. Prince SouphanouVong became head of the Pathet Lao (Free Lao) movement and formed an alliance with the Communist Vietminh. Prince Phetserath, the "elder statesman," announced his withdrawal from politics.

Then in 1953 the Communist Vietminh invaded north Laos from Viet Nam and joined forces with the Pathet Lao. Under the terms of the armistice drawn up at the Geneva Conference in 1954, the Pathet Lao withdrew their forces to the two northern provinces of Sam Neua and Phong Saly, which are to be administered by the Royal Government "in collaboration with the Pathet Lao." Several attempts were made by SouvannaPhouma and SouphanouVong (with Prince Phetserath acting as mediator) to form some sort of "collaboration." They had not been successful up to the time I left Laos in the fall of 1957.

This "family affair," I soon learned, was a very delicate subject in Laos. Members of the Lao Government always spoke kindly of the Pathet Lao as "our dissident brothers." They insisted that Prince SouphanouVong and the Pathet Lao were not Communists. Even in Nam Tha, the Chao Khuong would never admit that the Communist "bandits" who were responsible for the atrocity cases we saw were Lao. He insisted that they were Burmese, Chinese, Vietnamese, or members of the non-Lao tribes.

Inevitably, this kindly attitude toward the Pathet Lao reminded me of the "harmless agrarian reformers" in China prior to the Red victory. There was also another point of similarity to pre-Communist China that frightened me—the political innocence of the great mass of Lao peasants.

The Lao people, particularly in the north, knew nothing about Communism or democracy. They were neither pro- nor anti-western. These were big issues far beyond their knowledge or understanding. There was unrest among them, and there is no doubt that this unrest was being stimulated. I am convinced that the Chao Khuong was right in suspecting the village "teachers" as the chief agitators.

But this agitation was shrewdly keyed to things the people could comprehend. It was directed against the Royal Lao Government, and against foreigners and, particularly, against the white man. It was anti-*farange*.

At first, I was greatly puzzled by that word *farange*, which is heard everywhere in Laos. People often addressed me as *Thanh Mo Farange. Thanh* means Honorable, and *Mo* means medicine or doctor. It was some time before I learned that *farange* is the Lao corruption of the word *français* or French. Originally it was applied to the despised colonial rulers, but eventually it came to mean all white foreigners. Our interpreters told the people that I was not *farange*, and should be called *Thanh Mo American* or simply *Thanh Mo*.

I was never able to find much comfort in the Lao's lack of political knowledge or their ignorance of Communist ideology. On the contrary, remembering China, I found the condition frightening. It meant that any political force—Royal Lao or Pathet Lao, democratic or Communist—that promised these people something better than what they had could probably claim their hearts and minds.

Suddenly we were told that His Highness Prince Phetserath, Viceroy of Laos, would visit our village in two days. Indubitably he would meet the American medical team. We were trying to steer clear of politics and now perhaps we were about to be thrust into it.

The afternoon and following morning the whole village was feverishly making preparations for the royal visit. They were constructing floral arches, cleaning up their lawns, and hanging out Lao flags that the Chao Khuong distributed. Prince Phetserath is a much loved figure in Laos.

On the appointed day, a little before high noon, the military, the villagers, all the children and almost everyone present in Nam Tha (including four Americans) were lined up on the path from the airstrip to the Chao Khuong's house. The Chao Khuong, Mayor and village officials were all dressed in starched white jackets that looked like the U. S. Navy summer uniform. With the jackets they wore purple knee-britches of silk with a fold of cloth between the legs, hitched to the waist in the back. Long black stockings and black shoes completed the royal uniform.

Noon passed, and several more hours. The children had broken ranks, so had everyone else. We sat around the little shack at the airport, wondering whether the Prince would arrive that day or next week. John deVitry was rehearsing Pete's French. Though Pete knew a great number of medical terms in French, and frequently could understand the gist of a conversation, he still did not exactly know how to greet a Prince. Neither did John and I, so we asked the Chao Khuong. The proper greeting was: "*Mes respects, Votre Altesse*," which roughly means, "My respects, Your Highness."

Finally a plane was heard. All lined up in place again, the Buddhist monks marked the area where the plane would unload the Prince, and we ran down to the middle of the line, and stood at our appointed spot. The plane landed, taxied up, and unloaded a few sleepy-eyed soldiers. It was not the Prince's plane, but an advance military guard for His Highness. Disappointment was manifested by groans, the Chao Khuong's being the loudest.

Soon afterwards another plane throbbed overhead, and the Royal Prince descended to Nam Tha. The spry old gentleman had on a felt hat. He was also dressed in white and royal purple, and carried a gnarled walking-stick which he did not use for support. He knelt before the priests and made his obeisances, then briskly walked down between the lines of scrubbed-up children. Each child handed him a little handful of flowers which he handed to his following entourage. They in turn placed the bouquets in silver bowls brought for the occasion. Everyone got down on one knee, pressed their palms together in front of their chests, fingers touching the nose, and bowed over their hands—a sort of a modified kow-tow. This is the way a Lao meets his Prince. We quickly decided that that would be un-American, so we would just shake hands, respectfully.

Pete happened to be first in our line. When the Prince saw his Texas face, he registered royal astonishment. He turned to the Chao Khuong who quickly explained that this was a member of the medical team of Americans living in Nam Tha. Peter, in the moment's fluster, thrust out his hand and said: *"Je suis Pierre."* When I heard him say "I am Peter," I had an almost uncontrollable impulse to add: "And upon this rock I shall build my church." The Prince just smiled. I said something (I don't remember what, but it was not *"Mes respects, Votre Altesse"*). Bob shook hands and said "Hello, sir" and John, the diplomat, with flamboyant ease uttered the proper words of respectful greeting.

That evening the Chao Khuong gave a small dinner. We had not been invited, nor did we expect to be, since this was an official visit of a Prince to a Lao village. However, the Prince apparently had other ideas and, at the last moment, I was commanded to present myself for dinner at seven o'clock. I had no suit with me in Nam Tha, just khakis and work clothes for mountain living. I quickly found a clean pair of pants and borrowed a coat from Cauvin. I had one white shirt and a green tie of my own. So I made my appearance for my first meal with royalty dressed in khaki pants, white shirt, green tie, and gray coat four sizes too small.

The Prince completely disarmed me. He was charming, extremely interested in my work, and did not ask me any of those "dangerous" political questions that I was so fearful of stumbling over. We did not discuss race riots in America, Mr. Dulles' beliefs, or Ambassador Parson's politics. He did not ask for a frank opinion of his brother, nor did he mention the word Communism. We talked about delivering babies, raising chickens, keeping

water buffalo off the front lawn, and instructing the villagers in the relationships of polluted water to diarrhea. We spoke in French.

I told him of our CARE midwife kits, and he asked me to go over to the
hospital and get one, as he would like to see it. I replied, "Now?" The
Chao Khuong sank in his chair at my lack of diplomacy, and the prince
replied, "Of course, now!" So around eleven p. m. I brought a midwife kit
from the hospital. The Prince laid all the contents out on the table and
went into each packet. He was acutely aware of a great many things that I
thought Princes didn't know anything about.

When the time came to leave (I could tell, the Chao Khuong was staring
at me) I made obeisance; standing fully erect (American), I pressed my
hands together and bowed my head in the attitude of prayer (Lao), and
said: *"Bonne nuit, monsieur"* (French). The Prince asked what time we
ate breakfast. I said, "Around dawn." "Fine, I'll be there," he replied.

I woke the boys up at the house and told them we were having royalty
for breakfast. We cleaned our house up as best we could right away, which
was around midnight. Early the next morning John was cooking the best
coffee he could make, and our interpreters, Si, Chai and Kieu were waiting
in frozen terror. Si did not see how he could serve coffee because if he
approached the Prince seated at a table, Si must crawl on his knees in order
to keep his head lower than that of the Prince. "And how can I do this with
a pot of hot coffee in my hands?" We had no solution.

Suddenly, at the bottom of the ladder, the Prince appeared, with his
whole entourage. Should I go down the steps and bump into him? Standing
there with my head ten feet higher than his, this seemed impolite even by
American standards. However the Prince solved the crisis by coming up the
stairs quickly, and without calamity. He then proceeded to examine every
item of our place. The mats, the walls, our pictures of President Eisenhower and the King of Laos, the beams, the wash basins, the shower barrel,
the bar, the bookcase, the boxes, the two "sofas," the medicine shelf, the
kerosene lights, the Coleman kerosene stove, the odds and ends around the
place.

Then, with royal aplomb, he sat down. John said meekly: "Coffee anyone?" The Prince did not eat any breakfast, so no one did. He gets up
several hours before dawn every day, eats, prays and then goes to work.

He spied my tape recorder, and became very interested in this. We examined it, and I ran a tape for him, explaining that I used it to send recordings
home to my local radio station in St. Louis. He asked me what I spoke of
and I said: "The same things we spoke of last night." He grunted, *"Bon!"*
He visited the hospital and the grounds, then suddenly returned to his plane

and flew away. We slumped back into the house and collapsed on the chairs. The royal ordeal was over. Peter was still mumbling something like, *"Mes respects, Votre Altesse."* We did not know it then, but we were destined to see this Prince again.

NINE ·

BAN PHU VAN AND "ATOMIC FLU"

Pete Kessey's scheduled departure coincided with the beginning of the monsoon rains in May. The plane would arrive in Nam Tha around midday and because of the unpredictable weather, had to take off almost immediately in order to reach Vientiane before dark.

However, on the morning Pete was to leave, we received word that one of the midwives in an outlying village was faced with an emergency. The woman was hemorrhaging badly, and needed immediate help. I couldn't leave the hospital, and Pete was the only other person capable of handling the situation. Despite my warning that he would miss the plane and, hence, his connections all along the line, Pete insisted that he could handle the case and get back in plenty of time. So he grabbed a bag, summoned one of the Lao nurses, and together they set off afoot.

Pete prided himself on being an ornery, plain-talking Texan, which indeed he was. He was tough, raw-boned, fearless; but beneath his unpolished surface there were great depths of gentleness, compassion, fine sensitivity, and devotion to duty. The kids of Nam Tha loved him. Some evenings they would swarm around him on the porch, raising such a rumpus that I'd order him to send them all home, or else—

"Aw, whathehell, Doc," he would say, "leave the kids alone. It's good for public relations!"

Pete never grumbled when it was his turn to be routed out of bed in the middle of the night to answer an emergency call. Yet it was always Pete who argued that I ought to take it easy. Often I would debate whether to go off into the mountains on an emergency involving surgery that only I could handle, or to forget about it and stick to my hospital schedule. Pete would say, "Stay where you are! You can't do everything—something's got to give!"

"No," I'd say, "I just can't let the guy die. There's a *moral* responsibility involved here." Pete always hooted when I said that; to him the word "moral" meant just one thing—sex!

On this particular morning, Pete's plane arrived just about the time the black storm clouds began socking in. John was waiting on the landing strip with orders to bring the pilot to the hospital where he could sit on him if necessary. The Frenchman appeared, arguing volubly about the weather and the delay. I stalled, coaxed, and cajoled, meanwhile praying that the weather would hold until Pete returned.

I was a nervous wreck when he finally showed up, exhausted but with a big, satisfied grin that told me his patient was okay. Nevertheless, I lit into him.

"Didn't you know we'd have trouble getting this crazy Frenchman to wait for you?" I demanded. "Why didn't you just pack the patient and leave the midwife in charge until I could get there?"

Pete looked at me with astonishment, and then he blew his top. "How the hell could I do that, you idiot?" he shouted. Then he began to smile. "Besides," he said, "you ought to know I had a *moral responsibility* to stay on the case."

We both laughed until the tears streamed down our faces. The angry Frenchman was gunning his engine impatiently when we got to the airstrip, and I watched the plane take off and skim under the lowering clouds. Good old Pete! He had promised me six months of his young life and given me ten. I hope he won't get lost among all the illustrious Tall Men of Texas. For lots of simple people in Indo-China, he'll always stand head and shoulders above the crowd.

As the word of the white-man's clinic in Nam Tha spread, we became accustomed to getting patients from afar. But I was surprised by the increasing number of Chinese. Some, of course, were refugees who had settled in northern Laos; but by discreet questioning I learned that a good many of our patients came across the border from Yunnan province in Red China. We even had a number of cases from Canton, which is over 800 miles away via North Viet Nam.

Once an extremely well-educated Chinese appeared at the hospital with his 15-year-old daughter whose face was disfigured by an unsightly harelip. He made no attempt to hide the fact that he came from Yunnan and had entered Laos via Muong Sing, an entry point on the Burma border.

The Chao Khuong was very suspicious of him, and insisted that he was an officer of the Red Chinese Army. Perhaps he was. I only know that he was grateful for the operation which transformed his ugly little daughter into a very attractive girl. If, indeed, he was a Red officer I feel reasonably confident that he now entertains some doubts, at least, about any anti-American propaganda he hears.

This case had another curious aftermath. The Chinese girl was by no means my first harelip operation in Nam Tha; but shortly after it I began to see an increasing number of harelips. It was publicity, I suppose, that spread my fame through the mountains and made me the first plastic surgeon in northern Laos!

As the months went on Bob and John became hardened veterans, performing a splendid job. And Dooley is no easy boss. These young men had been quickly flung into misery such as they never dreamed existed. Neither had had any military experience, and were not accustomed to too much discipline. I would not tolerate anyone talking back, and ran my unit like a military unit. This they took very well, though thrown into it suddenly. Our constant awareness that we might be taken prisoners by the Communists kept us all on our toes. Military experience has proven that, in such a situation, there must be one chief and good Indians.

John's quiet diplomatic way of doing things was an excellent balancing lever for my sometimes impetuous actions. Much of the credit for the success of our last six months goes to John deVitry. Bob Waters, though not yet twenty-one, had the hands and heart of healing. Bob could not speak French, though he did study it constantly and caught the gist of most conversations. He was always studying medical textbooks and asking me questions. He became very proficient in operating-room techniques, and took over this command when Denny left. Both boys were capable of hard physical work in spite of frequent attacks of malaria, dysentery, and fatigue. None of these can be avoided when you live as we were forced to live.

Bob had a fixation on rats. Knowing that rats are intermediate carriers of typhus, plague and other diseases, Bob was constantly laying traps for them. Each morning he would take the caught culprits outside and burn them to be sure the fleas were killed. But no matter how many of these loathsome creatures Bob would destroy, more would always appear.

John and Chai became the closest of friends, spending long hours in conversation. Chai became a superb assistant and possessed the most important qualification of a medical man, compassion. With the dirtiest leper, bloated and wretched, Chai was tender. To howling kids, Chai would manage a patient smile, and wave a mother's anxiety aside. To children consumed with terror of the "white witch doctor Dooley," Chai's reassuring words would bring them within my stethoscope's reach. In giving out balloons and toys Chai was the epitome of fairness, and when he went shopping in the market place he was sharp. Chai was the most important member of our mission, along with his phantoms, ghosts and spirits, with whom we learned to live in peaceful coexistence.

Time and again, sick people would tell me that they came from a place called Ban Phu Van, some 30 miles distant, high in the mountains, near the Burma border. Ban Phu Van, they said, was a progressive village, but with many sick people who could not make the long journey to Nam Tha.

I was eager to stage at least one sick-call in Ban Phu Van, but the Chao Khuong, who felt personally responsible for my safety, argued against it. He said the mountain trails were treacherous, that the region was infested with bandits, and that the Communists would like nothing better than to get their hands on the white witch doctors of Nam Tha. Finally, he gave in when I consented to take along a number of coolies and several of his armed guards.

We packed our camping equipment and medical supplies on the backs of three little Tibetan ponies, and placed Bob Waters in charge. This main party was to go on ahead, and set up camp in the valley beyond the next mountain west of Nam Tha, where John and I would join them the next day.

The evening after Bob's departure a curious thing happened. I was asked to come immediately to the house of Ah Chan, probably the richest man in the village and owner of the only rice mill in Nam Tha. John and I ran down the road, pushed through a crowd of weeping and wailing villagers, and found Ah Chan lying on the floor. There was no heart beat, but the body was still warm; so we tried artificial respiration and I injected adrenalin directly into the heart muscle. We were too late. Ah Chan was dead.

The circumstances surrounding the death were puzzling. Ah Chan had been in perfect health. Less than ten minutes ago, he was talking and laughing with friends. Suddenly, without giving any sign of pain or distress, he simply keeled over. I arrived within a matter of minutes and found him dead.

Of course, it could have been some kind of heart attack or cerebral embolism. But cardiovascular diseases are extremely rare in this part of the world. Besides, Ah Chan was not yet 30 years old. I did not have the facilities for an autopsy, and I doubt that the family would permit it. So I could only speculate.

Ah Chan was one of the most beloved men in Nam Tha, and his death

Norman Baker with a very dead jungle prowler. Notice Chai on his right, surveying the situation, wondering if he dare suggest that the Americans try a tiger rump steak.

The ceremony of *baci*, with the old sorcerer chanting and our nurses making offerings and wishes.

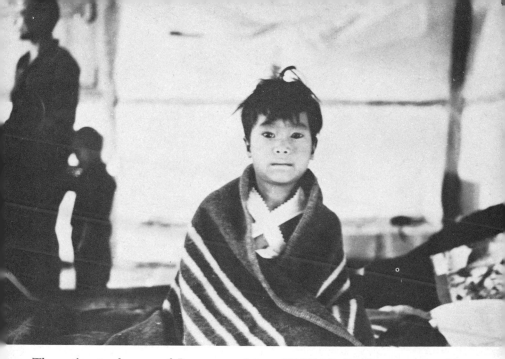

The pathos in the eyes of Ion, wrapped in a CARE blanket, but not sure of anything.

"Meals for Millions," along with Sustagen (the *"Ya mi henh,"* or medicine of strength, for the mountain people).

Mother and child, dressed in a gift sweater from U.S. school children.

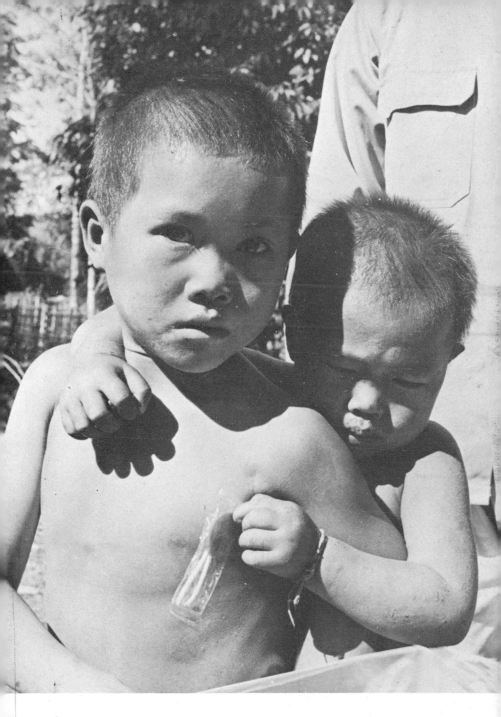

"He's my brother." With fungus of the scalp and scabies of the skin, they depict the true internationalist, disease.

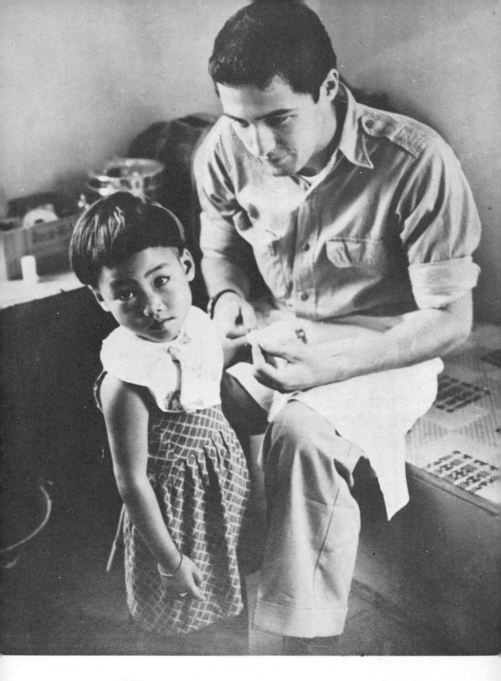

Bob Waters dressing the hand of a girl who has already received her bib and dress as reward for good behavior. Ask this girl if she thinks Americans are monsters.

A child blinded by the pus of trachoma, too late to be helped. But here a child is receiving terramycin, and will not be blinded.

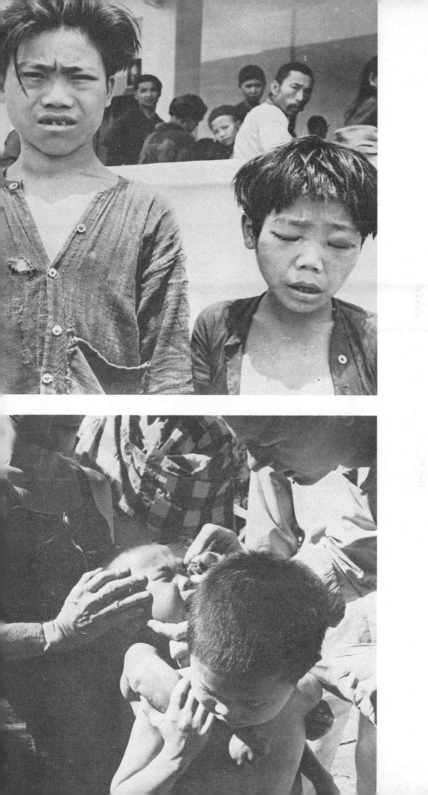

My favorite picture: our house and clinic in Muong Sing.
In the background a storm is gathering over Red China.

The doctor's post of honor in the clinic.

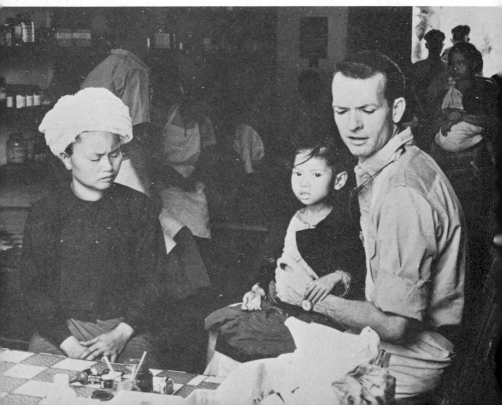

created quite a stir. While no one showed any animosity toward me, I could tell from the way people looked at me that my reputation as the great "white witch doctor" would suffer because of my inability to do anything for Ah Chan. The aftermath, however, was even more surprising.

The following morning, still worrying about Ah Chan's death, John and I traveled by bicycle over the 10 miserable miles of Cauvin's "road." At the end of the trail, we left our bikes in the jungle and crossed over the first mountain to Bob's campsite. The rest of the day we spent climbing up the steep trails to the summit of the next mountain.

The guides led on and we hiked up and up. We stopped once to chew on candy bars and eat rice from the hollow bamboo storage tubes. We had plenty of water to drink and found some fruit in the jungle that tasted like raspberries. The deep jungle was magnificent, with mists of air steaming up from patches of light. At high noon the jungle was bright, but within an hour we were thrust back into darkness save for pools of light. When the sun shone directly down, it could pierce the trees. At an angle the sun could not penetrate and we were flung into a dusk-like atmosphere. We felt like small animals crawling on the jungle floor. The trees reached up with such majestic ease. Wild deer darted about and birds splashed through in a constant dazzlement of color. This seething, steaming jungle puts one in awe of God's magnificence.

Everywhere we saw the banana tree, heavy with fruit, yellow and succulent, shaded from the sun by thick fronds. There were monstrous fig trees and vines. We plunged into pale green glades of softness, a bend in the trail, and suddenly a towering wall so thick that the eye could only penetrate a few feet. Along the winding trails we hiked, then up another steep mountain slope, heavily laden with foliage. Suddenly we came out of the dark jungle, to the fringe of forest. We were near the top, and the air was ineffably clean and pure. We had a glorious view of the surrounding mountains, and felt as though we were on the top of the world. Our panting made us sure of it. The village was just a little further up, and we arrived around noon.

Ban Phu Van was not unlike other villages of Laos, though a bit dirtier. They had no water nearby, no stream save down in the valley. Therefore they could not bathe as often as they should have. The houses of Ban Phu Van were rectangular, built entirely of wooden planks and bamboo, the whole house elevated high on wooden piling. Their roofs were thatched. The beams, door and rafters were all very carefully fitted and tied with rattan cord.

These typical mountain houses have a corridor running along one side of the interior and the sleeping rooms open onto it. There is one huge room where all the family lives. There is usually a veranda on the side where the mother plucks her chickens and washes her babies. Beneath part of the house is a workroom primarily for weaving and dyeing cloth, for repairing and building tools. The animals are stabled under the main part of the house on the ground around the pilings. This odor is staggering to American nostrils, but to a tribesman this odor represents wealth.

Ban Phu Van was one of the most isolated villages that we had seen in Laos. It gave us an eerie feeling, as though we were not in this century but in a time-machine which had taken us back to Biblical days.

Hundreds stood around the house, and dozens inside. The air was oppressive and the stench of their bodies nearly overwhelming. We opened the chests of medicines, bags of pills, and the minor surgical gear. Water was brought to us in bamboo buckets and a partition of the wall removed to allow for some light. We boiled quantities of water, and laid out instruments for minor surgery. During the next four or five hours, with the help of Chai, Bob, and John, I treated about 150 sick people.

The local schoolteacher, an intelligent young man named Phya Vong, remained by my side during sick-call. He told us that he was born in the village, but had gone to school in North Viet Nam in 1954. This interested me because it is standard procedure for the Communists to select the brightest boy in each remote village, give him some brief training (or indoctrination) in China or North Viet Nam, and then send him back home as a teacher. The Chao Khuong always insisted that these "teachers" were the most active Communist agents in northern Laos.

Phya Vong, who spoke French well, was cooperative and utterly charming. But he would not be drawn into any discussion of politics. Since he was by far the best educated man in the village I left a substantial supply of basic medicines with him, and he promised to send seriously sick people to the clinic in Nam Tha in the future. I had no idea of how he really felt toward us; but, at least, like the rest of the villagers, he knew now that all white men are not monsters.

On the way back, near the bottom of the valley, a man stopped us. He asked us to visit his child who was sick "in the head." It was only off the trail a bit, and there were less than ten huts in his village. We agreed. He walked ahead swiftly, determined, and frightened. Finally we came to his near-dead village. Inside his hut I crept past an oil lamp, and then he pointed to a pool of darkness. He said "ni." There was his son. A child of about four, he was whimpering like a wretched little dog. On examination I found he had some sort of cerebral spasticity and complete muscle atrophy.

His legs and arms were little knobby rods and his bloated stomach bespoke heavy worm infestation. He was lying on a mat soaked with his own urine. He had no contact with reality and had definite signs of cerebral damage.

There was absolutely nothing that I could do. Nor could I think of anything in all the chests of hope that even a sterile American Medical Center could offer to this lad. I explained as best I could. The father accepted my verdict with philosophical understanding. I, the white witch doctor, was absolutely his last hope for his son. Remembering I should never rob a patient of his last hope, I was apprehensive about painting the true totally black picture. I tried to leave a little light, but conscience forbade me to offer much. The father said that there were several in the village like this. Later when I discussed it with John and Bob, we decided that this must be a familial thing.

It was not yet dark when we arrived at the camp where we had left the bicycles. Remembering Bob's tale of trying to sleep in the jungle campsite the night before, we decided that we three would ride our bicycles back to Nam Tha. The coolies and Kieu could return the next day with the horses. It was still an hour or so before nightfall, so we felt we would be able to make it. For the first hour we pumped up and coasted down. We were speeding as much as our aching legs would let us. The road was dry, though occasionally we would hit a puddle.

At one spot we were coasting down too fast, considering the rough narrowness of the road. There was a drop of several hundred feet off the side of this path. While shooting around a corner I lost control of my bicycle. The tires slid on the trail and I was flung over the handlebars. I skidded on my belly across the road surface, directly toward the edge of the cliff. I remember throwing my arms out in front of me, digging my hands into the road to brake myself. That's all I remember.

I was unconscious for only a moment. When I came to I was perched on the edge of the trail, but still on it. I had deep abrasions along my chest and stomach, and the front of my shirt was a dirty mixture of blood and dust. I looked at my hand and to my horror found my left thumb protruding out at a right angle of my wrist. It was dislocated and a wrist bone was fractured. I remembered what to do, and pulled on it, slowly, as hard as I could. With a swift excruciating pain, it slipped back into place.

By that time Bob and John were around the corner and had to skid to a stop to keep from running over my tangled bike. All they could do was comment, "Lucky you didn't go over the edge." Suddenly we both realized something. I would have to get to a doctor and to an X-ray machine. But I was the only doctor around, and we had no X-ray.

A physician is taught never to self-medicate. In this case however, self-reduction of a fracture-dislocation was imperative. To a man whose hands are as important to his livelihood as a doctor's, this kind of injury seemed ghastly. However, the fracture-dislocation of Dr. Tom Dooley on the path to Ban Phu Van was a very minor footnote in the history of Operation Laos.

The bicycle was bent up a bit, but we pounded it straight. I had the small medical kit on the back of my bike and found a large Ace elastic bandage to wrap my rapidly swelling hand in. We then went on. During the last thirty minutes of the trip it rained heavily.

It was dusk when we arrived at Nam Tha. Si was sitting on the top stair waiting for us. The lad had a premonition that we would be back a day early. Never did our house look so good as that twilight moment when we returned. We made a pathetic sight. I was bloodstained and muddy, my hand in a big bandage. Bob was so tired and sore and bug bitten that he could hardly crawl. John was numb with fatigue. We lay on the floor for an hour or so, with Si serving us coffee off the mat. Finally we took turns at the shower, and collapsed in bed. My hand was throbbing and swelling, and I was trying to decide how I would ever get to an X-ray machine. I never did. A posterior plaster cast, the luck of the Irish, and the grace of God produced good approximation and a functioning joint.

The next morning we got to the hospital early, and found the whole town excited by the lavish plans for Ah Chan's funeral and, more surprising, aghast over the "cause" of Ah Chan's death.

Everyone in Nam Tha now knew that Ah Chan had died of something called *kia atomique* (atomic fever) which can be translated roughly as Atomic Flu! The Chao Khuong himself was the first to tell us about it. Of course, he said, the story was absurd. He knew that no fever or influenza could kill with such lightning speed. But, he said, the rumor had spread like wildfire, and everyone else believed it!

How had the rumor started? I'll never know. There were only two or three radio sets in all Nam Tha. Si, our houseboy, swore that the report had not been on Radio Peking (which was the only station we could get on our small set); and the Chao Khuong, who had the only powerful receiver in the province, said he had never heard *kia atomique* mentioned on any broadcast.

Ah Chan's funeral lasted nine days. Runners had been sent out with the news, and friends and relatives from the most remote villages had gathered in Nam Tha. The long period of mourning was more grotesque even than an old-fashioned Irish wake. The Buddhist *bonzes* (monks) prayed and burned joss sticks, the mourners wailed, the musicians twanged their stringed instruments and clashed cymbals, and the feasting and drinking went on far into the night. Finally, on the ninth day, Ah Chan's coffin was placed high on a wooden platform, with the head toward Luang Prabang, the ancient religious capital of Laos, and the funeral pyre was lighted.

But the buzz-buzz about *kia atomique* didn't die with the flames. Strangely, at that moment, in June 1957, the western world was worrying about Asian Flu. Yet in this remote corner of the Far East, practically cut off from the lines of world communication, someone had dreamed up a counterpart that was Made in America. To me this was a masterpiece of subtle propaganda—and a telling blow at the White-Man's Medicine which, apparently, was getting to be too popular in Nam Tha.

This series of events—Ah Chan's unexplained death; the dying mountain child near Ban Phu Van, in whose presence I felt absolutely hopeless; the injury to my hand; the fatigue of our journey; the feeling of frustration at the smallness of our accomplishment and the enormity of the task, the millions we could not treat—brought me almost to the brink of despair. Then a letter arrived and it was just what I needed.

It was from Dr. Melvin Casberg, the former dean of my medical school. He wrote: "Tom, you will face periods of abject discouragement, when all your efforts will appear negligible in the face of such a tremendous task. But remember, Tom, one can trace all major steps in the progress of humanity to the individual, to the minority. So keep up your courage, and as Saint Paul said so many years ago, 'Be steadfast in faith.'"

TEN ·

THE GREAT FLOAT

The "Great Float" was John deVitry's idea. As the time for "phasing out" of Nam Tha approached, he argued that instead of going directly to Vientiane we ought to travel down the Nam Tha River in small boats holding sick-call in the isolated villages along the way.

The Chao Khuong was violently opposed to the scheme. He insisted that the river was treacherous and impassable, and that the people in the isolated villages were hostile to white men. Most of the political prisoners in his stockade, he said, came from this region, yet his soldiers did not dare venture more than a few miles down the river for mopping-up operations. Moreover, he doubted that we could find boatmen who would risk their necks on the trip.

I sent a message to Dr. Oudom, and he promptly sent back his approval. The old Governor threw up his hands, and said he was no longer responsible. However, he did insist upon sending out a party of armed guards in advance, and assigned four gun-toting to accompany us.

We were to travel in *pirogues*, dugout canoes about 12 feet long, which were the only boats capable of shooting the rapids. As the Governor predicted, we had plenty of trouble signing up the boatmen. No one had ever made the trip before; and, in addition to bandits and impassable rapids, we would have to contend with the heavy rains of the monsoon season. However, extra pay plus some persuasion by the Chao Khuong prevailed.

John lined up three *pirogues*, each with a crew of four men. Two men sat in the middle of the dugout and paddled; the others mounted the "flying platforms" fore and aft and used the long oars for steering. We carefully divided our medical supplies, food, and camping equipment among the three boats, so that if one was lost we would still be able to eat, sleep and hold sick-call.

The departure time was set at dawn, but following the usual Lao pattern we heaved anchor a little before lunchtime. We were ready to go and were down at the *pirogues* with our equipment. The chief boatman was to come down in just a few minutes. An hour later he ambled down, took a look at us, and then said that he would have to go back to the Chao Khuong to get a paper of some sort. The interpreters said that they were afraid the boatmen were getting cold feet; they knew the banditry and the river and demanded more money for such a risky trip. I cannot say I blamed them.

When they finally returned from the Governor's, we said another farewell to our dozen friends who were squatting under a tree trying to avoid the constant drizzle. I squatted inside the little bamboo hut in the middle of this long dugout and when the boatman got aboard I yelled in good Navy style, "Heave anchor," but we did not heave anchor. The chief boatman did not like the way his assistants, and the Americans, had loaded the canoes.

We then had to unpack and rearrange all the gear following the boatman's orders concerning weights, and my orders concerning value of equipment. Finally we seemed to be loaded properly and, without adieu, we sort of drifted away from the shore. It was pouring in torrents by this time; it did not stop for the next four days. We waved a listless goodbye to our dampened friends.

That first afternoon's float, as we blithely refer to rapid shooting, was as frightening as it was interesting. One boatman stood on the bow of the slender dugout and one on the stern, each with a huge paddle for steering. Two other men squatted just inboard of them with short oars, used for thrusting us along. They did not have to stroke very much because the Nam Tha River current took care of us, propelling us with alternating heaves.

Anticipating that the cargo was tender, to say nothing of us, the boatmen wove a palm leaf covering which allowed us to sit, hunched over on the wet floor of the canoe, and just fit our heads under this curved roof. But during the incessant rains even this was a blessing. However, it did not take long for the rain to break through the leaves and we were just as wet inside as we were out.

Our first stop was about three hours down the river. The boatmen got out and waded into the jungle to hack down some more of these large green bamboo logs to attach to the side of the boat. This is because we were rocking so very badly and the rapids were more severe than he had anticipated. The river here had no bank. The monsoon flooded waters had risen so high that there were large bushes and trees smack in the middle of the river, and the edges were not banks at all but simply trees on which the water had climbed up several feet. When we came to the first rapid of any size, the *pirogues* pulled over to the side once again.

This time we had to get out with the most valuable equipment, and plunge through the deep jungle on foot. We walked along the side of the river while the boats shot the rough part of the rapid, bouncing off of rocks, between logs and over the wild, white foam. Suddenly they came out into a small, quiet whirlpool and were able to paddle over to the edge where we were standing, knee-deep in water, with camera and gear over our heads—as the rain poured down on them. And so passed our first day, stopping, diving along the edge of the rapid, getting back aboard again, and that constant, drenching, chilly monsoon rain.

The first night we reached a small village where only a few old women could be found. With four gun-toting guards we looked more like an invading force than a benevolent medical mission. The somewhat frightened women told us that the menfolk were in the jungle hunting but would be back later. We said that all we wanted to do was get into an empty or abandoned hut, dry off, and eat. We were shown the village guest house, a miserable one. We somehow washed up, dried around the fire, heated up some C-rations and promptly tied up the mosquito nets, unrolled the bedding and fell into the dry warm arms of Morpheus, dreaming of martinis and hard, hard land.

The next morning I woke up to the sound of all the village mulling around our hut. We had no fear because this village was still close enough to Nam Tha that we knew many here had been to our hospital. Some we recognized as old patients. There were not too many people here who needed medicine because they frequently came on to Nam Tha.

Although the weather remained unchanged the trip became ten times more interesting. We were plunging down deep gorges, but instead of Colorado River-like cliffs on each side, we were closed in by huge luxuriant jungle giants. I was constantly yelling to the boys in the other boat, and they were calling back to me: "Look at that animal!" "Did you see that, was it a bird? Was it a monkey?"

We stopped at several villages that day and at one we ate our C-ration lunch. Each village along this river seemed to have its own epidemic. None of the epidemics seemed to cross or go up and down the river. These villages live in complete isolation from one another with no commerce and no trading. Although this is evil, as far as progress is concerned, it is good insofar as it prevents the spread of epidemic diseases. In some villages there was cholera, in others dysentery. Everywhere there were scabies, ringworm, beri

beri, the alternating fevers of malaria, intestinal worms and yaws. I will never get hardened to this misery.

In the village where we planned to spend our second night, we thought the propagandists might have made some headway and we were a bit apprehensive. It was a poor village and extremely isolated, even from Nam Tha. As we walked up the side of the jungle into the cleared area where the village stood, clinging to the mountain slope, we asked for the house of the chieftain. We were given directions and all the village stirred and walked behind us. Suddenly from the crowd a man stepped forward with his small son. The father, evidently an important man in the village, came up to us, fell on his knees, clasped his hands before his face and thanked us again for what we had done. He then welcomed us to his village. His son had been one of the first cases of Kwashiorkor's disease that we had in Nam Tha. We had cured him and were able to explain to his father how to prevent a relapse. The son walked up to John and put his arms around John's waist. He had absolutely no fear, for he had known the tenderness and compassion of my boys. This made us acceptable to the village immediately, and the Tassieng came to the top of his stairs and beckoned us to enter into his home.

This Tassieng was a grand old fellow and answered a lot of questions for us. We asked him if he had ever seen white men here before. "No." We asked if he, or his family who were sitting around, found us droll. His truthful answer was, "Yes." As the evening progressed we became more interesting to them and they to us. We asked him if he had ever seen Chinese in this village. The old man said, "Oh, yes. Chinese have come here frequently, but not recently." I asked, "How long?" The old man said, "Oh, not for about ten seasons."

If propagandizing was being done in this village, it was being done by people of this very same tribe, and not by the Chinese. The communists had frequently offered silver to young men and women of the tribes of Northern Laos and invited them to come to Yunnan and Canton. Here in the Chinese communist states the people were gently but firmly and inexorably indoctrinated into the communist belief. The communists dangled all sorts of glib allurements in front of these people and offered to them especially "progress." The young men and women believed with all their hearts that the new land reformers would offer something better to their backward villagers. They then returned to the village of their ancestors and became teachers, of untruths. To the ignorant people of their village they would say, "Let us build a school, for we know how to read and write and we wish you, our people, to know also." And the people wished for this knowledge and would cooperate.

These villagers have no concept of what happened in the political field. They have no idea of the rift the world has suffered. They understand nothing about the two camps of ideas, the God-loving men and the Godless men. They have no idea of what America is and certainly no idea of where it is located.

It is hard to make these people hate. It is the custom of the land that a stranger in the village must be well treated. We were usually met at the river's edge by some elder of the village with a small silver bowl containing some flowers, candles and other offerings of welcome to the visitors.

This little village was remarkable: it had sidewalks. It was the only village that I have seen in the Kingdom with sidewalks. Only here it was a center-walk. The mud was so deep and so slippery in the monsoon rains, that the villagers had a raised path bordered on each side. Here caked mud and rocks a bit more solid were laid so that one could walk without slipping.

They found the spectacle of us Americans very interesting. They enjoyed watching us open our cans, cooking dinner, eating with bizarre instruments, mixing the black powder of Borden's, the white powder of Pream, the granules of sugar, and adding boiling water—these are strange-looking ceremonies to one who has never seen them before. To these villagers we were the greatest show on earth and the miraculousness of our medicines were most welcome. They had heard a little bit about us, and were very anxious to see us here in the flesh. Again many in this village seemed to have something wrong, but there were no psychosomatic diseases in Laos. For the record, during my year I never saw one case of neurosis.

According to the ancient map the halfway point for us would be the village of Nale. We arrived there in the late afternoon of the third day. This was not much different from other villages save it was a bit larger, and there was a police outpost there. Of course it was still raining when the village chief came out to welcome us. This man could read and write, and spoke some French, and had a fine substantial house. He had spent several years of his life in the capital of Vientiane, during the French occupation.

Next door to his home was a thatched sickbay with a "nurse" working there. This nurse had nothing in the way of medicines, not even aspirins, quinine or adhesive tape. He legally came under the Public Health Department of the Royal Kingdom but there was no way to get medicines to his outpost on anything like a regular schedule. The Royal Government was afraid to send any quantity of bulk medicines to this area for fear that it would fall into the hands of the bandits.

We had a long sick-call here lasting late into the night. There was a woman with a fibroid tumor; a boy with a type of ophthalmia which turns the eyeball into a whitish protruding globe; and several women with goiters; and one man here with a huge hernia.

We left many crates of medicines with the nurse, who seemed quite bright and very appreciative. I later told the Minister all about this.

The village chieftain gave us a fine little dinner mixed with our own food, and showed us then to the guest room. Because the advance *pirogue* of guards had told him we were coming, he had hastily constructed for the use of the white man some beds. "You know those bizarre white men do not sleep on stuffed leaf mats on the floor like normal people do. For some reason they put their mattresses up on a wooden frame and call it a bed." (Why do we?) He had had these beds constructed for us. But the measurements were a little off. They were only wide enough to lie perfectly still either on your back or on your stomach. If you rolled over, you would roll off for sure. Poor Bob with his husky six-foot frame really had a dangerous night.

We started up early the next day and several hours later we were over-taken by another *pirogue*. There was a frantic father in this boat who lived north of Nale. The night before, when we had arrived in Nale, his sister found out that we were the white doctors from Nam Tha. They had heard of us. She immediately set out by foot north to the village of her brother, and returned with him in the morning. They brought his dying daughter. We had already left the village so they borrowed a boat and came down to catch us.

We could not land anywhere because of the river and the jungle. He shot on down the rapids with us to the next village and carried his daughter into the guest hut. She had fulminating pneumonia. Her respiration was already a death rattle. Her heartbeat was so faint that I could hardly hear it and her lips were blue from lack of oxygen. We did everything we could, gave her medicines and infusions, and finally turned to the father and offered him enough medicines to continue the treatment for several days. I knew that the treatment would be futile. I knew she could not possibly live. And she was only about three, the age of my own brother's daughter.

That night we spent in a Kha Kho village. It was an abhorrent little place where we were looked upon with real suspicion. Every child in that village had fulminating whooping cough. The night's air was torn by their hacking. We had plenty of terramycin which is specific against this organism, but the thick tenacious mucus clogging the throats of the children was the worst thing that I had ever seen. After a sleepless night, we packed up again. We loaded our gear, now considerably lighter, and continued on down the river. We stopped at several villages and around noon the sun came out. It was most welcome.

We went on down and reached the Mekong River by nightfall. At the village of Ban Pak Tha, the Nam Tha River weds the mighty Mekong. This is a fine old village built on a lush piece of land between the two rivers. It was small and of course very muddy, but it had something about it that was dignified.

The village chief took us to a big, decrepit, termite-infested house that had in former times been quite a beautiful place. It had belonged to the Provincial Governor. But years of monsoons, disuse and tropical ravages had nearly converted this to the dust from which it came. And the Governor had moved north to Nam Tha. However this house was the very best that he could offer to us and to our eyes it looked like Buckingham Palace. We held sick-call that night after dinner and it lasted until midnight. Kieu had come with us as interpreter for this trip. We sent Chai on to Vientiane by air, with all of the boys' baggage, as they were going to America at the end of this float. Their personal baggage was too valuable to risk on the river.

Kieu had been a good interpreter. I will never forget how he gently reprimanded me for riding a bicycle to the Governor's house one night in Nam Tha. It was only down the lane a bit and I did not feel like walking. I asked why in the world I should not ride a bike. He replied, "Ce n'est pas chic." He was awfully worried about "face"; apparently I did not think about it enough. John, with a Continental background, was much more aware of this sort of thing. John always knew the right words and never gave offense, whereas my hot Irish temper sometimes caused embarrassment.

This particular night I was tired and cross. The crowds at sick-call were doing what so frequently happens, they were closing in on me so tightly that I could hardly breathe, much less listen to a man's chest through a stethoscope. I instructed Kieu to tell them to move back as I was being suffocated. In his well-trained, gentlemanly manner, he said something. They did not move. I told him to get the mob back, I was getting a little frightened. He repeated something sotto voce. Finally I turned and yelled at him to tell the people to get back or I would stop sick-call. I had no idea that yelling at my interpreter would cause him to lose that much face. Kieu, being as tired and perhaps as cross as I was, just walked away and refused to work. John went to try to apologize for me and get him to come back, but he could not, for he would lose face. So we held sick-call without him. We were all under a terrible strain, even the Lao themselves. It is no wonder that we were all edgy, cross and irritable.

While we were bathing from a bucket of river water, eating our dinner, or holding sick-call, we would always be watched by that audience of people, hacking, spitting, and being sick at both ends. But their smiles were so gracious and they were so genuine that I could never get really angry with them.

Late that night after sick-call when we were so beat we could hardly hold our heads up, the village chief of Ban Pak Tha asked us to come to his house. We wanted to get out of it, but we went and were glad. We found that he had laid out a little private dinner for us. We had some good Lao soup, Lao alcohol, and for one of the few times in Asia, potatoes.

The next morning we changed boats. We were now nearing civilization, on the Mekong. Here there were larger boats that had motors on them. These haul rice up and down the wide river from Luang Prabang to Ban Pak Tha and then further up along the Burma border. We were able to get a place on one of these on top of several tons of burlap rice bags. We left all remaining medicines at Ban Pak Tha with the schoolteacher. Even the bags and the small black footlocker in which we carried the supplies were left behind. With just our personal gear, plus a few gifts that were given to us, we left Ban Pak Tha for Luang Prabang.

These large motor-driven riverboats are built on Mississippi houseboat lines. Should we sit in the burlap on the main deck and slap at the bugs, or lie on the tin roof of the second deck and burn in the blazing sun? Being fair-skinned and having a certain amount of tolerance to fleas by this time, I took the lower berth, but the boys decided to go and sit on top and did get a good tan. I had had enough foresight to bring a book along, so sitting up on top of burlap bags, I read *The Great Alliance*, one of the volumes of Winston Churchill's history of the war. What more felicitous place in the wide world to read about our great ally England than on Asia's mighty Mekong?

On the afternoon of the eighth day we were still sprawled in confusion amidst the howling livestock, nursing mothers, sweating coolies, dried meats and other accoutrements of this Mekong *Queen Mary*. Kieu, now in better spirits, told us he had just heard the pilot say that we would soon be in Luang Prabang. We climbed out the side and up on the roof to watch beautiful, ancient Luang Prabang loom into view. The high golden spire of the main pagoda was the first thing that we saw. If it had been Paris in springtime or autumn in Manhattan, it could not have looked more beautiful to us.

As soon as the crew had a piece of planking down, we scrambled off the boat and climbed up the banks to the road. Here, with the solid earth beneath us, we felt that the river trip was at last completed. We felt as though the last days had been more fruitful than perhaps the whole preceding month. We really had taken American humanity into the most unknown, untouched hinterlands. We felt as though we had done some service in the name of our country, our fellow man and our God.

We grabbed two bicycle-propelled rickshaws and headed to the house of Dolf Droge, the head of USIS in Luang Prabang. When Dolf first looked at us, he said that we resembled prisoners who had just been released from communism. But after a hot shower and a cold beer our looks were markedly improved, to say nothing of our spirits.

Although Vientiane is the administrative capital of Laos, Luang Prabang is the ancient religious capital. Here is the palace of the King. Here is where all the princes live and the court is held. We decided on our second afternoon to pay our respects to His Highness Prince Phetserath, the Viceroy of Laos. As the boys were going to fly on to Bangkok in a few days, we thought that this was the opportune time. We asked Dolf to come along with some camera equipment and get a few snapshots for us. This was especially interesting to Dolf, since Prince Phetserath has not always been interpreted as pro-American in his comments. Whatever may have been the Prince's political leanings, his social and native leanings were wonderful. He was genuinely interested in his people and he showed it. He had sent us a gift of some husky chickens of fine breed from Thailand.

We went to his palace which is beautifully situated, gardened and groomed on a bend of the river just outside Luang Prabang. We visited with His Royal Highness for an hour, during which time Dolf took some candid pictures. The Prince was tremendously interested in our river trip and in the sicknesses encountered. He then asked me about hospital problems, how much it was costing per patient for rice.

Dolf Droge, like his boss Hank Miller, is one of those excellent men who walk with kings and do not lose the common touch. Son of an immigrant who became a cowboy in Montana, Dolf has done all sorts of work from newspaper reporting to acting as a nightclub comedian. He stands over six-foot seven inches (Hank Miller being a mere six-foot-six). Dolf explained to the Prince that when he was in Thailand the people used to call him "Pret". The Prince knew the legend immediately. It seems that "Pret" of ancient Siam was a huge monster, larger than a coconut tree and just as thin. This monster would reach down and pick evil people up in his hands and devour them. I took the occasion to tell the Prince a little of my plans. I told him that my money was almost entirely exhausted now. My two assistants had to return to America because they would enter Notre Dame in the fall semester. This was already the month of August.

We explained that our locals had been well trained and that we hoped they would take over from us. I laughingly explained that I had come to give aid to the Lao and had succeeded in working myself out of a job. The Prince exclaimed, "Good!" When he saw my surprise at this he said, "This is what aid should be, doctor. It should not make the people more dependent upon the aider, or upon the country from which he has come. Aid should work itself into a position where it abolishes any further need of itself." After thinking about this, I agree.

We discussed some other ideas and he told me to see the Minister of Health and the Prime Minister when I returned to Vientiane. We intended to fly down on the Veha Akhat's small plane the following day. The two boys would leave in a few days for Bangkok and then on back to the States. I would call upon the Ministers.

As we left, the Prince walked out of his palace and down to the jeep with us. He turned to us, holding out his hand in democratic fashion, and said, "Thank you for what you have done for my people, and come back again."

ELEVEN ·

THE MINISTER AGREES

We arrived in Vientiane in early August. John and Bob since February had been living in Nam Tha, with only a rare break from their work. And they had done an excellent job. With no previous medical training, they had not thought that they would ever be able to learn the things they had to know. Very little time elapsed before they had accomplished extraordinary tasks. Pain, hunger, ignorance, these are the things that go on forever, and these are the greatest internationalists of them all. These are the things which Americans are so well armed to fight against. Gentleness, intelligence and will can conquer. My boys illustrated this. And in this conquest John and Bob felt the vivid and intense joy of being able to serve. The best thing I can say of them is that they are fine Americans. I am proud to have had them on my team.

After they flew out of Vientiane, I was alone. But the job was not quite completed. I went to see the Minister of Health to present my "phase-out" plan. I had prepared a schedule, and intended to offer my proposals, and to make a request. I wanted the continuity of my program guaranteed. We had established the hospital at Nam Tha, and wanted to insure that after our departure it would continue to flourish. All the things we had done were so carried out that our departure would not create a void. We installed no X-ray machines, nor any large electrical plant. We had no complicated or extremely delicate instruments. We utilized ten or twelve basic antibiotics and other medicines, so that their exact usage and dosage was well understood by the local nurses. We turned over to midwives the CARE kits making them completely self-sufficient. The vaccination program, carried out by the locals themselves, would add a marked degree of immunity to many thousands of people in the high valley. The instructions would make them more cognizant of the relationships between dirt and disease. I did not want these accomplishments lost after our departure. I wanted to make sure that we would leave something real and substantial behind us.

I proposed three points to the Minister. I asked first, that he give our hospital a charter. This would mean that a specific amount of money would be earmarked for the hospital based on the number of patients treated, and hospitalized. This would mean that certain monies would be allotted for upkeep, and care of the buildings. Instead of paint and wood being bought with my own money, the hospital would now be administered and financed by the government of Laos, and their medicines would come from the government warehouse.

Second, I asked that he send to Nam Tha two Bangkok-trained nurses to replace my men. These nurses were well trained in Thailand's school of nursing. There were only a few in the whole Kingdom of Laos, but I asked for two for Nam Tha.

Third, I asked that a *médecin indochinois* be sent to replace me. There are no other doctors by international standards in the kingdom, except the Minister himself. There are 15 men who have had some medical training, though by our standards very little. These men could practice medicine in Laos.

If Dr. Oudom, the Minister of Health would agree to this, I in turn would agree to leave everything that we had brought to Laos in the hospital at Nam Tha. This meant that absolutely everything would stay there, beds, mosquito nets, linens, drapes, surgical instruments, stethoscopes, otoscopes, house gear, and about $25,000 worth of antibiotics. All these we would turn over to the *médecin indochinois*. Then I would myself return to America.

The Minister immediately agreed, but expressed some surprise that I wanted to become expendable. I told him that in my mind America should not attempt to build a dynasty in a foreign land. We should not attempt to make a foreign land dependent on us for its maintenance.

Dr. Oudom was pleased with this point of view. I also remembered the rapidity with which Prince Phetsareth had said "Good" when I told him that I had worked myself out of a job. The Minister asked, "Are you content to be replaced by a man who does not measure up to your ability as a physician?" I said that I believed the *médecin indochinois* to be the best that the Lao government had in the medical program, and that I would be very pleased if he would take over what we had built. I felt that if I had closed down the hospital at my departure, this would have intimated that no one else could do the job as well as we could.

Guardedly I added, "I hope you are not too pleased with my departure because I hope to return to Laos again."

With a smile, Dr. Oudom said: "You and your men have had the cotton strings of *baci* tied on your arms, and the heart of the Lao put in your hands. You may return whenever you wish."

I left to return to the north for a six weeks' phase-out period. The plane was forced down in Luang Prabang for several days, but when the rains lessened a bit in their fury, I was able to get on up to Nam Tha.

Most of the village met the plane, and all were relieved to know we had completed the great float without mishap. They also noted that the cast I had been wearing for so long was now off my wrist. They were not nearly as pleased as I was. Now I was a little more mobile, and could do surgery again.

Si was glad to be back in his domain in our kitchen again, but felt as though his job as a cook had shrunk to almost nothing. All he had to do was feed me. And our hut of a house seemed enormous. I was entirely alone, and rattled around in the place as though it was a huge barn. The new "doctor," who had just arrived, was going to move into my house and I intended to fulfill my promise of leaving everything for him. For the present time, however, he lived in the house of the Chao Khuong.

I explained to him how we had urged our patients to pay us for our medicines. I believed this important for two reasons. First of all, we needed the food; running and stocking the hospital was expensive enough without having to go to the village markets and buy chickens and eggs. Secondly, Operation Laos was not supposed to be a charity program. We were not here for hand-outs. The people of Laos are proud, and were pleased to pay for what we offered to them. This increased their prestige and mine too. One of the most touching of these payments was a gift that an old Yao once gave me. It was a small towel that she had found somewhere. She had embroidered with her home-grown cotton thread the words in Chinese characters for "A Cheery Good Morning".

The Lao doctor agreed about "fees" and said he would continue it. One of the first things he did was to start the villagers building a large fence around the hospital compound. This would keep the water buffalo from meandering around the front lawn of the surgical ward. I wondered why I had never thought of it.

This young doctor had had his *lycée* graduation in Vientiane. He then went to a "medical school" for two years in Cambodia, and became a "doctor". He was very young, very bright and anxious to please and impress all about him. He was typical of the new generation of Asia complete with wrist watch, expensive shoes, and high ideals. Yet he still respected the words of his grandfather with childlike humility.

We spent many hours together going over the medicines and instruments. I taught him how to run the sterilizer and how to put up surgical packs and instrument kits. He assisted me in a lot of surgery himself, with Lao nurses and midwives working as scrub and circulating nurses. He was conscious of his new duties and took them very seriously. He ran the sick-call line every day and I would go over just before noon to see certain cases upon which he wished to have my opinion. Then in the afternoons we would do surgery.

All the villagers knew that the new Lao doctor was replacing me, and the two new nurses were the replacements for John and Bob. Whenever they expressed fear, we tried to transfer to the Lao doctor all allegiance that we had won from a year in this country. He would need it.

The governor gave a going-away party for me with all the village in attendance. A Lam Vong, the national dance of Laos, was held. We had done it frequently; in fact, Pete and John were quite expert at it. I was sorry they were not with me that night in September.

A platform was built in the village square, and the amplifier from our movie projector was used for the local orchestra of drums, khenes, and string instruments. The dancers all lined up but do not touch each other. Placed side by side they moved rhythmically around in a large circle. They twisted their arms and hands with great delicacy. The dancers become experts in keeping masklike faces, while weaving around the dance floor. During the previous year, whenever a Lam Vong was held, you could always find a member of the Dooley mission there. Tonight I was alone.

Everyday villagers and mountain tribesmen would come to my house and give me going-away gifts. They would sit and chat about this or that, ask me how far it was to my village in America, and when would I return to Nam Tha. I knew they were sorry to see me go. The children would laugh a little, and I kept up "face". Even in the depths of their misery the children seemed always to manage a little laugh.

The Asian smile is more overwhelming than anywhere else. The Asian uses his smile as the mask or the mirror of his heart. Anger, fear, hurt, apprehension, these can all be manifested with a smile. I have seen the Asian smiling to explain how something pains him. I have seen the Asian smiling when he knows he will soon be operated on. I have seen the Asian smiling when he fears what the spirits or the white medicine man will do next.

The old witch doctors came to say goodbye. The teller of old legends, tales of love and sweet grief, he too came and wished me all happiness. He said that he hoped a butterfly would perch on my shoulder and that this good omen would bring me happiness. An old sorcerer came and sat before me and shook her joss sticks in their cylinders. She threw the half-moon clappers on the ground before me and said that my future looked bright, and in it she could see my return to her village. As she left, she fell into a spasm of coughing; the agony of rampaging tuberculosis.

Now that the boys were gone, my life was desperately singular. I used to look in the mirror and talk to myself just to hear English: "Good morning, Dooley, you look like the devil today." Si and Chai knew my loneliness and would come and sit at the table with me during meals. We spoke of our plans. I had found jobs for them in the American community down in Vientiane. They would work there until I returned. And my own plans—simple.

I wanted to tell America about Laos, and to point out the fact that we can span the gap between nations with a bridge whose fibers are woven of compassion. Someone had written to me and said that I must feel awfully limited in my work in Laos—limited by lack of transportation and communication, by custom and isolation. He wrote: "Give me a wider horizon." I wanted to show how vast the horizons of the spirit can be. And especially I wanted to show that we Americans possess an instrument not too well developed, more powerful than any bomb yet devised. It is the force that can relieve ugliness and tragedy. It is the force of gentleness.

On the morning of my departure hundreds upon hundreds of villagers were milling around the strip when I walked out with Si and Chai. How different these people seemed now—from the preceding February when we first walked down this lane from the landing strip. Now I knew each one, remembered their suffering, had lived part of their life, had become involved in some portion of their existence. As I walked through the crowd many reached out and thanked me with the simple eloquence of a touch.

I felt some guilt in leaving, but some pride in knowing that there was now a hospital in Nam Tha and things would run well. Strangely enough, these people had become important to me. I had learned to love them.

The plane took off. In the air the French pilot, usually untouched by the peasantry of the north, turned and said to me, *"Ils vous aiment bien."* Yes, I believe they did love me too.

TWELVE ·

SUNLIGHT ON THE EDGE

As the plane flew quietly on south to Vientiane, I thought of the thousands of hours I had spent in these villages. I remembered the long talks with the ancient old folk, many who seemed to be Father Asia personified—Ojisan, Old Joe, Maggie, the Chao Khuong, Cauvin. I looked at Chai and Si cramped in the small back seat and the words of James Michener came to my mind. I had read them long ago, and now the sentences took on a muscle and flesh, a hue and tone. They were applicable here with astonishing accuracy. He wrote:

"Most people in Asia will go to bed hungry tonight.

Most people in Asia live in grinding poverty.

Most people in Asia have never seen a doctor.

Most people in Asia believe anything different would be better than what they have, and they are determined to get it.

Most people in Asia have never known civil liberties.

Most people in Asia believe that freedom of enterprise means the right of the Western Colonial powers to exploit them.

Most people in Asia distrust people with white skins.

Most people in Asia are determined never again to be ruled by foreigners."

Many say that, until the villagers learn to read and write, democracy can never exist in Asia. They say that the masses of the peoples, the land people, are really not a power in Asia. Perhaps villagers do not wax eloquent on political affairs, but let their personal lives be affected to their dislike, and they will speak with massive action. An example is the exodus of nearly a million North Vietnamese to the south, for one reason: people did not wish to live under a political rule that was godless. Perhaps their own inaction, coupled with the white man's errors, helped to bring this ogre to their land.

But they have action now. There is great conflict now, and there are many errors. Perhaps there will be greater anguish in the future. But these are the birth pains of freedom.

Suddenly the little plane pitched into a steep bank and circled the airstrip at Vientiane. Down and down it flew, then we hit the runway with a gentle bump, a bounce, and the softer bump of the tail wheel. There was a rumbling race along the runway, an awkward turn, and we taxied to the parking area. I was back in Vientiane for a goodbye.

I went to pay my respects to Ambassador Parsons, who wished me all success in my hopes for return. I visited the administrators of the economic aid program. I felt that now I had much more insight into the situation than before. It is trite to reiterate that economic aid is essential to the life of Laos. But what should we expect in return? Their alliance, their friendship, their adherence to our policies? If the Lao government does not always follow the "American Line," let us not immediately attack them. Asian nations, newly independent and fiercely proud, will never accept any kind of American domination, however benevolent our intentions may be.

When a man chooses to "do good" in this world, it has been said that he cannot expect other men to roll boulders off his path. On the contrary, he can expect some people to roll them on it.

There is a glaring contrast in the yet underdeveloped Asia. One sees beauty and decay, and at the same time a massive potential for a new and throbbing life. Amidst the beauty there is horror, and the constant stalking threat of Communist conquest.

Many Americans are working in Asia to prevent this conquest. Most Americans are doing a superb job, yet there are great errors, easy to see. The most devastating is an attitude, held by some, that, simply because people in Laos live close to the earth, away from traffic, smoke, miltown, and cocktails, they are therefore *ad hoc* healthy and happy. "Don't change them, they're happy in their ignorance." "Why show them what they can never achieve themselves?" "They don't want to advance, they are perfectly unruffled and content." This pseudo-sophisticated attitude is not only wrong, it is malicious.

Let us stop all this blather and bleat about the beatitudes of democracy. Let us get out and show, with simple spontaneity and love, our ability to work at the level of the people we aim to aid. Let us stop proclaiming ourselves as the world standard. Democracy, as championed by the United States, does not translate well into Lao. Not yet. We evolved it from 1776 to 1958. Let us be patient with the Asian. The Lao need only time, education, and stimulation.

I believe that we would gain more for our own country (and this is certainly part of the incentive behind our foreign aid) if we emphasized the connections that exist between peoples. Let us show that we believe these connections to be greater than the differences. The cables binding humanity around the world are stronger than national rivalries. Let us re-affirm, and then live, our belief in the family of man. Let us prove again that America understands that "God hath made of one blood all men for to dwell upon the earth."

I said goodbye to the Ministers and restated my desire to return. They said that my mission would always be welcome, no matter what the political circumstances. To Chai and Si I offered my sincere thanks for their aid and fellowship. And on the third day I slipped out to the airfield for the flight to Bangkok. In Bangkok I changed to the huge plane and within a few hours of my departure I was listening to the clipped, precise English of the PAA stewardess. Her words sounded almost foreign to my ears.

As the plane lunged through the night, I reviewed what had passed through the turbulent fifteen months. Suddenly a little ray of morning came across the sky and I saw some sunlight on the edge of tomorrow. I said a prayer of thanks to God. I used to be selfish in my prayers, always asking for something. This prayer was different. I am now tremendously aware of my gratitude to Him.

I was back in America last November when the news broke that the Royal Government had settled its differences with the "dissident brothers" of northern Laos. A new coalition government was formed with two cabinet posts going to the Pathet Lao, including Prince SouphanouVong as Minister of Reconstruction and Town Planning. The Prince disavowed his allegiance to Communism, and denied that he was unfriendly to the West. Still, there were skeptics who said that the move marked the beginning of Communist infiltration. Who knows? Certainly not I.

Laos was still first on my own order of unfinished business. I was in Washington to meet for the first time a man who had been my most sympathetic and inspiring correspondent for nearly a year. He was Dr. Peter Commanduras, a distinguished Washington physician and associate professor of Clinical Medicine at the George Washington University Medical School.

We met in the lobby of the Mayflower Hotel and went in to luncheon. Dr. Comanduras was a handsome, dignified man in his early 50s, with a youthful face topped by greying hair. As we talked through luncheon, I began to understand his interest in my work. His clear concept of American medical aid to foreign countries, independent of government control and performed by individual doctors, went far beyond my own thinking.

Dr. Comanduras had tried and failed to sell his commonsense approach to foreign-aid officials who are impatient with anything less than multimillion dollar projects. Like me, he advocated keeping things simple, making a modest start, building slowly. He was delighted when I produced figures to show that our sixteen months' mission had cost less than $50,000 plus the contributions of pharmaceuticals and supplies.

But he also had what I lacked—the experience, temperament and ability to plan and direct operations. I see myself as just another worker in the vineyard. Hence his next remark took me completely by surprise.

"I have been thinking seriously of taking up this work myself," he said. "My children are about through college, the family is fairly well provided for, my wife goes along wholeheartedly with my ideas." He paused for a moment, and then looked at me with a twinkle in his eyes. "I feel pretty much as you do, Dooley," he said. "How can we go around preaching this idea to others unless we're willing to practice it ourselves?"

One week later I stood in the board room of the International Rescue Committee and faced the distinguished group of directors seated around the big table. Leo Cherne, the chairman, introduced me and asked me to tell my story. When I had finished with my report on Operation Laos, I sat down and waited.

"Well, doctor," someone asked, "what do you have to propose?"

"From the modest beginning I have made," I said, "I propose that we carry the work another step forward. I believe I have demonstrated that a medical team like mine can be kept in the field for sixteen months on a budget of $50,000. Dr. Commanduras and I have drawn up a plan for sending out six such teams. My team will return to Laos, the other five can be sent into other critical areas. I propose that our plan be adopted and sponsored by the International Rescue Committee."

There was silence. I sat down and waited for discussion.

Angier Biddle Duke, president of the International Rescue Committee, said: "The IRC has previously helped refugees from totalitarian oppression. Under the proposed medical program we can help a different kind of refugee, refugees from pain, from wretchedness, from misery, refugees in their own country."

Most of the board members agreed that this concept of humanitarian work, free from the stigma of proselytizing or policy peddling, was indeed a fine thing. But apparently the program was not consistent with the traditional approach of IRC, for someone then said: "We'll have to change the charter, but it's not that easy."

Well, I thought, *Bau pinh yanh,* as we say in Lao.

"Why not?" I blithely asked.

They all laughed good-naturedly at my brashness and naïveté, and then began to discuss the point. Then suddenly a motion was made to amend the charter enabling us to "accept the task of providing humanitarian medical aid to threatened parts of the world." The motion was seconded, and passed by a unanimous vote. I felt like swooning in my leather-cushioned chair.

That was the birth of MEDICO—officially Medical International Cooperation, a division of the International Rescue Committee. Dr. Gordon Seagrave, the world famous Burma Surgeon, will head up the work in Burma. Early this summer I will be on my way back to Laos. The four other teams are being shaped up under the direction of Dr. Comanduras. We already have a great many volunteers—doctors and dentists who are ready to sacrifice their practices; nurses, technicians, social workers, and plain college students like John deVitry and Bob Waters who are eager to serve on the teams.

The medical profession has rallied to our support. There's a plan afoot for a roving team of medical specialists—an eye man, an obstetrician, an orthopedic surgeon, a tropical medicine expert, etc.—who will rotate among the MEDICO outposts, treating patients and teaching native doctors and nurses.

MEDICO won't be big or fancy. (The global planners will probably sneer at us as pretty small potatoes.) But we'll be doctors doing what God meant us to do—treating sick people, and probably some of the most desperately sick people in the world.

We will do our level best, wherever we go, and with what little we have, to let the plain people of the world know that Americans really care.

At this juncture I thought of Dr. Schweitzer. I wrote at once and told him of our program, our high hopes, our belief that Americans would back us with the help we needed. MEDICO's teams can only be the hands; the heart is always in America. I pointed out that through MEDICO Americans could show to the world not only how Americans will care for and help other men, but how men can care for and help other men.

I asked that he accept a position such as he has never before accepted in his eighty-four years. The warmest and proudest statement we can make is that Dr. Albert Schweitzer has accepted the position of Honorary Patron of MEDICO.

With those who have helped us in the past, and with those who will work on and support MEDICO teams in the future, I wish to share these words I received in a letter from Dr. Schweitzer:

"I do not know what your destiny will ever be, but this I do know . . . You will always have happiness if you seek and find: how to serve."

THE
NIGHT
THEY BURNED
THE
MOUNTAIN

To My Mother
with deep gratitude for giving me her tender
love as a shield against life's winds and storms.

To Dwight Davis and Earl Rhine
with whom I've shared joys and worries, dis-
appointments and quiet triumphs in the fog-
shrouded valley of Muong Sing.

CONTENTS

ONE ·

BEFORE MY HIGHEST MOUNTAIN

It was a Saturday, at high noon, when the tired-looking Lao soldier came into my clinic in the little village of Muong Sing in northern Laos. He snapped to a slightly languid salute and said, *"Thanh Mo America, mi tayah.* Doctor America, you have a telegram."

What could this mean? Coming on the military radio, it must be about the war. My heart jumped a little and with a dry mouth I said, *"Ou he kai.* Give it to me."

He said that it was being held at the radio shack in the fortress, and I should accompany him there. I turned the line of patients over to Earl Rhine, one of my assistants, and walked out into the rain, across the road to the fortress.

There was war in Laos, and there were rumors of more war. Only four days before, the Voice of America had broadcast that over four thousand Red troops were in the two provinces of Sam Neua and Phong Saly. Other troops were massing on the Vietnamese side of the frontier and a new attack was expected. Would it spread to the China frontier? Would we be able to go on practising medicine much longer in this little village located at a point where Laos, China, and Burma meet?

In the mud radio shack another Lao soldier thrust a flimsy, crumpled sheet of blue paper into my hand. He said it had been forwarded from the Lao Army headquarters in the capital. He was sorry he was so many hours late in getting it to me but *"het punh,"* the war, you know. This limp piece of paper was to become a turning-point in my life. Noon, Saturday, August 15, in the year 1959.

My knees were shaking. I sat down on the wooden bench beside the radio operator, and smoothed out the thin blue paper on the table. I tried to make out the sentences. As the Lao language has no Roman letters, French is used in telegraph messages. Each letter of the telegram was in a box by itself. When I wrote out the message with its long introductory order to the local Commandant, the part addressed to me looked like this:

FROMPE TER COMAND URAS DOCTOR DOOLEY URGENT RETURN TOUS
IMMEDIATELY

The message made no sense to me. I asked that it be retransmitted. The operator said that this would take hours, but I insisted. I went back to the clinic and showed the garbled words to the boys. Dwight Davis, my other assistant, took out a pencil and immediately divided the letters so that the sentence read in English as follows:

FROM PETER COMANDURAS: DOCTOR DOOLEY, URGENT RETURN TO U.S.
IMMEDIATELY

How quickly Dwight grasped and understood that telegram—how strangely quick.

Suddenly the earth seemed to open up underneath me. Return to the U.S. now? I was intending to go in three months anyway. Why *now?* Had something happened to my mother? Had something bad happened to MEDICO? Had the Ambassador to Laos notified the State Department of my refusal to leave and had they in turn requested Dr. Peter Comanduras, as chief of MEDICO, to order me out? Why didn't Peter explain himself? Why did he just say "Urgent, return to U.S.?" Didn't he know that we were involved in a war? Didn't he know that the wounded might start flowing into this hospital tomorrow? Didn't he know that the mountains of Laos were on fire? What could be so urgent that I must come home *now,* instead of when I was due to go home in a few months? Didn't Peter know that Laos was moving deeper and deeper into the shadows? This was not the time to abandon my work. Didn't he know what the Communists would say if I deserted my hospital? "A typical American reactionary imperialistic coward."

I had complete confidence in Doctor Peter Comanduras as Chief of MEDICO, but why was he ordering me out now, without explanation? He was living in the civilized world. I was living in the world beyond. More than mere miles separated us. How could he judge what must be done when he was not on the scene? It seemed to me that the sky was full of the sound of thunder. It seemed to me that the night was coming at high noon. "Urgent Doctor Dooley return to U.S. immediately." This meant that I must abandon my hospital, abandon all I had done, abandon all the work of the last year. "Urgent, return to U.S. immediately." The letters in that telegram stared up at me and stabbed my soul.

The things that I felt in my heart I said with my mouth. I asked all these questions of my two Texan assistants, Earl and Dwight. They offered no answers. They didn't even try to present anything good, except that Earl said, "Maybe you're going home to do a TV show," at which I growled back in anger.

The message had been sent by the Lao army. How did they get it? Why did Peter wire me through the Lao army? Why didn't he send the telegram through the usual civilian channels? The army had filed it as TOP SECRET, URGENT. Had the message come so marked from America? How did it get to the Army in the first place? Was it sent to the Ambassador who requested the army to forward it to me? I was terribly concerned. My mind began to conjure up monstrous thoughts. Could it possibly have anything to do with the small tumor that Dr. Van Valin had cut off my chest? At once I banished that thought as sheer impossibility.

I decided that the wire must have something to do with the economic situation of MEDICO. It seemed to me that we were always on the brink of broke. I was going to have to go home and raise money. This infuriated me. Several times during the night I woke up suddenly, startled. I sat up in my bunk when thoughts came crowding to my mind. I did not sleep that night, nor the next night, nor for many nights to follow. By mid-week I had convinced myself that Dr. Comanduras had had a heart attack and that I was going to have to go and work at our MEDICO office. I, jungle physician, would have to sit at a desk in a New York office.

I sent a telegram down to Vientiane to Horace Smith, the American Ambassador, on Sunday. I asked him if he would please send up a plane to take me out. This was difficult to ask because only a few days before I had sent him a message pointing out that I was autonomous and that we could take care of ourselves despite the threat of war in our village. Now I had to reverse myself and ask him for his plane. I was sure the Ambassador knew about the New York telegram because I decided in my confused mind that the Lao government had received it from him.

No plane came Sunday, no plane came Monday, no plane came Tuesday. I felt as though I was tightly sealed in a coffin, my valley gray and grim. I walked around my village and talked to the people to explain to them that I had to leave quickly. They could not understand. They asked if I was afraid of the war. I tried to explain to them why I must go home, though I did not know myself. How could I explain to other ears what my own heart did not know?

On Tuesday afternoon the horizon could only be seen in dim outline; the mountains were veiled in the mist. No plane could come in now. Soon black clouds would roll across the heavens again and we would be surrounded by the monsoon storm of wind and water. These were wild and gloomy times, wild and gloomy in the valley, wild and gloomy in my heart. Yet this dirty, barren, underdeveloped Asian village of stink and misery and wretchedness suddenly seemed warm and good and close. I did not want to leave it. I did not want to abandon it. I did not want to go to America now. I could feel the dampness of soggy sentimentalism taking hold of me.

I thought, "Now, Dooley, you've got a job, and it doesn't necessarily mean that you must stay in this village. You must go where you can do the greatest good." But deeper inside me a voice said, "Stay in your village, stay wrapped in the love of being needed. Here Asians need you and you need that need." I remembered the words of a Chinese philosopher who said that life was like a tightrope. On this tightrope man walks, balanced between what he must do and what he wishes to do. If these two remain in perfect balance, he can walk forward on the rope with ease. If they do not remain in balance, he falls down on one side or the other. I must keep walking, I must walk straight forward. I must.

Suddenly, while we were sitting at a very late lunch, we heard the unmistakable drone of a small twin-engine plane. We rushed out of the house and looked up. We could see no hole in the murky clouds where the plane could pierce into our valley. I grabbed a small brief-case that I had packed and went out to the airstrip and waited. I could hear the plane as it circled and circled almost as though the fury of its engines would dispel the clouds. And they did, just as Chinese firecrackers dispel evil spirits. The Ambassador's small Beechcraft landed on our airstrip and out climbed my friend Bob Burns of USIS. There were no other passengers.

I asked Bob immediately if he knew what had happened, or why. He said, "All I know is that the Ambassador received a telegram from you saying you must leave immediately. He wishes to help and so he sent his plane. He told me to tell you that if you want to take your crew out, there is plenty of room on the plane. If you wish to leave your crew here, you must remember the immense responsibility that you place on them." "Who said that specifically?" I asked. He repeated, "The Ambassador himself." I was faced with another decision which I could not make alone. More fear.

I turned to Dwight and Earl and said, "Then this is your decision too, boys. You can get on this plane and leave with me, stay in the capital until we find out what this is all about, or you can stay here and continue to work alone." Without any hesitation they said, "Doctor, you go on, we will stay here and take care of things until you come back." I thanked God for men like mine. Yet involuntarily a hideous picture flashed in my mind— the impaled heads along the village airstrip which a French pilot had told me about. What if Earl and Dwight were captured by the Communists and beheaded as imperialistic Americans?

Dwight interrupted this ghastly thought by saying, "Do you want to take this, sir?" He held out a large crucifix given to me when I was made an honorary Oblate of Mary Immaculate. The Pope himself had blessed it and handed it to me. I said, "Why should I take it with me now? You keep it here in my house where it belongs. I will be back real soon." Dwight was again being solicitous, kind and good—something which I did not at the time understand. Instead I was depressed, angry, and irritable.

The plane revved up its motors. As it took off, I looked back at two young men standing on the very rim of Red hell, under the threat of war. Surrounding them were my nurses and interpreters who had come out to the airfield to say goodbye to me, each with more sadness in his voice than I ever remembered at a normal departure. I did not understand this. At that time I did not know what it meant.

The plane slowly corkscrewed its way up to gain enough altitude to jump the rim of the mountain. I watched the boys below until the mist swirled around and I could no longer see them. In their hearts was the same great spirit that made people cross the plains of America years ago. It is the same spirit that can keep this world free for free men to live in.

The plane flew high towards the capital. I spoke to Bob Burns. In quick words I poured out my fear, my anguish, my concern. Why, why, why? Bob kept putting his hands on my shoulders and saying, "Now don't worry about it, doctor. Don't give it another thought; you are probably going to be on a TV show." I said, "If Peter ordered me out of Laos just to appear on some TV show, I would use adjectives on the network that would shut TV down forever. I mean it."

Bob just smiled, and tried to change the subject, without success. I kept vocalizing the fear in my heart, and took refuge in wordy violence.

The plane landed at Vientiane's military airport and a car was waiting to take me to the house of absent Hank Miller. There I changed my clothes. Hank was in Bangkok, his house was full of war correspondents, and I had no desire to talk to anybody. Bob Burns told me the Ambassador had invited me to dinner so I cleaned up, put on my only suit, slightly mildewed, and walked to the Ambassador's house.

To my surprise I found that just the Ambassador, the Deputy Chief of Mission and I were to have dinner. I discussed all my fears again. Each listened to me with the patience of a father. I did not know at that time that the Ambassador was fully aware of why I was going home to America. Bob Burns knew, Hank Miller knew, Earl, Dwight and all of my crew knew. The point was, Tom Dooley did not!

I told the Ambassador that I wanted to get to Bangkok as soon as possible in order to telephone to the United States and find out what this was all about. I said, "Maybe I won't have to go home. Maybe I can handle this whole thing over long-distance telephone for a couple of hundred dollars instead of spending fifteen hundred dollars for an around-the-world plane ticket."

The Ambassador said kindly, "Tom, go ahead home for a few weeks. If you fly jets you can go home, do what you have to do, and return quickly."

The next plane to Bangkok was at five the following evening and the Ambassador said, "My plane can take you down in the morning, it is going to be going down early, and we will be glad to make room for you." I thanked him and went back to Hank Miller's for the night. I did not sleep at all. At dawn I got up and walked along the edge of the river.

In the mist of early morning I went to Mass in the Catholic church of Vientiane. Once again I heard the same familiar words in Latin, "Ad Deum qui laetificat. To the altar of God I will go, to God who is the joy of my youth." These are the same words I have heard in the cathedrals of Paris, of St. Louis, of Rome, and in the village chapels of Laos and Viet Nam. These same words in Latin had given me peace and solace when I was plunged into the hideousness and atrocity of Northern Viet Nam in 1954. These words had given me comfort in the strain and stress of medical school. These words had given me faith as a young man. Why did they seem to give me little solace now?

At eight o'clock the next morning I was at the airport once again, good Bob Burns acting as driver and friend. He put me on the Ambassador's plane and by nine-thirty we were winging our way across the emerald green paddies of the Korat plains of Thailand. Two hours later we landed at the sleek international airport at Bangkok. Some friends from the Thai airlines office met me and drove me to a hotel in town. I went immediately to the post-office building to place a phone call to America. I spent most of the afternoon trying to get a call through. I had to get through, I had to find out —four days of not knowing was already taking its toll. I had neither eaten a square meal nor held down much liquid; the agony of not knowing was the most terrible thing I had ever undergone.

My chest was sore from Dr. Van Valin's surgery. The fact that my whole shoulder ached must, I thought, have been due to the long flights.

By seven that evening it was obvious that I would not be able to get my phone call through, so I telephoned the airport and told them that it was urgent that I get to Hong Kong immediately. Although Hong Kong was not in the direct route to New York, it was only a six-hour flight and telephone connections out of Hong Kong are always good.

They said they could put me on a midnight plane. I took a taxi to the hotel where I put on the only white shirt I had brought with me, and then went to a small restaurant that I liked in Bangkok.

After a miserable dinner there (it kept bouncing in my stomach) I asked the owner if I could play the piano. I frequently spent time there whenever I was in Bangkok and always played their piano. I tried to dissipate the tensions that were in me through the dexterity of my fingers and through the warmth of Chopin. However, Chopin did not seem to help, nor did Schumann, nor did anything which was soft and light and airy. I soon found myself playing the crashing chords of Rachmaninoff and the thundering opening of Tchaikowsky's concerto. After two hours of playing, some people who were sitting at a shadowy table in the corner came over within the circle of the light and said: "Hi, Tom, how are you?"

I looked up and saw the faces of my close friends, Hank Miller, and his wonderful wife, Annie. Never was I so glad to see friends as at that moment. I said I wanted to talk to them right away, I was so worried, so concerned. They said, "Don't worry, Tom; play something soft and light and lilting." I tried, but I could not make my fingers play like this. I hurt in my heart, in my shoulder, in my side. I was tired, I was sick, I was worried.

We went back to Hank's table and Hank looked at me and said, "Tom, I have never seen you in this state, even during wars, even during crisis. What's wrong?" I let flood out of my head and heart the things that had come to pass, the fear which existed because I did not know.

Hank looked at me and coolly said, "I know why you are going home. I will tell you, Tom." I leaned forward, took a deep breath and pleaded, "What's wrong, Hank?" My tension was at its peak. I thought I would burst. Slowly, deliberately, he said, "The tumor that Dr. Van Valin removed has been diagnosed as a secondary stage of malignant melanoma."

I had no reaction. The words entered my head like a fist jammed into a pillow. I felt nothing. I neither felt elation at finding that MEDICO was not in a state of chaos, nor did I feel great dejection at finding out that I had a hideously malignant growth of cancer. It just seemed for a moment that all was quiet. All was tranquil for now. At last, I knew.

I knew? Yes, I knew, as a doctor, that malignant melanoma is one of the quickest killers of flesh and blood that is known in the history of cancer.

Looking back on that night, I do not remember much more. They drove me to the airport but I do not remember what we talked about. I only remember the warmth of Annie's goodbye embrace. I only remember the strength and warmth of Hank's handclasp and his words as I climbed the plane ramp, "We'll see you soon, Tom."

On the plane the reading lights blinked out and once again I was the sleepless traveler. By dawn the plane was in Hong Kong. Listlessly I went through Customs, took a cab and checked into a hotel. I did not want to see anybody. There was nothing that I wanted to do. No need to telephone now. I might as well get the fastest plane home.

At three p.m. on Wednesday I took a jet plane headed for London. On the plane I did a great deal of thinking. Somewhere the thought came, "Blessed are they that mourn." But there must be no black pit of melancholy, no inertness, no fog, no void. I had much to do. Now there was a new urgency.

How did this cancer come about? I had always thought the months of aching and pain in my right shoulder and chest wall were due to my fall down an embankment on my last river trip. A few weeks after the fall a small lump had grown on the side of my chest wall, but I thought it was just a cyst.

When I weighed myself on the scales at the Hong Kong airport, I found that I had lost over 30 pounds. I thought, "Is my life gutted?" I tried to think with detachment; I tried to think objectively about illness and cancer, but I am a miser of life. All I could think about was the statistic I had studied in med school, "Only about 50 percent of the people who have a malignant melanoma in the metastatic (second state) survive a year. Less than 30 percent live two years." Yet I knew I was not going to abandon what I think is the correct thing to do in life because of shadows on a page. Nor was I going to quit this living, loving passion for life that I possess simply because of a statistic. I was not abandoning the beauty and tenderness that man can give to man, just for a statistic.

Memories surged into my mind and blocked out words, memories of my villagers and their needs. Memories of the fetid pestilence and decay of the refugee camps of Haiphong. Memories of the red humid heat of Vang Vieng. Memories of the oppressive sick-call at the Nam Tha hospital.

I realized that I had become more aware of myself and my soul's adventure in the raw material of Asian life. There was still much to do. I must continue to do this work as long as God allows me time on this earth to do it. I must continue to be tender, for to be tender one must be courageous. Now before my own highest mountain I must be braver than ever, even though bravery is sometimes a sad song. No, my candle was not gutted.

Looking out of the window in the moon-shimmering night I felt a cloudy out-of-touchness with everything. I had a pleasant disembodiment from my own self. The physical tiredness of the trip from Muong Sing to Hong Kong had drained me. My mind put me somewhere else where I could look back at the body of Tom Dooley.

Once many years ago, as I sat on a small stool in the candlelit room of Dr. Albert Schweitzer on the banks of the Ogowe, in French Equatorial Africa, the great old gentleman said to me, "The significance of a man, Tom, is not in what he attains, but rather in what he longs to attain." I thought to myself, I must continue to long to attain.

The value of love is stronger than that of hate, and I was confident that many people loved me and the work I was doing. I must now draw new strength from the knowledge of their love, strength because I needed it. In my detachment everything suddenly became intent and vivid. I cried a bit and at one moment I laughed out loud. The woman sitting in the seat beside me asked if I was all right. I replied, "Yes, I'm just fine."

There were some hours on that plane trip when I was surfeited with contentment, for I felt as though I had completed a job well done. The plane roared on east, flying over Thailand, Burma, India and up through Europe.

I thought about the kind of village medicine that I was doing. It would be hard for me to do anything else. This kind of medicine is my salvation, my hold on life. It is my means of expression. Also flowing and surging in me was the passionate desire to tell others of this work, of this kind of medicine, of this life. I did not see how I could ever quit village work. I must treat patients with my own hands, reach out and give personal help every day. I feel that I must go out of my way to do it and to do it with tenderness.

I thought of Earl and Dwight back at work in Muong Sing. And I thought of my other crews in former years. And one thing stirred me, the fact that so many people gave me something or were something to me without my knowing it. There were some people I had never exchanged a word with, but had merely heard of by report. There were others that I had known and loved. All these people had a decisive influence on me. They entered into my life and became a power within me, almost without my knowledge.

I had left Muong Sing so rapidly that I had forgotten to say "So long" to the boys, at least "So long" as warmly as I would had I known I would be gone for months. I began to go over in my mind all the events of the past months. I remembered the day I arrived in Laos, and the press conference announcing the start of MEDICO which was held in New York before my departure. It was February 4, 1958. What had I said to the reporters? I must try to remember . . .

TWO ·

THE START OF *MEDICO*

"Ladies and gentlemen, a few weeks ago I turned over to my publisher the manuscript of my book, *The Edge of Tomorrow*. It ended on the encouragement of Dr. Albert Schweitzer's word of hope. When we told Dr. Schweitzer of the plan we are going to announce to you today, he accepted Honorary Chairmanship and he sent us this message: 'I do not know what your destinies will ever be, but this I do know: you will always have happiness if you seek and find, how to serve.'

"Now today, on the fourth of February, 1958, I feel as though I were on the verge of the longest journey I have ever taken."

In trying to communicate to the newsmen before me, I felt I had become a little stiff. I must grope and find *me* again. It had been so long since I had had to express myself to fellow-Americans like this. I felt a strong confidence welling up within me, forming my words. This same confidence, blended with sweat, effort and hope, must form the action of MEDICO.

"On this day a new organization is being founded. It will be entitled MEDICO, which stands for Medical International Cooperation Organization. MEDICO's reason for existence is simple. We wish to take care of people who are sick, in areas where they have little or no chance of receiving medical aid.

"We are in no way a religious or political organization. We're not intending to convert anyone to Catholicism, or Protestantism, nor are we trying to make them new Republicans or old Democrats. We are not trying to replace any already existing programs in the field of health. We feel that the World Health Organization and the International Cooperation Administration of our government's foreign aid program are doing excellent jobs in preventive medicine. What we wish to do is a job in simple therapeutic medicine."

I wondered if the meaning of therapeutic was clear. "By therapeutic I mean the simple act of passing out pills. Sometimes foreign aid becomes enmeshed in an obscure tangle of programs. The simplicity of MEDICO's program is this: we actually believe that we can win the friendship of people only by getting down on the ground and working beside them, on equal terms, humans-to-humans, towards goals that they understand and seek themselves. MEDICO is a person-to-person, heart-to-heart program. There is no more personal relationship than that of a doctor and his patient. We feel that therapeutic medicine will have a double effect: it will aid those who are sick and by that simple act it will win friendship for America."

Someone in the audience raised his hand and asked, "Where did the idea of MEDICO come from?"

"The idea of MEDICO is a blend of three ideas. We have taken some of the philosophy of Dr. Schweitzer, who believes that man belongs to man, that man has claims on man, and we have given it today's accent. We feel that man has claims on man but that this idea must be modernized into a program of self-help, a program that produces something *now*—today and tomorrow, not next year or next decade. That dream of Schweitzer's was part of my work in the small village of Nam Tha in Laos. We tried to show the villagers of Nam Tha that we five Americans really believed that Asians had claims on us. We left America to go live amongst them, to be an intimate and integral part of their community life. In Nam Tha we cared for thousands of their sick and wounded. We delivered their babies, we went to their weddings and their funerals, and we joked with their young military. We tried to show, with love, that we understood the responsibility of those who have towards those who have not.

"We therefore added a little modern touch to this fundamental philosophy, and in correspondence with Dr. Peter Comanduras we matured this idea. Dooley and his boys can care for about 36,000 people a year; however, there are about 36 million times some other multiple who still need help. We should really enlarge our program. When I returned to America just a few months ago, Dr. Peter Comanduras and I met in Washington and we talked about our mutual dreams. It was from this that MEDICO was born.

"Dr. Peter Comanduras is the Secretary General of our program. He has superb abilities that will earn for our program the position of respect it deserves among our fellow-Americans. He is giving up his private practice and teaching to devote all of his time and talent to MEDICO. He is making a great sacrifice.

"On the village level, I have had several years of practice and experience.

Both of our lives are permeated with the Schweitzer concept of brotherhood. This is the combination that gave birth to MEDICO.

"In summing it up, let me say this—MEDICO wishes to render a service to people of foreign lands and at the same time render service to our own country. We wish to clear up some of the fears and misconceptions of America that are held by people of some foreign lands. We wish to take care of their sick, and in return we wish only their love and understanding. We believe that medicine is above the give-and-take of national rivalry.

"Dr. Comanduras is leaving immediately on a tour of the world. On this tour he will speak to the leading medical people of many nations to see if they can utilize the services of MEDICO.

"I'm leaving on a lecture tour in order to raise three things: men of medicine to work in the various MEDICO teams around the world. Second, the medicines and surgical supplies that our village hospitals will need. And thirdly, the dollar donations from the general public upon which MEDICO must exist."

Then the questions started . . .

"No, MEDICO will not necessarily work in Asia alone but in any nation that asks us."

"Yes, MEDICO will demand much from the host nation. They must give free Customs entry, furnish internal transportation, kerosene, gasoline, give us *carte blanche* for their medical warehouse. Most important, the host nation must promise to sustain and maintain what we establish, after our departure."

"Yes, the host government will also be asked to pay indigenous salaries."

"How long will our teams stay in one area? That depends. In Laos I believe that we can build a hospital, stock it, run this hospital, train the personnel to handle it, and turn it over to them within a period of two to four years. In other areas this length of time might be longer."

As quickly as it had started, the press conference ended. Peter and I looked at each other, took a deep breath, and then realized what lay ahead of us—many months of begging, of organization, of talking. We had built our castle in the air. Now we must put a solid foundation under it.

I left the very next day to begin a lecture tour of America, covering all parts of the country. I spoke in high schools, in women's clubs, in medical societies. I spoke to people on trains and planes. Everywhere I tried to point out how MEDICO does not conflict with any existing organization. I stayed in cheap hotels in small towns, in magnificent suites in large cities. The lecture tour consisted of 188 speeches in 79 different cities over 5 months.

I went to the leading pharmaceutical houses of America, and once again they demonstrated their great generosity. Chas. Pfizer & Co., Mead Johnson & Co., and Eli Lilly & Co. were especially generous to me as they always had been in the past. We set up MEDICO in the beginning as a division of the International Rescue Committee. We needed a mother organization to help us get started. Through the good offices of the International Rescue Committee we acquired a warehouse, and soon the medicines and supplies began to pour in. Later we became an independent organization.

The A. S. Aloe Company of St. Louis, Missouri, supplied me once again with all the surgical equipment that we needed. Their Vice President, Henry Scherck, became MEDICO's most powerful friend. He headed our Committee for Procurement of Surgical Supplies.

When my lecture tour was finished in June, MEDICO had over one million dollars worth of medicines donated to it, and about three hundred thousand dollars in cash donations. My book, *The Edge of Tomorrow*, was condensed in "The Reader's Digest" in the issue of May, 1958. This brought a tremendous response in dollars, and also illuminated the purpose of MEDICO to millions of people around the world. Everywhere I went in America people showed their warm admiration towards our program—warm admiration portrayed by cold cash.

Over six hundred doctors, corpsmen and nurses had applied to join the various MEDICO teams. I had started out to raise money, men and medicine. And with the luck of the Irish and the grace of God, MEDICO had these three. After the tour ended, Dooley was nearly voiceless. Well, almost. When Peter returned from his round-the-world tour, he told me we had been invited by 23 nations of the world to do our kind of work in their nations.

It had been at the end of 1957, after turning my hospital at Nam Tha over to the Lao government (the story I tell in *The Edge of Tomorrow*), that I had come home, via Africa. In Lambarene I had one of the greatest privileges of my life—working at the hospital of Dr. Albert Schweitzer. And there I had dreamed up and solidified much of the plan for a world-wide miracle: MEDICO! Now that our plan was really launched, I would soon leave for Laos once again.

THREE ·
PICKING A NEW MEDICAL TEAM

I was pleased and grateful that over six hundred men and women had written in the opening months to volunteer to work with me in Laos or on other MEDICO teams around the world. Yet how would I ever choose my new men? This would be a risky thing. My last team was made up of men with whom I had worked before. They had been my Navy corpsmen, I knew what they were like. I knew that their abilities and friendship would be a help to me. For the new team I would have to choose unknown, untried men, and this would be really difficult.

Throughout the lecture tour, after each speech, people would come up and say, "Doctor, I'd like to do that kind of work with you in Asia. I am an ex-Army or ex-Navy corpsman. May I help you?" I would always set up plans to have breakfast with them, or coffee later on. After I spoke with them, I would go back and write prodigious notes about each person, covering everything from their personalities to their medical and surgical abilities.

The choice of Earl Rhine and Dwight Davis was almost accidental. On March 17th, *Life* magazine did a picture story on my lecture tour. Two young men working in a hospital in Austin, Texas, read that story, turned and said to each other, "This is the kind of work for us." Both these men were veterans, and both were surgical technicians working at Brackenridge Hospital while in pre-med at the University of Texas.

They then sat down and composed a lengthy letter of application, including a list of every single surgical experience that they had had, every operation on which they had assisted, and all of their sundry talents. Then they slept on it and in the morning they decided the letter was no good. They then wrote a very terse and succinct letter, offering their services to me and asking for an immediate reply.

They went one step further. They telephoned my mother. The fact that they obtained her number and had the intelligence to find the city in which she lived was a pleasing thing to me. My mother has a very good sense of business about her and endorsed the boys practically by "the sound of their voices" and their go-to-itiveness.

Their letter came to me like all the other letters, but when I saw the Texas address I telephoned Pete Kessey, one of my old crew who lived in Austin. I asked Pete to interview these two volunteers. I pointed out to Pete that he must give only the blackest picture of working in Asia, and especially point out what a hard-headed, stubborn, difficult and irascible son-of-a-gun Dooley was to work for.

The next night Pete called me and said he'd interviewed these two men and thought "they were both tops." Knowing me as well as he did and knowing what these two men would be involved in, working and living with me, Pete was an excellent judge. After all, like most humble Irishmen, I think I'm practically faultless. Pete does not exactly agree, so he could warn potential candidates about the guy for whom they would work. I didn't want some juvenile enthusiast who would sour and quit on me when proximity dulled the edge of admiration.

A week later I called the men and set up an appointment in Houston, Texas. I had a speech in New York on a Monday and in Washington on a Wednesday, so that gave me all of Tuesday free. I took an early morning plane on Tuesday and arrived in Houston, where Earl and Dwight met me at the airport.

They told me many months later, with a laugh in their voices, how they stood so nervously at the ramp, watching various people get off the plane. Earl would say, "That's him," and Dwight would respond, "Oh, no, he's too fat." Then Dwight would say, "Maybe that's him," and Earl would reply, "Oh, no, he's too old." Their nervousness led in this guessing game. Finally they did spot me and I spotted them. My first impression was, "These guys are too well dressed to work for me in a dirty Asian village."

Yet after about four hours of speaking with them, I had made up my mind that these were the men I wanted. They were the best of any I had interviewed. They possessed innumerable qualities that I wanted. They were not in any way religious fanatics and their idealism was balanced by a sense of realism because, in their overseas' duties they had seen the stink and misery in which idealism must rub its nose. Yet they had enough youthful idealism to be willing to accept the challenge of any kind of a job. They were in good health and had superb medical technician training.

They both were seniors at the University of Texas and wanted to go on to become doctors. They had an obvious amount of admiration for Tom Dooley, yet neither was too full of hero worship. They seemed, after a four-hour interview, to have a good sense of balance between right and wrong, duty and pleasure. My own opinion, blended with what Pete had told me and my mother's intuitive knowledge, convinced me that these were my new crew. We then went to dinner at a glorious hotel in Houston to enjoy the first meal that we would ever have together, including the last steak that we would eat together for a long time.

Several times during the conversation I mentioned that they both had on the same kind of dark blue pin-stripe necktie. Each time I mentioned it, they gulped. Later, Dwight asked, "Doctor, would it make any difference if we were married?" I said, "Of course it would. I would not take a married man with me. On my last trip, Denny Shepard and Norm Baker were married. Things were doubly tough for them than for the bachelors of my team. I feel that to do this kind of work one must devote to it all his time, all his energy, and all his emotions. He could not be involved with nostalgia and homesickness for wife and family."

Dwight again said, "You mean that if we were married you would not take us?" To which I replied, "Probably not. Why? You're certainly not married, are you?"

With this they both slumped in their chairs, took a deep breath, and said, "Yes, we are both married."

They proceeded to spend the next hour, explaining how happy their wives were that they were going to Asia. This I found hard to believe. They insisted. They said they had no children and both their wives were working independently and would continue their nursing work. Their wives said that their salaries and the $150 a month I planned to pay the boys would be enough. Earl was quick to point out that he'd been married seven years though only 26, and "we are not exactly honeymooners, sir." I had been convinced that these were the top men of all that I had interviewed. I was pleased with Pete's opinion of them, so once again I decided that I'd better change my mind. After all, isn't changing one's mind a sign of intelligence?

At dinner I again commented that they looked like the Bobbsey Twins with their identical neckties. They burst out laughing and said, "We wore these neckties at Dwight's wedding several years ago. By accident we both put them on tonight, and almost let the cat out of the bag when you noticed that they are identical."

We smiled that evening and laughed with the warm laughter that comes from good companionship. I took a midnight plane back to the east and the boys drove back to their homes in Austin. The decision was made. Their wives were not opposed to their doing this kind of work as they intelligently realized what fine men this experience would make them. My team was formed. All of us were happier men by dawn that next day.

Dwight Davis is 27 years old. He was born and raised in the state of Washington. While he was in the Air Force, he was stationed in Korea. He had plenty of time to see some of the wretchedness into which he was now plunging his life, the wretchedness of Asia. In 1955, as a civilian, he started college in Austin, Texas, and began to work nights at Brackenridge Hospital. It was at that time that he met a fellow veteran, Earl Rhine. Dwight and Earl became fast friends and this friendship was one of the things that pleased me about their application. "They sound like a good pair. Two for the price of one," I thought to myself. I smiled because I thought it was good to have a pair. It is good for two men who work together to be friends because they would have mutual solace when I got angry with one, and angry I do get.

Dwight is tall and very slender, with a tightness in his facial features. When his horn-rimmed glasses slip down off his nose a bit, he looks something like Arthur Miller. With an immobile face he sometimes seems stern, but he is not at all; quite the contrary. He has a heart so big that it suffuses his character. He has a wonderful love for children. He calls village kids "Mr. Bigger-eyes-than-mine" or "Tex" or "Hi, buddy." Dwight walks with a lithe gait, but in a long and lanky step, not unlike a Texan even though Texas is his adopted state. He speaks with a clipped accent of the northwest, but has adopted the expansiveness of Texans. His eyes are deep-set, penetrating, and blue in color. You rarely see them, however, because the rim of his low-slung glasses hides his eyes. His hair is close-cropped, almost a crew cut, though it gets a little long and scraggly at the back of his neck. His wife is a Mexican girl and, as a consequence, Dwight speaks good Spanish. In the mountains of Indo-China, when upset, he would break out into a spate of Spanish.

Dwight is a quiet man, and I used to think that he was almost invisible, saying very little, though always working much. In seventeen months of working with me, he never expressed any particular emotional response to having Dooley for his boss nor to working amongst these people of Asia. However, like the proverb of the way still water runs deep, I always knew that Dwight Davis was deep. Over a year later, in a hospital bed in New York, I was to receive a letter from him which proved this adage.

Earl Rhine is 26 years old. "Rhine like the river," he would say. Though born in Illinois, Earl had lived in Texas long enough to become "Texan." (In spite of this language barrier I was able to communicate with him.)

After many years of marriage, just a few weeks before Earl left for Laos, he found out that his wife was pregnant. He nevertheless felt as though he could afford a year and a half out of his life to invest in Asia. He had a valiant little gal for a wife who said that she would take care of herself and their child while Earl was out taking care of thousands of kids in Asia. Indeed, she did.

Earl is shorter than Dwight. The thing about Earl that you noticed immediately was the extreme gentleness of his manner. This later became doubly obvious when I watched how he handled his patients. His black curly hair had earned him the nickname "Marcel"; he likes neither the nickname nor the hair. His features are round and though not fat he is somewhere between chubby and normal. He has large brown eyes and at six o'clock at night he looks like he should shave again. As I was later to observe with satisfaction, he does his tasks quietly and he does them well.

In Earl and Dwight I was confident I had as good a medical team as I could possibly have found to work with me in the unknown months ahead. I could soon fly towards the edge of tomorrow once more.

FOUR ·

ARRIVAL IN LAOS

In June I boarded a plane for Hawaii. MEDICO was not yet five months old. My mind was flooded with plans and my heart was warmed by the generosity of my country. I was pleased at having had contact with the abrasive minds of some of the young students of America; I was still dizzy from the questions asked by thousands of them on my lecture tour. I looked out of the window of the magnificent Pan American plane and watched a little sunlight come over America. That same sunlight would soon be over Asia. I hoped that this sunlight would warm the hearts of the people of Asia whom I had grown so to love.

As the plane swooped into the airport at Hawaii, I remembered landing here as a young Navy officer. In 1954 I first came here as a Navy doctor, just having finished my internship. I was en route to duty in Yokosuka, Japan. After only a few weeks in Japan I was transferred into the chaos that was to become the evacuation of North Viet Nam. For one year I stayed in North Viet Nam, working in a huge refugee camp. In my first book, *Deliver Us From Evil*, I told how more than 600,000 miserable, wretched and beaten but valiant people passed through my camp. I had the good fortune of being an intimate part of one of the greatest tributes to the majesty of the human spirit. I saw it, I was there. I had the joy of seeing white-capped sailors respond to a call, a need, a cry for help: North Viet Nam in 1954 and 1955!

I stayed in Hawaii a week. More Americans came to the help of MEDICO. Especially grand to me was a small group of young men and women called the Junior Chinese Catholic Club and their leader, Fred Luning. Later we were to have an even more eloquent testimonial of their effectiveness.

The following weekend Earl Rhine and Dwight Davis flew to Hawaii and spent two days. This was only the second time that I had seen them in my life. I looked at these two men and thought to myself, "Dooley, you're going to live with these two guys for two years. You had better get accustomed to them, and they to you."

In the first week of July we flew to Japan and on to Hong Kong. At the latter place we had a lot of things to buy. We spent many hours walking up and down the streets of Hong Kong, arguing over prices. The Wilson Club of Bridgeport, Connecticut, had sent me a generous donation. They had written and said that they did not want to contribute any money to MEDICO itself but rather wanted to contribute something personally to me. They asked what I would like to have. I blithely answered, "A piano so I can take Chopin to North Laos." Two months later, they sent me the money. And now in Hong Kong I must find a piano.

It was an enjoyable hunt. After several days of testing every for-sale piano in Hong Kong, I finally found the zinc-lined one I wanted. But the price was almost twice as much as the Wilson Club had sent. Fortunately, the Chinese man knew of my work (after I not-so-humbly told him about it), so he generously cut the price in half. This blessed piano proved to be my most constant friend.

We flew to Saigon, where we stayed at the orphanage of Madame Vu Thi Ngai, the gallant woman of North Viet Nam whose 500 refugee children had come with her. She was now established in her new orphanage buildings in Saigon, supported by the fine American community there. Earl, Dwight and I climbed into a newly arrived jeep, painted Kelly green, which was a gift from the Willys Corporation, and began our drive across the belly of southeast Asia.

Several days later, in Cambodia, we talked to the health officials and the American Ambassador in order to make the final preparations for our MEDICO team in Cambodia. Then we went to the ancient jungle ruin of Ankor Wat.

The first night of our arrival we went out to the pool behind the Court of the Leper King. I had loved this place from years back, and wanted to go now and take a swim under the night sky. We did, and then sat around and talked. Things seemed so tranquil here. What would the next year show? Would our new hospital in Laos be successful or would it merely be a wasted effort? Would the Communist threat become more powerful and the atrocities of Yunnan, China, reach out into northern Laos? Was my former hospital at Nam Tha, which we had turned over to the government of Laos, continuing or had it already collapsed?

Were those who criticized me in southeast Asia as powerful and vitriolic in their anti-Dooley ideas as they had been in the past? Would those who could think only in terms of multi-million-dollar projects snigger at my paltry efforts, or would they see that if the darkness is black enough a small candle can give a brilliant light? But worst of all, would the ogre of Communism conquer and consume the country into which we were going to move? Sitting on the mossy stones around the side of the pool behind the Court of the Leper King, I thought of how I had grown to love these people of southeast Asia. I tried to tell Earl and Dwight of how quickly they would lose their hearts to these primitive people. I tried to tell them something of the problems that would soon face them, and I wanted to steel them for the stink and death of their next two years. We sat and talked about a realization that we all possessed—the realization that the only way man can achieve his own happiness is to strive for the happiness of others. This is a simple guide: every man has a responsibility to every other man. These two boys volunteered to go to the high rain-forest of northern Laos to act out their responsibility to other men.

I warned them of the difficulties they would encounter, hostilities from the enemy as well as green-eyed hostility from fellow Americans. I warned them of the stupidity and the ignorance, the stubbornness and the cling-to-the-pastness of the mountain tribes of northern Laos. I tried to tell them that there would be many moments in each of their days that would involve someone's very life; therefore, those moments involve eternities.

We talked of the valley of Muong Sing where we expected to work, a valley just over the mountain from Nam Tha, my former village. I told them that what comes to the valley of Muong Sing in the tide of time will affect other valleys and other lands and other people.

Earl said, "It seems so hard to realize that we are soon to be thrown into such chaos. Here at Ankor things are so tranquil."

"That is exactly the point of Asia," I said. "Earl, you will spend your days being amazed at contradictions like this. The magnificence of a wild and wonderful jungle contrasted with the wretchedness of the people who live in it; the glories of God's nature and the seeming injustices that God puts on this earth; the tranquility of a pool at the Court of the Leper King and the hideous atrocities of northern Viet Nam; the red-hot heat of a humid day and the blue cool breeze of the mountain night."

While we were swimming, Dwight noticed a gold medal around my neck and asked to see it. He read on the back of the St. Christopher medal the words that have guided my life since 1954, the words of Robert Frost:

"The woods are lovely, dark and deep,
But I have promises to keep,
And miles to go before I sleep."

Quietly we got back into our jeep and returned to the hotel.

Two days later we arrived in Bangkok. The boys took the jeep in for its first checkup while I flew on to Vientiane, the capital of Laos. I have a warm feeling towards many of the officials and the people of Laos. And I know that they possess the same toward me. My book on their country had been successful in America, and the Lao Government had formally thanked me for telling Americans something of their Kingdom, its trials, and its needs. The Lao Government, both officially and as my friends, was looking forward to welcoming me back to their Kingdom. And deep in my heart I was looking forward to my return, first to the capital, and then to my old village. Although I had been gone only eight months, I felt no less near to them than I ever had. My heart was bursting as the plane landed at the hot metal landing strip at the capital. I had returned to Laos. I promised I would. Excitement made my mouth dry while sweat rolled down my body. I was the first to push out the door and down the steps.

There were no Lao to meet me. Nor were there any Americans. Was the plane early? No. Why had none of my Lao friends come to welcome me back? The chief of the United States Information Service, Hank Miller and his wife, probably my closest friends in all Asia, were on home-leave in America. I had wired my date of arrival well in advance to the USIS in Vientiane. I was checking my bags off the plane when an official American car pulled up with one of the USIS men. This official said to me, "Good heavens! Your plane came in on time. Planes never come in on time. We usually don't come out until much later." I immediately flushed with anger at this haughty attitude of the white man toward the Asians and their efforts at running an airline. I asked him, "Did you notify the Lao government of the time of my arrival?" He replied, "Oh, I intended to, but I'm awfully sorry, I never had a chance. I told one of my Lao assistants to go tell the Prime Minister, however. I don't know whether he did or not."

The next morning I went to the office of this same American and asked if he had made the requested appointment for me with the Premier. He apologized for "not having had a chance to get around to it but he would send an assistant over immediately." I said, "Don't bother." I then walked two blocks to the office of the Prime Minister and asked his secretary if I could see him. His secretary beamed excitement, and within five minutes I was sitting near my good friend, Premier Phoui Sananikone. He expressed regret that no one had met me at the airlines. He knew I was en route back to my "second home" and said, "We are very unhappy that we did not have a chance to extend to you the warm welcome and the affection that all of us hold for you, our *Thanh Mo America.*" How good to hear my old title again, "Doctor America."

I told the Premier of our new plans for the village of Muong Sing and the new hospital there. This choice had been made by many members of his Cabinet months before my return. He told me that things in my old hospital at Nam Tha were going well. I intended to return to Bangkok the next day and drive our jeep across Thailand, straight north to the Mekong River. We would then cross on the ferry and come into Vientiane. He again said, "My King has ordered us to extend to your mission all of the facilities of his government. This we do with great pleasure." They had done exactly this for me for the previous two years.

Again they were affirming their desire to help me to help them. They pledged to me Customs-free entry, all free kerosene and gasoline, and all indigenous salaries to be paid by them. We could have medicines that they had available at their pharmacy, and any other help that I could possibly need. The Prime Minister said, "We have the enthusiasm, we have the basic potential. You bring to us your American talents and your American medicines and teach us so that we can care for our own people."

I went to spend the night at Hank Miller's home, in his absence, and there met another man who was soon to become one of my closest friends. His name was Bob Burns. He worked for USIS, though when you asked him what he did, he would modestly reply, "I'm simply a typist in the army of the Lord." As he was non-Catholic, I always kidded him that he had "the right Lord but wrong army." It was a standing joke from that day for us to call Bob Burns "simply that typist."

I visited the Minister of Health who informed me that the warehouse would be ready for us the following week so I could transship the thirty-two tons of medicines from Bangkok. In the morning I flew back to Bangkok.

The crew loaded up the jeep, arranged for the transshipment, and a few days later we drove on to Vientiane. We arrived at the river late at night, left our jeep on the Thailand side of the Mekong River and crossed over in a small boat. The outboard motor pooped out and we were swept down river in the rapid current, away from the capital of Vientiane. I smiled and thought to myself, "A fine way to introduce my two men to their new Kingdom, down the river, motorless."

However, in about fifteen minutes the motor sputtered to life again, being resuscitated by the Lao mechanic who repaired it with string, spit, sweat, and ingenuity. On the Lao side of the Mekong we hitched a ride to Hank Miller's house where Bob Burns was waiting for us with bourbon on the rocks. After a clean shower, we collapsed into bed—the first night that Earl and Dwight were to spend in Laos. They would see many, many more nights before their task was done.

By previous plans, all our equipment arrived the next day. It was brought across the river and driven on trucks up to the capital. The Lao government warehouse, where the equipment would be stored, was near the Customs House. However, things were "not quite ready" and we could not put the medicine in the warehouse. I asked the American Economic Mission if they had a warehouse available for a few days. They "regretted." I looked around town for a high enough space to store this medicine for a short length of time, but no luck. As I could not leave the medicine on the trucks, there was only one alternative. The rest of the afternoon was spent unloading thirty-two tons of equipment on the lawn around Hank Miller's house. When Bob Burns returned from work, he found Hank's house practically engulfed by thirty-two tons of crates whose cubic measurements were about the size of a solid football field, ten feet high.

While the boys were unloading (as the Commanding Officer I try to do as little physical labor as possible), I had gone to find Chai. Those of you who have read my other books know that Chai is my very good friend, corpsman, interpreter, and entrepreneur. I found Chai out near his old home on the outskirts of Vientiane. This was only a few blocks from where I had met him at a love-court, when he was courting a young girl in June, 1956. Here, two years later, Chai was now living, married to that girl.

I told Chai of our problem and he said, "Ban pinh yanh," which means rustically: "To hell with it," or just about anything else you want it to mean. He immediately rounded up a half dozen of his friends and they all drove with me to Hank's house and gleefully perched themselves on top of the boxes to stand guard for the night. With no more concern than that, with complete confidence in their honesty, Earl, Dwight and I dragged ourselves into bed, the day's work done. With nearly a quarter of a million dollars worth of medicines and equipment piled around the house, covered with palm leaves, and guarded by Chai's languid friends, we slept well.

FIVE ·

THE VILLAGE OF MUONG SING

Muong Sing is the valley just west and a little north of Nam Tha. It is a full day's walk, but only a fifteen-minute flight, from the site of my former hospital, because the mountain which divides Nam Tha from Muong Sing rises to about 8,000 feet. Muong Sing is located just five or six miles south of the China border. It is on a direct line north from Bangkok through Vientiane to the China frontier. This is the northwest corner of northern Laos.

The almost enchanted village of Muong Sing sleeps on the floor of the valley at about 2,000 feet. All around it are purple, jagged mountains. Some of the peaks run 10,000 feet high but the average is 8,000 feet. They encircle three sides of Muong Sing, leaving only the south end of the valley open. From peak to peak is a distance of only some 25 miles.

The Prime Minister had given me a letter to the Commandant of the Lao Army, authorizing all internal transportation. That afternoon I met with the Commandant in Vientiane and chose the following morning for my reconnaissance flight to Muong Sing while the boys worked at the warehouse.

The flight from the capital to the north is a spectacular thing. Flying over the Kingdom of Laos you see craggy mountain peaks whose spires stick up into the blue sky. In the space between these spires are broad valleys, checkerboard flat. Most are filled with small, green rice paddies. Each paddy looks like a square of beads all strung together, or a tangle of beads, or beads in a row, or in a coil, or beads twisting upon each other like a rosary dropped on a flat surface. The beads of green are in dovetailing knots, and sometimes the large beads seem to engulf the small. Between each square of rice field is a small brown-black dam of earth.

In almost every valley's central portion is a small clear river. From high in the sky it looks like a small vein or artery of clear, cool water. As you look you think, "What a lovely Shangri-La," but it is not that at all. It is another unsanitary, underdeveloped Asian village.

The further north, the more mountainous the countryside becomes, and down deep in the foliage of those mountains is wild and wonderful jungle. When the plane flies low, it seems as though the trees are reaching up to grab the plane. In some areas the mountain has been burned; I was to learn a great deal about this native custom.

It is understandable why the plane must corkscrew down in order to land on the floor of the valley. Although I had spent much time flying in Asia, when the plane suddenly lurched to the starboard and began to drop into the valley, I felt my heart go up to my mouth.

The road of the Muong Sing valley is cut out of the thick green of the jungle floor. From my plane it looked like a gray bony streak. Dotted along on both sides of the road are small little clusters of huts—these are the villages. Each village has its complement of dogs, chickens, cats, and children all of whom mix together and stray around under the houses. Asian houses are built up on stilts to protect them against the mud of the rains. Also the family animals can get under the house for warmth and their odor is considered to be a sign of wealth. These villages sure are wealthy!

The village of Muong Sing at first glance is a sleepy little place. It is a typical Asian village, wretchedly underdeveloped, but rich with potential for future progress. The nearby rice paddies are flooded much of the year, and the emerald green of ripened rice is a beautiful thing.

The plane finally landed. From the airstrip one must walk about twenty minutes to get to "downtown" Muong Sing. There are really several villages for the quadrangle of Muong Sing has a village dangling on the top of each of its four corners. Muong Sing, with appendages, has about 4,000 inhabitants. Along one edge of the village is a large "Beau-Geste"-type mud fortress, complete with moat. Adjacent to the military encampment is a house of the village Mayor, or Chao Muong.

First of all, I went to see the Chao Muong. He was a nice little man, socially charming, and not very effective. He took me over to two forlorn and dilapidated straw-mud-cement huts. "Our dispensary," he said. So these were the buildings that would be turned over to us to rebuild and to make into a hospital! This was not a new challenge. It was just as it had been in Nam Tha not so long ago. I had only to look at the buildings to know how much work stood ahead. I checked on the nearness of the water supply (it was far away), and the nearness of the military (very close). In fact, our hospital would be across the road from the fortress. I wondered how much aid the languid-looking Chao Muong would give to us.

A few hours later I flew out of the valley. The plane plunged into the misty evening sky, just skimming the treetops. It then circled over up and up and finally leveled out and rode on the very crest of the jungle for just a moment. It suddenly banked tightly, making one more circle in order to rise above the crest, and vaulted over the mountains on to the south. I looked at the horizon ahead and it seemed to sink and slowly rotate, and suddenly we were in the marshmallow mist of the clouds. I looked again at the valley below, jeweled and precise. It lay quietly. It seemed tranquil. Would it be this way for long, I wondered, or would war soon wound it and burn it and scar it? In less than three hours the plane took me back to the heat of Vientiane.

In the capital we then went to work, loading planes to bring equipment to the north. I knew it would take about eight round trips and so we planned to take the first load of essential living equipment up and leave Earl, Dwight, Chai and Si, my former chief cook and bottle washer, who had rejoined us. I would return on the empty plane. The following day I could return to the north with another load, and back again. By this process we figured that within a week we could move about eight tons of essential equipment and medicines to start our project. The remaining 24 tons would be brought up as needed, over the ensuing months.

The next morning at dawn we loaded two tons onto borrowed trucks and drove to the military airport just outside the city of Vientiane. We loaded the planes. Earl and Dwight spent much of their time on this flight north looking out of the windows. They were heading to the village where they had come to invest two years of their lives. As the plane flew northward, their tension built and mine did too. Several hours later we bounced to a landing on the thick grass strip of Muong Sing.

We then unloaded the plane, but we were not alone. We had the help of many villagers who were all watching and wondering what this spectacular thing that had come to them really was. They would soon know. From the landing strip into town there is a trail. On either side of the trail there is a high wall of jungle trees, almost inextricable vegetation. There is always a soft and sweetish smell in this valley, and almost always strange and savage sounds. While the villagers were unloading the plane, under the direction of Chai and Si, Dwight, Earl and I walked fast into town. I wanted to show them the huts that would be ours.

Earl and Dwight were aghast. The main house in which we were to live had just a yawning hole instead of a door. The floor was sunken and there were pools of brackish water in the center of each room. There was a cesspool-like area that I wanted converted into the kitchen. On the grounds of what would be the hospital compound were buffalo wallows deep in mud and filth. There were several paths running right across the compound and in the back a string of dirty grass huts. The whole area looked miserable. We would have to remake this place completely to build what we were seeking, a nice, neat MEDICO compound.

I outlined to the boys the first essentials: doors on the buildings, cover for the newly arrived gear, the construction of a functioning outhouse, cement for the holes in the walls, patches for the roofs, and ceilings. I told them to emphasize the house first, making it livable, so that from this base they could work on the second building, the hospital. We had dreams of building a third building for a ward, at a later date. They took a deep breath and said, "O.K., sir, the Davis-Rhine Home Construction Gang will go to work. The Lord only knows what will come of it, however." I wasn't worried. I don't think the Lord was, either.

We hiked back to the airport. The plane was unloaded and the pilot was tinkering with the right engine. I said good-by to the boys, climbed into the empty plane, and sat on the floor, looking out of a window. For some reason the plane had to rev up its props for about twenty minutes. Earl and Dwight were sitting on top of the equipment. Sheets of corrugated metal that we had purchased for roofing were flapping in a propwash. It had begun to rain, and they looked forlorn and drenched.

While the pilot held the plane on the end of the landing strip, I kept looking back at these two young men. Here they were, twenty-six and twenty-seven years old, more than half a world away from their wives, out beyond the beyond. They were sitting on a primitive landing strip in an ancient land, just a few miles from the hostile frontier of Red China. When this plane took off, there would be no further transportation into this valley until I returned. Here were two young men who did not speak the native dialect, relying on interpreters whose English was highly inadequate. Here were two very brave young Americans. Suddenly, with a jerk, the plane leaped forward and began its flight up and out of the valley. As the plane flew on, the boys looked like small specks in the distance. They became smaller and smaller. In the months to follow, they became larger and larger.

I spent the next two weeks loading up the military planes from the south and sending them up to the north. I was especially anxious to get a shipment of food off to the boys. They were living off the village market.

My zinc-lined piano was in the warehouse but I did not feel that I could morally send it north on the Lao military aircraft. I went to the commercial airline and asked them if they would fly it up for me. The Frenchmen who ran the airline were so amused at the idea of a piano in the foothills of the Himalayas that they promptly agreed to do it as a contribution to civilization. I took the piano out to the airlines the following day and they shipped it on up to Muong Sing.

I was told a few weeks later that the reaction at Muong Sing was strange. The boys had been eating bizarre native food, and their gastro-intestinal tracts were a bit angry. Each day they thought that the next plane would have canned food aboard it. They went out to the airstrip on this particular day and were positive that good old Dr. Dooley would come through with the food. Instead of the military cargo plane, a commercial plane arrived and unloaded a huge box. They opened it eagerly and found—a piano! Earl said to Dwight, "What can we do with it? We can't play it and we can't eat it." They contemplated just leaving it at the airstrip, but finally they loaded it into an ox-cart and dragged it, strings, hammers, ivories, zinc lining and all, to our newly repaired house.

The boys were doing a lot of construction on the house and the hospital buildings and were getting everything into good shape. Down in the capital I finished handling the formalities with Customs and the government. After I saw that all the essential gear had been shipped up, I flew north again. We would soon be ready to start our hospital work at Muong Sing.

On my arrival, I found that the house was livable and the hospital almost workable.

Our house has three rooms, each about 18 x 23 feet in size. In the center room we put crates up against the wall and covered them with thin mattresses, forming couches on one side and a chair on the other side. The "dining room" table stands in front of one of these couches and some chairs are around its free side. Against one wall, in splendor, stands my piano. On the other side of the door is a bookcase (which has a distinct list to the starboard). We had a very small fireplace which was used as a cooking area until the boys knocked it down; they dug a much larger one and now we boast quite a noble and proud fireplace. One wonders about the need for a fireplace in a tropical land but in this high valley the early morning is quite brisk. At night the cold mist lays low in our valley. Chill enters the night air, but we do not feel it. Warmed by an inner sense of accomplishment we warm ourselves even more by sitting in a semicircle in front of man's most ancient friend, the fire.

The walls of our hut were constructed of a plaster-like substance made of a great deal of mud and a very little cement. The ceiling is high and the floor is stone. Later we laid cement on top of the stone and leveled the floor out so the water did not collect in the middle. Unlike most of the village huts, our house was built on the ground. Many, many months later we put up a corrugated sheet-metal ceiling. This was necessary because the birds collected in our eaves and kept messing up our house, to say nothing of interfering with our meals. The room to the west of the center room is our bedroom. Here we built a platform along the wall and laid five mattresses and bedding rolls on top. Mosquito nets were hung above and we slept Asian style, along one long platform rather than in individual beds. On the top of the platform along each side we built small shelves to keep our clothes in and at the foot of the platform we kept our locker boxes. Along the other wall we had one bed for our rare female guests, and most of our male guests just slept on the platform in Asian style.

The east side of the living room was where our Lao helpers slept, in the same style as ours. They hung more pictures on the whitewashed mud wall than we did. They had more sense. Whereas our wall crumbled when bugs got into the plaster, you could never see what was happening to their wall because it was covered with calendar art.

Staggering along the front of our house was a porch. Where the porch ended in front of the main door, there was an extension covered over and closed in. This became Si's kitchen. We laid a good cement floor, built him a large cooking table upon which he could put his kerosene stoves, and large shelves were built against the wall to store the food.

Back in the corner we built a shower. This was not a shower such as Peter Kessey built in Vang Vieng, ("la douche du Pierre"); however, the fundamentals were the same. In Vientiane we had a large 50-gallon tank made with a gooseneck coming out and a shower head on the end of this. This tank was placed on a large flat board connected with lines which went through pulleys and came down near the other side of the kitchen. We could lower this huge tank of water through the system of pulleys to easy filling-level, and dump buckets of heated water from the well into the tank. Then the tank would be pulled up by the lines until it was about eight feet high. We hung a piece of tarpaulin for a shower curtain, built a drainage pit and a bamboo floor as the shower deck, and enjoyed all the comforts of a hot-shower-at-home.

Out in the back we built an outhouse in magnificent style. While I was away on a village trip one day, the boys painted over its door, "Uncle Tom's Cabin." On the inside of the door facing the seat, I put up a large piece of paper with all the Lao alphabet on it so that we could learn the script in our leisure moments.

On the front porch we built a shaving area consisting of nothing but a wooden board with two circle holes cut into it and enameled basins countersunk into these holes. Underneath the basins we put a metal drain joining a rubber tube which then ran into the ground. Under the ground the boys planted some large green bamboo pipes which drained out into a ditch in front of the compound. Quite an ingenious Asian water system. On the side of this washing area was another large 55-gallon water barrel made out of an empty gasoline drum. This was kept filled from the well.

The well? This was a personal gift of Ambassador Horace Smith. Within a few weeks after we arrived, Ambassador Smith came to visit us. This was an extremely nice gesture. Never before, when I was in Laos, did any high American dignitary ever visit me. We were tremendously thrilled that he came. He said, "Tom, what can I specifically give to you?" I said, "Sir, two wells and a jeep." He laughed and asked me to explain myself. I pointed out that we wanted to build a cement well and that cement was heavy, therefore costly, I did not want to be so expensive to the Lao Ministry of Health so early. And I wished to transport my jeep to the north. This too was a heavy problem in transportation. Both of these were "luxuries," because we really could get our water from the local river and walk instead of ride in a jeep. The Ambassador said he would take care of it and within three days the Embassy plane returned bringing us a jeep and the cement rings for two wells.

There is a story about the jeep. Muong Sing has one "road" that runs the length of our valley. I use the word road in quotation marks advisedly because this road, which runs about 20 miles, is a single buffalo-cart lane. No other type of vehicle had been used on this road until the Army brought a jeep up and, a few months later, we received our jeep. In all of northern Laos, for hundreds of square miles, there were only two jeeps and only twenty miles of "road." Nevertheless, one day a few months later, these two jeeps actually ran into each other.

We loved to put titles on things and after the well was completed and a little well-house above it, we tried for weeks to think of an appropriate title. "Smith's Water Hole" sounded a little fresh for three young men to use in honor of an Ambassador. "American-Nam," meaning American water, sounded a bit too nationalistic. Ambassador Smith's name does not lend itself to rhyme and so his well remained unnamed but not unappreciated.

The Laos Minister of Public Works sent us an old carpenter friend from Nam Tha to help us build our buildings. We called him "Bolum," which means "uncle." Bolum didn't believe in any of this modern stuff, like nails or gasoline-run buzz saws; everything had to be wedged and cut by hand.

It took Bolum quite some time to get these done, but never can we complain of architectural shoddiness. Our buildings certainly do not look as though they were built in haste. We asked him to build a small roof over the well house and he ended up building something massive enough to be a pagoda.

Every little thing is a problem in Laos. To make a building you have to chop the tree down, skin the bark off of it, cut it into planks, then cut the planks to fit and then groove and wedge and paint. Nothing is easy in the primeval forest, as we knew when we came to Asia.

Since Chai was now a married man, we had to build a house for him on the back of the compound. The poor boys needed Chai very badly during the opening months, but Chai had come down with a case of yellow jaundice. He spent his first three weeks in Muong Sing as the first patient in our new hospital. When his house was finished, he moved into it.

Once in Nam Tha I had a patient, Owi, whose leg had been hideously bloated by infection and then withered up. When Owi heard that I had returned to Muong Sing, a full day's walk from Nam Tha, he came to me to join our team. We were delighted to hire him, as he is a very bright boy. He became the assistant to Si. When Owi had to have an assistant he found La, a Thai Lu tribe boy, to help him. Therefore the staff of the house consisted of Si, Owi and La—Owi, a Thai Dam tribe boy; La, a Thai Lu; Si, a Lao, each speaking a dialect a little different. Each of them had their own small specialization (not unlike the American Medical Association). Face is tremendously important in the Orient. I would offend Si if I went directly to Owi to ask for something. Si had given to Owi responsibility for the grounds and for the food contributed by the patients as payment in the clinic. Owi had given La responsibility for the house—cleaning, dusting, and making of the beds. The two boys helped serve dinner while Si, who had previously cooked the dinner, would sit down at the table and eat with us.

This division of authority is important, and we would always go to Si to have him tell La and Owi to do various things. Owi had a battalion of small kids from the village who assisted him. When the lawn had too much debris on it, when the water buffaloes had gotten in and made a wallow somewhere, when a bad wind had broken a lot of palm trees and their fronds were all over the ground, Owi would call his battalion together and they would sweep over the compound, cleaning it much as hordes of locusts clean a field of corn.

As none of us believe in exploitation, these children were paid for their work. They were paid by being allowed to pick out some jewelry from the huge chest of costume jewelry that had been collected for us by children all around America. The children of our village would come and say to Owi, "Do you have some work for us?" What this really meant was, "May we have a piece of costume jewelry?" They knew us well enough to know that we "gave" nothing away, and that they must earn these things. It appealed to their pride and we felt this was important.

On the same theory we demanded that all of our patients pay us to the best of their ability. They cannot pay in money but they can pay in kind. An operation would cost several chickens. A delivery, one chicken. Pills would cost eggs or rice or fruit. When the pineapple season came, we would get as many as twenty or thirty pineapples at the end of the day's sick-call. We needed this food, we had a staff of some ten or fifteen to feed, and a hospital full of patients; we put all of the donated food to good use. I think that easy and condescending charity robs people, and perhaps nations, of their self-respect.

Once the clinic began to run, it became important that we find a student staff. I was not too concerned with the training of Earl and Dwight myself. I am not interested alone in the amount of antibiotics that circulate in the bodies of our patients. But I am most interested in the amount of education that circulates in the hearts and minds of the people of our high valley. After our departure this will last longer than will their blood level of penicillin.

Therefore, we needed to find students and begin our training program. We went to the Military Commandant and suggested to him that we open a training school for the military. He was delighted and said that he would have some men sent over to us the next day. The next day ten men came and never have I seen such a motley crew. (I suppose my professor at St. Louis University Medical School said the same thing after he met his new freshman class.) The Lao army students were made up of several tribes, the Thai Dam, Thai Lu, Yao and Lao. Each tribe considers the others just a little bit inferior.

My first glance at the students made one boy almost an immediate favorite. His name was Deng. Deng was very short and looked about fourteen, although he claimed to be twenty-one. He was very olive-skinned, with a dark heavy shank of hair and two of the widest doe eyes I have ever seen. Months later as he would see surgery, see medical miracles, see the progress of patients, his eyes would get bigger and bigger. It looked as though his whole face were engulfed by the whites of his eyes. Deng stayed on with us while other students came and went. Deng became a very intricate part of the

The daily sick-call line.

photo by Erica Anderson

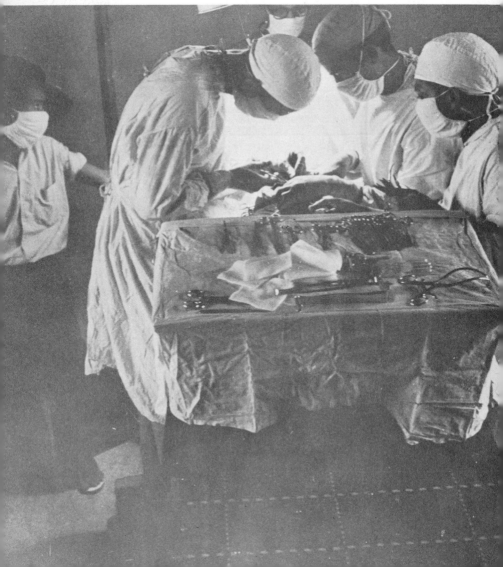

photo by Erica Anderson

Earl, Chai, Dooley and Dwight unload newly-arrived drugs, the gift of Pfizer.

Little girls are the same the world over — and so are little boys, even young Buddhist monks.

Dwight Davis with his favorite nurse, Changtip.

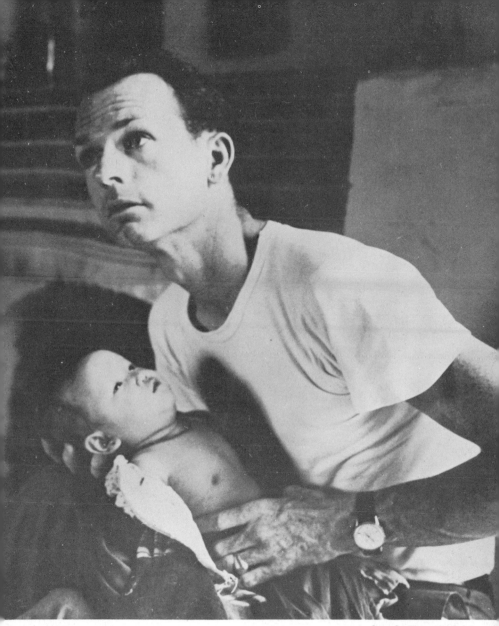

photo by Erica Anderson

When a doctor feels helpless: a tiny life, which he knows will be brief.

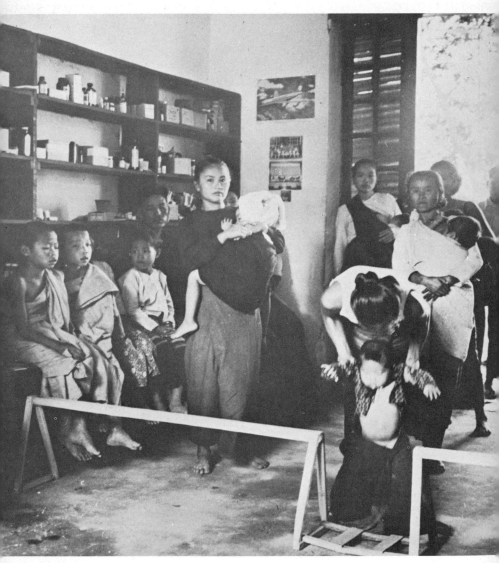

photo by Erica Anderson

With his mother's help, a young patient enters our clinic.

Dooley and his two Texans.

photo by Erica Anderson

House call brings me inside a typical village dwelling.

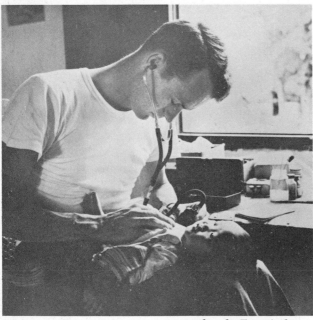

The heart-beat of Asia.

Dooley team at Muong Sing. We all grew to love him very much. He became a competent compassionate corpsman.

The first thing we had to do was to explain to students that they must not pick their noses. There were a few other commandments, such as:

"Thou shalt not spit on the deck.

"Thou shalt not scratch thyself.

"When thou wearest rubber gloves, thou shalt not shake hands with thy friend.

"Thou shalt not toss the left-over water on the floor.

"Thou shalt not open capsules and dump powder in hand of patient, but thou shalt push pill in mouth of patient.

"Thou shalt cut thy fingernails to the quick, including the fifth fingernail.

"Thou *shalt* and thou *shalt not* one thousand times."

The next step was to try to get them to be a little better group of men. The first thing this entailed was teeth cleaning. Earl, who had a penchant for dentistry, began to scrape the tartar off their teeth, and for their first pay we gave them toothbrushes and toothpaste. We introduced our student staff to the bizarre habit of daily toothbrushing.

Then we had to reteach ourselves that patience is the companion of wisdom.

As the months went on we grew more and more fond of these boys. Later we brought three girls into study with us. However, the same problems that arise in coeducational schools began to arise in our hospital. A little pinching here and there, a little play here and there, and a slight deterioration of the work level.

People talk about the differences between Americans and the Asians. It is obvious that there are differences, but these are good. We have no desire in Laos to build a mirror image of an American hospital. We have no desire that my staff mimic the staff of anybody else anywhere. We just want to illustrate to these people what we are, and if they wish to adopt our system, fine. If they do not, then though we believe it's their loss, it is their decision to make.

Differences of race and culture are not accurate measurements of superiority or inferiority. As I see it, uniformity is something to be abhorred. The world would be a very unattractive place if everything conformed. China through her commune system is trying to build such conformity. It is not a pleasant thought, because it is an offense against freedom.

The great richness of our universe is due above all to its diversity. We should take honorable pride in the distinct accomplishments of the Irish, the French, the Asian, the Negro. We must be equally aware that the accomplishments of others are proper subjects for their pride too. These thoughts were present in each day's work. These differences were obvious and pleasing to us.

Our students pitched into each day's work with a wonderful vitality. They soon grew to have no fear of us. They came to our house in the morning and mixed their own coffee, sat around and read magazines (looking at the pictures), and were very much members of the team, not employees of a Westerner. Some things were hard for them. I imagine that we three Americans made an appalling sight: we talked so fast, we walked so fast, we did such bizarre things. It must have been more difficult for them to adjust to us than it was for us to adjust to them. The instinctive pride that these young men and women had in becoming members of our team was a very bright and precious thing. We had to care for that pride and nurture it. We had to take their abilities and their youthfulness and teach them to grow tall and straight, glowing and strong.

There was much they had not seen of raw life even in their own Asian land. The sick and the wretched often live and die in the corners of their huts, out of the sight of other villagers. Suddenly our student staff were slapped with all the drudgery and frustration of medical work. They knew some of the hopelessness, and the unremitting, grinding treadmill of work. They saw that the sick vomit, the dying die, the maimed limp forever. We had to show our students that along with the ugly part of life they would also see that precious thing called hope. Just as the rain-forest trees soar over even our mountaintops, these young men must soar over the heads of their compatriots.

I treated these men as I treated my own two Americans. To an outsider one would notice little difference in the way I spoke to or dealt with any of them. This is as Earl and Dwight would have wished it, and it was essential for our students. I am their brother, yes, but their older brother. Though Asians seldom speak roughly to each other, I frequently spoke strongly to my students. Once when Deng, for about the forty-fifth time, had put an instrument back into the case unwashed, I blew my stack. In front of several of his student friends, I told him that he was not a capable man and that I had no room in my hospital for men who did not do things as I told them. I told Deng to go. I would replace him with someone else. I know I spoke to him very sternly but this had been an offense committed too many times. Deng slunk outside and cried his eyes red. Several hours later he came back and pleaded, "*Kho tot kenoi, Thanh Mo America, dai*. I'm sorry, Doctor America, please. . . ." Of course he was forgiven and has never put an unclean instrument away since that time.

It is a very wonderful thing to watch the young men grow and mature. It was feeling the pulse of existence in our high valley. They watched people dying, suffering, being healed, being born. Our working together in the languid afternoon, hiking together down mountain trails, our shooting the rapids on boats, gave us a common touch of humanity and made it evident that the brotherhood of man exists as surely as does the Fatherhood of God.

Asians respond to the help of brotherhood with affection. With these men of Asia I found my life's work. My convictions have gained in strength whatever, from time to time, they may have lost in disillusion. I will work amongst these people. I will train them as best I can. But I must do more than just treat the sick. I must bear witness, I must speak up as often as possible and according to my ability. I must tell other Americans of these Asians. I think all men should reaffirm what they know, what they believe. I want to speak of the spirit of Asia.

The spirit of man is not a nebulous thing. The spirit of man is this palpable thing in the hearts of Deng and Chai, Earl and Dwight. On this earth each man must find his field of work. For Tom Dooley the workbench is Asia. Here where the mountains mingle with the night, where there is the anguish of living and dying, here in these high valleys I will work for all my days.

A few weeks after our arrival in Muong Sing a man came to our still unfinished house, with a huge basket of flowers and fruits. He wanted to perform a *baci*. When we first arrived in Nam Tha in 1957, there was a certain hostility and coldness amongst the people of the valley. We were new, we were white men who had strange techniques, we did strange things. They had never seen us before, and they had heard much from the Communists and from the jungle rulers, both good and bad. The situation was not the same when we arrived in Muong Sing. The word of our work in Nam Tha in the preceding years had spread, and this man's visit was proof.

The traditional ceremony of *baci* consists of tying the white cotton string of friendship around the wrists of those to whom the *baci* is offered. As each string is tied, one makes the wish, "I wish you happiness," "I wish you longevity," "I wish you much love," "I wish you wives and many children," "I wish you blue skies, bright night and good health."

We did not know why these people had come to us to offer us a *baci*, as we had yet to treat them. The man brought his wife, sister, aunt, uncle and a half a dozen children. We talked about many things, always trying to figure out exactly why he was offering this *baci* for us. Then he pulled over his little son, yanked down his pants and showed me a neat hairline scar. I had done a herniorrhaphy on the boy in 1957. He remembered us well and was grateful for our returning to North Laos. I remembered that when his son had been my patient they had walked all the way across the mountain that separates Muong Sing from Nam Tha. Now I live on his side of that mountain.

With men like him speaking in our behalf it took no time at all before we were a most accepted group in town. Within a few weeks people didn't even notice us in the market place. This was a pleasant thing. We wanted to become an intimate and integral part of the community life of the villagers. We were friends with these people of the valley, but we wondered about the people of the mountain.

Good fortune shone on us. Only a few days after our arrival, a young man was brought to us whose face had been hideously mauled by a bear. This lad belonged to the high mountain tribe called the Kha Kho. The boy had a filthy wound and a huge hole in the cheek. You could shove two fingers into a yawning, foul-smelling wound just below the eye and the fingers poked out of the roof of his mouth. This pus-filled hole had been stuffed with tobacco and monkey fur. His right eye was torn loose and many of his teeth were broken. The whole upper jawbone was fractured in several places.

We had to do a series of operations on him, first removing the loosened maxillary plate. It took us several days of cleaning him up with antibiotics and daily washings in order to find what tissue was worth saving. We had to remove what was left of his lacerated eyeball. Then under general anesthesia we were able to loosen the good skin from around the jaw, the eye, the side of the nose, and the cheekbone. Without tension we pulled good tissue over and closed up the hole in his face. It healed well, leaving only a jagged scar. Though to us this still looked awful, to him it was a near miracle. From a miserable youngster with a horribly dirty, foul face, this lad had become quite an acceptable sight. We discharged him from the hospital but he returned in a few days with a very small dog. He got on his knees and held this dog up to us as an offering of gratitude. I smiled at him and said "*Cup Chai*," and added, "*Het menh yanh*. What can I do with it?" The boy looked at me in surprise and responded, "Eat it." We were adopted into the Kha Kho family of men.

Many people became our friends. So did this little dog. Dwight named him Fang because he was so utterly harmless and cowardly. All of the children in our area called the dog Fang too. Occasionally Dwight would get angry, growl at the dog and say, "Come here, Fang, son of Claw." When the Asians would try to repeat that, the sound that came out was unprintable in Lao or English.

SIX ·

"RESPECTFUL MEN OF MEDICINE"

Perhaps our hospital at Muong Sing was unattractive, whitewashed, utilitarian, and ugly. But it was also a compassionate candle in the darkness.

It only took a few weeks to put the clinic building in useable shape. The clinic building, like our house, had three major rooms, plus two smaller ones on the side. One room was temporarily used as a ward. Later when the new ward building was finished, we made it over into an operating room. The room on the west side of the building was the dressing room and the small room behind it was the shot room. The large central room was the clinic.

The clinic was a long rectangular room, with the window at one end and the door at the other. Along each side the boys had built long high shelves. On the bottom of these shelves were five crates in which our gear had been shipped from America. These crates had been painted green and covered with linoleum. Everything in our hospital was painted green and covered with linoleum, a Dooley fixation.

We put up a foot-high railing across the center of the room. I sat in front of the window at the opposite end from the door. I had a desk on one side, the patient's chair in front of me, and interpreters on each side of me. Two students would stand against the shelves on my left. Two other students would stand in the shot room and watch from the adjoining door.

The sick man would come through an opening in the center railing, walk up to me and sit on the chair. With my interpreters and forty or fifty people behind the railing listening in, we would discuss this man's ailments. By having everyone listening in, many other people learned. "Oh, can you cure that kind of a thing, doctor?" they would ask. "My mother has the same problem." "Oh explain yourself better than that, Houmpenh," they would urge an old man. "Tell them what your problem is." It really added a touch of togetherness to our work, and after all there was a certain propaganda element in what we were doing.

After I discussed the problem with the patient and my students, the patient was sent to the shelves. There he would receive medicine from the students. I never gave any medicine to anyone. Nor did my two Americans. The Asian students would be told, "This man has pneumonia. Give him something for his pneumonia, some terramycin." The Asian student would then take the terramycin bottle from the shelf, put the correct number of capsules into an envelope, and give them to the patient. The Asian student would explain to the patient the dosage schedule, and would make such comments as "Why don't you wash your hands?" "Why didn't you bring your child back here last week?" "Why haven't you done what the doctor told you to do last week?"

This idea of Asians helping Asians is much superior to Americans helping Asians. When the patient received the medicine, he would turn to the Asian student and say, *"Cup Chai."* They knew the help was American but they were grateful to the Asian student too. My Asian students will be here all their lives, I will not. I dispensed nothing, the Asians did.

The main theme of our work was to establish things so that Asians could maintain them. This included prestige, position, and pride.

If the patient had to have a shot, he was sent in through the door on my right, where we would tell the two students what to give—penicillin, streptomycin, dramamine, and so on. A card was given to the patient with the number of shots that he would need. As the shot was given, the student would mark it off the card.

If the patient needed a dressing, he was sent to the dressing room which was the west end of the building. There on many low tables the patients would sit. Earl and Dwight would run this room much like a symphony conductor. With all the patients sitting, the Lao students would begin to treat the wounds, washing them, suturing them, cleaning them. Earl would say, "Wash that one with hydrogen peroxide." "Clean that one up with a little soap and water." "You had better take the stitches out of that one, they have been in long enough." "Better call Thanh Mo America in to look at this wound. It's kind of bad." By this system it was the Asians who cared for the wounds of the Asians and not the white men. To be sure, Earl and Dwight and I looked at many a wound and sutured hundreds of them. But as often as possible and to every extent possible the Asians took care of their own.

Earl and Dwight, though reluctant at first, later saw the wisdom of this action and carried it out even better than I. They taught the students how to suture by having them practice sewing their pants legs together. Many times a suture job would have to be done and I would merely tell Dwight to do it. Dwight in turn supervised Deng or some other student in doing the job. The Lao boys who did the suture job would take great pride in their work and give the patient their daily dressings with much compassion and interest.

The sick-call started early in the morning, and ended up after high noon. The patients paid us in chickens, eggs and corn, and would say to our students, and to us, the most sublime utterance in any language—the words of gratitude. Two words, "Thank you."

The villagers who came to our clinic were wonderful people to see and know. Some were as frail as an El Greco saint. Others looked like mystic holy men, with wispy little beards of a hundred hairs. Others were fat and corpulent women who laughed and smiled, their bodies rippling with them. Many brought their spindly-legged, pot-bellied little children glumly perched on their hips, the pathos in the eyes of the mother almost matching the bleak look of death in the eyes of their children.

Many of the patients had beautiful Mongol features, delicate creamy skins and deep-set eyes. Others had bright almond eyes, or eyes so deep that one looked into bottomless pools. The children with bulging bellies and gaping wounds rapidly became healthy and husky. Several times the wretched sick came from huts where they lived on miserable straw pallets in dark rooms. They came to our bright clinic with colorful pictures on the walls and put themselves in the tender hands of my crew. And they were better even before they received their antibiotics. Some of the old men were like little walnuts, browned and wrinkled and withered. Sometimes straggling primitive hordes of human beings known as refugees would come. These silent people, witnesses to such horrors of Communism, are the sad song of humanity in our time.

Then there would be the bouncing healthy children who would wait for sick-call more interested in the show than in any particular illness. They would be energetically swishing, swatting, and thwacking, to keep the bugs away. The people at our clinic, in the high valley of Muong Sing, were just like the people who came to me in clinics in America. They had their share of meanness and magnificence. But there is something different about them because the prospect of curing sickness was a totally revolutionary concept to them. The villagers all their lives had thought it was impossible to be rid of malaria, goiter, rickets, dysentery and boils.

When we demonstrated to them that they need not have these things, it was an amazing and wonderful thing. The scarlet and black wounds that burst in their superb olive flesh were closed up with simple cleanliness. The dirty stumps of teeth were extracted with ease; no longer did they have a fetid or foul mouth. Soon the wretched patients with green-black sores, or inflamed bellies, would quietly become cured. They were the better for our having been there.

I also watched my American assistants at work. Earl Rhine's ease at handling people was beautiful to behold. He showered his time and attention on the wretched sick with a sad kind of joy. With grand aplomb he treated them all like visiting royalty. For example, one day a wizened old man came to him and gesticulated how he had an excruciating pain in his left knee. The old man explained very carefully that "the pain begins in my left knee and runs up the inside of my leg. The pain plunges into my pelvis, continues on up to my face and into my head." He went on to say that with some dizziness the pain would come out the tip of his nose and "then it falls to my knee, the other one." Earl listened very seriously and nodded his head with a solemn and professional mien that would have pleased the President of the American Medical Association. Then, with insight and knowledge, he said, "Oh, yes, of course. I completely understand. I suggest hot soaks for both knees."

Dwight Davis would jokingly call some haggard, snaggle-toothed old gal "honey," though this in no way ever indicated any superficiality of concern. Earl in turn examined each patient as though he were examining the king himself. Both men did a magnificent job. My patients risked too much compassion.

Each person was important as a person. I tried to get this view across to Earl and Dwight, only to find that they already fully realized its importance. Whether the child was a bleating mountain boy or the son of the local Mayor, he was important to Dwight and Earl because he was a child.

Earl had a love affair. Only Earl's "love" was a five-year-old girl whose slim little body had all the delicacy of the proverbial lotus flower. This midnight-eyed Asian girl would come to see Earl frequently. At the mature age of five she would blithely walk into our house and sit down, folding her hands gracefully in her lap as though they were simply two leaves that had fallen into her sarong. When she walked, she put each foot down as softly as trembling light. She never said one word to Earl during all the time that he knew her. And yet she came almost every day. From time to time Earl would be out on a river trip and she would come to the house, look around for Earl, and when she realized he was not there, she would go home. She had nothing to do with Dwight and me. She was Earl's love.

If Earl was there she would climb up on his lap, no matter what he was doing, and sit there in utter contentment until Earl was forced to put her down to do his work. She would then smile, clasp her hands in front of her face in the prayerful fashion of saying adieu, and "silently steal away."

It has been stated on high echelons in Washington that the success of American foreign policy in Asia depends primarily upon the image we create of America and Americans in the minds of Asian people. If this is true (and I believe it to be so), the image of Americans in the eyes of thousands of people in Muong Sing is the image of the gentility, compassion, and love of Dwight Davis and Earl Rhine.

Earl seemed more interested in dentistry than he did in medicine. His mossy-toothed dental patients swore by him. No matter what the dental problem might be, however, he had only one treatment, extraction. When I had to leave Laos on an emergency a year later, the first letter that I received from the boys included the statement that they had found a very small foot-powered dental drill and had purchased it—"hope you don't mind."

We all wore white coats in the clinic and Earl had one of the Lao student midwives embroider his name in Lao on his coat. The word Thanh Mo means "respectful man of medicine," though "Mo" also includes witch doctors. I am called Thanh Mo America. Earl was referred to as Thanh Mo Chep Keo which literally means "respectful man of medicine for pain in the teeth." This is the closest our village dialect comes to the word dentist.

Just before dawn, one of the first weeks we were in North Laos, we were torn from our sleep by the shrieks of a screaming woman. She was only a few feet from our window. I lunged to the window and saw several men huddled over something. The moonlight was bright. I jumped out of the window to the ground a few feet below, yelling for Earl and Dwight. They leaped after me and immediately the clump of men raced away. They left a sagging limp figure on the ground. I bent down and recognized the bloody mass of a young woman we had recently hired. She was working for us as payment for the delivery of her child. She had no home, her husband was in the army, and she had come quite some distance to our new American hospital for her delivery. We had hired her to give her a place to eat and live for a few months.

Even by moonlight I could tell she had been brutally stabbed with long dagger-like knives. Dozens of deep wounds pumped blood from her body. The bundle on the ground by her side was her newborn baby. He had also been stabbed. The men that we saw running away were the ones who had attacked them. Why?

We carried her bleeding body into the hospital a few feet away, and tried to get her blood-soaked clothes off. Intravenous fluid was started immediately and we began to try to stop the bleeding from all of the stab wounds around her body. It was futile. Within a few minutes she stopped breathing entirely. She had lost too much blood. The floor underneath the operating room table was wet with congealed blood. We baptized her and turned our attention to the baby.

Meanwhile, quite a large crowd had gathered, including the Chief of the Military Battalion and the Chief of Police. Chai, Earl, Dwight and I were operating on the baby to sew up the multiple deep lacerations, which tore through the muscles and down to the bone of both the arm and leg. We repaired the infant, and gave him to a nurse who took the child from the awesome scene. Then we went to the house and collapsed from the shock of it all. Everything seemed so useless. Why would anyone attack this young woman? What ever prompted such a hideous atrocity so close to our house? Was this an indication of hatred for us?

We carefully wrapped the dead girl's body, and she was buried the next morning. Her child was adopted by some people in the neighborhood. For many weeks everyone was speaking about the murder—and there were many reasons given for it. The one that seemed to be generally adopted was that she was having a love affair with a soldier and the soldier killed her.

This seemed hard to understand, as she had just given birth to a child a few days beforehand. Also the Chief of the Military claimed that he had caught the soldier and put him in prison, though no one else ever saw him. This included our Lao military students who lived in the fortress just a few feet from this prison cell. It is my personal belief that this was a Communist maneuver in order to frighten us out of North Laos. It frightened us indeed, but not out of North Laos.

What it did do was bring several things sharply and clearly into focus for all three of us. It was not a new experience for me; I have seen the anguish of atrocity. All my years of training, of study and experience were focused that night on that mutilated young girl before me. Yet at dawn the girl was devoid of breath and blood and life itself—dead. The horror of this night was simply an introduction for Dwight and Earl to what they would have to bear for the many months ahead.

From the date of our arrival we were constantly in the processes of building. As soon as we got the house in order and the clinic finished, we started to work building the new ward. Behind the clinic building some 50 yards was a small shell of an old building. Attached to this building on three sides were a series of grass huts, occupied by the wives of some of the military. We gently, yet firmly, had these ladies evicted and we took over this area for our ward. The huts were torn off, a wall or two was knocked down, another built up, much cementing, scrubbing and painting and we soon had for ourselves a three-roomed ward. The ward had mat space for twenty or twenty-five and I suppose in an emergency we could jam in a few more. We covered all the holes and spots that would not take paint with pictures and postcards sent to us from people all over the world.

We also found that our patients, of their own free will, painted some of our walls. They painted them with signs and symbols of witchcraft and black magic. The tribal people of North Laos wallow in superstition, black magic, necromancy and sorcery. There are as many legends as there are mountain peaks. There are as many herbs as there are trees. Our working in this area demanded a constant awareness of the power of witchcraft and black magic. So our walls even displayed our peaceful coexistence with witchcraft.

The army sent over to us daily working parties to help build. The whole compound was leveled off. What had been a patchwork of sinkholes, buffalo wallows, ditches and hillocks became a level, clean hospital compound. We even transplanted grass. Around the hospital compound (about the size of a football field) we had a ditch dug and a barbed wire fence erected. The ditch was to keep out water and the fence to keep out buffaloes; both had a tendency to collect on our compound. Earl, with all of the knowledge of a Midwestern farmer, planted a vegetable garden. The tomatoes grew to be succulent and large, but we rarely got a chance to eat them. The jungle monkeys got there first. Si planted flower gardens all around the hospital and they grew in profusion. We soon had a lovely looking hospital compound, primitive, utilitarian, but neat, clean, and whitewashed.

As far as witch doctors are concerned, they have several techniques. One of the types of magic that they use is a defensive thing. They have fetishes and objects that are endowed with certain magical powers. I have a gift given me by people of a mountain village. It is a stone with a Buddha carved on it. The stone is wrapped in a tiny net of silver. This will protect me against two things, bullets and black magic. The people believe these chains around their necks and little bags with pieces of silver are extremely powerful, not unlike certain talismans used in Africa. However, when I was at medical school I saw many a patient wearing a copper penny on a chain around his neck. And as a matter of fact, I know one very sophisticated woman in the American community in Laos who wears copper bracelets to keep arthritis away. (Perhaps we really shouldn't attack witchcraft too vehemently.)

When the witch doctor talks to patients, he really elicits something like a clinical history. He asks the patient what he is wearing and how long he's been wearing it. He asks if the patient has any talismans or amulets around. He asks what was the position of the moon when the sickness began. What dreams had he been having? The witch doctor then sits down to read long passages from folded "bibles."

One afternoon Chai's wife was quite sick and he called me over to her house. I found one of the old gentlemen of the village, a sorcerer, sitting cross-legged with a long fan-fold of something like cardboard. He was reading ancient Pali script. On the floor before him Chai was sitting in a white surgical gown from my modern hospital, listening and offering worship to witchcraft. If you can't fight 'em, join 'em.

Often the witch doctor would tie black and white strings around the affected part, or rub ashes on the forehead, or lay leaves under the ground around the sick patient. They also fill a small bowl with eggs and rice and a small candle. In some areas I have seen them make little mud images of horses and cows and elephants and lay these on the bowl of rice as offerings to the evil spirits.

When I had a visiting surgeon with me one time, we went to see a child who was lying on a bank of leaves. Herbs are of importance to these people. The villagers believe that illness is due to the presence of an evil spirit and that lying on these herbs would chase the spirit away.

I found that the primitive people of our high valley were very anxious to be cut open. They have no fear of my scalpel and seem to think that I can actually cut the evil spirit out. One man of the Kha Kho tribe was delighted to have me operate on his wife because he knew that I would have to turn on the light in the operating room. He seemed to think that to chase the evil spirit, all I had to do was make a cut, let the light shine in, and the evil spirit would flee. I wish it were that simple.

The Kha Kho tribe, of the high hills, paint their teeth black. We spoke to one of our friends of this tribe asking about the black teeth. He summed the whole thing up in words that I had heard many years previously in North Viet Nam: "Who would want white teeth like a dog?" The men paint their teeth black when they begin to get interested in girls. The girls paint their teeth at puberty. This ceremony takes place with a celebration. The substance with which they paint their teeth stays on for a lifetime. They take the bark of a certain tree and cook it down until it becomes a thick paste. This is mixed with other ingredients and then is rubbed on the teeth every day for seven days. The only time they reapply this is when they become very sick. They believe that by reapplying it, they will have better health. Many times I have seen patients sitting in my ward, blackening their teeth again.

There are many different tribes in the area. The Kha Kho are the most primitive, and the Thai Lu the most predominant. The Thai Lu, who have a more developed civilization than the Kha Kho, stand tall and straight. They are angular and thin, and though they have Mongoloid features they are not as squat as the hill people. The Thai Lu tattoo their bodies, the men from the knees to the waistline, covering practically every inch of that area, and the women tattoo small figures on their arms and words across their backs. All this is supposed to give them "strength," and protect them by inserting good spirits under their skins.

In all of Indo-China this custom of tattooing goes back to prehistoric times. There is an ancient legend which says that a mythical king ordered the fishermen of all his realm to tattoo the monsters of the sea on their arms. This, it was believed, would protect them against crocodiles. In the ancient court of Annam, in central Viet Nam, the kings tattooed images of dragons on themselves. The dragon is not only the symbol of Viet Nam but of all Indo-China. You often see dragons undulating across the roofs of pagodas, tattooed on people's skins, painted on walls, carved in homes. The dragon is one of the four symbolic animals engraved in Buddhism, the others being the unicorn, the phoenix, and the turtle.

Although I have never run across a dragon personally, many people have described them to me. Chai claims he has seen many. They tell me that the dragon has a head which is shaped like a deer's, with great horns, and his monster eyes stick way out of their sockets. The dragons of North Laos, I was told, have the ears of a water buffalo and the long body and tail of a reptile. Chai says they have scales like fish, but where the fins should be there are large claws, like a vulture's.

The dragon is a very marvelous creature. "He's even more marvelous than Americans," Chai says. The top of the dragon's head always has a decorative area which is supposed to be the mark of intelligence. The dragon can live either underground, in the water, or in the air. He can swim, walk or fly. And the dragon spits a certain kind of vapor which he can transform into fire or water at will. Of course everybody knows that dragons are immortal. The people of North Laos reconfirm this frequently. There is one dragon in the area who is supposed to have lived down our road for 5,000 years. In spite of these terrible characteristics, the dragon is not considered an evil thing. On the contrary, the dragon has always been a symbol of nobility and power in China, and some of this dragon culture has sifted down to North Laos too.

In view of their more positive qualities of durability, intelligence and power, I sometimes think I would like to have an official dragon attached to each of the MEDICO teams around the world. How about it, Dr. Comanduras?

SEVEN ·

TAKE A WALK WITH ME

Our ward is something unique to see. We have three rooms which we majestically call "Ward A," "Ward B," and "Ward C." Each room is small, about eighteen feet in width and just about the length of two average American beds. As you enter the door there is a bed to the left and another to the right. At the other end of the room is one large platform. We lay bamboo mats on the platforms and hang individual mosquito nets; in this way a platform can sleep five or six.

On a typical day of making rounds, you would find a small girl of the Kha Mou tribe on Mat 1 in Ward A. She is a little reluctant to talk to you, but her father and mother who are staying here with her are not. The mother herself had a large tumor which we removed surgically. While she was here we realized that her child was wracked with pneumonia. We are treating both of them.

On Mat 4, we have an old Yao man who lives high in the mountains in a village called Ban Chao Mai. He had had a bladder stone almost all of his life, but the old goat was sort of indestructible. We had a lot of trouble with him before surgery, but finally we removed a stone just a little smaller than a tennis ball. Yes, a tennis ball. I cannot speak his dialect, but Chai can. The old man said: "Doctor America, you can have my bladder stone. I don't want it." It was obvious, however, that this old gent was doing fine—not complaining for a change and, by all signs and symptoms, much improved. We call him "Old Indestructible" because he has had such a difficult time post-surgically.

Over on the other part of the platform we have another Yao, a small boy nearly blind in both eyes. He has an entropion, a disease that is caused from the scarring of the lower or upper eyelid. The inside of the eyelid scars from many repeated or from constant infections. The scar makes the eyelids turn in. The eyelashes therefore constantly rubbing on the eyeball causing more irritation to the eye. This in turn causes more scar, more contraction and more inturning of the lash on the eyeball. The surgical correction is merely to excise an eliptical piece of skin off of the top of the eyelid, leaving a gap in the skin. The lower portion of this area is then pulled up over the denuded area to the top part of the eliptical excised area. The eyelid is made narrow and in pulling the skin up it turns the eyelid up, too. The eyelashes no longer rub on the eyeball. If surgery is not done, the repeated infections will cause the boy to be totally blind by the time he is ten. After surgery he looks a great deal better. With cortisone drops in the eyes, the corneal irritation diminishes rapidly and vision returns. Now he will see as well as any child.

A third patient on the platform is a lady getting over a blazing attack of malaria. As is so often the case, these people exist on the brink of malnutrition. One or two days of high fever will push them off this ledge and they fall into a negative balance. Their ankles and bellies bloat up, they become extremely sick and emaciated in a staggeringly short time. This woman's malaria was cured with Camesquin, about eighty cents worth in a day. Now she is on protein extracts like Sustagen and the Meals for Millions. Her condition is mightily improved and after a few more days of convalescence she can go home.

Walk out on the porch now to the next door, into Ward B. Here we have a small boy whose name is Guntar. He is on Mat 1 on the left. Guntar belongs to the Kha Kho tribe. He claims to be seven years old. By the Buddhist calendar this may be true. By our calendar he is closer to six. A few weeks ago his father shot a tiger with an old flintlock. In wild exuberance the lad ran up to the body of the tiger. The animal, not yet dead, lunged at the child mauling him terribly. The boy's whole leg was practically torn off and blood loss and shock brought him close to death. By the time they got him to us his leg was just a bloated glob of infected flesh and pus. We feared it would be necessary to amputate at the thigh to prevent the poison of that nearly gangrenous limb from permeating his frail body. But we tried antibiotics on him first. The lad is doing very well now, after many days of hot soaks, terramycin, and good old-fashioned TLC ("tender loving care").

Frequently at night we show a movie on the wall of our house. Some 1,000 people sit on the grass and watch in wonder. Little Guntar loves the movies. I think movies have just as much therapeutic value as antibiotics. Walt Disney gave me a 16 mm. version of *Dumbo*. *Dumbo* has enchanted

North Laos, and the children watch for him every time we show this movie. They never seem to tire of it. "What a wonderful land America must be," they say. "They have huge elephants and the elephants are pink and green and blue and purple. And some of these elephants have ears so big that they can fly through the air." *Dumbo* is winning friends in the ten-year-old bracket for sure.

The other patients in this ward are a sad assortment of malaria, dysentery, skin disease, malnutrition, and other maladies of filth, ignorance, and privation.

In Ward C we have a Meo woman and her husband. The Meo woman has a tumor in the abdomen which we are going to remove very soon. She is too anemic and too loaded with intestinal worms now. After these are cleaned out and her blood iron brought closer to normal, we will operate.

There are also some Kha Kho tribesmen in Ward C. One of them is a leper. There is not much we can do for him except keep him clean. Leprosy is not very contagious, contrary to Biblical beliefs.

We have several tuberculars in this ward, one of them a thirty-five-year-old man, who belongs to the Thai Dam tribe. We also have in this ward a very attractive young woman who came to us from the village near Nam Tha. Her husband is a member of the police force and he was able to get her on a special plane to be sent to us. She has tuberculosis and other diseases of malnutrition. However, she is doing very well now; her eyes are brightening up and she is a very lovable person. All of the police officers in town here (eight of them) come over every day to visit and bring her food. They take very good care of her. The deep sense of family among these Asians is a wonderful thing to behold.

Now I can hear someone saying, "My gosh, keeping children in the same room with tuberculars." Yes, it's bad, but there is such a tremendous amount of tuberculosis here. We gave our cases streptomycin for fourteen days, and built up their cachetic bodies with Deca Vi Sol and Sustagen. Though not cured, they are always discharged improved, with instructions in diet and some explanation of the principles of contagion.

I do not want to enlarge upon the incidence of tuberculosis in Laos, because to be scientifically correct I would have to have laboratory smears and X-rays, but I would estimate that one in ten over the age of forty has tuberculosis; and one in five over the age of fifty. We do not use any new drugs and we do not devote a great deal of time to the treatment of tuberculosis because I am more interested in cases which can be readily cured rather than the chronic cases that require long-term treatment. Our emphasis is on the more readily treatable diseases.

In Ward C we have a lady with a bad dental infection. The whole side of her left cheek is missing and there is a gaping hole. She can stick her tongue out the side of her face where her cheek should be. There is just one thin bridge of tissue on the side of the mouth running from the upper lip to the lower lip. We tried plastic surgery on her, but it was unsuccessful. We will wait now until a visiting plastic surgeon comes and we can do a more complicated skin graft.

Ward rounds are held by Dwight and Earl every morning just a little after dawn. I make rounds in the afternoon, seeing only the cases Earl and Dwight feel I must see. These two American boys are really tops. It is a wondrous thing to watch them care for the wretched. They use so well the hot towels of caution and the aspirin of compassion. They soothe the small child and they help and quiet and give strength to the old. My men have high courage, goodness, patience, and constancy. Our small ward is a veritable chapel of compassion.

My interpreter Chai has been with me since I first came to Asia in 1956. In *The Edge of Tomorrow* I told how I met him, and how he refused to swim in the Nam Lick River because he hadn't been checked out with the spirits. Chai is a very competent Asian corpsman, yet he still reverts back to his black magic when he feels that my terramycin and surgery are not quite adequate. After he recovered from his first month having yellow jaundice, he pitched in with the enthusiasm which so endeared him to us.

Neither Earl nor Dwight speak French, though Dwight does understand some due to his ability in Spanish. As soon as we arrived in Laos I knew I would have to find an English-speaking interpreter. They used to be difficult to find, but since American influence in Laos is increasing and all Asians want to learn English, the situation is improving. A friend in the American Economic Mission runs an English language school. This is not under any formal program, but just his own personal contribution to the people of Asia. I asked him if he would find someone in his school who could work for us, and he said he would.

The next night he brought to the home of Hank Miller a short, slightly stooped young boy, who didn't look a day over fourteen, as a candidate to be my interpreter. I was a little aghast to think that my conversations with certain of the tougher tribes would have to be handled through this little boy. I spoke to him in English and though he did have some competence, he was reluctant, fearful and overly polite. At first I thought that this lad would never work. On the other hand I realized how frightened he must be, how anxious he was for the job, and his youth perhaps would make him malleable. I put him on the next plane to the north and told him he would be interpreter for Earl and Dwight. His name was Ngoan.

It took no time at all for Ngoan to become a very intimate part of the team, and to become as beloved as a brother. Chai would interpret for me and Ngoan would interpret for Earl and Dwight. Chai has always been my shadow, Ngoan is now shadow for Earl and Dwight. We kidded him so much about being stoop-shouldered that he soon learned to stand up straight. Eating the kind of food that we ate, he soon filled out and became a healthier and stronger boy. He was constantly studying. Every free moment that he had he was studying one of his books.

Later we had correspondence courses in simple language sent from America on which he worked diligently. Every time someone would say a word that he did not understand, he would write it in his little notebook and look it up later. Although his translations were a bit stiff, nevertheless they were accurate. The great strides that this boy made in the fifteen months he was with us were impressive.

One day we went up to the China frontier to see if any refugees were escaping, and to take a general look around it. We drove to a village a few miles from ours, climbed out of the jeep and began to hike. We had some of our soldier students with us as well as Si, Owi, and La. Just for comfort we brought along a map that showed the cartographic presence of the Communistic frontier. In these heavy hills and jungles I am always afraid of stepping three feet too far and ending up in China.

It was a beautiful day, the sun high, the sky blue, and there was a certain feeling of abandonment. This break from the dull monotony of misery was a good thing. As we walked in the high rain-forest, Ngoan told us this story:

"The village where I was born looks like this valley. I was born in a village called Song La which is not very far from Dien Bien Phu. I, of the tribe of the Black Thai Dam, do not really live in Viet Nam or in Laos. Our tribe lives all across this land. This land belonged to our tribe long before France divided it up and called one part Viet Nam and one part Laos.

"My country is very beautiful, but I do not ever remember anything but the blood of war in my days. In 1946 war was tearing the flesh of the valley of Song La. When the war destroyed my own village, my family was scattered. Some were taken prisoners, some of us escaped, and I got a job with a French soldier. I did his laundry. The soldier was very good to me. I was only eight or nine or ten, depending upon how you count. When this soldier was transferred to Dien Bien Phu, he took me with him. I then went to Hanoi, the great capital of North Viet Nam. I was his coolie. When 1954 came the fortress of Dien Bien Phu fell to the Communists, and I am told they had some big treaty somewhere and that the war was over."

(I thought to myself as Ngoan spoke that I, too, remember the fall of the fortress of Dien Bien Phu and for good reason. In 1954 this fortress was conquered by the Communists, just after June's Geneva Treaty. At that moment I was a Navy doctor running the refugee camp, not more than sixty kilometers from where Ngoan was living in North Viet Nam.)

"When I was in Hanoi," Ngoan continued, "I heard of the people leaving the north because they did not want to live under Communism. I did not want to live under the Communists because I had seen what their war had done, and I decided that I would leave too. I asked the soldier if he would take me, but he said that he could not. He said that he was very sorry but that they were unable to take their coolies with them." (However, the French did make a request to the American representatives in Saigon, and one day early in 1955, a few months before the Communists took over Hanoi, a group of American airplanes came to Hanoi.)

"All of the tribe of the Black Thai who were scattered in the mountains and in the city of Hanoi got together, because we were told that American airplanes would fly us to a free land very near by. We all climbed on airplanes which scared me and amazed me very much. I found my brother at the airport. He, too, was waiting for escape. I had not seen him for many years. The American airplanes were large and terribly frightening. They flew us to a village called Xieng Khouang in North Laos." Xieng Khouang is about a hundred miles straight west of the Vietnamese Black Thai tribal area of Song La. The area of Xieng Khouang is a tribal area of the Thai Dam also, though geographically it is in Laos. The Communists had not taken over this part of Indo-China. Here the Thai Dam could live in peace.

We sat by a mountain stream, as Ngoan continued: "I lived in Xieng Khouang for another year. Now that I was a man of thirteen or fourteen years old, I had to do gardening and farming work. I never owned any land, so I always had to work for other people and I did not like this. When I heard from my friends that the Lao government was going to resettle the Black Thai refugees further away from the Viet Nam border, I decided to go too.

"I was then herded on more airplanes and flown down to the capital of Laos, Vientiane. In Vientiane I got a job as a waiter in a restaurant. When my brother came he got a job working in the garage for the United States Overseas Mission people. While he was there he met a Doctor Taeed, who was a member of the Bahai faith. Doctor Taeed was very good to my brother, and my brother told Doctor Taeed about me.

"A few days later Dr. Taeed took me to his small clinic. You know, Dr. Taeed takes care of the Americans in U.S.O.M., so I worked in his clinic as the clean-up boy. He also let me go to his school to begin to study English. I was very pleased and proud to have an opportunity to study English. Dr. Taeed is a good man. He has done a great deal for my tribe, Black Thai. Everybody else says that we are no good, that we are only a tribe to be servants, to be slaves. I do not think this is true."

Earl, Dwight and I listened to Ngoan intently. We were enchanted by the way he spoke, by the clarity of his statements, the poignancy and tragedy that had been his very young life. Today he is only eighteen years old and yet he has seen more unhappiness and tragedy than most people who live to be eighty.

I said to him, "Well, Ngoan, how did you ever get to me?" Ngoan said, "I worked for Dr. Taeed for a period of eight months. I worked very hard to learn to speak English and then one day Dr. Taeed came to me and said, 'Ngoan, would you like to have a job with Dr. Dooley, the Thanh Mo America?' But I did not know what the word 'job' meant. When he explained it to me, I was frightened because I did not think my English was strong enough to be an interpreter for a doctor. But I did want to have the chance, and so he took me to the house of Mr. Miller to meet you. And now I am with you and I am very happy."

We frequently heard what life was like on the other side of the Bamboo Curtain, the curtain of terror. The most vivid example came one afternoon when Earl, Dwight and I were building a small cage. We had been given a tiny Himalaya sun-bear as a gift. We were building a cage which was only a few feet high and a few feet wide. This cage was going to be put up in a tree at the back of the house, and the little bear would be kept in it.

While we were building the cage, a man came and squatted on his haunches and watched us. He kept watching us. Finally he began to cry. I called for my Yunnanese interpreter who came and spoke to the man. Soon the interpreter began to cry. The man had told him this story:

"I live in the large village on the other side of that mountain slope. The Communists came to our village several months ago to build a commune. You know the communes of China, doctor. The Communists come into a village of some 600 huts and they destroy 50 huts in the middle of the village. And all the men are put into the huts on the south side and all the women into the huts on the north side. The children are taken away to live in another village. The old folks are taken to the village with the children. The Communists thus break up the family.

"All the cooking utensils are smelted down into one general cooking area. All the harvested rice must be put into the village commune. There is no tax, all the rice goes into the same basket."

The man continued to cry, sobbing more strongly than before. Earl, Dwight and I sat down on a log and listened to him more intently. He continued: "My wife had beriberi because she did not eat enough rice. One day my son and I were harvesting our rice, and my son put two handfuls of harvested rice into his pocket instead of putting it into the village commune. He was caught as he returned to the village.

"He had committed a crime against the state, as all food belongs to the state. This was the highest crime he could be accused of. The rice had not even been decorticated, it was just the raw rice. Because he had committed a crime against the state, the state punished him. The chief of the commune built a small cage just about the size of this cage that you are building for your bear. My son was put into the cage. It was so small that he could not stand nor sit, but had to bend over with his head jammed down hard and one leg thrust out through the bars on the side of the cage. The cage was put into the middle of the village square. Around it was put a roll of barbed wire, and around that the guards.

"Under the direct sun my son stood in this cage, having all of the body functions, never being allowed to eat or drink, no one being allowed to come near the cage. The ants and flies became something awful. The stink of death soon came. And my wife and I and all the village witnessed the starvation and agony and death of our son in that cage."

The man told me that he and his wife waited until late one night, many days after the death of their son, and then escaped across the frontier, and came on down to the village of Muong Sing. I asked the man to come to my house and I gave him some tea. He said something which I put into my notes. He said, "In our village the people are nothing but bricks in the wall of the state." I remembered that in America our state exists only of the people and by the people and for the people.

As the months went on, we suddenly realized that it was almost Christmas time. A few days before Christmas, a plane flew in with dozens of packages of Christmas gifts that had been sent by foresighted people. They probably mailed them sometime in June. The amusing thing was that Christmas gifts continued to come in up to the following Easter. On Easter we had a fake

Christmas tree on our piano; on the Fourth of July we received some chocolate Easter eggs. This is how it is in anachronistic Asia.

I do not believe in days off. My crew works every day, all day. Every six
months I might give them a week or ten days off, but there are no Saturday
afternoons or Sundays off. When a child is brought to us hideously mauled
by a tiger, how can we close the hospital and say, "No work today." Hospitals and doctors in America can't do this, nor can we in Muong Sing.

I did, however, give half a day's vacation at Christmas. All during the
following year when the boys would ask for a day off, I would say: "Why, I
gave you guys a half-day off last year."

On Christmas we had all of our staff over for a lunch and we attached
to this lunch all of the elegance of Christmas Day at home. The meal was
served buffet style, because there were not enough chairs for everybody. We
sat on the porch, on the steps, on the table, and on the bed platform, eating
and laughing. We explained the American Christmas. We explained the
religious significance of Christmas implicit in the very word itself. No doubt
the Communists might make grist out of this for their propaganda mill and
say, "You see, Doolcy is a Jesuit in disguise."

We drank champagne we had bought in Bangkok months before. We
cooled it and drank out of coffee mugs. Chai sipped the champagne, and
not liking its taste, he spat it out on the floor. Then he apologized for spitting on the floor, but not for spitting the champagne. Everyone had a grand
time and all of the gifts we received we gave to our students. Each was
individually wrapped and the ribbons and colored papers were just as much
a part of the gift as were the T-shirts, sweaters and candy.

All of our Lao student staff agreed they like this custom of the West very
much. Ngoan said that he certainly hoped he could live in America for a
while and then he could enjoy both Thai Dam holidays and American holidays. We just couldn't tell him that most cities in America do not celebrate
the Thai Dam holidays.

I had a task to do on Christmas Day. I was asked by radio station KMOX
of St. Louis to send a Christmas message to America from the Kingdom of
a Million Elephants. Into a tape recorder I was to speak a message that
would be played on the radio for all America. What could I say? How could
I take the huge emotions and thoughts that were in my heart and in neat,
clipped and precise form put them into a few minutes? I had too many
thoughts, but I went ahead and into my battery-run tape-recorder I tried to
express in fragile words our feelings on that Christmas night in the high
valley of Muong Sing:

"This is Dr. Tom Dooley speaking to you from half a world away. I know you will not hear this message during the Christmas season, but I believe that the spirit of Christmas throughout the whole world lasts more than just the days around December 25th. I think the Christmas spirit should last each day, each week, each month, each year of all our lives. So what I want to say to you tonight, even though it may be the end of January when you hear me, is this: Christmas is a timeless thing.

"I have a very beautiful card in front of me that was sent to me from Rome. It expresses my feelings towards Christmas better than I could ever do with my own faint breath of talent. Let me read to you my Christmas wish, my Christmas hope, my Christmas thought:

It is a good thing to observe Christmas Day but it is better to hold the spirit of Christmas through the year. To hold it helps one to feel the supremacy of the common life over the individual life. It reminds a man to set his own little watch now and then by the great clock of humanity which runs on sun time. There is a better thing than the observance of Christmas Day and this is, keeping Christmas. Are you willing to forget what you have done for other people and to remember what other people have done for you? Are you willing to ignore what the world owes to you and to think of what you owe to the world? To put your rights in the background and your duties in the middle distance and your chances to do a little more than your duty in the foreground? Are you willing to see that your fellowmen are just as real as you are and try to look beyond their faces into their hearts, hungry for joy?

Are you willing to admit that probably the only good reason for your existence is not what you are going to get out of life but what you are going to put into it? To close your book of complaints against the management of the Universe and to look around for a place where you can sow a few seeds of happiness? Are you willing to do these things even for a day? Then you can keep Christmas.

Are you willing to stoop down and consider the needs and the desires of little children, to remember the weakness and loneliness of people who are growing old, to stop asking how much your friends love you and ask yourself whether you love them or not? Are you willing to bear in mind the things that other people have to bear in their hearts? To try to understand what those who live in the same house with you really want, without waiting for them to tell you? Are you willing to trim your lamp so that it will give more light and less smoke and to carry it in front so that your shadow will fall behind you? Are you willing to make a grave for your ugly thoughts and a garden for your kindly feelings with the gates wide open? Are you willing to do these things even for a day? Then you can keep Christmas. Are you willing to believe that love is the strongest thing in the world, stronger than hate, stronger than evil, stronger than death? And that the Blessed Life which began in Bethlehem over nineteen hundred years ago is the image and brightness of eternal love? Then you can keep Christmas, and if you keep it for a day why not keep it always.

"From Africa, Europe, Sweden, India, from Taipai, Viet Nam, Indonesia, and from all over America we have received Christmas cards this year. These cards have come here to the mountain valley of Muong Sing and the cards all cry the same thought. In this season there is a great unity—a unity of the world, of all races, of all faiths. There is a unity of Protestant, of Jew, of Catholic, of Mohammedan, of Buddhist. They all unite in this spirit. Why? Why can't this same battered, beaten world unite in a newer, firmer, more meaningful reaffirmation of the splendid basic truths of this Universe? The truth that the brotherhood of man exists as certainly as does the Father-hood of God. The truth that service to humanity is the greatest work of all.

"At Bandung, several years ago, President Sukarno said that great chasms yawned between nations and groups of nations. Our unhappy world is torn and tortured and the people of all countries walk in fear, lest through no fault of theirs the dogs of war are unchained once again. The life of man today is corroded and made bitter by fear, fear of the future, fear of the hydrogen bomb, fear of an enemy, fear of an ideology. Perhaps this fear is greater than the danger itself because it is fear which drives men to act foolishly, to act thoughtlessly, to act dangerously.

"We know the danger. We know the danger in this era of time and in this area of Asia. We know the leaders of Soviet and Red Chinese communism, the leaders of these nations who denounce God, who despise freedom, who deny individual rights, who exalt treachery, who counsel deceit, who prac-tice terror and intimidation and torture as part of their day's work; who have everywhere possible exterminated every human being in any human institution that has opposed them. We know that Communism has acknowl-edged as its supreme mission in life the destruction of the last vestiges of our way of life.

"We have also learned something of the new young nations of Asia. We have learned that they are stirring and trying to find a new place in the sun. I have walked with the people of these nations. I have eaten with their princes and in their village huts. I have argued with these voices in the world, with the voices of people who are destined to have a lot more to say about their future than they ever had in the past. I have sensed and known the bitterness, the confusion, the resentfulness. I know now that there stirs in the hearts of many nations in young Asia a new awareness, a new spirit, a new drive. Often it is aimless but it is always stirring, seeking, endeavoring, trying to find that new place under the sun, the Asian sun, the world sun.

"So when Christmas time comes and we think of this day, we should remember that there must be courage now. There must be, because how can there be peace among men if there is no courage among men? We Americans can be courageous without being pugnacious about it. We can stand up bigger than bitterness. We can reject thoughts of revenge. These don't belong in the minds of moral and peaceful men anyway. We can remind ourselves that love is indeed one of the strongest forces on earth. We can remember that we have had to struggle, that the liberty of our forefathers was secured for us through struggle, and that it must be struggled for and resecured by each succeeding generation.

"So, ladies and gentlemen who listen to me back in America, Christmas of 1958 shows to we three men in Laos the unity of a man's spirit, and a potential of this unity. Christmas of 1958 quietly reminds us that the challenge of our era is the godlessness of Communism. Christmas of 1958 reilluminates for us again the young nations of the world. It sums itself up with the thought that the keynote of 1959 must be for us, each and every one, for America and for all nations of the world, to seek more ways on a world-wide basis, more ways to serve, with courage and love, the humanity of man. This is Tom Dooley signing off from Northern Laos. So long for now."

EIGHT ·

THE HEART OF IT ALL

An ancient Buddhist prayer says, "O Lord Buddha, O Lord of light and love, give my roots rain." For Dooley, Rhine and Davis our mail from America was rain for our roots.

While I was home on my lecture tour I tried to tell high school boys and girls of some of my feelings. I urged them not to be bland and indifferent young boys and girls. I told them not to keep safely within their own confines and customs. They must listen to the rest of the world, to the voices of conflict, the voices of Asia and Africa. They must hear of civilizations that are being torn apart, of peoples dying, of families being uprooted and scattered. They must be exposed to shattering new ideas and strange new forces, the potential that makes their destiny. I tried to point out that most of the people of the world hate them. They must know why they are hated and they must not be afraid of hate. The weapon against that hate, based on ignorance, is love, based on knowledge. Students must look for new distances, reach out for wider horizons.

While I spoke of horizons, they would always bring me down from my pedantic heights with the question, "Well, doctor, what can we, the seventh grade pupils of St. Anthony's, do for you?"

I remember Dr. Schweitzer once telling me, "In America you must only attempt to create awareness, nothing more. Awareness will then act by just being there." I just do not believe this is true amongst the school boys and girls of America. Too many of them bob on waters like boats torn from their moorings. They need direction. They need a clearly marked channel where they can sail. And when put on this channel, or often when the channel is merely indicated, the kids take over the tillers and sail proudly and well. From Hawaii to New York, from Maine to California, from Seattle to

Miami, school students had projects for Dooley. They warm the cockles of my heart. Some of these projects:

"Do-It-For-Dr. Dooley Day." (I don't know what they did, but they charged for it, and they sent me a check for several hundred dollars.)

"Eat-A-Hamburger-For-Dr. Dooley Day." This project was explained to me with the following note: "Dear Dr. Dooley, We had an 'eat a hamburger for Dr. Dooley day' and we charged a dollar a hamburger. Doctor, those hamburgers weren't worth a nickel. Enclosed please find $114."

"Shake Rattle and Roll for Dr. Tom." This performance by some young Texans brought in several hundred dollars. And old man Dooley can't rattle or roll even though he does shake a little bit just naturally.

"Popcorn Balls for Dr. Tom." "Money for MEDICO." "Dollars for Dooley." "Duds for Dooley." A group in Detroit had a "Doughnuts-for-Dooley Day." In Hawaii the Junior Chinese Catholic Club had a "Buy-a-Bar Dance" and collected over two tons of soap. (Hawaii must think that Dooley is the dirtiest doctor in Asia.) Not only did these young men and women collect this soap but the president of their club, Fred Luning, then proceeded to con the Navy out of the transportation. We have enough soap to wash almost every child and elephant in Asia.

The flow of gifts is endless. The most stalwart club that has helped me for several years is the Metropolitan Life Insurance Dooley Aid Club. They have sent to us everything from coffee mugs to skivvies. Teresa Gallagher has been their adrenal gland, and is one of these rare girls who understands that along with the prayin' there must also be a little payin'. Not only did she have people praying but she also had them contributing from all around the Metropolitan Life Insurance building. From MLI several thousand dollars came to our high village. And with the money an endless cable of love and help.

The Wilson Club in Bridgeport, Connecticut, sent me the wherewithal for the zinc-lined piano whose story I have already related. They also sent some fine Easter candy which we received in July.

A Mrs. P. G. Spring and Mrs. Leonard sent us a monthly box of cookies from Hawaii, always wonderfully packed and a welcome treat.

Miss Florence Jacko sends us boxes of stuffed animals and toys month after month. However, Miss Jacko made one drastic mistake. She sent us a large box with 40 little tin xylophones. All around the mountain slopes and deep in the valley, from dawn till dusk and back to dawn again, you could hear this endless clinking and clanking of xylophones. Thank you, Miss Jacko, but please—no more xylophones.

One of the most priceless programs through which money and material were earned for us was through a Mr. Lorenz Aggens of the North Shore Country Day School in Winnetka, Illinois. He sent a letter to our New York office which said:

"Here at North Shore Country Day School we are busily engaged in a campaign to collect soap for Dr. Dooley. The students have set the goal themselves, which is equivalent to the combined weights of a selected representative from each grade through 12th. These students climb on one end of a balancing beam. The accumulated soap is piled on the other end. When the total affair is in balance, we will have made it. The total weight is 871 pounds, which is a good deal of soap for just 250 kids. To accomplish this each class is trying to organize a project, the proceeds of which are soap. One class is running a bake sale, another a sweet shop and the three lower grades are having square dances and charging soap for admission. Some of the older boys will have a car rally, and we hope to be able to organize a car wash for some Saturday before the end of the term. If all the kids flunk out of school this year, it will be Dr. Tom's fault."

This letter came to my office on the same day that the Hawaiian soap shipment came. The password in the foothills of the Himalayas in Muong Sing is "Soap, anyone?" But it can be used!

Some kids, ages 4 to 8, baked cookies to help my hospital in Laos. They sold them under the title "Lousy Cookies."

Earl, Dwight and I are simply the hands. The heart is America. I wish that I could extend to everyone personally some of the warmth of the blanket of thanks that comes to us from our villagers. Each one of their gifts adds a stone to the structure of MEDICO and in so doing strengthens the slightly shaky structure of world peace.

My mail ran into thousands of letters each month. Much of it was handled by Gloria Sassano in the New York office of MEDICO. I had to handle a great deal myself. For many years I have followed a personal law which says that I will write ten letters a night. Now I decided to increase it to fourteen. Many people wrote and said that they would like to join my team. It was impossible to invite all these good young men and women to Laos. If, however, they could pay their plane fares themselves, I was glad to give them a chance to invest some of their humanity in Laos. Such a boy was Jack Regan, of Boston, Massachusetts.

I had met Jack in Boston several times when lecturing there. For a graduation gift his father gave him a trip to Laos. Jack had no medical training whatsoever, nor did he have much mechanical aptitude. However he cheerfully contributed his services in building, chopping wood and working as a general handyman around the compound. Soon he learned to give shots and we utilized him as a corpsman too. Poor Jack, he suffered from any job that happened to be needed. "Jack, build that bear pen, would you please?" "Jack, drive the jeep out to Ban Nam Di and pick up that patient." "Jack, get that thing painted would you? It doesn't look very well." "Jack, put a dressing on that patient and tell him to come back tomorrow."

Such was life in Laos for Jack Regan, and he spent several months with us. One of his greatest contributions to Tom Dooley was his faith. Dwight and Earl were not Catholics, Jack was. As a consequence I had someone with whom to say my nightly rosary. This rosary meant a great deal to me. It was impossible to taste fully the passing moments of our life. There was no time in Laos to pause, one had to keep running. But during the peaceful silence of night those few quiet moments with my rosary seemed to be the only time that I could get completely out of myself and be tranquil.

Jack was quick to learn the philosophy of our program. He did not agree with many things when he first got there. He thought we were too simple, too down to earth, as indeed we were. We had none of the more complicated things of modern life. He soon realized that to be effective in Asia a program must have an answer expressed in Asian terms and values. What we were trying to do on a medical level was something that the villagers could easily understand. And when they understood it, they were happy.

There are many who bless our work, but there are also some who criticize it. Several of the critics of what we are trying to do are in high places; their main criticism of our work is that we are short-ranged. I believe basically as follows: we should go to places to which we are asked, build and stock a small hospital, train the villagers to run the hospital on a simple level, and after a few years—two, three or four—turn the hospital over to the host governments. Though each MEDICO team is a little different, most of them are based on this concept. The host government where each MEDICO team is situated must furnish many things. In Laos all of the indigenous salaries of my personnel, students and interpreters, cook and housemen are paid by the Lao Minister of Finance. I have *carte blanche* for the Lao medical warehouse and some thirty or forty per cent of my supplies come from them monthly. The Lao Government furnishes all internal transportation and of course Customs-free entry. Whenever I'm in need of things such as cement or metal roofing I get this from the Lao Government. The Lao Government on a local level gives me my working parties and our mason, carpenter and any help we ever need here. We have a medical evacuation program set up with the Ministry of Health so that if anybody at the Nam Tha hospital cannot be treated by the Lao staff there he can be flown to us in Muong Sing on a government requisition.

When I first heard of the formation of the Woman's Division of the Lao Red Cross I wrote them a letter and asked for blankets for my hospital. They were delighted and immediately dispatched 100 brand new blankets. I thanked them, pointing out that I believe Lao aiding the Lao is much better than the Americans aiding the Lao. The hospital at Muong Sing is *not* an American hospital. Rather it is a Lao hospital that Americans are running for a while.

The powerful and sometimes immaculate dispensers of American aid believe that my philosophy is short-sighted. They claim that the villages cannot maintain what I build. I admit they perhaps cannot maintain it at my level, but I am confident that they can at a lesser level which is still superbly higher than the medical level of the area. I have had many, many visitors to my hospital from Washington. Most of them arrive with that chip on their shoulder, looking around to find the weak spots. Among "jungle doctors" the world over adaption to the environment in an effort to maintain simplicity is the keynote of survival.

Nam Tha furnished my critics a chance to find grist for their mills. Two years earlier we had come to Nam Tha with my former team and had started a hospital. We trained the personnel to a certain level, then turned the hospital over to the Lao Government on our departure at the end of 1957. The Lao Government then sent a "doctor" to the area. There are only two M.D.'s by international standards in the Kingdom of Laos, but there are some 25 *médecins indochinois*. These men have not had the equivalent training of an international M.D. At the end of their *lycée*, which is second-year high school (the highest education that France left to this kingdom after almost a century of occupation), these students went to Cambodia or to Hanoi. They pursued a four-year course of medicine which by our educational system in America would merely be two years of high school and two years of college. They were then diploma-ed as "doctors." I know many of these *médecins indochinois* and some of them are excellent men, but unfortunately not all of them are.

The one who was sent to take over my hospital was a young man. As sometimes happens when young men are taken from villages for education, in returning to their village they feel haughty and superior. So it was with this young man. He felt that, having become a *médecin indochinois*, he should live in the capital and have life a little easier. He did not like being rusticated in the villages of the north.

As soon as I returned to Laos in 1958, I was told how "terrible" the situation was at Nam Tha. The USOM representatives who handle American foreign aid told me with delight and glee how inadequate the *médecin indochinois* at Nam Tha was, how poorly the hospital was being run, and how only 30 or so patients were being seen a day. If they had remembered that before we got there, no patients were seen, they would have to admit that 30 a day was an improvement, even though less than the 100 a day we had seen.

I was urged by all of the USOM types (a) to go to Nam Tha and straighten that situation up, or (b) to return to Nam Tha and resume my work. I refused. I claimed that I had begun this program and turned it over to the Lao Government. It was a Lao responsibility and a Lao problem, and none of my business. I had no right to go stomping into the area and demanding this and that.

Instead, we went and built our new hospital at Muong Sing. After a few weeks I dropped down to Nam Tha for a visit. All of my former students came to me and complained about the doctor, pointing out how inadequate he was, how he came to work late, how he kept all the medicines locked up so that they could not take care of people, how all the minor surgical instruments and sutures that the student staff knew how to utilize were unavailable because they too were locked up. I told them, as I had told the Americans, that I could do nothing about it and suggested that they go to their own government representatives and complain. I suggested that every time a Lao official came up, some member of the community should speak to him about this unhappy situation.

I reminded the "doctor" in front of his staff that the Lao Government had established an evacuation program. If ever there were a patient with a surgical problem or a disease that he did not feel capable of handling, he should fly him to me at Muong Sing. The doctor agreed, smiling broadly. And that was all he ever did, smile broadly.

This "doctor" at Nam Tha was also Chief of Medical Affairs in the province, and my hospital at Muong Sing came under him administratively. On several occasions I was obliged to send a military telegram to ask permission for a plane ticket, or a working party, or some quite minor matter. Several times he refused me flatly. But there was nothing I could do. I was an invited guest in this foreign land, and I was not going to make the kind of mistake that too often is the white man's error in Asia. I was not about to storm around criticizing, complaining, and demanding.

I believed that if enough Lao heard about Nam Tha they would finally do something. Indeed they did. Many months later when I was in the capital the Minister of Social Welfare and Health, Colonel Sananikone, called

me and said, "Thanh Mo America, what is the trouble up at Nam Tha?" I
was delighted that he had asked me and I related the whole messy situation
to him. He said that he would like to act immediately but that he had no
one else to send up there. I suggested that he take one of my male nurses,
a graduate of the school in Vientiane, and send him to Nam Tha, pointing
out that then there would be superb collaboration between Muong Sing
and Nam Tha. Colonel Sananikone agreed; a few weeks later the doctor
was transferred and my man ordered to Nam Tha. We were all pleased,
especially my nurse who was then promoted to Chief of Medical Affairs
for the province. My former assistant was very cooperative about giving me
permission to buy a plane ticket.

Under the tutelage of the new man, the young men and women at Nam
Tha pitched into things with a vitality that I remembered them as having
possessed. Earl and Dwight at various intervals have visited the Nam Tha
hospital and are delighted with the way that the students are carrying on.
The province is happier, we are able to send down more medicine and aid,
and they in turn send us patients that they feel they cannot handle. Because
we treat this as routine, there is never any loss of face. As for certain criti-
cisms of the ability of the crew at Nam Tha I can only say what I always
say: "In America doctors run 20th century hospitals. In Asia I run a 19th
century hospital. Upon my departure the hospital may drop to the 18th
century. This is fine, because previously the tribes in the high valleys lived,
medically speaking, in the 15th century."

On two of our visits to Nam Tha, we continued on down the Nam Tha
River to a village called Ban Houei Sai, repeating the river trip that I had
made in the fall of 1957. We made this *pirogue* trip twice in December,
1958 and later in February, 1959. This February trip became a turning-
point in my whole destiny.

At first we were reluctant to make the river trip in February because
there were rumblings of war again in the Kingdom of a Million Elephants.
We had heard radio reports of guerilla murders and of many areas where
small infiltrations and skirmishes were taking place. We knew that the
Communists had been kicked out of the coalition government and the new
pro-Western government of Premier Phoui Sananikone was an honest one,
yet still shaky.

Communism had not seized any major chunk of land for several years
in this part of the world, and it looked as though there was going to be
another try. Therefore we were apprehensive about starting out on a 15-
day river trip in the most distant corner of Asia. Some of the territory
through which we would pass is territory where there had been former bat-

tles. We talked to the Chief of the Military and to the Ministry of Health; they said that they would furnish us with police and military protection. They thought this would be adequate, though they were reluctant themselves to accept any kind of responsibility for us. I always smile when people want to "accept responsibility for Dooley." As I see it, only Dooley is responsible for Dooley.

The people whose villages crouch along the sides of the Nam Tha River in North Laos are some of the most wretched, sick and diseased people I have ever seen. They had nothing in the way of medicines, only the brews concocted by the witch doctor.

The allegiance of these people to their central royal government was a tenuous thing. This royal government, as an independent unit, has existed in name since the 1949 treaty of acceptance into the French Union. But this was in name only. In actuality the Geneva Treaty in 1954 gave birth to a really free government. The people recognize the King and local important officials; but without communication, and the woeful lack of schools, they have little knowledge of the government which guides their country—or even about the country itself. Just the presence of the military men standing guard for us was a complete reverse of the customary situation of Westerner with Asian. I felt it essential to our task in Laos to take our medical aid to these villages as often as possible. As we were sent and supported by the Lao Government, there was a good political overtone to the trip. The existence of unrest there increased the need for our river trip in February, 1959.

Earl stayed in Muong Sing this second trip, while Dwight, Chai, Ngoan and several military corpsmen came along with me. We did a great deal of planning, separation of equipment, and calculation of how much to take with us. The Lao Government had sent us an Army DC-3 and we flew all our gear, including nearly 1,000 pounds of medicine, to Nam Tha.

In the few days we spent there, walking around Nam Tha flooded my mind with memories. There is the hut where we had that difficult delivery; here a place where a child died of smallpox; here the house of the school teacher who was our best English student; here we worked all night to save a burnt child; there is where the villagers gave a dance for us; here is where we all lived and laughed and loved.

Returning was a very nostalgic thing. All of our former nurses gave a big party for us. Now that my man from Muong Sing was in charge, all was going well. I think that the most important component of a hospital is not lavish air-conditioning, nor electricity, nor fancy electronic paraphernalia, but rather compassion. Nam Tha, completely maintained and financed by the Lao Government, had plenty of this.

Some former students of ours lived in our old house in Nam Tha. I couldn't help noticing that our interior decorating scheme was changed markedly. Where Eisenhower's picture had hung, there was now the photo of the King of Laos, and our kelly-green paint had turned a dusty green-brown. However, the old house flooded our minds with memories of Johnny and Pete and Denny and Bob and Dammit too. We had been sitting on the porch only a few minutes, when visitors began to arrive.

Remember Ion, the lad who had been so hideously burned? He was the boy we had found in a dirty hovel of a hut, his burned and charred flesh covered with maggots. Remember how he was in our hospital for many months in 1957? He's quite a grown-up lad now, well healed, and he smiles more enchantingly than ever before. As usual he brought me a gift, just as he had done every day two years ago. His gift was three eggs and a coconut.

Old Maggie, the village sorceress, dropped in for a chitchat. I really cannot say that we discussed any of the new antibiotics on the pharmaceutical market, but we did have a good reunion. She had the same crummy towel wrapped around her head as she had two years ago. I gave her a can of shaving cream for a present. No, she doesn't shave but the soap comes out of the aerosol in such a magic way, and if she puts this on wounds it will be a lot more sanitary than her own beetle-juice-cock's-blood-uric-acid compound.

I was glad to find out that the local whisky at Nam Tha had improved slightly. It was still as powerful as ever but some of the kerosene taste had left. If you drop a little on your skin, it blisters.

Nam Tha now boasted four jeeps and a truck and one caterpillar tractor, the last having been parachuted in. American aid was building a road from Nam Tha to Muong Sing. Every vehicle to be used on this road will have to be flown in.

A neighboring tribal village, the Dam village of Ban Nam Mieng, asked if we would come over for a banquet. I use the word "banquet" very loosely. I believe that at one time or another every villager from Ban Nam Mieng had been in my clinic at Nam Tha. When they heard that their Thanh Mo America had returned, they insisted on entertaining us. We accepted. I have always believed that to get nearer to the heart of Asia, Americans must use their own heart more. But in Ban Nam Mieng it has been proven that occasionally one has to use his digestive tract as well.

On long, low tables some twenty-five feet in length many wooden bowls of food had been laid out for us. The dinner was given in the house of the Tassieng, or village chief. They had palm branches and leaves along the floor with silver bowls and planks of wood. Various assorted pieces of meat, vegetables and greens were set on top of leaves. The food represented every imaginable kind of thing to eat, plus a few unimaginable. There were pig's feet, bat wings, tripe, fish sauces, buffalo steaks, and various herbs, sweet-smelling and otherwise. There were some fetid cuts of meat and an anemic, limp-looking salad that we jokingly call "a dysentery dish." There were several bowls of raw frogs, assorted insects, fried beetles, tubers, cooked bark and roots, and some emaciated sparrow carcasses. But there was one large, lovely dish, the masterpiece of the evening. This hand-hammered silver bowl, set in the middle of the table, crowned the whole repast. It was full of warm, freshly congealed pig's blood. That's right, pig's blood!

We stayed on late, enjoying the warm comradeship of old friends. Villagers brought us the babies I had delivered a year or two ago. Former surgical patients dropped in to the chief's hut to show me how well their scars had healed or their bones knit. Many asked about my former team, Johnny and Bob; many wanted to know whether Pete had put on any weight. The visit was just like the homecoming of any country doctor in America when he goes to a county fair. A doctor's life lights up when he sees his former patients in good health. He helped them regain it, and his inner joy is quiet and good.

The next day we spent making the final arrangements for our trip. The governor had already called for the long dugout canoes, *pirogues*. They were waiting for us down on the river bank. On the following day, we loaded into four *pirogues*. We started about dawn. We now had over 1,000 pounds of medicines, plus bedding rolls, knapsacks, mosquito nettings, foot lockers full of cooking gear, canned foods and assorted bric-a-brac. Three police guards came along with their packs and rifles. Three of my Lao military student corpsmen came: Deng, Panh and Dam. Each of these boys had his pack and a basket of glutinous rice. Chai, my interpreter, had his gear (and, I suspect, a little herbal medicine). We looked more like an invasion party in war than a medical team in peace.

Because of problems similar to those encountered by any family leaving for a Sunday picnic, we didn't really get shoved off until noon. Just as we pushed off, Dwight gingerly opened up his shirt and held up a six-pound baby monkey that someone at Nam Tha had given to him. He was afraid to show it to me until we got out on the river, in case Dooley's humanitarian instinct would demand that the animal be released rather than brought along. "O.K. We have one more passenger," I said. "At least he doesn't have a full pack of gear."

Just a few minutes out of Nam Tha we hit our first set of rapids. The boat plunged into the center of the stream. It then thudded heavily against the underwater rocks. Water poured into the dugout canoe on each side, thoroughly soaking the seats on the bottom. These canoes, about 30 feet long, are made from huge trees that are halved in center, burned and cut out. They have no motors or outriggers. They capsize very easily, though the villagers keep saying, "Don't worry, doctor, they can't sink." (Little consolation to me with thousands of dollars worth of medicines that *can* sink.) Though the rapids lasted only a few minutes, at each set of them I aged a few years.

The first night we slept in a little splash of a village called Ban Saly. There are only about 100 people who live here and 80 per cent of them were at sick-call in the morning. Real illnesses—malaria, tuberculosis, pneumonia, chronic coughs, hookworm anemia and always, always the pathetic pot-bellied children of malnutrition. The people of Laos are not a happy, care-free people. They laugh and smile, but they suffer. Their existence is eked out of this life with great effort, just as their villages are hacked from their savage jungles with great difficulty.

This village story was repeated again and again, day after day for the next twelve days. It was not unlike our work at Muong Sing, but here the misery seemed to be in greater intensity. There was greater desolation and everything seemed to be more difficult.

In most of the villages we saw absolutely no indication of American aid in the north—no wells, no rural sanitation, no posters, no roads, no schoolhouses, no farming techniques, no development programs, none of the things that newly independent nations so badly need.

The fault is not with American aid alone. The fault is not all because of apathy in high places in the Lao Government. But I feel that if both parties concerned do not show better results soon, the Communist propaganda may succeed, just because it sounds like "a change," even though they are promising pie in the sky bye and bye, as they accuse us of doing. But while we preach of our good intentions and loudly proclaim our plans, programs and blueprints, the Communists move in amongst the naked masses of people and seize power.

Recently an educational program was opened up under the American Economic Aid Mission. It is training village teachers, and it is superb. We met two Lao teachers on this trip, and they are indicative of real progress. I feel we have to stop thinking of hydroelectric plants, dams, super-high-ways and vast import-export programs. I think we should work more for objectives within the villagers' capability. We should find out what they want and help them to achieve this.

In these villages there is always hunger. Not the dramatic starvation of famine, but daily privation. One of the greatest medicines that we possess is a protein extract called Meals for Millions. This foundation in Los Angeles has given us over 10,000 pounds, and has pledged 5,000 pounds of this extract for every one of the MEDICO teams around the world. I have seen the spindly-legged, pot-bellied children stand taller and straighter, and become bright-eyed and happier. The people who make and support this program, Meals for Millions, should also stand tall and hold their heads high, for they have exercised the greatest power that God has given to man—they have helped their fellow man.

We did not have to fight a barrier of fear and apprehension. Within five minutes after we climbed out of our canoes, half of the village was helping us unload and carry our boxes to the house of the Chief. We had been in their village before, and were returning as friends. We would sit outdoors before the Chief's house in a large semicircle, surrounded by our medicines and our students. We tried to maintain a little order in the chaos of the sick-call, but the important thing was that we maintained distribution rather than order. I would examine the patients and then they would go down to the next person in line, one of my Asian corpsmen. He would give them their medicines, or they would go to the other end of the line for their shots. I'm sure many people came just to chitchat, and others came to "see the show." But as long as they were there, they might just as well bring up that old backache of theirs.

Dwight's new-found friend, the always-unnamed monkey, was tied to the nearest tree to distract the children and the adults too. They could not understand why we didn't eat the monkey, so young, so succulent, so tender. Fried monkey meat? No, thank you.

There were many things that vividly impressed themselves on my mind on this trip. One was an awareness of God, of the great pattern of the universe, the similarity of all the world, the magnificence of the dense green jungle, the majestic cathedral-like colors of the rain-forest, the rapids and rivers flowing one into another. All this cries of a Creator; this speaks of God. For me it is harder to know God in the tumult of plenty, in city traffic, in giant buildings, in cocktail bars, or riding in a car with a body by Fisher. But just as a maker is stamped on America's products so is His stamp on all the universe.

Here was God, even in the decay of the villages, because in the death of yesterday there was a birth of tomorrow. We were very lucky to be in the middle of this mystery and wretchedness. We had seen, known, felt and held great beauty. Yet there was a dull, dreary monotony of misery to all sick-calls. Even beside the river, with its constantly changing panorama, this monotony was all-enveloping. Quickly, all could become over-luxurious, over-green, too dense. The rain-forest trees would seem too high, too majestic. And each night seemed a little more uncomfortable than the night before. Here in its essence was the contrast I had tried to point out to Earl and Dwight many months before beside the pool of the Leper King—magnificence holding misery.

We would pull into a village to spend the night. We could not plan ahead of time, because there was no way of judging how far down the next village was or when we would get there. The people here did not lead any kind of life governed by watches strapped on their wrists. If you asked how far or how long it took to get to the next village, they would just say, "Well, you will get there before the sun sets." Even that, we found, was not always reliable.

When we pulled into the village where we were going to have evening sick-call, we held our clinic first and then went down to the river to bathe. Though not really cold in the evenings, it was definitely too chilly for river bathing. Anyway, we never came out feeling very clean. Every day I threatened to abandon my nightly bath (but I had not abandoned it yet). We would then eat a dinner composed of a mixture of canned rations, local chickens, eggs, and anything else we could pick up. The chickens of Laos lead a very independent life; not penned up, they run loose in the village and forage around, and each of them is wiry, tough and brawny. To us, however, they tasted good; we were a hungry crew.

We always slept in the hut of some village Chief. Our nights were not very comfortable. It is strange how the sleeping habits of the Westerner depend upon a mattress of some sort. We become addicted to it. At least I have; I don't care how thin, there must be a mattress between me and the bamboo floor. At Muong Sing we had them, on the river trip we did not.

In several of the villages on the river we saw a disease that I had not seen frequently since Nam Tha. It is the hideous scourge of this area, and it is known as Kwashiorkor. It is a massive protein and vitamin deficiency, and the disease was first found in a tribe called the Akra in Africa. Kwashi is a name meaning "a boy who was born on the seventh day." In Africa Kwashi is as common a name as Tom or John, but it is also used to refer to any country fellow, a simple man, a kwashi. The kwashi of Africa often suffer from malignant malnutrition. But others in the world are hungry too, and Kwashiorkor has become known everywhere as a hated and dreaded disease.

What does the victim of Kwashiorkor look like? A child first becomes peevish, irritable; soon he becomes apathetic, his belly bloats, and he sickens. He then becomes indifferent, shows none of the interests, liveliness, or smiles of childhood. If disturbed, he becomes resentful, but shows no vigor in this resentment. He just becomes listless. He doesn't cry, or laugh, or smile. He shows no response to stimulation. Soon he stops eating completely, and then he dies.

However, this is one of the most easily treated diseases. Mead Johnson gave every MEDICO team a large supply of vitamins and proteins. More important than the vitamins and the proteins is education. It does little good for me to give children the medicines and have them fall right back into the same malnutrition environment due to poor dietary care and ignorance. We educate the parents; we explain patiently and tediously about good diet. The people listen. They are eager to know. They do not want the scourge of Kwashiorkor in their village.

The hospitality of the villagers along the river is a warming thing. Their simplicity is delightful. There's no complexity to their lives. Disease and suffering, yes; but also simplicity and kindness. When we come to a village they come down to the river's edge and present a bowl of flowers to us. Sometimes the girls throw a silken scarf across their shoulders and tie it around their waists, and present to us an offering of eggs and fruit.

My boys and I talked a great deal about fundamental questions. Here we were living with some of the most primitive peoples of the world, but they were all men and women of the same human race. Such questions came to mind as these: Is it true that all men are created equal? Or is it true for only some of them? Is it true that they are all endowed by their Creator with the same inalienable rights, or only some? Is it true that among these rights for all are life, liberty and the pursuit of happiness, or only for some? And doesn't the pursuit of happiness include health? I believe that poverty and malnutrition and wretchedness, which make health impossible, are not God-made, but wholly man-made, but the cure for the scourges, the compassion to want to cure, this also comes from God.

We continued plunging down the river. Seven days, eight days, nine days, ten days. On the eleventh morning the river lurched. Wretchedness, misery, stink, poverty. Southward the mighty Mekong River loomed up before us. Here, in an area of deep swirling water, the small Nam Tha River dumps into the large Mekong.

The Mekong River rises from the high plateaus of Tibet at an altitude of about 15,000 feet. It is over 3,000 miles long. It descends slowly through the Chinese province of Yunnan and then forms a frontier between Laos and Burma and later Laos and Thailand. The river continues south, crosses Cambodia and enters into southern Indo-China. It is a benevolent river. It rises slowly in the rainy season and in Vientiane when it reaches its summit it is 40 feet higher than the dry season height. The river rises and falls slowly. The villagers never have to worry about floods, they do not have to build dikes, they can plant fertile rice and vegetable fields along the banks. The Mekong River is a major artery in this part of the world, as well as a good friend of the villages.

Twenty miles up the Mekong River from its junction with the Nam Tha River is a village called Ban Houei Sai. At Ban Houei Sai there is a border patrol station, a landing strip, and a short-wave radio. By this eleventh day we had dispensed the two boatloads of medicines, and we were able to jam ourselves into one small outboard motor boat and one large canoe. We then began the most difficult task of poling up to Ban Houei Sai. It took the whole of one day and the morning of the following day to cover this distance. The boats go along close to the banks of the river, and the natives put bamboo poles onto the earth and rock, pushing upstream. The canoes that we had used to come down from the village of Nam Tha now returned. It would take them nearly a month to pole their way back up to Nam Tha.

At the end of the first day poling upriver, we were really exhausted. We stopped for the night along the eastern bank of the river, where there was a long bed of sand, with a rapidly rising cliff covered with craggy rocks. About 25 feet almost straight up in this jungle, there was a small village of only a few huts.

Chai and I walked across the sand and climbed up the slope to ask the village Chief if we could stop over night in his area. He said we could, and we started to go down the slope to the canoe where the crew was waiting to unload our gear onto the beach. In coming down the side of the slope, just after stepping down carefully on a precarious rock, I tripped and lost my balance. Head over heels I fell down the cliff, banging my chest and my head, gashing open a small spot behind the hair line, and badly hurting my chest. When I hit bottom, I had to lie doubled up for a few minutes to get my breath.

Chai immediately came down to my side and asked if I was all right. I told him that as soon as I could get my breath I would be, though I had badly skinned and bruised the right side of my chest wall, just below the shoulder. I realized then that my boots were unlaced. We do not wear our boots in the canoes, and I had slipped mine on before getting out without lacing them all the way. Through my own stupidity, I had tripped on the lace of my boot, plunging headlong down this 25-foot drop, bouncing my rib cage off a few of the rocks. I was really sore.

I did not of course realize it, but that fall was to become a pivotal point in my life.

We arrived in Ban Houei Sai around mid-morning. The landing strip was large enough for a small single-engine plane. At the radio station I sent a message to the capital requesting the Lao Government to send us a plane. I also sent a requisition telegram to the civilian airline, knowing that probably one or the other would not make it.

I sent the messages at 10 o'clock, and we sat on the airfield all that afternoon. No plane. We rolled our bags out and slept on the ground at the airstrip that night. The next morning we started our vigil again. Day two passed and no plane; the third day dawned. This was the morning of the day that I was supposed to be in Vientiane, to speak to several hundred people at the International Community. With a three-day leeway, I thought I couldn't miss. If a plane did not get there by three o'clock, we would not be able to fly to Vientiane by sundown. No flying was then allowed in the Kingdom of Laos at night because there are no airports with lights on the landing strip.

We wondered whether the war had flared up. Was all of Laos now in the flames of combat? Were no planes allowed to come for us? Would we be isolated and left abandoned in this village? While talking about all this, we heard the distant drone of a motor. At 2:30 in the afternoon, the small plane landed and we clambered aboard as fast as we could.

In the air I glanced down at an opening in the jungle and I could see the Nam Tha River curlicuing between the ranges of mountains and I thought over what we had seen and done in these river villages for the last fifteen days. I thought less about my fall than about other incidents on the trip, but later I was to have good reason to remember it.

NINE ·

THE HANOI BROADCASTS

Over 14,000 refugees from China had escaped into our valley in the past year. The Communists were furious and proclaimed loudly that Laos was aiding and abetting people to leave China. In order to prevent provocation, the police in our area were ordering the refugees to return to China. We recognized the familiar Red tactics: they wanted border "incidents" in order to justify infiltration and invasion. The simple people who had escaped, fearing they would be ordered back to certain death, invented hunting accidents such as the following.

A young Kha Kho tribesman was brought down from the mountains, carried on a large stretcher. His whole upper left arm had been completely torn away by bullets. The lead had also peppered his belly and chest. His wounded arm, wrapped in monkey-skins and packed with tobacco and dung, was of course highly infected. The muscles had been brutally torn and the main arm vessels lacerated. We gave him antibiotics, vitamins, intravenous infusions of glucose and proteins, anti-malarials, and a complete bath. Then we put him on the operating-table. Dwight gave him sodium pentathol and Earl, in spite of having a mild case of infectious hepatitis, came over to the hospital to assist me in the surgery. We were able to close his arm up, but in a few days the swelling from lymph obstruction tore the suture line open. A few weeks later we had a visiting surgeon who helped me to do a skin graft. The skin graft had about an 80 per cent "take"; in short, the Kha Kho boy came through all right.

The Kha Kho are a warm and simple people. We became very fond of this boy while he was a patient of ours. He often came to the house and thumbed through picture magazines. His friends gave him a haircut, leaving just a pigtail. He delighted in washing himself several times a day with soap, which was something he had never seen before. We had one inter-preter for his dialect who would come over several times a day to visit.

The boy came from the frontier and I was convinced that, in attempting to escape from China, he was shot by the frontier patrol. If he had admitted that he was a refugee, the police would have had to send him back to China. Nevertheless, because of the circumstances of the case, the police had to be brought in and the boy claimed that he had been hunting, had climbed up a tree, and that another hunter had mistaken him for a bear and shot him. I was glad for the boy's sake that the police accepted this story, and it was obvious to me from the nature of the wound that his assailant *was* a hunter —a hunter of escapees on border patrol, who had too good an eye to mistake a man for a bear.

There was much rumor of war now, and foreboding through all the North. Once again it seemed as though the dogs of war were going to be unchained. These border skirmishes along the Viet Nam frontier and along the China border were increasing. Radio Hanoi and Radio Peking were be-coming more vehement in their attacks on Laos. The broadcasts of Radio Peking are required listening for all who live in China. The same is true of the Vietnamese, who must listen to Radio Hanoi. The refugees tell us that they were harangued hour after hour by speeches, denunciations and propa-ganda. Over the air the anti-American venom was devastating, with such words as "imperialist" and "colonialist" appearing frequently. Every vacil-lation of our foreign policy in Washington, every news story about the school situation in Little Rock, every single piece of bad news in the U.S. was instantly exploited by the Communist radio, and more verbal violence was unleashed against the western world.

Never had I heard of a medical program being attacked until the month of March, 1959, although anything that is accomplishing something of value for the Free World is usually attacked in an attempt to destroy its efficacy.

The Communists were accusing us of espionage activities. By shouting day and night about this sort of thing they were creating a certain doubt. If you accuse someone over and over, week after week, month after month, the listener begins to believe what he hears. The repetition induces sus-picion and finally belief.

Recently in Vientiane, a Minister himself had said to me, "Dr. Dooley, Radio Peking accuses you of espionage in North Laos."

"That's absurd, isn't it?" I replied.

"You don't work for any agencies of America, do you?"

The mere fact that he added the Lao equivalent of "do you" indicated to me that suspicion was being implanted even in his mind by these radio attacks.

This is exactly the kind of vulnerability the Communists aim for. That is how they could destroy my mission in Laos. If they repeated lies about us long and loud enough, soon the lies might seem like the truth to the government leaders in Laos. The Communist plan was obvious. Why did they want my medical program out of here? Because they are basically opposed to medicine? No. Because they realize that our hospital is helping the free Royal Lao Government to establish itself firmly. At the same time it is helping to unite ties of friendship between the people of Laos and the people of America.

To force this hospital to go home, the Communists would have to fill the Lao Government officials with suspicion that perhaps we are doing more than they are aware of. If we were selling opium or spying or running around with their village women, the Lao Government would be alarmed. And if they felt that our presence is a threat to the peace and security of their country, obviously they would be forced to ask us politely to leave. I was sure that the Lao Government realized that the mere fact that the Reds were attacking us was proof positive that our actions were having a good effect. Otherwise they would leave us alone. The very fact that the leaders all the way up in Peking, China, were denouncing our three small buildings indicated that we must be doing something worthwhile.

"U.S. secret agents have established permanent organizations in that area under the guise of performing medical services, of running a village hospital. The United States is plotting to provoke conflict on the China-Lao border with the aim of creating a pretext for armed intervention by the United States and other aggressive blocs, and for dragging Laos step by step into war."

Hearing these things said about us did not in any way make us feel secure or safe. In fact, the broadcasts from Hanoi and Peking added a touch of terror to our days and nights.

Another recent Radio Hanoi broadcast said: "The Lao authorities have been acting in collusion with secret agents and organizations . . . permitting them to use the Muong Sing area of Laos to carry out espionage and sabotage activities against China. They have taken advantage of trade across the border to send special agents into China repeatedly to collect information, spread rumors and create disturbances. . . .

"The above mentioned provocations by Lao authorities . . . in the region of Muong Sing and Nam Tha . . . in the last six months . . . are being done under the guise of a medical team. . . ."

The greatest problem that we had to put up with in our kind of work was loneliness. There was loneliness in Laos, but not of a bitter kind; not the loneliness of dead friendships or lost awareness. Rather we had that strange kind of loneliness that men have who find themselves swinging out beyond the boundaries of normal existence, who find that there suddenly bursts upon their view a fleeting moment of almost devastating awareness. We felt as though we were standing on the mountain peak and had, just for a quick moment, a tremendous view of all the world. This kind of loneliness was a good thing, for it made us more aware, and there was no exhaustion of the spirit.

The dull rounds of our daily work, and its accompanying misery, had a tendency to submerge us. We usually found some small thing to prevent this routine from stifling us, but such escape was never peaceful. Since I started medical school I have had to struggle, first with myself, later with an enemy, and now with both. It seemed that complete tranquility, in my time, was just about the rarest parenthesis in life.

The loneliness that I knew was different from the loneliness of my boys. They both missed their wives and Earl his unseen child. Our relationship as a team was such as would exist on a ship with an officer who was liked but who was nevertheless the Commanding Officer. Earl and Dwight always referred to me as "Dr. Dooley," and there was a "sir" at the end of every sentence. Though we shared a deep bond of comradeship, and a deeper bond of common interest and love of our work, there was nevertheless a kind of wall between us, and also putting up with the irascible burrs of my personality is tough on my crew. I drive them hard. I suppose in many ways Dooley is really tyrannical. Earl and Dwight developed a plan of escape from me. They fixed up a den out of a small room (more like a large broom closet) in the hospital. Every night after dinner they would take a kerosene pressure lamp, the battery-run tape-recorder, and retreat to the Bird Room (so named in honor of a single sad old crow Earl had stuffed). There they were free of Dooley's hyperthyroid totalitarianism. The Bird Room was my crew's inviolate cloister.

We had come to the mountains to do our work. The daily routine of our life in this valley jungle, with its habits and techniques, its daily wretchedness, could make one sink almost into lethargy—until terror struck from across the border and plunged us into fear.

One day Chai and I went to a border village to see a very sick man. While there, we were asked to go down the trail and see two new refugees who had just arrived, one of whom was critically ill. We went to a small grass hut built up on stilts; it was poorly erected, rickety and unstable. Inside we found an old man and his daughter.

The young girl's name was Nung Di. She belonged to the Chinese portion of the Thai Lu tribe, living 50 miles inside China. This girl was lying on her side deep in her own filth, with various herbs and incense around her. She was doubled up in acute agony. When I touched her hand, she trembled like a frightened pup and pulled away from me in fear. Nung Di had a massive infection of the hip joint which had spread to the muscles and tissues of the thigh and leg and onto the abdomen. She was a sick and wretched little girl.

I could not speak her dialect and sent Chai to find someone who could. We instructed him to tell her that she would have to be taken to the hospital immediately so that we could give her anesthesia, incise and drain that leg. Otherwise she would either die, or, if she did not die, would be hideously crippled all her life. I watched her face as the interpreter slowly and softly told her my words. She started to cry and became almost hysterical. I touched her hand and tried to reassure her, but again she pulled away from me and became hysterical. She said she would not go to my hospital. The interpreter again was told to tell her that if she did not, she would die. She said, "I don't care. I will die here. I do not want to die in your hospital."

Other villagers who knew me and our work came to talk to her. They patiently explained to her that our medicines would help, that our hands would heal. She sobbed and whimpered like a beaten dog and she and her father both said, "No, no. We will not go to the hospital at Muong Sing. It is a white man's hospital. It has an American doctor." I went outside and sat on the front ladder of the hut, while the Lao talked to them. I knew that Chai would find out the real reason behind her fear. He explained that it was not the usual reticence. Her fear of the hospital had nothing to do with good and evil spirits, with witchcraft, our biggest competitor. The girl was deathly frightened of the American monsters that she had heard so much about.

In her village of Muong Pun in China, the Communist Commissar had held several hundred hours of lectures about the American monsters. He specifically cited the Dooley-Davis-Rhine hospital program at Muong Sing. He said that we were not medical people at all, but secret agents of America. The Commissar said, "The Americans commit heinous crimes, especially against girls. They inject germs into the bodies of young people." They accused us of brutally beating children who would not take our medicines. They accused us of being corrupt and depraved. They said that we had injected medicines into old people and that they died right away, and that we had crippled many people and had foul plans of hurting more. This little girl had been exposed to this for week after week. No wonder she was afraid to come.

After much talking by all of the villagers, she consented to come to our jeep but only if her father and half a dozen people came with her. I carried her down the stairs myself. Her frail, half-bloated body was trembling terribly. We got her to the hospital and onto the operating-table, though it was quite a task. After a little anesthesia, we drained quarts of purple-green pus from her leg, put her on antibiotics immediately, and then moved her to the ward.

The little girl remained a pathetically frightened wisp for several days until our medicines began to have a marked effect. Her temperature dropped, and as the pain disappeared she realized that she was going to be better.

By this time the eloquent compassion of my crew showed its effect. On the fourth day she and her father broke down and told us why they were so fearful; they were sorry that they had been wrong. They fully realized that the lies were part of anti-American hatred, and we knew that China was plunging such hatred into the hearts and minds of the people of that country. How tragic, how inhumane, how miserable must existence be for those who live under the lies of Red China.

In six surrounding villages around Muong Sing we established substations, run by our Lao military students. Each substation consists of a small hut with the minimum amount of medicines. The students work in these areas for a month, coming back to stock in more supplies, and to compare notes with me. Dam or Boun Tung would sit beside me as I was holding sick-call at the hospital and say, "Oh, yes, I had a case similar to that just a few days ago. I find that terramycin is most efficacious." It always amused me that the boys who only a few months ago were on the backs of water buffalos were now talking as one physician would to another at St. Mary's hospital in downtown St. Louis.

Though the work of these Lao military students might be considered amateurish by American standards, they did have talent and they were improving the health of their respective villages. These intense young corpsmen were sparkling and clean. They were very proud of their newly acquired knowledge. They saw *"meh penh yats"* everywhere and must have possessed a microscopic vision to be able to see "germs" so readily. Earl was teacher for the students of these substations. The students were learning, and Earl was surviving.

One of our favorite patients was a young lad of the Thai Dam tribe, called Tao Koo. Tao Koo was seven years old. He had a scorching fever accompanied by diarrhea several months before he came to us. The family put him into bed, the village witch doctor incanted something or other, and within two weeks, on a diet of rice and water, the child developed a bed sore. Within a month this had spread until all the flesh of his lower back and buttocks had sloughed off. Over each bony hip he had a dirty ulcer. He became incontinent and this constant soilage only worsened things. He shrank and withered until he was just a shadow of a child. Finally the father brought him to us in Muong Sing, a three-day walk.

Earl and Dwight immediately took the child to their hearts. They took that little urinoid glob of flesh and washed him with all the tenderness they could muster. With gentle hearts and hands and a little of the grace of God, they treated and dressed his sores. The child showed no reaction. He was too sick, too dulled by pain to respond even to this much compassion. They rigged a special bed for him, tying balloons on the cross-bars and pasting pictures on the wall beside him. They gave him a color book and a little rabbit that squeaked and in the few days of sunlight left before the early monsoon season, they took his bed outside and draped a mosquito net over it and let him lie in the sun. The dressings were removed and the sores were aired.

About a week after admission Tao Koo's eyes, so bleak with dying, began to brighten a little. His terrified father learned how to treat him, how to feed him properly, how to bathe him and tend him without injuring what little good tissue was left. The boys rigged a method so that his incontinence would not soil everything. This wistful little lad, God's compromise between flower and dung, an interval between birth and death, once again began to live. He began to smile and answer questions with a word instead of a whimper. This emaciated skeleton, his withered skin tightly pulled around small bones, was now picking up weight and filling out, and his sores were closing. He was perhaps the happiest and definitely the cleanest boy in Asia.

As the sun set and the boys were putting Tao Koo's bed back in the ward, I would sit on the back steps and watch them. There was an immense, quiet happiness in the faces of my two Americans. There was peace in the faces of the Asians around the compound. There was much beauty in the purple glow of the sunset over the Burmese hills. There was an extraordinary amount of exertion here, danger, some choking futility, and much loneliness. But there were also these moments in the evening when the chaos and sadness of the day melted into the peaceful silence of the night.

At such moments my mind would embrace much. I remembered that my teachers had taught me that humanity is God on earth. I remembered that a doctor's job is to cure sometimes, to relieve often, to comfort always. I remembered the strong vine of friendship that joined my hospital with all our good people of America. I remembered reading Lincoln's "freedom is for all men in all lands everywhere." I remembered just why we were here. And in watching Earl and Dwight care for that little wisp of a lad I was positive that the human spirit can rise supreme, and that man can develop a feeling of oneness with other men. All beings of blood and breath are brothers, here to help one another.

Maybe the dream of Anne Frank is closer than we know: "Things will change and men become good again and these pitiless days will come to an end and the world will once more know order, rest, and peace."

TEN ·
THE NIGHT THEY BURNED THE MOUNTAIN

The month of May brought the hot, dry season to an end. The jungle though still green was dryer than ever. The stream and gullies were dry, and the wet humid dampness of the jungle was no longer present. Though there were not many changes in the color of the leaves, there was definitely an aridness to the high mountain slopes.

The tribes of the Kha Kho and the Thai Dam now began to prepare for their great planting season, called the Duong Pet. The Duong Pet means the eighth month, since in their calendar it is the eighth month, the month when the rice must be planted, the month before the rains begin.

For us Americans it was a most uncomfortable period of time. On one particularly warm night I was vividly aware of how anxiously I was awaiting the coolness of the monsoon season. Though each monsoon season I cursed the rains and the gales, I was now eagerly anticipating the cool wild mornings. The soaking rains would be a relief from the oppressive heat that came at the end of this dry season.

The war scare was worse than ever now, with definite shooting in many areas. The rainy season might slow the war down, because the jungles become impassable during the heavy rains. However, under such conditions the war might also take a twist and increase in intensity and it would certainly be a more difficult war to fight, especially by modern means.

Late one night I was sitting in the main room of our house with a kerosene lamp on the table, my typewriter papers and stacks of unanswered mail around me. My T-shirt was soaked from sweat and the kerosene lamp was hissing at me. Earl and Dwight were asleep in the other room, Ngoan and the Lao were in the room on the left. I was writing to my family and friends in America, but more than ever they seemed distant to me now. I had a vague uncomfortable feeling. I wasn't especially worried about the war, yet on the other hand I feared the poison of China flowing into our valley. I had pain in my right shoulder and chest dating from my fall of several months before. The pain had never eased; in fact, several times I sneaked over to the hospital and took some codein. On that particular night I had a feeling of apprehension that was difficult to describe to myself, more difficult to explain.

The night seemed noisier. I had a sensation that there was activity outside the house, so I took a flashlight and walked out on our front porch. The mountains all around us looked as though they were covered by swarms of lightning bugs. As I looked at these blinking, flickering lights moving in all directions, I thought to myself, "Almost like Japanese lanterns in a parade."

Suddenly as I watched I saw one whole section of the jungle catch on fire. Then more fire. And more fire. Suddenly and almost in a flash the whole mountain slope on the Burmese hill burst into a blinding glare of yellow flames. The flickering lights I had seen were people moving down with torches to set fire to the jungle. I walked out to the field across from our house and a whole panorama opened up—the jungles to my south, north, and east were also aflame. Huge billows of clouds were spraying up from the ground and heading towards the sky.

Oppressive rolls of heat poured down into our valley. I had an almost terrifying feeling. Were these Communists? Burning the jungle down? Aiming at the complete annihilation of our village of Muong Sing? Just a few weeks ago they had completely destroyed a village only a few miles away from us, in retaliation for the village taking refugees from China into their huts. Was this another Communist atrocity?

In a few minutes Earl and Dwight, awakened by the heat, ran to the porch and looked with amazement at the sky and the night on fire. The whole jungle covering the mountains around us was alive with flames. In the bottom of the bowl of the Muong Sing valley it seemed as though all three sides of us were blazing, the yellow flames licking at the clear sky, the smoke rolling higher and higher. Ngoan came out, looked at the mountain slope, then looked at us, and said, "Do not fear, Thanh Mo America, this is the night they burn the mountain."

I then remembered seeing such Maytime fires far off on previous occasions in Laos. But never had the geographical pattern been as close and tight and menacing as now.

For the mountain tribes the last week of the Duong Pet is a time of great feasting and great work. These tribes do not plant their rice in water-paddies, as do those who live in the valley, but rather on the burnt slopes of the mountains. The village sorcerers and astrologists choose the felicitous night, and after several days of feasting the people light their bamboo torches. The legend is that someone lit a fire in this land dynasties before the conquest of Kublai Khan. Since that time there has always been a fire somewhere, in some homes, over some cooking-areas, outside some huts. When a villager wants to light a fire, having no matches, he merely goes to the house of his neighbor with a piece of flayed bamboo and steals some fire and takes it to his home. On this night all the mountain tribes had lit torches and had gone up to set the mountain slope on fire. The jungle would burn for several days. Then ashes would cover the slopes of the mountain—blackened ashes, and dead earth. But when the rains came, in a few days, the water on the ashes would make rich, fertilized ground. And in this black scorched earth the tribes would plant their rice roots. From the seedlings would grow their rice—not paddy rice, but poor rice, mountain rice.

Earl, Dwight and I watched the mountain burn for many hours. The strange, vague forboding feeling that I had had in the house seemed all the stronger now. What would become of these mountains and these tribes? What would happen to their Kingdom of Laos? Would the flames of Communism conquer it? Would the flames of disease destroy the people? Would there ever be another free May when the people would burn their mountains and plant their rice in this blackened earth?

Finally fatigue completely conquered me. In spite of the heat and the still roaring flames all around, I went to bed. Ngoan had explained that the flames would not come below a certain area because the mountain people had dug trenches as fire stops. I went to bed and slept until dawn came over the scorched mountains. It seemed as though the sorcerers and astrologists were right. Only a few days later, before the earth was even cool, the Nyam Fon came.

Nyam Fon, the season of the rains and monsoons. Back at my University of Notre Dame, this was the season of lilacs. Here it was a time of crashing violence and tropical thunder-storms, of gray, dark and murky days. The tropical night no longer whispered, but roared with a torrent of monsoon rain. The rains lashed the high valley, whipped the palms and frangipani, and flooded the earth. Clouds piled high, and downpours crashed all day and night.

The magnificent sun rose unseen. Steamy breaks of blue weather came, but with it came bugs, rot, mud, and a foggy sash of sunset. This was the season of Nyam Fon, when the whole earth was sodden. In the breadth of the night's storm, the black bats tumbled and darted, the huge insects brushed and flapped and fluttered about.

It was a season when, more than ever, God was everywhere. We saw Him in the mountains, we saw Him in the air, in the mist, in the morning fog. We heard Him in the monsoon rain on the thatched roof. We saw Him outstretching His arms in the lightning and in the thunder of the Nyam Fon. We saw His hand of life in the wind. Even during the rains the village days went on imperturbably with the same rhythms. The villagers prayed to the gods for more rain, to the lord of thunder and the goddess of lightning. They threw firecrackers up into the air to chase away the evil spirits. They wanted the rain and the wind. Their rice hungered and yearned for it; without it, the rice would die.

The trees across the field from my hospital, always clear to see, were now lost. The mountains rimming the valley, the skies and earth alike, all grew dim and vanished in the tide of gray rain. The noonday's silence of a little while ago became the rustle of the wind. Then the wind hummed, and the hum grew deeper and wilder. Then the sound of thunder, the rain, the wind. The thunder and the lightning crashed and rolled and broke overhead. Around the hospital compound were tall palm-tree tops. Above them the sky was blue and violet and blue and dark and then gray again.

The town of Muong Sing was lovely and hideous at the same time. It was lovely in its majestic site, a deep green valley with the rain-forested hills around it and the thrusting mountains just beyond it. Our valley was beautiful when the sky was high and clear and the horizon was wide. It was beautiful even when the skies were dark and we were surrounded by the all-protecting gods of strength, the mountains of Muong Sing. But how hideous the village could be in its filth and its squalor, how odorous the close-packed fetid huts. The streets were now a sea of filth and garbage. The wretched of the village hacked out their lung tissues and their lives. Great splotches of red betel could be seen all over the ground. The chickens and pigs and water buffalos and cows roamed loose all around the town. Beauty and hideousness—they were both here at one and the same time.

When the monsoon torrent of water flowed down the mountain slopes, the valley floods and the fields grew rich with jade-green rice. The palm trees bowed to the wind as acolytes bow at the *Confiteor*. The people of our valley were completely the victims of external circumstance. They could not control the rain coming, nor counteract the bacteria that flooded their lives, they did not know how to improve their plows, they lacked so much.

Those of us in the world who have these things must not ignore the essential needs of human nature the world over. I used to think: These people will die of misery. I have learned something, an unpalatable truth: No one ever dies solely of misery. I wondered just how these people would live on. I looked at this tranquil, almost sleepy green jungle and realized that neither the earth nor the bulk of its human inhabitants really know much of what is going on. All humans are in some way incomprehensible. Yet all human beings can be understood—and must be. The effort must be made.

Life continued in the village in spite of the rains. In fact, everyone worked harder at this time of the year. With their broad-brimmed Chinese conical hats, the villagers went out into the flooded paddies and planted their rice. In a few weeks their closely packed rice would be pulled up and spaced in the replanting season. All of the villagers got together and worked in one large communal movement. They sang while they worked and there was a wonderful vitality to the air.

Many came to our hospital for sick-call during this time with sores on their legs because their feet had become shriveled and bloodless from long immersion in their paddy water. Also the fungus skin diseases increased at this time.

We were the only ones that the rains seemed to bother. We were unaccustomed to such incessant downpouring, and built rain ramps connecting our buildings—thatched covered walks so that we could go back and forth without becoming drenched.

The Muong Sing landing strip, though it became sodden, was still useful. Though the strip at Nam Tha could not be used, the Muong Sing landing field could handle small planes the year round. Soon after the rains came, I flew to Vientiane to make a quick trip to Phnom Penh, the capital of Cambodia. Dr. Emmanuel Voulgaropoulos, head of our Cambodia MEDICO team, had invited me to come down and visit his hospital. At Phnom Penh the chief of the Economic Mission lent me his small plane to fly to the village of Kratie, where Manny has his hospital.

Manny's hospital comes closer to the realization of my dream of MEDICO than any other. The small hospital that we have in Kenya is, I would say, second. We have surgical programs in Jordan and Viet Nam, eye programs in India, dental programs in Africa, but closest to my heart is a village team such as Manny's.

Dr. Manny was a 28-year-old bachelor when he came to join MEDICO in December, 1958. Soon after his arrival in Kratie he sent for his fiancée and, for the first time in the ancient history of Cambodia, an American wedding was held. The Governor of the Province first gave Rose away in a

Buddhist ceremony, and Rose wore the full costume of the ancient Khmer wedding ceremony. After this ceremony had been conducted with all the ancient pomp and circumstance, a smaller Christian ceremony was held. The whole Kingdom of Cambodia had heard about this American and his bride being married according to the customs of their country, and they loved it.

Manny had with him two young American corpsmen. One of them was a former Navy corpsman, Tony Jagger, which pleased this old salt's heart. Their hospital, a little larger than mine, was located in a large city, with electricity and running water, though primitive and spasmodic. There was a road running through this city connecting with the capital in a murderous 12-hour drive.

Manny was working in close cooperation with the Cambodia government, and although he was having to surmount many obstacles, this was simply part of his occupational hazards. He was doing a wonderful job and his heart had found its mooring in his work. The touch of a woman was very easy to see—curtains on the windows, flowers in the vases, a little study fixed up over the main clinic. Maybe there is something to this connubial bliss.

While I was in Cambodia I heard a very beautiful legend. In origin it belongs to Viet Nam, but it is known and loved throughout all of Indo-China. It is a story of the season of Nyam Fon, and the legend goes like this: Once upon a time, long ago, there lived a very rich king, who had a beautiful daughter. Many young princes came from neighboring countries to beg for her hand, but the king refused them all. One day two handsome young men happened to arrive at the palace at the same time. The first introduced himself as the god of the Mountain, the other as the god of Water. The king's embarrassment was great. Here were two suitors for his daughter's hand, equally handsome, equally rich, and equally powerful. What would the old king do? After much thought, he said, "I will give my daughter's hand to the prince who arrives first on the morrow with the most exotic and fabulous of wedding gifts."

The next day the god of the Mountains arrived first, bringing, silver, gold, ivory and jade. True to his promise, the king gave him his daughter, even though the god of Water had not yet appeared. The couple then left immediately to go to the high mountain castle for their honeymoon. When the other suitor arrived, with even more magnificent gifts, the princess was gone. The god of Water was furious and swore to the blue sky above and to the black earth below that he would win back this lovely young princess. He would wage war against the Mountain. And so the battle began. The god of Water amassed all of his powers to wage war.

First, the elements burst forth, the skies opened up, and rain pelted the earth mercilessly. Tidal waves and floods and typhoons and tornados devastated enormous areas. Amidst all this fury the sea fauna were suddenly turned into soldiers and marched in huge columns to the fortress of the god of the Mountain. The god of the Mountain had power no less great. He transformed all the highland fauna of his mountain into warriors, and turned the stones into white elephants. Dreadful battles took place, and the number of casualties in this war of the gods was tremendous. The damage to the fields of the ancient kingdom was incalculable, for the war dragged on for years and years. Finally the god of the Mountain defeated the god of Water. The latter was forced to withdraw his forces into the sea and the sky. However, he bore with him a grudge and a vow of vengeance that has never left his heart. Every year since that time, the god of Water returns to earth. He floods and thunders and plagues the people of the mountains in an attempt to win the lovely princess. And ever since that first battle, the season when the god of Water returns is called Nyam Fon.

I returned to Laos in a few days, and they were sick days for me. We have a tremendous amount of malaria in our territory of northern Laos and we take malaria suppressives weekly. When I went to visit Manny in Cambodia I did not take a suppressive; I forgot it. When I returned to Laos I spent the night at the house of Hank Miller. We talked of the war problems, and I mentioned my aching body. I felt quite bad that night, with much generalized fatigue. I thought it was simply because I grow old. The next morning I realized that I had a blazing temperature. I was due to fly out at dawn and I preferred to be sick at my own hospital rather than in the capital.

I climbed into the plane and had the most awful trip of my life. Every little bump, every little air pocket was excruciating. I thought my head would split into pieces. When I arrived, the boys came out in the jeep to meet me and made some comment like "My gosh, you look like hell, Doctor." I agreed with them wholeheartedly, climbed into the jeep, and we rolled into town, each bump pushing me a little bit closer to the brink of death. Or so it seemed.

By the time I got to the house it was obvious that I was having a first-class malaria attack, complete with chills and 105 degrees of fever. I took the malaria medicines and went right to bed, with half of my hospital staff around to help, aid and succor me. Never was a patient so overtreated as the boss when he got sick. Twenty-four hours in bed and the fever was gone and the chills had stopped. Although I felt tremendously exhausted, I was able to go back to work. I did not get malaria from Manny; it was evidently in my bloodstream when I flew down and the incubation period elapsed while I was in Cambodia. But from that day on we preferred to blame the Kingdom of Cambodia for Dooley's malaria.

While passing through the capital of Laos once again I heard more of war; more skirmishes, more shootings. It looked as though along with the burning of the mountains, the land of Laos might be thoroughly burned by the flames of war.

During the month of June the pain in my chest increased. A lump on my upper chest was getting larger, and had increased from the size of a pea almost to that of a golf ball. My arm ached so badly that I did not play the piano anymore at night. One day, driving the jeep with Chai in the back seat, I had to ask him to lean forward and massage my neck and back because it hurt so much to keep my arm lifted. I thought the lump must be a large sebaceous cyst or a boil that was growing rapidly in size and affecting the nerves and muscles of my chest. Or maybe this was a deep bone bruise, with a blood clot below the bruise, pressing on tender nerves of the rib cage.

Sometimes it even hurt when I took a deep breath, a stabbing kind of pain into my lung. Some years back I had been badly clobbered on the chest by some angry people of North Viet Nam. Every once in awhile I had vague aching pains in my chest. Was this a left-over of that incident of many years ago, its pain accentuated by the recent fall? While I was at Hank Miller's house in the capital, he noticed the lump under my T-shirt and asked about it. I jokingly said, "Oh don't worry, Hank, it's just cancer of the lung."

One day in July, during Nyam Fon, the clouds unexpectedly cleared and the sun burst forth in a blinding flash. Almost instantaneously we heard the small roar of a twin-engine airplane and ran out of the clinic yelling, "*Hua bin, hua bin, hua bin,*" (which, as your ears should tell you, means "airplane"). It was good to see that the plane had an American flag on it. We all drove with the jeep out through the water and the mud to the landing strip. Out of the plane stepped an old friend of mine from Solvang, California, Doctor Bill Van Valin. Years ago Bill had promised that he would come and visit my hospital someday and give me a hand with surgery. Now, during the height of the wet season, when the North was consumed in a war, Bill Van Valin blithely arrived in Laos to spend a week.

One of the first things I asked Dr. Van to do was to take a look at my chest. It was now causing me quite a good deal of pain. He saw the lump and immediately suggested that he remove it surgically, agreeing with my pre-operative diagnosis of a rapidly growing sebaceous cyst. The next afternoon, in an almost joking manner, we went to the hospital and I climbed up on the operating-table. Several of my students thought that this was a very funny moment and had many comments to make, such as: "Thanh Mo America himself is getting operated on, instead of doing the operating." "Do you want me to call the witch doctor?" "Lie still, doctor, it won't hurt." Chai leaned over me and moaned and groaned and made comments in Lao while the girls walked in and out of the room smiling.

All the while Dr. Van was busily opening up the skin of my chest to remove the lesion. I remember now in retrospect the cloudy look that came across his face when he finally got down to the tumor itself. Lying as I was I could not see what he was removing. It was not until he finished and I saw the tumor that I said, "It's jet black, Van?" He said, "Yes, it is."

After my chest wall was sutured we examined the tumor more closely. It was hard, circumscribed, and completely black. There is only one tumor that is jet black. I was not in the least concerned that this was melanoma, truthfully believing the tumor had something to do with a fall, perhaps an old, hardened and partially calcified blood clot. Van agreed with me but was very insistent that the tumor be taken to a hospital in Bangkok for analysis.

He asked me if I had any formalin. I laughed and said, "I should say not, doctor. Do you think you're at the National Institute of Health? If you want to preserve that tumor you will have to be content with just old 90 per cent alcohol." He smiled and said, "No. We must get formalin." Earl came to the rescue and went to his Bird Room and brought back a bottle that he was using in his taxidermy work. Doctor Van prepared a solution of the proper strength and put part of the tumor into the bottle. He would take it with him when he left Muong Sing. In Bangkok there was a large Seventh Day Adventist hospital with a superb pathologist, and Van would have my tumor examined there.

I dismissed the thought of cancer from my mind, and plunged back into my work. Being a doctor with a heavy patient load and a war on my mind, I really didn't have much time for negative thinking. And yet, after a night of good sleep with drugs, the area still hurt plenty.

I was awakened a little after dawn by the work that I was put on this earth to do. A villager had come to take me to Ban Ting That. The chieftain of the village had sent him to say that there was a man who was terribly sick, so sick that he could not allow the man to stay in the village. He had built a thatched lean-to in the field, and put the man in it. With the rest of the symptoms, this sounded very serious to us, like cholera. We climbed into the jeep to splash our way down the soggy trail to the village of Ban Ting That.

In the field outside of the village we found the hut. Not even a hut, really, just four pieces of thatch on a two-foot high wooden frame. Underneath this frame was the most wretched-looking human I had ever seen. The man was desperately sick and was covered with his own excrement. He had a severe infection of the lungs. He was foul-smelling and as he inhaled and exhaled there was a rattling in his chest, a death rattle. His eyes were glazed and the opium gourd on his side indicated to us that he had been taking a great deal in the past days. He was completely dehydrated and responded very sluggishly to even the most violent stimulation. I was seized by a sudden urge to leave the man there and let him die. What could we possibly do for him in such a filthy state? But this was wrong. A doctor shouldn't feel this way. My business is wretchedness, but he was the most disgusting human I have ever seen in my life. We baptized him immediately as I was sure he would die. Ngoan and I picked him up and carried him over to our jeep.

We drove to Muong Sing and were surprised to find he survived the thirty-minute trip. We carried him in to the dressing table and all of my staff pitched in and helped clean him up. We burned his clothes and washed him over and over again until he was clean. Having some guilt about my original feelings towards the man, I bent over backwards to give him full attention every day. We tried to get him to walk, to get him to eat, to get him to breathe deeply. Only after four days did he begin to respond at all and then he began to beg for his opium pipe. He was a hopeless, helpless addict. I started giving him some morphine but soon realized that we could not support him on morphine alone. On the fifth day I withdrew the morphine. We found him dead in bed on the sixth.

We had a little boy in the hospital at this time, a boy whose name was Thai Noi. His brightness helped to offset the sadness of the man's death. Although he was about nine years old, he looked like a withered up little boy of five. He had a huge bladder stone that had taken everything out of his life. He was never able to put on weight, to grow strong, and was constantly racked with kidney infections. We surgically removed the stone, about the size and weight of a golf ball. He convalesced well but when we removed the stitches he developed a fistula. We re-operated on him a second time, attempting to close the fistula, but were unsuccessful. He stayed on at the hospital for many weeks on protein extracts and vitamins and soon the wound healed up and the fistula closed.

Thai Noi's round big eyes grew brighter and cheerier and he put on weight. Soon we had him working around the hospital to earn his living and his father became one of our chief water-carriers; we are constantly carrying water from the well to the hospital and the house. Thai Noi used to come and sit in our house and talk with Ngoan, as they were both of the same tribe. He became very much an intimate part of the family and we loved him very dearly. When he left to go back to his village a stronger, healthier, finer boy, he was better because of us and we were a lot better for having had him as our friend.

ELEVEN ·
THE WAR

Laos has been threatened by war ever since 1954 when she first established herself as a completely independent nation under the Geneva Agreement which followed the war in Indo-China. Sometimes in our village hospital high in the foothills of the Himalayas this threat of war seemed remote—the people were so gentle, the mountains were so impenetrable, the situation so apparently calm.

While I was in America in 1958 from January till June, Laos was run by a coalition government. An agreement had been reached at the end of 1957 by the two half-brothers, neutralist Prince Souvanna Phouma, then Prime Minister, and the Communist Prince Souphanouvong. Prince Souphanouvong's forces, the Pathet Lao, controlled the two large northeastern provinces, of Sam Neua and Phong Saly. He skillfully used his control of these two provinces as a lever to bargain his way into the royal government of Prince Souvanna Phouma. The neutralist Prince Souvanna Phouma did not seem to object, as long as the *status quo* were maintained. Many American, British and French advocates of Lao independence tried to point out to Souvanna Phouma the lessons of recent history, especially that of Czechoslovakia where only a few months after a "coalition" with Communists was completed, the nation fell. Nevertheless Prince Souvanna Phouma agreed to form a coalition government that included Communists.

Two Communist members, including Prince Souphanouvong, were given portfolios as Ministers, and 10 or 12 seats in the National Assembly were held by the Communist representatives of the two northeastern provinces. A plan was worked out to integrate the Pathet Lao army of 6,000 men into the Royal Lao Army of 25,000 men. The Communist Pathet Lao force changed to a political party called the Neo Lao Hak Xat.

At this point, Prince Souvanna Phouma was replaced by a new Premier, Phoui Sananikone. He had been Premier for only a short time when I brought my team back to Laos in the summer of 1958. Sananikone had no confidence in the concept of a coalition government, when it was clearly the intention of part of the coalition to seize power at the earliest opportunity and remake Laos into a Communist country. In January, 1959, at his request the National Assembly scrapped the constitution. Then they voted the Premier special powers for a period of twelve months. Premier Sananikone then decided that the Pathet Lao soldiers who were still not integrated into the national army either had to be assimilated completely or disbanded. He also made matters extremely difficult for Communist politicians and kicked the two Communist leaders out of his Cabinet.

By July, 1959, it was obvious that the plan of integrating the Lao army was failing and that the Communist soldiers had no intentions of being assimilated into the national forces. They were being maintained as an independent Pathet Lao Army by the Communist brass within the Royal Lao Army.

We first heard of the problem of army integration in June, when the leader of the military battalion in Muong Sing called me over to the fortress to tell me that I was not to leave the village at night without an armed military escort. When I asked why, he said that the situation was becoming "très grave." He told me that some Pathet Lao (Communist) troops south of us had forcibly resisted integration. When ordered to Luang Prabang, they had not obeyed, but deserted and fled into the mountains towards the borders of North (Communist) Viet Nam.

We had sporadic reports of war from our radio during the next few summer months. As usual the terrorist technique was monotonously familiar. Small, well-trained Communist bands would come out of hiding at midnight and attack a small isolated Lao army post or a house, killing, mauling and mutilating. Occasionally a story of atrocity and slow death would come to us. We listened to these reports and tried not to let them create fear, for fear is exactly the weapon that the Communists use in this whispering warfare of Laos.

The monsoon rains were pouring down and the sick were flooding into our hospital. We tried not to think about war. However, by the middle of the summer the distant rumblings became more like near thunder. Our Lao students were coming in late for work and often, when they did come, they were desperately exhausted. They had spent many hours the night before on patrol. During the daytime we would see the patrols marching out, and we would listen to their reports of the build-up of Communist forces on the China side of our northern frontier, five or six miles away.

The Lao army was doing an excellent job in eradicating internal jealousies among the soldiers. In each army battalion were Thai Dam, Thai Lu and others, as well as Lao themselves. The internal friction that existed between these tribes for centuries was being lessened by the new training programs which told the soldiers of their duties to their King, their nation and their flag. Our corpsmen came to our hospital filled with this new patriotism and new enthusiasm. We would hear them singing patriotic songs in the fort at night. Lao army training was progressing very well.

One afternoon out on a sick-call I came on a group of soldiers sitting in a field with their officer reciting on a melodic scale the fundamentals of the trigger-assembly of their rifle: "This is the trigger, this is the hammer, this is the head, and this is the screw," went their chant, just the way we sang our lessons as children.

The Lao are very touchy about their beliefs and superstitions relating to the origins of different tribes. Each tribe thinks itself superior to the others; the Lao group, for example, believe that their race is strongest. The legend about the origin of these races begins with a sacred pumpkin. An envoy of one of their ancient kings split this pumpkin up with a red hot poker. The first people to tumble out of the pumpkin were the aboriginal Kha, whose skin is a little dark because it was seared by the heat. Next came the lighter-colored mountain tribe of the Meo; finally came the lightest-skinned of them all, the Lao. There are anthropologists who take another view and believe that the people of Laos are simply the result of centuries of blending between the bloods of the Tibetan, the Burman, the Thai and the Yunnanese.

What were the origins of the Communist group in Laos? They go back to 1953, during the Indo-China War, when the group was formed by Prince Souphanouvong, aided by Ho Chi Minh. They attacked Laos in 1953 and the armies of this force (the Pathet Lao) came perilously close to the capital. In May, 1954, the war ended after the fall of the ill-fated fortress of Dien Bien Phu. Viet Nam was divided at the 17th parallel and in July, 1954, the United States Navy steamed into the harbor of Haiphong, to begin the historic evacuation of Vietnamese escapees from Communism.

That first day I looked upon the rocks of northern Indo-China, over five years ago, I wondered what this strange and mysterious area would be like. Now I was living in North Laos only a few hundred miles west, as the vulture flies, of my former refugee camps in Haiphong, centuries apart in some ways, and yet very close in the similarity of suffering.

The 1954 Geneva Agreement recognized the independence of Laos and its three million inhabitants. It also called for the withdrawal of all the Pathet Lao Communist fighting units into the provinces of Phong Saly and Sam Neua. The Geneva Treaty also provided for the withdrawal of the Viet Nam Communist forces. And there was established an International Control Commission composed of representatives of India, a neutral; Canada, a pro-Western; and Poland, a Communist nation. After the political settlement was signed by Prince Souphanouvong and Prince Souvanna Phouma in November, 1957, the two northern provinces were surrendered.

Early in 1958 the Lao Government, under Premier Phoui Sananikone, stated that they believed that the unity of the nation was established, the armies were being integrated, and therefore the presence of the International Control Commission was no longer necessary. Any remaining problems should be dealt with by the elected government.

The political party called the Neo Lao Hak Xat, which is just another name for Communism, had become a strong internal threat. They had an organization that went right to the villages of Asia, whereas the other political parties, in the sudden sophistication of independence, sometimes did not reach deeply enough into the villages. How could they? These non-Communist parties had the arduous task of running the government, whereas the Neo Lao Hak Xat was free to criticize, condemn and poison.

On our river trips we would find the Neo Lao Hak Xat newspaper in every village along the river valley, and many young men and women trained to believe and accept the teachings of the Communists. Of course, they did not call themselves Communists, or advocate that they be made part of China. They spoke of the "terrible errors" of the Lao Royal Government and of the need for ox-carts instead of limousines. They constantly harped on the mistakes of Premier Sananikone's government, and the errors of American foreign aid. They magnified these out of all proportion.

My students loved to listen to our small transistor-run radio. There are two news broadcasts, one after lunch and one late in the evening. They would sit on the window sill, looking over into the sky of China, and hold the radio close against their ears. Earl once said to me, "There sits young Asia listening to her future."

On July 15, 1959, rebel attacks sharply increased in the two provinces of Sam Neua and Phong Saly. We heard that an emergency telegram was sent on July 24th asking the United States to supply experts to help train the army immediately in the use and maintenance of equipment.

Later in July the rebel guerrillas attacked a 35-mile front in northeastern Sam Neua, not far from the famous fortress of Dien Bien Phu. Some radio reports said that as many as eight villages fell to the Communists. Others said there was heavy howitzer fire.

The people are a drowsy people, and the country is a landlocked country. It has been invaded repeatedly, but still it keeps its craggy individuality and the people fight courageously for their independence when they understand that it is threatened.

It seemed that it was threatened now. We often talked to our students about this threat to their nation. They understood that the Pathet Lao was simply an extension of the Communist Viet Minh movement, which in turn is an extension of Red China, which in turn is allied with Soviet Communism. They also seemed to understand that the simple fact that Premier Sananikone was making so much progress towards a strong, free nation had alarmed the Communists, who had decided to act immediately.

The Communists announced that the arrival of a 130-man American training mission for the Lao army was the cause of the blowup in August. They screamed on Radio Peking accusing the United States of "engineering" the Lao war and warning that the war in Laos could set all of Asia ablaze. Radio Peking and Radio Hanoi used language that was reminiscent of the Chinese intervention in Korea. The Chinese Communists called for an "abolition of all U.S. military bases" in Laos and warned that Washington must "bear full responsibility" for the Laos situation. In Hanoi the defense minister for the Communist leader Ho Chi Minh said that the fighting was a dangerous thing and Communist North Viet Nam would "not stand idly by."

The students understood that this propaganda was perfectly idiotic. They knew that no military bases were being built by the Americans, though certain former French bases were being improved in their physical setup by the Lao Government forces. They were quick to distinguish lies from truth, and I think my young students were typical of all the young Laos. We tell them the truth, and their intelligence does the rest.

It is known that a considerable number of Pathet Lao were taken into North Viet Nam, armed by North Vietnamese (Viet Minh) guns and formed into battalions. They were trained in the newer, more insidious techniques of the whispering war—the psychological battles. Their own rank and file were stiffened with Viet Minh hard-core Communist leaders. Now these troops were being sent back across the Lao border into their own land, to begin guerrilla war against the Lao Government. Their ways were devious: a midnight raid where only the village chieftain is slaughtered; an ambush killing a patrol of six men—never a large classical battle. Yet no one will ever prove that there was any "outside" intervention. Little did I realize that the United Nations itself would soon be involved in trying to prove who was fighting whom. My men were quick to see that indeed this was the same picture as the Communists' conquests elsewhere throughout the world.

By the month of August all of the land was ablaze with the news of the war. Airplanes came into the valley only rarely. The pilots told us that all planes had been requisitioned by the military, and no civilian regular runs were being made. "Four weeks and no mail plane yet; kind of tough on a guy with a six-months-old baby at home," commented Earl. Dwight, a little more staid, just said, "It sure gets lonesome without that airplane." I could only think of the danger. Should I consider taking my outfit out of a war-threatened area? Certainly, if war broke out along the Vietnamese frontier just a little east of us. China, close on our northern side, will be looking for provocative instances. Would they consider our hospital a provocation?

The Communist radio announcements became more and more arrogant. They brandished threats and accused us Americans in Muong Sing, while busily passing out cough medicine, of setting up spy stations and planning programs for eventual take-over of all of North Laos. Earl, Dwight and I smiled at each other. "We don't even entirely run our own hospital, so much of the work is done by our Lao student staff. So how are we possibly going to run North Laos?"

Every morning I would go across the muddy road (the monsoon turns the whole valley into a sea of mud) and speak to the Commandant. He was a bright young man, fast-talking and quick-thinking. I enjoyed being with him, and he did give me a good deal of information when I asked for it. But I always had to ask or, rather, wring it out of him. We listened to our radio, read the papers that came to us monthly, and blended this with the information from the Commandant.

The figures were staggering—1,500 men, 2,000 men, 15,000 men—invading Laos from Communist North Viet Nam. It seemed unreal that people were dying again in war. We knew that aggression, if expanded, could easily get out of hand. And we realized most of all that the tiny Kingdom of Laos, and the valleys just over our mountainside, possessed the potential for a catastrophe whose consequences might well alter the history of the world.

These things gave us many sleepless nights. Was their goal war, or just unrest? To foment small local uprisings would keep the Lao Government tremendously concerned in the expense and preparation of war. Perhaps this was part of the "initiate confusion within the Kingdom" program. The Communist government had attempted, by parliamentary means, to win over Laos but due to the bravery and strength of Premier Phoui Sananikone, they had failed. Now they were attempting to discredit western military help, western political aid, and especially American Economic Aid. Would they succeed?

One night while I was making a tape-recording, machine-gun fire broke out in the field across from my house. The whole sky was lit up with torches. My heart flipped, goose-flesh popped out all over, and I ran to the front porch of our house thinking, "They are attacking our village." The boys jumped out of bed and we looked quickly at the sky, alive with flares. The ratatatat of machine-gun fire was deafening.

We noticed that flares were falling right over the fortress. The sky was lit up with the blinding white brilliance of day. Another flare shot up from within the fortress. On looking closer, with cooler heads, we noticed that the machine-gun firing was coming from within the fortress. A few minutes later one of our student soldiers quietly ambled over to the hospital. We asked him, "Tao Souk, what are they doing? What is happening? Are they attacking Muong Sing?" Tao Souk looked at us, smiled at the perturbed Americans and said, "Oh, no, we just received a new shipment of ammunition by paradrop. You know, 50 per cent of the ammunition that we get is no good. We are just trying it out to see that it works."

I thought to myself, "What an alarmist you are, Dooley! Who's scared around here?" Nevertheless that night seemed a preview of the nights of horror that we feared would come. The local Commandant especially alarmed us when he told us that there was definite proof now of a build-up of Chinese troops on the Yunnan border six miles north of us. It seemed as though they were going to push east from this border into Phong Saly at the same time that they were pushing west from North Viet Nam.

Few supply planes came in. I flew down to Vientiane on an airplane that came in the month of August, to have a long visit with Colonel Oudone Sananikone. Colonel Sananikone was a nephew of the Premier and belonged to one of the most capable and famous families of Laos. Colonel Oudone's wife was leader of the activities of the Lao women, and he was the Minister of Public Welfare and Health. This made him my boss, and an excellent boss he was. He gave me a free hand in the running of my hospital, yet he seemed to know every aspect of administration involved. He had visited my hospital twice in the past. As a Colonel, he was the most interested in our army training program. He was pleased that I did not make my hospital into a white man's hospital with a few Asian assistants, but rather an Asian hospital with three Americans working in it.

Colonel Oudone was a young man, about 34, stocky, and a veteran of many years of fighting. He was well-known through his land not only as a fighter, but as a thinker. Though not a heavy-set man, as are most of the Lao, he had extremely broad shoulders and a chin that jutted forward in almost arrogant fashion. His eyes were wide set and he had a heavy shank of hair over which his military cap perched straight and proper. Along with many other young Lao such as Sisouk Na Champassak, Impeng Suryadhay, Keo Viphathong, and others the Colonel made up the powerful political group called the C.D.I.N. which stand for Comité pour la Defense des Intérets Nationaux, or Committee for the Defense of National Interests. These young men hold the future of the Kingdom in their capable hands. These men are dynamic and have a surging vitality. They also have a deep and profound love of their country, and are determined to serve it with loyalty. Upon attaining some power in the Phoui Sananikone government early in 1958 they attacked the corruption that had taken hold of the nation. They helped to abolish the former sloth and old corruption. They established rural self-help programs, village school programs, civic action programs, and made it their task to see that the young people became aware of their duties as citizens of the Kingdom of Laos.

A youth rally had been held in Vientiane and when Colonel Sananikone told me about this his eyes gleamed with pride. The youth rally had been set up by the Minister of Youth, Sisouk Na Champassak. Sisouk had formerly been in New York with the UN and I knew him well. The rally was the first of its kind, an old-fashioned rally, boy scout-jamboree and political convention combined. Thousands of students marched in parades through the city and out to a temple ground area several miles outside the capital. Here they had an encampment, sang songs, made a huge bonfire, and listened to many talks. Colonel Sananikone told me how dynamic the young people were at this rally, and how anxious they were to improve themselves and their parents. They know now that there are better things in the world than they have yet achieved within their kingdom and they are determined to have them. In this same kind of search some have turned to Communism as the quicker way, forgetting that they must give up freedom they will never regain. With leaders like Sisouk, Colonel Sananikone, Impeng and Keo, the young people of the nation will be guided correctly. And I believe they will achieve what they seek. But I believe they need more assurance of the fact that the young men of the Western World will also respond to their challenge. They need our hands, our hearts, our economic support, and our diplomatic prestige.

Colonel Sananikone told me that at present they were not evacuating any wounded to the hospital at Muong Sing. They felt that this would be simply increasing the danger in the area, taking wounded men from one war zone and moving them into another threatened zone. He did, however, ask me to keep my hospital alerted for emergencies, and increase our training program to make more corpsmen capable of handling battle casualties. I pledged that we would.

He also told me of a program that had been in effect for several months wherein the Lao military groups around the country were trying to win the villages over to their side. I had seen evidence of this under the civilian program headed by Colonel Sananikone called Civic Action. The Colonel pointed out that there was also a Military Civic Action program whereby the military would aid the people of various villages. He said that this was tremendously important in the two provinces where the war was going on. I left the Colonel pleased and proud to be working hand in hand with a government such as his.

Premier Phoui Sananikone invited me to a small stag dinner in his home, which was his way of saying, "God bless, and we're glad to have you here, Dooley." There was a lot of friendly give-and-take at this dinner, and although politics were not discussed and very little was said about the war, I returned to Muong Sing feeling that the capital was fully aware of the danger of Laos being pushed into war deeper and deeper.

A few days later I loaded another plane with supplies, and returned to my village. I was reassured of the Lao Government's support and interest in my mission, though I was apprehensive about the turn for the worse that the war was taking.

(*Postscript in 1960*. As this book goes to press in the early months of 1960, the political situation in Laos has changed from what it was during the period covered above. Late in 1959 Premier Phoui Sananikone reversed his anti-Communist stance in favor of "neutralism." Seven members of his Cabinet resigned and the C.D.I.N. demanded that a provisional government be established. The Prime Minister thereupon handed in his resignation to King Savang Vatthana. A new Cabinet headed by Kou Abhay as Premier, and his brother, Nhouy, as Vice Premier, became the compromise administration and restored civil authority after a week of army rule. Dag Hammarskjold, Secretary General of the UN, had wired the King: "I permit myself to express the hope that the line of independent neutrality . . . will be firmly maintained." *Time* reported the news of the civilian compromise

Cabinet by saying, "It was, everyone in Vientiane delightedly agreed, a truly Lao solution: though Premier Phoui Sananikone had been ousted, his new, more neutralist policy, at least for the time being, had won." The Abhay interim government is to rule until the national elections scheduled for April, 1960.)

TWELVE ·
A SHEET OF BLUE PAPER

Now we spent every noon listening to the radio news. Occasionally we listened to the Voice of America. More often we heard British news stations better. In the evenings we listened to Communist Radio Hanoi, realizing that, though most of what they said were macabre lies, they revealed their aims and tactics "between the lines." We learned that the Communists had attacked several villages in the area of Phong Saly, though the radio broadcast said they were now retreating. The Royal Lao Army dropped parachutists between Communist rebel troops and their Viet Minh headquarters, thus cutting off their supply line. The guns captured during this maneuver were made in Communist Czechoslovakia. Everyone in this area knew these facts but they also knew that, in the event of the United Nations being brought into the matter, further more definite proof would probably be demanded.

Many people in Muong Sing were speaking of the fact that the Lao Government had sent airplanes to Sam Neua to evacuate families of the Lao Government employees. I considered this bad news. Seemingly the Lao Government was abandoning Sam Neua and letting the Communist come. On the night of August 5 the war news was very bleak indeed. The Lao Government put all northern provinces on an "alert."

My boys and I had put our hospital on an alert also and began war-training exercises. The next morning we started teaching all of the students how war wounded should be brought in. We discussed the unloading of wounded from an airplane, and decided how stretchers should be put on our jeep. We taught the men how to open and carry stretchers and how to make additional emergency stretchers from bamboo and blankets. We practiced such emergency measures as admitting 15, 20, and 25 patients into the wards at

one time. We showed the students how the patients should be stripped
their clothes put under their heads, and their bodies covered with blankets.
We discussed how they would be tagged on the foot and how morphine
when given would be marked on the forehead. We held classes on first-aid
and on triage. In essence we began a long course of training our men for
emergency work.

The boys and I discussed what we would do in a dangerous emergency
ourselves. Would we evacuate and abandon our hospital? We were told that
the Filipinos of Operation Brotherhood were forced to leave their village
hospital in the war-plagued province of Sam Neua. Operation Brotherhood
is that grand program of the Filipinos, who have several medical teams scattered throughout Laos—they are doing a topnotch job. They give of themselves. Now the problem must be considered: if I were ordered out by the
Lao or the American Ambassador, should I go, or should I refuse the order?
And if I went should I take all my civilian crew with me?

Abandoning my hospital would be difficult. If I thought this hospital were
to be destroyed, it would be doubly difficult. It would be destroying part of
me. I did not think the Communists could be that stupid; a hospital is above
politics. It can serve humanity, no matter what the political coloring of this
humanity.

It would be a difficult thing for me to take myself out of the geographical
position that demanded the presence of a doctor. I had been under threat for
many years. I had lived under the ogre of Communist conquest, and I had
seen Communism at close hand. I was not afraid of this any more. There
had been a time when I was; now I was not. I am a doctor, I am supposed
to take care of people who are sick, especially the wounded. The root, the
foundation, the heart of it all was that I am a doctor.

At one point Chai said, "Doctor, you go. You are American, the war is a
Lao war." But Ngoan said, "Deep down in my heart I know that you will
stick by us Lao." I too knew that we would stick by them.

I had seen what Communists do to Asians who work with Americans, for
I had Asians working with me in North Viet Nam when the Communists
took over. I knew that the six or eight of my star pupils would be taken out
and beheaded in front of the whole village and their heads, with the organs
of the neck hanging down, would be impaled upon stakes. I knew that the
Communists would take members of my Lao crew, stand them in a circle
facing inward, and with machetes would deftly cut the tendons in the
back of their knees. When the crew would fall to the ground the Communists would walk around and hack them to pieces. I have seen the Communists do this and just leave the men in the middle of a room or in a field.

When the tendons were cut, the Lao would not bleed to death. They would crawl like animals until they were caught and hacked to death. This is what they would do to Chai, to Si, to Ngoan, and to Deng. To the girls on my staff they would do even more dreadful things. These were the thoughts that burned the hours of my nights those early weeks of August. The decision was mine and only mine.

This is a time when we must be strong and courageous, even though fear might spread through our bones. The first week of August was even more difficult than usual because I was alone. I had sent Earl to Vientiane for supplies and Dwight was in Cambodia with our team there for a few days.

I wanted to indicate to my Lao students that I had confidence in them. I wanted to show them that I knew they could maintain and sustain me and my hospital when my two Americans were gone. And indeed they did. They bent over backwards helping each other and helping me, though they often spun their wheels just a little bit. They stepped on each other and on me; the operating-room was often so crowded that we continuously contaminated each other. Ngoan gave all of the anesthesia for me and the Lao scrubbed as surgical nurses. It pleased me to see how well they did these things.

Perhaps I felt a great deal more loneliness at this time because I had no one with whom to speak English. I frequently found myself looking in the mirror and saying, "Hello, Tom. My, you look fine today."

I had some difficulty with the Military Commandant while Earl and Dwight were gone. He wanted to take Deng and others, my finest crew, and transfer them down into the central portion of the province. Of all times I needed a trained crew more than ever at this moment. I had to argue with all my force to prove my point. I won it, but it was a constant irritation to both of us, to say nothing of the amount of effort required not to get something accomplished but merely preserved.

Very late in the afternoon of August 6th, a plane circled overhead. It was the first plane we had seen for several weeks. We went to the airfield to find Earl disembarking. Earl had left from Vientiane, but due to the war had been held up in Luang Prabang for several days. Finally he went to the Commandant of the Lao army in Luang Prabang and explained his predicament and they turned an airplane over to him. All military as well as civilian planes had been requisitioned for evacuation of civilians from the war-torn areas around Sam Neua. However the Commandant helped out and flew Earl back to us.

Earl was full of news of the war, and of the things that were happening in the capital, and I hungered for accuracy. It was strange that the only way we heard of the war was through rumors and the radio. That was the most deadly factor of the struggle—it was never black or white, always a nebulous gray.

After the Lao students greeted Earl and heard all the news from the capital, Earl said he would like to have a few minutes with me in private. The dark sincerity that came across his face frightened me. When we were alone, he pulled out a letter given to him by the American Ambassador to Laos, Mr. Horace Smith.

The letter was dated August 3rd and began: "Dear Tom, The Royal Government has reported many insurgent attacks on border posts in Sam Neua and considerable penetration into the Phong Saly from the east. Most of these attacks appear to involve incursions from across the border." I read that paragraph without alarm because we had heard this news of Phong Saly, a neighboring province of ours. The letter went on to point out that there were reports of recent Red Chinese troop movements, involving some three hundred to four hundred people, on our border some five miles away. We had also heard the same thing, although our figures were double.

The Ambassador wrote that "from information so far available, the American Embassy fears that the Royal Army may be unable to guarantee your continued security and, as you know, the Embassy is not in a position to guarantee that you or your assistants will have an opportunity to evacuate safely if the situation develops rapidly.

"I therefore urge you to consider carefully the desirability of either evacuating immediately your assistants and yourself at least temporarily, to a place of safety such as Luang Prabang or Vientiane until the situation is clarified, or of making arrangements that satisfy you that you will be able to do so whenever it becomes necessary."

This was it! A letter from the American Ambassador—not ordering me, for he knew he could not—yet "urging" that I consider the desirability of leaving—*now*. This was exactly what I had given so much thought to. This was the first step in a program that might end up in tragedy. I had already decided that I would not evacuate and this letter did not change my feeling. I had also sent a telegram to the Commandant of the First Military Region of the Lao Army, informing him that our hospital was ready and able to receive any war wounded that he wished to send here.

I then wrote a letter to the Ambassador, knowing it might not get out for many weeks. I informed him that I appreciated his letter and his consideration, but felt that my duty was here in the hospital. I wrote: "We are not going to evacuate at this time. From my rapport with the Royal Army both locally and at staff level, I am confident that if the situation warrants they will do all in their power to give us security and, if necessary, evacuation.

"I have requested the army to consider our hospital as a Lao military hospital. Further I have asked that we be evacuated only when and if it becomes necessary to evacuate the military units of this area. At such time I shall request first priority and am sure all possible aid will be given to us."

I went on to point out to the Ambassador that if the local civilian authorities ordered us to evacuate, I would turn the decision over to the Royal Army. If there were sick and wounded in Muong Sing, then it was our duty to stay with them. Above all else it must be remembered that we are a medical unit. I also said, "However, if ordered by the Lao Military we shall evacuate immediately."

I have great admiration for Ambassador Smith and I tried to explain fully my feeling: "I feel very strongly, sir, that we three Americans are now given a splendid opportunity to serve our nation and the Kingdom of Laos. By being present in this village at their time of need, by not seeking self-safety, we can reaffirm (in a minute way) America's policy: when free people are threatened, when Taiwans, Laos and Lebanons are intimidated, America will stand by their people and not abandon them." I wrote the letter and felt relieved that my decision had been reached and announced. I told Earl what I had done—he was 100 per cent in accord. We both wished that Dwight were with us now. We knew that when he heard the news of the increase in the war, he would come home immediately, though we also knew he would have the same difficulty that Earl had with transportation. There was strength in all three of us together.

The Lao Army now began an intense recruiting program in our area. In one week we had over 100 admission physical exams to do for them. Every day there were drills and marches on the fields beside our house. Every afternoon there was shooting out on the rifle-range. The whole village was alarmed. Early in the morning of August 8 we received a police radio message that Dwight was stranded in Nam Tha. His small plane was forced down by the rains.

The telegram came while we were eating breakfast but almost simultaneously, through the dawn's mist, we heard the motor of an airplane. We knew it must be Dwight so we raced out to the airport, as fast as we could in knee-deep mud. We watched the plane cut down through the mist and land in one of the worst landings that I had ever seen. Why the wheels weren't fractured off, I do not understand. Dwight shakily came off the plane along with Dr. John Keshishian, the head of the MEDICO team in Viet

Nam, who was here for a visit of several days. With them was our good friend, Bob Burns, the "typist in the army of the Lord."

They told me how their plane had taken off the day before and flown a terrible flight. They had circled Muong Sing, but could not land due to the fog. Instead they had gone to Nam Tha to land. Earlier this morning their plane had taxied to the end of the grass runway at Nam Tha to take off, but the wheels had sunk into the mud. The villagers at Nam Tha had grabbed the wheels and with the help of a jeep had managed to get the plane out of the mud. All baggage and passengers except Dwight and Doctor Keshishian had to get off to lighten the plane. The villagers laid a few extra bamboo mats, the pilot gunned the plane, released the brakes, and catapulted into the air, taking off almost vertically.

Dwight quietly said, "Worst flight I ever had." The French pilot was much more eloquent. "Twenty years I fly in Asia, always in these dangerous territories—never, never have I been as frightened as today." He added, "And for two Americans."

I quizzed the pilot about the war. He told me that the landing strips at Phong Saly and Sam Neua were under attack and were jammed with civilians and military refugees, waiting for a plane to evacuate them. There was no order or discipline whatever, people were all over the landing strip clogging and blocking it. Disorder and confusion reigned, the familiar chaos of Asian war.

The pilot told us that he saw one village landing strip where many people had been beheaded. Their heads were stuck up on posts along the side of the strip. As the plane came to land, the pilot spotted this atrocity, pulled back on the stick and flew away. The Communists fired on his plane with small weapons. I asked a foolish question: "Were the victims military or not?" The pilot said simply, "I saw only the head and the vessels of the neck hanging down. I could not tell if they were military or not." We heard another figure, over 300 killed and several hundred more wounded.

Dr. Keshishian obviously had little idea what he was getting himself involved in. He had come up to visit us on his way home from working with our team in Viet Nam, and we were glad to have a surgeon at a time like this. Bob Burns was always a welcome visitor; though he probably would pass out at the sight of blood, we had plans for him.

At midnight that night Earl, Dwight, Bob and I discussed what I had decided. I knew my refusal to evacuate was right. I said: "Nothing is obscure, nothing is in a tangle." I knew exactly what I must do. No one in Vientiane, in New York, or anywhere else could judge the situation as well as I could. We were lucky to have this chance. We would not abandon these people; we would stay here as long as we were needed. Bob Burns said he would carry our letter back to the Ambassador and explain our feelings more completely. He had come to sound us out thoroughly, for the Ambassador suspected I might refuse his "urging."

On the plane that brought Dwight and Dr. Keshishian we found a great deal of mail. It was full of clippings about the war in Laos, and we learned more from the clippings than we did from the government of the place where we were living. A great deal of the mail upset me this particular day. Ordinarily mail pleases me; when people write and say "God bless" or ask for my autograph, I am a typical Irishman and delighted. However, because of my frame of mind and the darkness all around us, on this day I was angry. Many months later I found a copy of the letter I had written to my mother in St. Louis on this night of August 8. What I said was not very pretty. This is what I wrote:

> Don't people in America know I've got my own problems just living from day to day? I am not interested in how much people are going to pay when I come to America for my lecture tour. I am very honored that Mutual of Omaha Company has decided to give me their Criss Award. I am tremendously pleased that they are giving me $10,000 to help run my hospital. I have planned to return the end of October to receive this Award and to stay on for a month's lecture tour. But this is months away and right now I have no time to think about this. Right now I must battle from day to day and work out the problems of war, death and chaos. People write and ask me to write another book, and tell me how I must find words. Don't they realize I have other things to do now?
>
> I am a doctor. This is the root of me—I am a doctor. Everything else, everyone, is second to that. First, I am a doctor. All my duties are entwined with that and they are clear and lucid. Everything else is second. Home life, social life, writing life, living life, loving life, family, friends, romance, fame, fortune, all these are secondary, because I am a doctor. Perhaps I take this too much to heart. It was a hard and humiliating fight for me to become a doctor. I want Ambassadors to stop thinking of me as an international figure and a threat to the tranquility of their post. I want publishers to stop thinking of me as a hand that holds a conversation with a typewriter, while a piece of paper listens in. I want broadcasting systems to stop thinking of me as a correspondent and stop sending me telegrams asking for my opinion of the news. I want the people who write to me simply asking for my auto-

graph to stop writing. There is nothing I can do about certain Senators' views on the excellency of my mission. I do not care whether the American Economic Mission considers me annoyingly autonomous or not. I disapprove of some people getting me so cheaply as a "wonderful" speaker and writing me how proud they are of this fact. Perhaps I am ranting and raving, but this is how I feel.

It is very late, close to three in the morning, and everyone is asleep in the house, even the frogs and insects of the jungle seem quiet tonight. Through the screen doors I can see tonight's moon. It is a lurid moon looking down on grisly things. Hundreds of dead in the north, major villages fallen to the Reds, a build-up of troops only a few miles away from us. Young men and women beheaded with their heads stuck on posts at the runway. The whole of the north suffering, bleating and crying, full of sadness. No wonder everything is quiet tonight. They are sad, soundlessly.

The letter stopped at this point and started again on Sunday, August 9, as follows:

The dawn came today wild and fiery. There was a turbulence of cloud and wind and rain. And then almost miraculously (and I expect miracles here all the time) the thunder stopped and the lightning no longer staggered across the sky and the whole valley fell into unearthly silence. We all noticed the noise of the silence. But then by noon the windless skies again grew disturbed and the sound of thunder was distant. Or was it the sound of guns? We never know now. The noise rolled and crashed overhead, and the skies streaked with lightning and opened up and once again flooded our valley. Dr. Keshishian is overwhelmed by the rains. The visiting Bob Burns is amazed at the downpour. I am scared. Scared.

I wrote letters like this, long letters to my friends all around the world, to my mother, knowing that it would take weeks and weeks before they would ever get these letters. But by writing I talked to people just as though they were sitting across from me. How grateful I was to be able to talk, to write, to communicate.

In my village, we still experienced the madness of not-knowing; that same madness that had frightened the people into another exodus out of the neighboring provinces. We spent August 10, 11, and 12 working at the hospital training, doing physical examinations for the new army men. We made up emergency evacuation packs and planned the route. I talked into the tape-recorder, keeping a log of the day by day occurrences, never realizing to what use I would put this at a later date.

As I write these pages, going in spirit back across those monsoon months I remember very vividly the bizarre behavior of Earl and Dwight after Dwight's return from Cambodia. I remember certain incidents that took place in those early weeks of August—especially the boys' solicitousness. They knew I had been alone for a while so I assumed that was the reason why they were overly attentive to me. They poured my coffee, heated the water, ran the bulk of sick-call. They told me, "Oh, let's not do that surgery today, doctor, you've already worked hard enough," whereas their usual comment was, "Oh, let's not quit, doctor; we have time to do one more operation."

The selection of food was made with great care during those evenings. Instead of just saying to Si, "Cook up another chicken," the boys were now saying, "Si, the doctor needs to gain a little weight, let's make some potatoes tonight." I vaguely noted these things at the time.

I also distinctly remember one late afternoon coming back from the hospital from surgery. Surgery is always tiring to me because of the intense concentration that it takes. I collapsed on the couch in the center room and one of my Lao students came over and asked me if I wanted a back rub. I thought this was nice of her and said: "Why, of course, give the old man a back rub. But be careful of the scar on my side." I meant the scar where that little lump had been removed by Dr. Van Valin a few weeks before. The student nurse gave me a fine back rub and I did feel better. There was still some aching around the shoulder and the chest and some tenderness where the lump had been taken out. Their solicitousness was a warm and heartening thing. I did not realize what was behind it until much later.

Every afternoon we would listen to the news. Things seemed quiet and there was little change. Bob agreed with my letter to the Ambassador and said that he intended to take the next plane out when and if one ever came. At noon on Wednesday, August 12, just after we had scheduled surgery, we heard a small plane fly in. It was an old and tired Beechcraft belonging to the civilian Lao airline. Dr. Keshishian and Bob went to the airport, climbed aboard, and we said farewell.

This plane brought in some more mail; once again we were able to find out a little more about what was happening in areas so very close and so very threatening to us. On the night of August 11 I wrote in my notes: "The Voice of America announced today that over 4,000 Red troops were in the area of Sam Neua and Phong Saly, massing on the Vietnamese side of the frontier, a new attack was expected soon, or at the time of the end of the rains in October."

Four days later was Saturday, August 15. This was the day on which I read the blue sheet of paper—the telegram from Dr. Peter Comanduras, which I describe in the opening chapter of this book.

THIRTEEN ·

NOR EAR CAN HEAR,
NOR TONGUE CAN TELL

Continuing the story from the point where I broke it off in Chapter One—
that is, during my airplane flight west towards England—I arrived at London
airport disheveled, crumpled and still depressed. I went to the Pan American
window, where they immediately put me on a connecting flight to New
York. On Thursday evening I arrived in New York, only a couple of days
after leaving Muong Sing.

As I walked through Customs at International Airport, I looked up at
the huge glass window and saw Dr. Peter Comanduras waiting for me.
How good it was to see him! That night Peter, Gloria Sassano and I, the
original three who had started MEDICO a short nineteen months previously,
talked of many things. It was strange that in talking to them about myself
I felt as though I were discussing the sickness of another person, not myself
at all.

It was good to have Peter with me because he spoke to me not only as a
doctor but as a father and a friend. He said, "The diagnosis has been con-
firmed with the National Institute of Health. It is malignant melanoma in
the metastatic stage." I knew melanoma to be one of the most rapid-growing
and most insidious kinds of tumors. I had malignant melanoma and in its
metastatic state it already involved the lymph nodes under my arm. It was
one of these nodes, the lowest one along the upper chest wall, that Doctor
Van Valin had excised that afternoon in Muong Sing. Peter questioned
me as a doctor, asking me whether or not I had a cough; I knew he was
concerned about a spread of the cancer to my lung. He asked me if I had
any soreness in the bones of my chest, fearing the cancer might have invaded
the bone structure of my thorax.

Now I understood why I was having all the discomfort and weight loss over the past several months. I kept associating this with the fall on the river trip. This was not the cause though it certainly might have been an aggravation.

That first long night in New York was also made a lot easier by my brother, Malcolm. He flew in from Detroit that night and we talked of the weeks ahead. He was a great help, a sheltering tree, and I thank God for such a brother.

Malcolm and Peter both agreed that I would have to notify my mother immediately. But how? If I just said, "I have cancer," it would be a terrible shock to her. She had had so many shocks, having lost two husbands and two children. I first called a friend of ours in St. Louis and asked her to go to my mother's and make sure that she would be all right when my call came. Malcolm and I planned how I would phrase this, and very carefully I called: "Hello, Mother. This is Tom. I am in New York. Yes, I'm all right but I have come home because I have to have some surgery done."

She immediately poured out questions. At first she was so relieved that I was no longer in North Laos that I thought she was having some kind of mental block. I said, "Mother, are you all right? Do you understand me? I am in New York."

"Yes, son. I know you are in New York and I'm so glad. I was so afraid you would be taken prisoner and tortured by the Communists. The war news has been so terrible. I worry about you and I sleep so little."

She sounded relieved and I knew I had to say then that I had cancer. "Mother, I have just discovered that I have a tumor which is believed to be malignant. Do you understand me, Mother?"

"Yes, I understand, dear. You have a tumor that may be malignant. Well, you take good care of yourself, dear."

I knew that I had still not broken through the fog of the initial shock. Later my mother told me that it wasn't until the next day, when she actually saw it in the newspaper, that she fully realized how serious was the cause of my returning to America.

Malcolm left and the following day I flew home to St. Louis. I had to see my mother and explain to her in person the truth of the cancer that I faced. Mother met me at the airport and soon I was home again. From her strength I was able to derive much. She had been through a great deal of unhappiness in her life, and had a staunch way of taking all this though I knew it was so terrible for her. At Mass the next morning, in the same Cathedral that I had attended as a child, I prayed to the same God to Whom I had prayed all around the world. I had some peace but little solace.

That same night I flew back to New York and the following morning entered Memorial Hospital. Peter sent me to the world-famous pathologist Dr. George Papanicolaou who in turn took me to the country's great specialist in this kind of cancer-surgery, Dr. Gordon McNeer. He made all the arrangements for me to enter this hospital.

I tried to feel that I was prepared for what was ahead, but one is never completely prepared. Everything was strange. Instead of the familiar feelings that I have when walking into a hospital, things now seemed new and I felt apprehensive. The hospital had the usual odor of ether and sterile solutions, well known to me, but today it was strangely peculiar. The hospital bed seemed much different now that I was in it, instead of standing over it speaking to a patient.

From the barrage of tests, needles, X-rays and examinations I knew that my doctors were probing around my body, digging deep into its recesses for evidence of extension of my cancer. The final decision as to how radical the surgery would be depended upon how deep the involvement was. If it extended into my neck and arm nodes, the operation might include amputation of my right arm at the shoulder. With one arm I could do little in Laos.

On my third day my doctor came into my room and said, "Tom, all tests have proven negative for extension of the cancer. It seems that the melanoma involves only the chest wall and the local lymph nodes. Tomorrow we will do an extensive removal of all the skin muscles, nodes, veins, nerves and tissue of the right side of your chest and axilla. We can graft skin from your legs to put on the bare chest wall. We'll operate tomorrow."

In spite of the weeks of pain that I knew would be ahead, I felt good. Maybe things would come out all right. I offered up a little prayer of thanks and said, "All right, Doctor, I'm ready." He grinned and said, "Good. Chin up, boy."

All the familiar preparations began, things that so many times in the past I had ordered for other patients. Now it was my turn for the presurgical bath, the premedications the night before, the shaving of axilla and all the chest wall. And then a very heavy night sleep, well drugged from premedication seconal.

The following morning the priest came early to bring me Holy Communion. I wondered then, as I so often do, how do people live without their faith? In whose hands can they put their troubled selves and the infinity of questions that come to a man at a time like this? After Holy Communion, I had a few moments of thanksgiving and felt serener, safer, stronger. I was in His hands now, wholly, and in resignation. Peace of soul and body flooded over me, a deep, warm, quiet peace. I was ready.

A few hours later they came in to give me my premedication hypo. I was scheduled for surgery after high noon. I smiled to myself and thought about "high noon" back in my valley in Muong Sing. I knew the medication was working, but fear was also gnawing deeply into me. A normal reaction, I knew, but this knowledge lessened the fear's intensity not one iota.

The man in the green operating-room gown rolled my nearly drugged body off my bed onto the hard stretcher and I was wheeled up to the operating-room. I felt sure that they had given me more than the usual dose. Sure is tough to quiet Dooley down. As we wheeled into the operating-room I remember noticing a lot of people standing around the room who seemed uncomfortable in their masks and gowns and caps. They were part of a television crew that was going to photograph the operation. Then my arm was strapped to the arm board and the anesthetist very gently put the needle in. I knew this would be sodium pentathol. As the drug was injected in my veins, two strong hands came over my eyelids and pushed them down shut. I remember nothing else, nothing else.

A day and a half later (I'm told) I had lucid moments. I remember waking up for a few minutes, looking around the recovery room, everything spinning around again and blurring, and then to sleep. A few hours later, or was it minutes, or was it days, I woke up once again. I remember very distinctly a recovery nurse, who had a heavy German accent. I was angry at her, because she wouldn't let me fling myself around the bed the way I wanted to. I remember cussing at her in German.

I remember seeing Dr. Peter Comanduras looking down over me in the recovery room. His cool mien gave me reassurance, even in the haze of anesthesia. Later when I was wheeled to my room I remember seeing mother, and her warm love gave me much confidence. Then came the slow recovering of consciousness, of focusing on objects in the room. I remember the tightness in my chest and the raw soreness in my legs. I knew that these were normal post-operative pains.

I was determined to take no morphine shots for pain. I was operated on Thursday, the 27th of August, less than a week after I left Laos. By Saturday the 30th I was wide awake, sitting up in bed, sore as hell all over.

On Sunday I had some visitors and a bourbon on the rocks. I felt much better now. By Monday they let me out of bed to walk around a little bit, though I walked around all bent over like an old man. Later, Gloria Sassano came over to the hospital, bringing several baskets of mail from the office of MEDICO. How the mail was pouring in and how wonderful the letters were from all around the world, wishing me good luck, and the blessing of God.

It seemed the newspapers were carrying every single development of Dooley's illness. I had had no idea what a personal shock my cancer was to so many people around the world. A lady in Ecuador wrote that she was praying for me; a litany was being offered by Carmelite nuns in Fort Worth, Texas; Hindu prayers were offered for me near Delhi where someone was sitting crosslegged on the floor, reading the *Bhagavad-Gita*. I knew that the public in America was interested in my work, but I was overwhelmed that my sickness would cause such reaction. For many years I have received as many as two and three thousand letters a month, but now I was receiving several thousand letters a day. The spiritual bouquets that were offered up for Dooley must have perfumed the halls of heaven. I felt their strength and knew their power.

I received many strange letters from well-meaning people. They kept me gratified though sometimes amused. One lady suggested that I check on the new research in vitamins and thyroid relationships, and a letter came from the University of Munich suggesting some animal gland injection. An Anglican bishop on the West Coast told me that he would pray for me "from time to time." A lady 77 years old suggested that I rub burnt alum on my chest, as this would make my cancer go away. Another wonderful lady suggested that I eat alfalfa and garlic, pointing out to me that quinine and digitalis were acquired from these sources by the early South American Indians. She told me that alfalfa contained every vitamin so far discovered, as well as ten of the eleven mineral elements. My dear correspondent also pointed out that although alfalfa lacks in carbohydrates I could supply that by eating potatoes, "But always raw, never cooked."

One man wrote and told me: "If it is any consolation to know that you have scores of friends you have never met who are deeply concerned for your welfare, then you should be much consoled. I am an elevator operator and in the course of my day I overhear, without eavesdropping, many conversations. You are the topic under discussion many, many times. I doubt that you know any of the people who work in this building. I certainly do not, but they all know of you and your work and your sickness to them was a personal blow." What a wonderful way to learn that people are rooting for you—on elevators.

Another woman wrote and said: "I do not know whether you have ever heard of the urine therapy. Probably not. It is far too simple for the medical profession as a whole to give credence to it. But since you are in the category far above the rank and file I hope you will see the wisdom of checking into this. I suggest you buy the book entitled *The Water of Life*." The spirit in which the letter was written was wonderful, though I was not quite ready to try her therapy.

A man in Joshua, Texas, had a particular weed concoction he wanted to send to me because he believed that it would help. The children of my favorite Texan family, the Womacks of Fort Worth, composed new words to the tune of "Hang Down Your Head, Tom Dooley," and they sent them on to me:

> Lift up your heart, Tom Dooley,
> Your work will never die.
> You taught us to love our neighbor
> And not just to pass him by.

> We'll pray for you, Tom Dooley,
> Your cure and your patients, too.
> We'll send in our dimes and dollars
> For work that's left to do.

> Lift up your head, Tom Dooley,
> Lift up your head, don't cry.
> Lift up your head, Tom Dooley,
> 'Cause you ain't a-goin' to die.

One lady just wrote a letter to my office, and said, "Here's another why for which there is no human answer. Did God raise Tom Dooley up, give him a certain fire to blaze a trail in the wilderness, to give his brilliant mind and healing hands to the lost and ignorant and diseased? Did God bring Tom Dooley up to leave his stamp of greatness on each person with whom he comes in contact that are never quite the same again and then perhaps recall him from this world, his mission fulfilled, and MEDICO his memorial?" I wondered to myself if this was what the Lord had intended. But I did not think so.

Another lady wrote and said, "It's too bad that his life so dedicated now is in mortal danger. His beloved Laos is besieged. It seems that both are besieged." Another said, "One moment I faced agonizing death. The next moment I face God, and now I have a new release." She said that I should get in contact with a man named Oral Roberts. She added a postscript and said, "You are too valuable and lots of happiness lays ahead of you, see Oral Roberts, be cured, be cured." Someone else wrote me enclosing a long mimeographed article entitled "My Operation." Nice light reading for a convalescent!

I received letters from Columbia, South America, Ecuador, Poland, India,

Australia. A lady from France suggested yogurt, black bread, no sugar, soy beans, and Vitamin E in large dosages. (Doesn't she know that Vitamin E is a sexual stimulant?)

Another man wrote: "My dear Doctor, Be of good courage. Cancer is caused by eating flesh foods. It can be healed by prayer. Do not fear cancer. You do not need surgery. Just pray." He signed it and then said, "I invite comments." Somehow or other the surgical staff of the Memorial Hospital does not completely agree with him, though we all give faith a lot of credit.

One of the most touching gifts I received was a scroll from a small village in Korea. On the scroll were written the Beatitudes in Korean, and with it the wish that my health would soon improve and that I would return to the people of Asia.

Another woman took a more aggressive attitude. She said, "Go ahead, throw your life away, but don't feel sorry for yourself. I and your friends feel bad enough about your troubles." Another woman sent me a lovely Biblical quotation which said, "Here, at whatever hour you come, you will find light, health and happiness, human kindness." I thought to myself if I ever write a book about this problem I am going to call it "at whatever hour you come." I will, the next one I write.

Another cheery card came from the bartender of a small bar I used to go to in St. Louis, called "Petit Pigalle." Some children wrote me and said they hoped my "lump glands" were not involved. I think they meant "lymph" but lump is more descriptive.

One lady wrote me and said, "I'm sending you my secret for good health. All you have to do is this (and keep it quiet). Keep all dishes boiled, never eat food that you or anyone else has handled unless the food is thoroughly cooked; and, above all things, do not eat out of aluminum pans." Evidently she has no friends at Alcoa.

A lady from Kankakee (through which I had traveled many a day when a student at Notre Dame) said, "Today I am sending you a miracle healing from my hands. By touching this paper and the writing of this pen the cancer will be burned out of your body. Now you are full of pep and vigor again. Do not doubt me or you will not get it."

I thank all these people who wrote. I thank them for the thought that was at hand. However foolish the suggestion seemed, however unrealistic the advice, the kind intention and the depth of spirit are what count.

One night I dreamed that I was walking up a steep trail, leading across my valley floor and weaving its way through the high rain-forest onto the mountaintop just east of us. My boys were with me, and some of my Lao students. And in the vivid flash of the moment, in my dream, I saw a century-old pagoda that nestles on this mountain slope. The pagoda is made of mud stones and is crowned by a high spire. Hanging from the spire are long white banners, the streamers of Buddhist prayers. There are miniature bells that tinkled in the wind.

I have often been there before. But in the dream I reconstructed it even more lucidly. The central stupa has a shrine below it. Black and silver images and cascades of bells, big and small, fall down from the slope of the stupa. As I looked around through the eyes of my dream I saw many areas of land around this mountain slope, where the jungle had been burned and the mountain's naked ground was dull black. I also saw tiny insignificant little figures of men on these patches of brown earth. These men were planting the new rice seedlings into the burnt soil. The month of my dream must have been May, the time of lilacs at my beloved Notre Dame. But in Laos, May is a time when the season is driest. These are the nights that they burn the mountain.

The mountain in my dream was burned, and now they were planting the new life into the near dead soil. I dreamed this clearly and when the blue turquoise of morning came, though perhaps neither ear could hear nor tongue could tell, I knew the meaning of my dream.

From my hospital bed in New York, with the same white light of revelation I had known once several years before, I saw what I must do. After Communion that morning, Tuesday, the first of September, my God and my dream commanded me. I must, into the burnt soil of my personal mountain of sadness, plant the new seedlings of my life—I must continue to live. I must cultivate my fields of food, to feed those who cannot feed themselves.

The concept came to me as strongly and as powerfully as if a peal of bronze bells proclaimed it. There was no more self-sadness, no darkness deep inside: no gritty annoyance at anyone or anything. No anger at God for my cancer, no hostility to anyone. I was out of the fog of confusion— standing under the clear light of duty.

The jagged, ugly cancer scar went no deeper than my flesh. There was no cancer in my spirit. The Lord saw to that. I would keep my appetite for fruitful activity and for a high quality of life. Whatever time was left, whether it was a year or a decade, would be more than just a duration. I would continue to help the clots and clusters of withered and wretched in Asia to the utmost of my ability. The words of Camus rang through, "In the midst of winter I suddenly found that there was in me an invincible summer."

Maybe I could now be tender in a better way. I was a member of the fellowship of those who know the mark of pain. The philosophical concept of Dr. Schweitzer that he used to talk to me about years ago was now a more vivid thing—I bore that mark.

The days went on and on. The hospital had a monotony to it, though there was some turmoil in my hospital room. MEDICO had to set up an independent office. We had formerly been a division of the International Rescue Committee. Now we were an independent organization. My return and the ensuing public interest in and contributions to MEDICO made the time right. On September first we became MEDICO, Inc.

Now we had to get offices, typewriters, stationery, employees and a thousand other things. Mr. Zeckendorf gave us a suite of rooms in the Graybar Building at a dollar a year, though I told him I was willing to pay two bucks. The Metropolitan Life Insurance Company gave us much office furniture. Our typewriters were given to us. The Soundscriber Company donated their wonderful battery-run dictating machines to us. All around the country once again people were helping us to help others help themselves. MEDICO's administrative overhead would therefore be extremely low.

The days were busy with dressing changes, inoculations, examinations and all the things that make hospital life far from restful. One night I was all scrunched up in bed, the dressings on my legs tight and sore, my ankle swollen, my back aching from having to sit in bed so long, and my chest a mass of dressings from the belly up over the shoulders. The bed was bent in a "V" and I was lying over on one side, far, far from comfortable. Using an instrument panel I was able to push one button and turn on the television set. I got the John Daly newscast. He flashed on the screen a picture of me taken many months before and said, "Dr. Dooley is resting comfortably tonight in Memorial Hospital." I quickly pushed the button off and wished the announcer could see how "comfortably" I was resting.

But when the night came and the peaceful silence once again flooded my room, my mind returned to my high valley. I could close my eyes and conjure up the village placidly floating before me like a Chinese landscape wrapped in a fine blue mist. I sometimes felt that familiar, cloudy out-of-touchness, that pleasant disembodiment from my own self. The physical tiredness after surgery melted away into liquid. I could see once again the mountains of my beloved northern Laos, its gulfs and gorges, the hosts of billowing clouds that roll off the slopes of the high rain-forest. I could see the green lush valleys, and see huddled in their thatched huts, the sick of Laos. The valleys become gray green in the evening sun. The mountains disappear in the sunset glare—and it seems as though the sun itself thunders drily, before the rains begin.

I could see, from my cool quiet bed in America, the sickness of the valleys where I knew my boys were working now in the depths of the rains. I could see the whole side of the mountain heave and slither. The monsoon landscape. The waterlogged sodden land of Laos buried beneath the rains of heaven.

Convalescence from any kind of surgery can be an exhilarating phenomenon, lifting out of depression into a state of health. Often I would think of the boys, and one day a letter came through from them. It was dated Muong Sing, August 26, and I thought to myself that a plane must have come into the valley very soon after I left in order to get it to me in the second week of September. It was the first letter from the boys since I had left North Laos. I found out that they had known all this time that I had cancer. Dwight, when returning from Cambodia August 6th, had seen Bob Burns and Hank Miller in Vientiane. They had been notified by Dr. Van Valin after the specimen Van took to Bangkok was diagnosed by microscopy. The three of them decided that it would be best *not* to tell me I had cancer. Knowing I was going home in October anyway, they thought (correctly so) that I would probably refuse to rush right home upon receipt of Dr. Comanduras' cable. So they kept it a secret from me. Dwight's letter explained their feelings:

> Dear Sir:
> Just a personal note to ask you to forgive us for having to practice a deception on you. I am sure you know that it had to be done that way or we would not have done it. At the time we felt right about it and if we had it to do over again, we would do it just the same. However, it was hard, very hard.

I knew it was doubly hard on them because they not only had to make the decision to get me out, but they had to make their decision as to whether they would stay on alone or not. They made their decision. They are fine men! The letter went on to say,

> What I want to say is this: We are more proud than you will ever realize at being members of the first MEDICO team out in the field. As a result of this pride we intend to fill your shoes to the best of our ability until you come back here, as you certainly will. Earl and I want you to concentrate on getting well, and not upon worrying about your hospital. We promise you that you will never have to worry about any

action of ours bringing anything but credit to you and to MEDICO. We realize that there are unbridgeable chasms that separate us. We realize that because of our relationship within the team we can never really be intimate friends. But we want you to know that we admire you greatly. We do or else we would all be back in the United States.

You know full well that we don't agree with you from time to time, but we hope you realize that if we didn't have the courage to disagree with you, we would not be men. And if we were not men, we would be of little use to you here in Laos.

It was signed with a Spanish expression that Dwight used so often, *"Anda con Dios."*

I missed them very much. It is easier to part with the dead than the living. How profound my depth of admiration was for these boys. I knew they were doing well, and I heard later that they really didn't need me at all. I had worked myself out of a job.

My immediate plans were not muddled. I knew what I had to do. I had with me in the hospital the very beautiful letter that I had received from Dr. Charles Mayo informing me that I was to receive the Mutual of Omaha's Criss Award. I had received this letter in Laos in June, and it said,

> Dr. Dooley, we are honoring you because of your outstanding contributions to the medically underprivileged peoples of the world. You have been an outstanding example of a free man helping other free men on a person-to-person basis. With this in mind, the Board of Judges has selected you as recipient of the 1959 Mutual of Omaha, Criss Award.

The letter had gone on to say that the Award would be given in Omaha on the 10th of November, and that they would pay for my ticket. Of course, I came home earlier for cancer and Mutual of Omaha paid for the ticket anyway.

Now I knew what I would do. I would spend the next couple of weeks in New York after discharge from the hospital. And then, as soon as possible, I would go out to Hawaii for my convalescence. In Hawaii I intended to give some speeches, make some money, and also write this book. I would return to America and go on a lecture tour. On November 10th I would go to Omaha to receive the Award, give a few more weeks of lectures, and then in December return to my high valley. I intended to be "home" in Laos for Christmas. I was.

When Dr. McNeer came in I told him of my plans and he gasped, "Well, if all dressings are finished and if the graft does not slough off, and if all goes well, I suppose there is really no reason that you can't." He knew as well as I that the internal "get up and fight" is half the battle against cancer. I had no intention to lie in a hospital bed and wither away. There was too much to do in this world. There is a line from a poem that my father gave to me long ago. It hung in my room as a child and said, "I must fill each minute full of sixty seconds' worth of distance run." On the night of the eighth day after my operation, I was discharged. They let me out at this time because I was very anxious to go to the United Nations on Labor Day.

The tiny Kingdom of Laos, to which I had devoted so much time and love, had brought its newest malady to the highest court on earth, the United Nations. The war was continuing in the provinces, the areas all around Earl and Dwight were aflame.

The government of Laos had sent a letter to the United Nations requesting that they investigate the situation in Laos, and bring to the attention of the whole world the fact that she was being invaded by outside forces.

The Secretary General, Dag Hammarskjold, called for an emergency meeting of the United Nations Security Council on Labor Day, an unprecedented thing. It made all of America wonder whether Laos would become another Korea. Would the land of Laos become the battleground where once again the blood of the young men of the world would be spilled? The Secretary General was in South America, but returned as speedily as possible to New York in time to preside at the special session of the Security Council on September 7, 1959—Labor Day. Dag Hammarskjold pointed out that the Lao plea was for the dispatch, as speedily as possible, of an emergency force to "halt aggression and to prevent its spreading." He pointed out that this was the first time in history that a specific request for action had been addressed to a main United Nations organ. Mr. Hammarskjold went on to indicate that the request of the Lao Government of the 4th of September confronted the United Nations with problems entirely different from any they had been confronted with so far. Would the UN respond immediately and precisely to the request of Laos, and dispatch an emergency force? Would it send a sub-committee, or an observer? Or would the UN merely get involved in a war of words, and help never emerge from the air-conditioned splendor of the conference halls on the East River?

I was able to secure a seat in the press section (I told them I represented the Bamboo Press of Muong Sing). Swathed in bandages from knee to nipple (I have only one left), I hobbled into the UN building on that fateful day. There were thousands of people standing outdoors waiting to get in. The whole world was focused upon the UN. Henry Cabot Lodge of the United States said that this plea from Laos was an appeal "which put us to the test." He went on to say that the appeal of a small state member such as Laos, which told of threats to its integrity by forces from the outside, could not be ignored. The United States had no doubt that aggression was being committed. The United States believed that Laos was a victim of this aggression and Mr. Lodge proposed a step to prevent spreading of the fires of war. In fact he went on to point out that there should be an emergency meeting that night, if necessary. He said that if the Security Council "presented to the world a spectacle of haggling and hair-splitting," the effectiveness of the UN would be greatly diminished.

The Security Council is a magnificent room. Seated before me were some of the great men in the world, representatives of England, France, Japan, Canada, Argentina, Tunisia, and many other countries. Here also was the Russian representative. Would he be able to block the adoption of the resolution?

Many hours were spent that afternoon while the Russian representative pointed out reasons why the resolution, in fact the whole Laos situation, could not legally be put on the agenda. However, by fine footwork and verbal skill, Mr. Lodge won out and indeed the question was put on the agenda.

I sat up in the balcony and looked at these people, in the glory of this magnificent building. I looked at the heavy drapes, the fine paintings, the thick rugs. But these are not the real marks of the greatness of the United Nations.

The whole magnificence of the United Nations is based upon a concept of the importance of the individual. Chai, Si, Ngoan, and my Kha Kho tribesmen were just as important as these delegates. This made me realize how wonderful it is to be a member of the community of free nations. How wonderful it is to see the free men of the world taking on themselves the responsibility of those in the world who are not free, who are threatened. The nation of Laos is small, obscure, and primitive. We all knew that Laos was being attacked by forces from without, but it is a hard thing to prove this against clever enemies. It is a hard thing to prove from just what area come the soldiers who pour down the high mountain valleys of North Laos. It is hard to "prove" anything in such a primitive land as this.

Had I seen in the future, I would have realized that before the end of November the whole Laos crisis would have quieted down, and the threat of war held off by firm action. America did a good job. Laos did a better one. The UN showed herself capable of answering a challenge.

The American Government stood by its promises to help safeguard the integrity of Laos. In September the small units that had been crossing the borders in Sam Neua and Phong Saly began to pull back. Everyone thought the town of Sam Neua would fall, yet in the next few days it was obvious that the Pathet Lao forces had received a pull-back order. We had shown Laos that we did indeed intend to back her. As one newspaper put it that very night: "Fingers crossed, in short, we can say that the Free World has had a significant success. Laos is free, and will probably maintain her freedom. America has stood by a threatened nation. We have shown ourselves to be the great nation of love and care for our brothers we profess that we are."

I knew that I would have to go on a lecture tour and once again try to raise money and men and medicines. MEDICO, Inc. with hospitals and programs now in nine nations should grow and grow. We need the awareness and the dollar support of all men. I knew that I would return to Laos, and would indeed be home for Christmas. But first I still had three months in the States. My mountain was now burned. Yes, but new life was planted in my heart. My night was now day. I must strive once again to help achieve that dream of Anne Frank's, "Things will change, and men become good again, and these pitiless days will come to an end, and the world will know once again order, trust, and peace."

I left the UN just as the sun was setting, hailed a cab and asked to be taken to my hotel. The driver adjusted the mirror, looked back at me and said, "You been at the UN, aintcha, Mac?" I said yes. He said, "You've seen a lot of Communism, aintcha?" I said yes. He adjusted the mirror and looked at me again, studying my face and the way I was hunched over in the back seat, just as he had watched the stiffness with which I had climbed into his taxi. Evidently he recognized me. As we pulled up to the hotel the fare was eighty cents and I gave the driver a dollar. He looked at me, thrust the dollar bill back in my hand and said, "Oh never mind, Dr. Dooley, I'll pay your fare. You keep that buck and get back as soon as possible to your Kingdom of Laos." I smiled and felt warm and good inside and turned to my fellow-American and said, "O.K., Mac. Shall do."